Neuropsychological Rorschach Assessment

AF837783

Neuropsychological Rorschach Assessment: Science and Practice examines both the empirical research literature addressing how the Rorschach can be applied as a method of neuropsychological assessment and case illustrations looking at the Rorschach performance of neuropsychologically impaired individuals.

This book is the first comprehensive resource to trace and integrate neuropsychological research with the Rorschach—from the early insights of Hermann Rorschach and Zygmunt Piotrowski to modern, evidence-based systems such as the Comprehensive System and the Rorschach Performance Assessment System. It is unique in synthesizing findings on the Rorschach's correlations with cognitive functioning, its applications in assessing neurocognitive and neurodevelopmental disorders, and its emerging role in neuroimaging research. Clinical case studies demonstrate the Rorschach's application in early-onset Alzheimer's dementia, attention-deficit/hyperactivity disorder, personality disorders, traumatic brain injury, autism spectrum disorder, alcohol dependence, and psychotic depression.

Featuring invaluable practical guidelines and rich clinical cases, this book equips psychologists, neuropsychologists, and students to use the Rorschach from a neuropsychological perspective, expanding the scope of Rorschach and multimethod assessment.

Emiliano Muzio is a licensed psychologist, psychotherapist, and international Rorschach expert with thirty years' experience in clinical practice, teaching, and psychological/neuropsychological assessment.

"Emiliano Muzio has given us a remarkable book of great merit, plumbing the complexities of Rorschach in neuropsychology. Impeccably researched and exceptionally well written with wonderful examples that increase its accessibility, this book will be THE standard reference against which all subsequent scholarship will be measured."

F. Barton Evans, Ph.D., *retired professor of psychiatry, East Tennessee State University, USA*

"This comprehensive and long-awaited book is remarkable, tracing the history of cognitive/neurological disorders in the Rorschach test, reviewing the evidence base, and offering detailed and fascinating analyses of four clinical cases. Essential reading for psychologists, neuropsychologists, psychiatrists, gerontologists, and a reference book for students."

Anne Andronikof, Ph.D., *emeritus professor of psychopathology, University of Paris Nanterre, France; past president of the International Society of the Rorschach and Projective Methods*

"This book bridges two centuries of Rorschach and neuropsychological research, linking early theory with modern findings from advanced neurophysiological techniques. It seamlessly connects clinical practice and empirical science, making complex, interdisciplinary concepts accessible to students, clinicians, and researchers alike—a rare and valuable resource."

Luciano Giromini, Ph.D., *associate professor of psychology, University of Turin, Italy*

"Kudos to Dr. Muzio for his extremely thorough and lucid synthesis of the Rorschach assessment of neuropsychological conditions! A gem of a resource for students, researchers, and seasoned clinicians, Muzio's contribution integrates CS and R-PAS perspectives in his review of a range of neurocognitive and neurodevelopmental disorders."

James H. Kleiger, Psy.D., *ABPP, ABAP, private practice, Maryland, USA*

"This book is an essential guide for clinicians looking to integrate the Rorschach test with neuropsychology. It blends rigorous research with vivid clinical cases. Emiliano Muzio provides practical solutions to complex diagnostic challenges. It is a very compelling resource for the modern psychological clinician."

Piero Porcelli, Ph.D., *professor of clinical psychology, University of Chieti-Pescara, Italy*

Neuropsychological Rorschach Assessment

Science and Practice

Emiliano Muzio

Routledge
Taylor & Francis Group
NEW YORK AND LONDON

Designed cover image:

First published 2026
by Routledge
605 Third Avenue, New York, NY 10158

and by Routledge
4 Park Square, Milton Park, Abingdon, Oxon OX14 4RN

Routledge is an imprint of the Taylor & Francis Group, an informa business

© 2026 Taylor & Francis

The right of Emiliano Muzio to be identified as author of this work has been asserted in accordance with sections 77 and 78 of the Copyright, Designs and Patents Act 1988.

All rights reserved. No part of this book may be reprinted or reproduced or utilised in any form or by any electronic, mechanical, or other means, now known or hereafter invented, including photocopying and recording, or in any information storage or retrieval system, without permission in writing from the publishers.

Trademark notice: Product or corporate names may be trademarks or registered trademarks, and are used only for identification and explanation without intent to infringe.

Library of Congress Cataloging-in-Publication Data
A catalog record for this title has been requested

ISBN: 978-0-367-53755-5 (hbk)
ISBN: 978-0-367-53754-8 (pbk)
ISBN: 978-1-003-73189-4 (ebk)

DOI: 10.4324/9781003731894

Typeset in Times New Roman
by Taylor & Francis Books

To my daughter, Maisa

Contents

List of illustrations x
About the Author xii
Preface xiv
Acknowledgements xvi

PART I
Empirical Research and Guidelines 1

1 Moving beyond the Mind–Body Dichotomy 3

2 Rorschach, Piotrowski, and Early Studies on Neurological Populations 15

Hermann Rorschach's Seminal Work 15
Zygmunt Piotrowski's Ten Organic Signs 17
The Long History of Rorschach Research with Neurological Populations 24

3 The Rorschach, Intelligence, and Cognitive Functions 28

Adaptive Resources, Mentalization, and the Coping Deficit Index 29
Perceptual–Cognitive Engagement, Cognitive Sophistication, and Complexity 38
Perceptual Accuracy, Conventionality, and Thought Organization 48
Additional Rorschach Variables Related to Intelligence and Cognitive Functions 51

4 Rorschach Performance of Patients with Specific Neurocognitive and Neurodevelopmental Disorders 60

Dementia of the Alzheimer's Type 61
Dementia with Lewy Bodies 65
Polycystic Lipomembranous Osteodysplasia with Sclerosing Leukoencephalopathy 66
Traumatic Brain Injury 67
Unilateral Brain Lesions and Hemispheric Asymmetry 70
Attention-Deficit/Hyperactivity Disorder 73
Autism Spectrum Disorders 77

5 Neuroimaging Studies of Specific Rorschach Variables 90

Unique Perception, Emotional Interference, and Amygdalar Structure and Function 91
The Human Movement Response, Embodied Mentalization, and the Mirror Neuron System 96
Color-Determinants, Affect Mentalization, and Functions of the Left Hemisphere 104

6 Practical Guidelines for Using the Rorschach from a Neuropsychological Perspective 120

PART II
Clinical Case Illustrations 139

7 "It Looks Like an Island": A Rapidly Progressing Case of Early-Onset Dementia of the Alzheimer's Type 141

Initial Assessment: Medical and Neuropsychological Assessment Findings 142
Initial Assessment: Contributions of the Rorschach 144
Diagnoses, Summary/Discussion Session, and Treatment Plan 147
Follow-up Assessment at Six Months 148
Follow-up Assessment at Fourteen Months 148
Follow-up Assessment at Twenty-Six Months 149
Follow-up Assessment at Twenty-Six Months: Contributions of the Rorschach 150
In Conclusion 151

8 "A Middle Finger": A Case of Attention-Deficit/Hyperactivity Disorder, Personality Disorder, and Traumatic Brain Injury 156

Neuropsychological and Self-Report-Based Assessment Findings 157
Contributions of the Rorschach 158
In Conclusion 161

9 "I'm Having Trouble Digesting": Grieving in a Case of Autism Spectrum Disorder 166

Neuropsychological Assessment Findings 168
Self-Report-Based and Other Assessment Findings 169
Contributions of the Rorschach 171
In Conclusion 174

10 "I'm Feeling Great!": Cognitive Deterioration in a Woman with a History of Alcoholism and Psychotic Depression 180

The First Assessment: Self-Report and Neuropsychological Assessment Findings 182
The First Assessment: Contributions of the Rorschach 183
The First Assessment: Final Observations and Conclusions 185
The Second Assessment: Self-Report and Neuropsychological Assessment Findings 186
The Second Assessment: Contributions of the Rorschach 188
The Second Assessment: Final Observations and Conclusions 191
In Conclusion 192

Appendix 197
Appendix A: Catherine's Rorschach Protocol, Sequence of Codes and Structural Summary from the Initial Assessment (Comprehensive System; Exner, 2003) 198
Appendix B: Catherine's Rorschach Protocol from the Follow-up Assessment at Twenty-Six Months (Comprehensive System; Exner, 2003) 203
Appendix C: Ville's Rorschach Protocol, Sequence of Codes and Structural Summary (Comprehensive System; Exner, 2003) 207
Appendix D: Pekka's Rorschach Protocol, Sequence of Codes and Structural Summary (Comprehensive System; Exner, 2003) 213

Appendix E: Tuula's First Rorschach Protocol, Sequence of Codes and Structural Summary (Comprehensive System; Exner, 2003) 218
Appendix F: Tuula's Second Rorschach Protocol (Five Years Later), Sequence of Codes and Structural Summary (Comprehensive System; Exner, 2003) 222
Index 229

Illustrations

Figures

3.1 Theoretical scatter plot model for significant positive correlations between neurocognitive performance variables and related Rorschach variables representing psychological resources 30
3.2 Theoretical scatter plot model for significant negative correlations between neurocognitive performance variables and related Rorschach variables representing psychological liabilities 30
A.1 Catherine's (female, forty-nine years) first structural summary (lower section) 202
C.1 Ville's (male, twenty-one years) structural summary (lower section) 212
D.1 Pekka's (male, forty-eight years) structural summary (lower section) 217
E.1 Tuula's (female, forty-three years) first structural summary (lower section) 221
F.1 Tuula's (female, forty-eight years) second structural summary (lower section) 228

Tables

2.1 Piotrowski's ten organic signs (Piotrowski, 1937) 19
6.1 Rorschach variables (CS and R-PAS) with neuropsychological correlates and guidelines for interpretation 124
A.1 Catherine's (female, forty-nine years) first Rorschach protocol 198
A.2 Catherine's (female, forty-nine years) first sequence of codes 201
B.1 Catherine's (female, fifty-one years) second Rorschach protocol 203
C.1 Ville's (male, twenty-one years) Rorschach protocol 207

C.2 Ville's (male, twenty-one years) sequence of codes 210
D.1 Pekka's (male, forty-eight years) Rorschach protocol 213
D.2 Pekka's (male, forty-eight years) sequence of codes 216
E.1 Tuula's (female, forty-three years) first Rorschach protocol 218
E.2 Tuula's (female, forty-three years) first sequence of codes 220
F.1 Tuula's (female, forty-eight years) second Rorschach protocol 222
F.2 Tuula's (female, forty-eight years) second sequence of codes 226

About the Author

Emiliano Muzio, Ph.D., is a licensed psychologist and psychotherapist in private practice in Helsinki, Finland, with thirty years of experience in clinical practice, teaching, and supervision of students, psychologists, and other mental-health professionals. He has served as a university lecturer and is an experienced educator, regularly teaching advanced courses in psychological and neuropsychological assessment, the Rorschach Comprehensive System and the Rorschach Performance Assessment System, the Wartegg Drawing Completion Test (Crisi Wartegg System), collaborative/therapeutic assessment, cognitive remediation therapy, and related topics.

Since 2018, Dr. Muzio has served as CEO of Terapiatalo Sointu, a private provider of psychological and psychotherapy services in Helsinki. He has been president of the Finnish Rorschach Association since 2015 and first vice president of the International Society of the Rorschach and Projective Methods since 2024. Dr. Muzio has also served as a member of the Test Committee of the Finnish Psychological Association since 2023 and as the representative of the Italian Institute of Wartegg for Finland since 2020.

Dr. Muzio earned his doctorate from the University of Paris in 2006, where he defended his dissertation on the neuropsychological correlates of the Rorschach in geriatric populations and dementia of the Alzheimer's type. While in France, he taught the Rorschach Comprehensive System at the University of Paris and psychological and neuropsychological assessment at the École de Psychologues Praticiens. He later held teaching appointments at the University of Jyväskylä and the University of Helsinki, and since 2011, he has directed a one-year Rorschach specialization program in Finland that is widely regarded as an international gold standard.

Dr. Muzio is a contributing author to *Using the Rorschach Performance Assessment System* (edited by Joni L. Mihura and Gregory J. Meyer, Guilford Press, 2018), served as guest editor for a special issue of *Rorschachiana* on neuroscience and the Rorschach (Hogrefe, 2016) and has authored or co-authored several peer-reviewed publications. He has been a regular presenter at international conferences on personality assessment (e.g., International Society of the Rorschach and Projective Methods, Society for Personality Assessment) and neuropsychology (e.g., International Neuropsychological Society) since 1996.

Dr. Muzio's career reflects a long-standing commitment to integrating personality and neuropsychological assessment and to using the assessment process as a collaborative, therapeutic intervention. His work emphasizes the Rorschach as a clinically rich and neuropsychologically meaningful tool when applied by appropriately trained professionals.

Preface

This textbook is primarily addressed to psychologists and neuropsychologists who use the Rorschach inkblot test as part of their personality assessment practice and wish to broaden the scope of their assessments by incorporating a neuropsychological perspective. Although the research literature examining associations between Rorschach variables and intelligence, cognitive functions, or neurocognitive disorders is broad, it remains relatively sparse and has not, to date, been summarized in the form of a practical textbook for clinicians and students.

The focus of the book is on research using the Rorschach administered, coded, scored, and interpreted according to one of the two leading international, evidence-based systems: the Comprehensive System (CS; Exner, 2003) and the Rorschach Performance Assessment System (R-PAS; Meyer et al., 2011). The more recent revised version of the CS (CS-R; Exner et al., 2022a, 2022b) was also considered but was ultimately set aside as a primary focus due to the lack of neuropsychological research using this version. Additionally, neuropsychologically relevant variables in the CS-R are the same as in the original CS, making references to it largely redundant in this context.

Although the primary emphasis is on neuropsychological research using the CS and the R-PAS, this book may also be of great interest to psychologists and neuropsychologists working with other systems. Additionally, Rorschach instructors, clinicians, or psychology students learning to use the Rorschach, and researchers interested in neuropsychological applications of the Rorschach may also find it to be a helpful resource.

It is important to note that this book is not a comprehensive manual for administering, coding, scoring, or interpreting the Rorschach and does not replace the basic manuals of the various Rorschach systems. Its aim is to serve as a useful adjunct by broadening the scope of Rorschach assessment.

The book is divided into two parts. The first part reviews the neuropsychological research literature involving the Rorschach and concludes with a summary of neuropsychological correlates and practical guidelines for interpretation. The second part presents four clinical case illustrations that demonstrate how the Rorschach can contribute to a more comprehensive understanding of neuropsychologically impaired patients—for purposes of differential diagnosis, identifying individual resources and vulnerabilities, treatment and rehabilitation planning, and tracking changes in neuropsychological functioning over time. All four cases are drawn from my clinical assessment practice across a variety of settings, including the clinical gerontology department of a major hospital (Paris, France), a rehabilitation center for traumatic brain and spinal-cord injury (Helsinki, Finland), and a psychiatric day hospital for adults (Helsinki, Finland). Neurocognitive, neurodevelopmental, and psychiatric conditions covered in these cases include dementia of the Alzheimer's type, traumatic brain injury, attention-deficit/hyperactivity disorder, autism spectrum disorder (Asperger's disorder), alcohol dependence, and depression-related cognitive deterioration.

References

Exner, J. E. (2003). *The Rorschach: A comprehensive system: Volume 1: Basic foundations and principles of interpretation* (4th ed.). Wiley.

Exner, J. E., Andronikof, A., & Fontan, P. (2022a). *The Rorschach: A comprehensive system—revised. Administration and coding manual.* Rorschach Workshops.

Exner, J. E., Fontan, P., & Andronikof, A. (2022b). *The Rorschach: A comprehensive system—revised. Interpretation and technical manual.* Rorschach Workshops.

Meyer, G. J., Erard, R. E., Erdberg, P., Mihura, J. L., & Viglione, D. J. (2011). *Rorschach Performance Assessment System: Administration, coding, interpretation, and technical manual.* Rorschach Performance Assessment System LLC.

Acknowledgements

First and foremost, I would like to express my deepest gratitude to my friend and colleague Barton Evans, without whom this project would never have come to fruition. His unwavering encouragement, thoughtful comments, chapter reviews, and continuous feedback throughout this work have been invaluable.

I am also indebted to my friends and peers—Anne Andronikof, Luciano Giromini, James Kleiger, Joni Mihura, Piero Porcelli, Jed Yalof, and Eric Zillmer—for taking time from their busy schedules to review and comment on chapter drafts and to help further elaborate or clarify specific sections of the book. Their expertise, insights, and generous support in various forms have enriched this work in many ways. I also wish to thank my personal assistant, Salla Skön, for her outstanding efficiency in gathering references and for her invaluable help in organizing the final version of the manuscript.

More broadly, I would like to acknowledge the many brilliant clinicians and scholars whose contributions to Rorschach research and practice form the foundation of this book. Through their dedication and hard work, they have deepened our understanding of how to make meaningful use of this fascinating and multifaceted tool for the benefit of our clients and patients. I salute their expertise, feel privileged to have known many of them personally over the years, and remain sincerely grateful—both to those still with us and to those no longer among the living.

Finally, I could not have written this book without the sustained support, flexibility, and patience of family and friends. To all of you, I am immensely grateful.

Acknowledgements

Part I

Empirical Research and Guidelines

Chapter 1

Moving beyond the Mind–Body Dichotomy

Hermann Rorschach's iconic inkblot test has been used by psychologists around the world for over a century and remains one of the most widely used psychological assessment tools. A recent survey in my home country—Finland—found that approximately 25 percent of psychologists who conduct assessments list the Rorschach among their ten most frequently used tests (Finnish Psychological Association, 2024). Other countries where the method remains widely used—evidenced by the broad membership and activity of the Society for Personality Assessment (SPA) and the International Society of the Rorschach and Projective Methods (ISR)—include the USA, Italy, France, Belgium, Spain, Denmark, Israel, Turkey, Argentina, Brazil, and Japan, among others.

It is important to note, however, that—for a variety of historical reasons—the popularity of the Rorschach varies considerably by country. A European survey on testing practice among psychologists (Evers et al., 2012) found that—across seventeen countries—the Rorschach was listed among the top ten most frequently used tests in eight (47 percent). While it ranked eighth overall and was used by 5.1 percent of all respondents throughout Europe (N = 11,017), its use was marginal in countries such as Germany or the UK, for example. In contrast, it ranked as high as second in Greece (79 percent) and the Czech Republic (28.9 percent), and as third in Slovenia (24.2 percent) and Slovakia (21.3 percent)—positions typically occupied by classic cognitive and intelligence tests.[1]

Although the Rorschach is also used in forensic (e.g., violence risk assessment), educational (e.g., assessing learning difficulties), and occupational or organizational settings (e.g., recruitment), it has historically been developed and applied primarily in clinical settings, typically within a multimethod assessment framework. According to preliminary results from an international survey conducted by Mihura et al. (2022), more than 50 percent of respondents reported using the Rorschach in clinical practice for purposes such as differential diagnosis, assessing psychosis, evaluating complex or ambiguous cases, identifying personality disorders, or simply as part of a routinely administered assessment battery. Use

DOI: 10.4324/9781003731894-2

within the context of collaborative/therapeutic assessment (e.g., Finn, 2007) was also among the most frequently cited applications internationally—but only among non-US respondents.

In the same survey, 20.5 percent of clinicians who use the Rorschach indicated that they apply it in the context of neuropsychological referral questions. Earlier surveys have also found that neuropsychologists tend to use many of the same instruments as clinical psychologists when assessing personality or emotional functioning. For instance, Zillmer (1994) reported a survey mailed to a random sample of 500 members of the International Neuropsychological Society (INS) in the early 1990s. Of the 331 respondents, nearly half reported administering the Minnesota Multiphasic Personality Inventory (MMPI-2; Butcher et al., 1989)—despite concerns about its validity in neurologically impaired populations[2]—followed by the Rorschach according to the Comprehensive System (CS; Exner, 2003), which was used by nearly one in four clinicians.[3] In a more recent survey targeting randomly selected members of the INS (final sample N = 404), 12.4 percent of respondents reported administering the Rorschach (CS) at least "sometimes," and overall usage rose to 32.8 percent when also considering those who used it "seldom" (Smith et al., 2010). According to the authors, results suggest, like prior surveys, that the assessment of personality or emotional functioning is relatively uncommon in neuropsychological practice and that the primary focus of neuropsychologists is on cognitive functions.

Hermann Rorschach considered his test to be primarily a psychological experiment about perception and apperception, not a personality or projective test (Rorschach, 2021).[4] As noted by Exner (2003, p. 20), "nearly two decades [after the publication of *Psychodiagnostics*] would pass before the notion of projection would be applied to Rorschach's test." According to Rorschach, the test did not involve free-flowing associations from the unconscious as in dreams but rather an exercise of adaptation to reality and external sensations (Rorschach, 2021, p. 25). In the introduction of *Psychodiagnostics*, he specifies that his work is "predominantly empirical," that the conclusions drawn from the experiment "are to be regarded more as findings than as theoretical deductions," and that "the theoretical reason for the experiment is, in part, still only in its infancy" (Rorschach, 2021, p. 31).[5] Coding different aspects of the response process and generating scores that described *how* the individual perceived the inkblot stimuli, with only secondary interest in *what* the individual perceived, was central to Rorschach's seminal work.

Interestingly, as Searls notes in his captivating review of the Rorschach's history (Searls, 2017, p. 48), "Rorschach both respected Sigmund Freud's ideas and preserved a certain skepticism towards them." He also attended lectures by Carl Gustav Jung in Zurich and used Jung's word-association test for many years (Jung, 1910). Eugen Bleuler, another key figure in early twentieth-century psychiatry, served as Rorschach's supervisor for a time and strongly influenced his thinking—particularly regarding the integration of psychodynamic concepts into psychiatric practice.

Rorschach followed with great interest the emerging debate on the nature of mental illness, for which Zurich was a central hub in the early twentieth century. At the heart of this debate were two competing perspectives: Bleuler's psychologically oriented view of schizophrenia, which used concepts such as *depth psychology* or *ambivalence*, and Emil Kraepelin's biologically based concept of *dementia praecox*. This division created a deep and often polarizing rift in the psychiatric community, with many professionals feeling compelled to align with one side or the other (Searls, 2017, pp. 38–52). Searls describes how Rorschach, like Kraepelin, valued empirical observation and diagnostic accuracy. At the same time, he was drawn to the subjective dimensions of mental life and psychoanalytic ideas, such as unconscious mental processes—an interest more aligned with Bleuler's, Jung's, and Freud's ideas.

Unlike many of his contemporaries, Rorschach chose to forge his own path, advocating for a comprehensive psychiatric approach that integrated both biological and psychological perspectives (Searls, 2017, pp. 53–64). His position between Kraepelin's biologically based psychiatry and Bleuler's psychodynamic orientation reflects more than a historical compromise—it represents a model for transcending the entrenched mind–body dichotomy that continues to shape psychiatric diagnosis, as well as psychological and neuropsychological assessment, to this day. Rorschach's inkblot method embodied this integration: it was grounded in observable, systematically coded behavior, yet also provided access to the affective and cognitive processes that shape perception and apperception. He combined structured administration, scoring, and empirical rigor with the aim of gaining deep insights into an individual's inner world and modes of experiencing. His approach offers a compelling invitation to move beyond dualistic models toward a more holistic understanding of human behavior—precisely the kind of integrative perspective from which contemporary psychological and neuropsychological assessment could greatly benefit.

After Rorschach's death in 1922—just one year after the publication of *Psychodiagnostics*—his empirically grounded and integrative approach gradually faded from view, as multiple systems of administration, scoring, and interpretation began to emerge in the USA, Europe, and beyond. Each system emphasized different theoretical orientations, aspects of the test, and potential applications. In the USA alone, five major systems competed with one another: the Beck System, with its emphasis on structured scoring, empirical validation, and a focus on thought organization and reality testing; the Klopfer System, emphasizing personality dynamics, symbolic interpretation, and intuitive content analysis; the Hertz System, focused not only on empirical validation but also psychoanalytic theory, defensive operations, and ego strength; the Rapaport–Schafer System, integrating thought organization and psychoanalytic theory within a broader multimethod assessment framework; and the Piotrowski System—further described in Chapter 2—which focused on Rorschach signs of neuropsychological impairment. (For a review of these pioneering systems, see Exner, 2003, pp. 12–27).

In the post-*Psychodiagnostics* era, it became common practice for practitioners and researchers to create their own individualized versions of the test—combining elements from different systems, inventing new codes, scores, and indexes, or, in some cases, abandoning formal coding altogether. Those in the latter group often focused instead on content analysis, typically grounded in psychoanalytic theory (e.g., Chabert, 1998). This lack of standardization contributed significantly to the decline in the test's professional credibility and popularity, particularly after its usage peaked in the 1950s (Searls, 2017, p. 212). In the absence of international standards for administration, scoring, and interpretation, conducting research and building an empirically grounded evidence base became extremely difficult. Although research with and on the Rorschach continued during this period, it was often impossible to compare findings across studies due to the use of different and largely incompatible systems.

Beginning with the publication of the first CS manual in 1974 (Exner, 1974), John Exner ultimately rescued the Rorschach from what might otherwise have been its decline into scientific irrelevance. By the 1970s, the test had begun to lose credibility within the scientific community due to the proliferation of inconsistent and competing systems. As this happened, Exner began his career as a psychologist and researcher by synthesizing the five major systems developed in the USA after Rorschach's death (Exner, 1969). In doing so, he systematically evaluated the empirical strengths and weaknesses of each system and, based on this assessment, made evidence-based decisions regarding administration, scoring, and interpretation procedures. These elements were then integrated into his new unified system, grounded in rigorous standards for reliability and validity. With the collaboration of hundreds of researchers and clinicians, Exner went on to develop a substantial body of research: introducing new variables and indexes, expanding the empirical foundation, eliminating unreliable or problematic elements, and refining interpretive principles. (For a review of the development of the system, see Exner, 2003, pp. 1–41.)

Although several different Rorschach systems still exist in various parts of the world, most are, at best, only marginally represented in the leading scientific literature on clinical psychology and personality assessment. By the 1990s, Exner had succeeded in building a broad international consensus around the CS, which many came to regard as the gold standard for state-of-the-art, evidence-based Rorschach research and practice. His perspective was closely aligned with Rorschach's original empirical orientation. Moreover, Exner's conceptualization of the Rorschach as a *perceptual–cognitive problem-solving task* framed the method in terms more familiar to neuropsychologists. This, in turn, helped bridge the gap between personality assessment and neuropsychology, as reflected in the growing number of neuropsychological publications on the Rorschach beginning in the 1990s (e.g., Acklin & Wu-Holt, 1996; Zillmer & Perry, 1996).

After Exner's death in 2006, a group composed of his closest collaborators—primarily members of the Rorschach Research Council—continued refining the method by addressing what they viewed as psychometric limitations of the CS. This core group of five highly qualified researchers and clinicians focused on improving administration, coding, and interpretation procedures with the aims of: (1) reducing assessor variability, (2) correcting normative anchors, (3) limiting error variance in the total number of responses (*R*), (4) aligning interpretation more closely with validity evidence, and (5) making interpretation easier and more accurate. This work came to fruition in a user-friendly, all-in-one manual introducing what the authors named the Rorschach Performance Assessment System (R-PAS; Meyer et al., 2011).

Like the CS, the R-PAS is a strongly evidence-based system. Moreover, its development benefited from more stringent criteria for variable selection, drawing heavily on recent meta-analytic findings on variable validity (particularly Mihura et al., 2013), as well as the integration of non-CS but well validated variables (e.g., Bornstein & Hopwood, 2017; Diener et al., 2011) and more recent research—including some of the neuropsychological studies referred to in this book. Also consistent with the CS, the R-PAS conceptualizes the Rorschach as a perceptual–cognitive task. Additionally, however, it also emphasizes the Rorschach as a *performance-based method* that enables the assessor to observe the individual's "personality in action" in a standardized situation. Finally, the R-PAS also highlights the *response process* itself, with the idea that "the best and most valid interpretations are those in which the coded behaviors observed in the microcosm of the task generalize to parallel mental, verbal, and perceptual behaviors in the external environment" (Meyer et al., 2011, p. 1). All these concepts frame the Rorschach in a way that resonates with concepts familiar to neuropsychologists. In other words, much like traditional neuropsychological tests, the Rorschach in the R-PAS framework offers a structured behavioral sample that can be coded, scored, and compared to reference data and validity research—forming the basis for sound interpretive inferences.

This reconceptualization of the Rorschach, from a projective test rooted in psychodynamic theory, to a perceptual–cognitive performance-based task grounded in observable behavior and empirical validation—as Hermann Rorschach had initially intended—represents a clear paradigm shift in both theory and practice. Rather than interpreting responses as projections—which in some instances do indeed occur[6]– both the CS and the R-PAS view the test primarily as a problem-solving task that reflects how individuals process, organize, and respond to complex, ambiguous stimuli as they go about their daily lives. This shift has aligned the Rorschach more closely with principles familiar to neuropsychologists and has helped position the method within the broader landscape of evidence-based psychological and neuropsychological assessment. Moreover, a change in the nomenclature recommended to refer to personality tests—suggesting that it is "time to retire 'objective' and 'projective' as personality test descriptors"—has further consolidated this paradigm shift for the Rorschach (Meyer & Kurtz, 2006).

In a recent effort to integrate Rorschach performance with brain functioning, Meyer and Friston (2022) proposed that the Bayesian model of brain function (see, e.g., Friston, 2009, 2010) offers a compelling framework for understanding the nature of the Rorschach task and what it measures. According to this model, the brain actively interprets the world by forming predictions based on prior experience and updating them in response to new sensory input. This ongoing process—known as *active inference*—guides perception, emotion, and behavior through dynamic hypothesis testing shaped by internal models (i.e., apperception-like processes). Rather than passively registering reality, the brain minimizes the discrepancy between expected and actual input through continual predictive modeling.

From a Bayesian perspective—aligned in many ways with Rorschach's original ideas—the Rorschach task provides a unique opportunity to observe how individuals construct meaning under conditions of uncertainty. The ambiguity of the inkblots necessitates reliance on expectations shaped by previous experiences, cognitive tendencies, and emotional response patterns. This makes the Rorschach uniquely useful for examining individual differences in perception, interpretation, and coping.

As further explored in Chapter 5 through neuroimaging research, Meyer and Friston illustrate how certain Rorschach responses exemplify active inference. For instance, unusual responses (*FQu*) or responses representing perceptual distortions (*FQ–*) may reflect difficulty adjusting internal predictions to external stimuli due to emotional interference. Another compelling example is the human movement response (*M*), which involves top-down processing. Perceiving movement in static inkblots requires high-level predictions not directly prompted by the stimulus, engaging internal models of motion, social cognition, and embodied mentalization (Porcelli, 2025)—likely activating higher-level processing networks, such as the mirror neuron system and mentalization networks (empathy and theory of mind networks; Schurz et al., 2021), as also discussed in Chapter 5. From a Bayesian standpoint, these responses illustrate how the brain applies rich prior knowledge to sparse sensory data, constructing meaning through inference. As described in subsequent chapters, individuals who produce well-integrated *M* responses tend to demonstrate higher levels of neurocognitive functioning and socially attuned, flexible inferential processes. In contrast, those who fail to produce such responses may show deficits in key adaptive resources such as intelligence, the capacity to mentalize, or the capacity to experience empathy. In this way, the Rorschach offers a standardized and structured context for exploring how people process ambiguity—illuminating the interplay between the brain's predictive systems and psychological functioning.

There is now strong empirical evidence and meta-analytic support for using the Rorschach in a variety of settings and for a variety of purposes (Mihura et al., 2013). In addition to excellent validity support for several key scores and indexes, a large survey of practicing clinicians found that these same measures are also perceived as highly valid in clinical practice, with strong correlations between quantitative research findings and perceived validity (Meyer et al., 2013). In other words, clinicians worldwide report that the Rorschach provides valid and valuable information about their clients—which helps explain the test's continued popularity—and their clinically informed opinions tend to be aligned with the evidence base.

Probably most importantly from a neuropsychological perspective, cognitive variables—such as those assessing psychotic phenomena in perception and thinking, or higher-level processing resources—are among the most strongly supported in terms of validity, even according to some of the test's staunchest critics (Mihura et al., 2013; Wood et al., 2015). Additionally, the use of R-optimized administration procedures in the R-PAS, designed to reduce the likelihood of excessively brief or lengthy protocols, has significantly improved the validity of several key variables (Dean et al., 2007). Finally, it is important to note that in response to recent critiques of the test's use in forensic settings, based on anecdotal evidence, it has been argued that the primary issue is not the *use* of the Rorschach by appropriately trained psychologists—who understand the test's strengths and limitations—but rather its *misuse* by those unfamiliar with the contemporary research literature and the appropriate evidence-based use of the test. These critiques were also found to be based on the application of unrealistic standards for assessing the reliability and validity of a psychological assessment measure and a fundamental misunderstanding of how the Rorschach works (de Ruiter et al., 2023). Beyond this recent debate in the forensic assessment literature, there is a longer history of misuse and misunderstanding of the Rorschach—as well as misconceptions about how the test is or should be applied—which has likely limited its broader acceptance and its potential for more widespread use (e.g., Meloy, 2005; Wood et al., 2003).

Throughout my career as a clinician—working in geriatric, psychiatric, neurological, and private practice settings as a clinician and integrative psychotherapist—I have consistently been impressed by how performance-based personality tests in general, and the Rorschach in particular, can be extremely useful in deepening our understanding of individual strengths and vulnerabilities, as well as the complex psychological and neuropsychological processes underlying various symptom presentations or inner struggles. Within the framework of multimethod assessment, I have repeatedly witnessed how the Rorschach can provide access to insights that are not attainable through other methods, such as interviews, self-report inventories, or traditional cognitive and intelligence tests. In other words, the Rorschach appears—and has been shown—to offer incremental validity when compared to other commonly used assessment tools (e.g., Weiner, 1999, 2005). This is in part because the Rorschach—and performance-based methods more broadly—tap right-hemisphere and subcortical brain functions and provide information about implicit neuropsychological processes that clients cannot directly report. By giving clients the opportunity to engage aspects of their neuropsychological functioning that lie outside conscious awareness, assessment can offer clinicians a deeper understanding of the psychological functioning of their clients while simultaneously providing clients with lifechanging insights and powerful emotional experiences which are often necessary to promote therapeutic shifts (Finn, 2012).

In addition to my long-standing interest in the Rorschach and other performance-based methods, I have also been deeply engaged with both psychodynamic theory and neuropsychology since the early stages of my career. However, as I first became actively involved in the international communities of personality assessment and neuropsychology in the late 1990s, regularly attending and presenting at conferences, I quickly realized—much to my regret—that there appeared to be an artificial divide between these two worlds, reminiscent of an outdated Cartesian version of mind–body dualism (Descartes, 1996). One widely held implicit assumption I observed among colleagues was the idea that brain functions—typically linked to cognitive domains such as attention, memory, and executive functioning and measured by traditional neuropsychological tests—play a more significant role in brain–behavior relationships than the functions of the mind. Valtonen et al. (2021) have referred to this assumption—which they empirically demonstrated to be widespread—as *neurodualism*, the belief that the brain affects the mind more than the mind affects the brain.

Despite the widespread persistence of dualistic and asymmetrical thinking about the relationship between the brain and the mind—a pattern also evident in the field of mental health, particularly in debates over the relative emphasis on psychopharmacological versus psychotherapeutic treatments—the movement of *neuropsychoanalysis* has, since the early 1990s, made significant contributions toward bridging the artificial gap between neuroscience, psychiatry, and psychoanalysis (e.g., Damasio,

1994; Solms & Turnbull, 2002). Although over two-thirds of neuropsychologists do not use the Rorschach (Smith et al., 2010) and some may even hold dismissive attitudes toward it, the development of the CS and the R-PAS—with their conceptualization of the test as a performance-based, perceptual–cognitive problem-solving task grounded in empirical evidence—has uniquely positioned the test to contribute to these ongoing integrative efforts, particularly in bridging the gap between personality and neuropsychological assessment.

As initially illustrated in my doctoral dissertation, which explored the neurocognitive correlates of the Rorschach in a geriatric population and in dementia of the Alzheimer's type (Muzio, 2006), my interest in integrating performance-based personality assessment and neuropsychology began three decades ago. Today, I believe the time has come to synthesize the extensive body of research that has since accumulated on the neuropsychological applications of the Rorschach. I also believe the time is right to finally make available a foundational textbook—one that can serve as a practical resource for clinicians seeking to broaden the scope of their assessment practice, and as a springboard for researchers aiming to further deepen our understanding of brain–behavior relationships from a more integrative perspective. Finally—and perhaps most importantly—I believe it is time to move beyond the mind–body dichotomy that still prevails in much of our field and toward a truly integrated model for understanding the complexity of brain–mind–behavior relationships.

Notes

1 Note that in both the Finnish and European survey, all psychological tests were considered, including intelligence and cognitive/neuropsychological tests, personality tests, measures of psychopathology, and other tests. Countries included in the European survey included Austria, Belgium, Croatia, Czech Republic, Germany, Greece, Lithuania, The Netherlands, Norway, Poland, Romania, Spain, Slovakia, Slovenia, Turkey, and the UK.

2 For example, in a study of 144 brain-injured patients, only scale L (Lie) was significantly correlated with the global level of neuropsychological impairment, raising concerns about profile validity in more impaired cases ($r = -.27$, $p < .05$; Gass, 1997). Additionally, the MMPI has been described as a "murky measure" in neuropsychological assessment, as several clinical scales may be elevated in neurologically impaired individuals simply because their symptoms are consistent with neuropsychological dysfunction—not necessarily due to psychopathology or poor emotional adjustment (Cripe, 1996).

3 Note that the manual for the Rorschach Performance Assessment System (R-PAS; Meyer et al., 2011) had not yet been published at that time.

4 While perception typically refers to the direct sensory registration of external stimuli, apperception goes a step further and involves how the individual interprets, organizes, or gives meaning to what is perceived.

5 Rorschach found that the final title of his book, which the editor insisted on, went beyond the scope of his research. He regretted it and would have preferred

the original title he selected for the monograph: Method and Results of a Perceptual-Diagnostic Experiment: Interpretation of Arbitrary Forms (Exner, 2003, pp. 5–6).

6 As Exner (2003, p. 184) describes: "Projections can and do occur in the Rorschach and their presence often adds considerably to the interpretive yield of the test, but it is important to discriminate projected material from that which is not." Popular and perceptually accurate responses based exclusively on the contours of the blots, for example, do not typically include projected material. Furthermore, Exner describes different types of projections (Exner, 2003, pp. 183–185).

References

Acklin, M. W., & Wu-Holt, P. (1996). Contributions of cognitive science to the Rorschach technique: Cognitive and neuropsychological correlates of the response process. *Journal of Personality Assessment*, 67(1), 169–178.

Bornstein, R. F., & Hopwood, C. J. (2017). Evidence-based assessment of interpersonal dependency. *Professional Psychology: Research and Practice*, 48(4), 251–258. doi:10.1037/pr00000036

Butcher, J. N., Dahlstrom, W. G., Graham, J. R., Tellegen, A., & Kaemmer, B. (1989). *Minnesota Multiphasic Personality Inventory–2 (MMPI-2): Manual for administration and scoring*. University of Minnesota Press.

Chabert, C. (1998). *Psychanalyse et méthodes projectives.* Dunod.

Cripe, L. I. (1996). The MMPI in neuropsychological assessment: A murky measure. *Applied Neuropsychology*, 3(3–4), 97–103. doi:10.1207/s15324826an0303-4_1.

Damasio, A. (1994). *Descartes' error: Emotion, reason, and the human brain*. Putnam.

de Ruiter, C., Giromini, L., Meyer, G. J., King, C. M., & Rubin, B. A. (2023). Clarifying sound and suspect use of the Rorschach in forensic mental health evaluations: A response to Areh et al. (2022). *Psychological Injury and Law*, 16 (2), 158–176. doi:10.1007/s12207-023-09472-6.

Dean, K. L., Viglione, D. J., Perry, W., & Meyer, G. J. (2007). A method to optimize the response range while maintaining Rorschach comprehensive system validity. *Journal of Personality Assessment*, 89(2), 149–161. doi:10.1080/00223890701468543.

Descartes, R. (1996). *Meditations on first philosophy* (J. Cottingham, Trans.). Cambridge University Press. First published 1641.

Diener, M. J., Hilsenroth, M. J., Shaffer, S. A., & Sexton, J. E. (2011). A meta-analysis of the relationship between the Rorschach Ego Impairment Index (EII) and psychiatric severity. *Clinical Psychology & Psychotherapy*, 18(6), 464–485.

Evers, A., Muñiz, J., Bartram, D., Boben, D., Egeland, J., Fernández-Hermida, J. R., Frans, Ö., Gintiliené, G., Hagemeister, C., Halama, P., Iliescu, D., Jaworowska, A., Jiménez, P., Manthouli, M., Matesic, K., Schittekatte, M., Sümer, H. C., & Urbánek, T. (2012). Testing practices in the 21st century: Developments and European psychologists' opinions. *European Psychologist*, 17(4), 300–319. doi:10.1027/1016-9040/a000102.

Exner, J. E. (1969). *The Rorschach systems.* Grune & Stratton.

Exner, J. E. (1974). *The Rorschach: A comprehensive system*. John Wiley & Sons.

Exner, J. E. (2003). *The Rorschach: A comprehensive system: Volume 1: Basic foundations and principles of interpretation* (4th ed.). Wiley.

Exner, J. E., Andronikof, A., & Fontan, P. (2022a). *The Rorschach: A comprehensive system—revised. Administration and coding manual.* Rorschach Workshops.

Exner, J. E., Fontan, P., & Andronikof, A. (2022b). *The Rorschach: A comprehensive system—revised. Interpretation and technical manual.* Rorschach Workshops.

Finn, S. E. (2007). *In our clients' shoes: Theory and techniques of therapeutic assessment.* Lawrence Erlbaum Associates.

Finn, S. E. (2012). Implications of recent research in neurobiology for psychological assessment. *Journal of Personality Assessment*, 94(5), 440–449. doi:10.1080/00223891.2012.700665.

Finnish Psychological Association. (2024). Datadiagnoosi: Testien käyttö tarkastelun alla [Data diagnosis: A closer look at the use of psychological tests]. *Psykologi*, 59(4), 24–25.

Friston, K. (2009). The free-energy principle: A rough guide to the brain? *Trends in Cognitive Sciences*, 13(7), 293–301. doi:10.1016/j.tics.2009.04.005.

Friston, K. (2010). The free-energy principle: A unified brain theory? *Nature Reviews Neuroscience*, 11(2), 127–138. doi:10.1038/nrn2787.

Gass, C. S. (1997). Assessing patients with neurological impairments. Paper presented at the University of Minnesota MMPI-2 Clinical Workshops and Symposia, Minneapolis, MN.

Jung, C. G. (1910). *Studies in word association.* Heinemann.

Meloy, J. R. (2005). Comment: Some reflections on what's wrong with the Rorschach? *Journal of Personality Assessment*, 85(3), 344–346. doi:10.1207/s15327752jpa8503_11.

Meyer, G. J., & Friston, K. J. (2022). The active Bayesian brain and the Rorschach task. *Rorschachiana*, 43(2), 128–150. doi:10.1027/1192-5604/a000158.

Meyer, G. J., & Kurtz, J. E. (2006). Advancing personality assessment terminology: Time to retire "objective" and "projective" as personality test descriptors. Editorial. *Journal of Personality Assessment*, 87(3), 223–225. doi:10.1207/s15327752jpa8703_01.

Meyer, G. J., Erard, R. E., Erdberg, P., Mihura, J. L., & Viglione, D. J. (2011). *Rorschach Performance Assessment System: Administration, coding, interpretation, and technical manual.* Rorschach Performance Assessment System LLC.

Meyer, G. J., Hsiao, W.-C., Viglione, D. J., Mihura, J. L., & Abraham, L. M. (2013). Rorschach scores in applied clinical practice: A survey of perceived validity by experienced clinicians. *Journal of Personality Assessment*, 95(4), 351–365. doi:10.1080/00223891.2013.770399.

Mihura, J. L., Jowers, C. E., Dumitrascu, N., van den Hurk, A. W. V., & Keddy, P. J. (2022). The specific uses of the Rorschach in clinical practice: Preliminary results from an international survey. Rorschachiana, 43(1), 25–41. doi:10.1027/1192-5604/a000155.

Mihura, J. L., Meyer, G. J., Dumitrascu, N., & Bombel, G. (2013). The validity of individual Rorschach variables: Systematic reviews and meta-analyses of the comprehensive system. *Psychological Bulletin*, 139(3), 548–605. doi:10.1037/a0029406.

Muzio, E. (2006). Vers une approche neuropsychologique intégrée de la personnalité à travers le Rorschach en gériatrie et dans la démence de type Alzheimer [Toward an integrated neuropsychological approach to personality through the Rorschach in geriatrics and dementia of the Alzheimer's type]. Doctoral dissertation. Université Paris X—Nanterre. https://theses.fr/2006PA100172.

Porcelli, P. (2025). Embodied mentalization: The case of human movement in the Rorschach. *Rorschachiana*, 46(1), 3–23. doi:10.1027/1192-5604/a000189.

Rorschach, H. (2021). *Hermann Rorschach's psychodiagnostics: Newly translated and annotated 100th anniversary edition.* (P. J. Keddy, R. Signer, P. Erdberg & A. Schneider-Stocking, Eds.). Hogrefe Publishing. First published 1921.

Schurz, M., Radua, J., Tholen, M. G., Maliske, L., Margulies, D. S., Mars, R. B., Sallet, J., & Kanske, P. (2021). Toward a hierarchical model of social cognition: A neuroimaging meta-analysis and integrative review of empathy and theory of mind. *Psychological Bulletin*, 147(3), 293–327. doi:10.1037/bul0000303.

Searls, D. (2017). *The inkblots: Hermann Rorschach, his iconic test, and the power of seeing*. Simon & Schuster.

Smith, S. R., Gorske, T. T., Wiggins, C., & Little, J. A. (2010). Personality assessment use by clinical neuropsychologists. *International Journal of Testing*, 10(1), 6–20. doi:10.1080/15305050903534787.

Solms, M., & Turnbull, O. (2002). *The brain and the inner world: An introduction to the neuroscience of subjective experience.* Karnac Books.

Valtonen, J., Ahn, W.-K., & Cimpian, A. (2021). Neurodualism: People assume that the brain affects the mind more than the mind affects the brain. *Cognitive Science*, 45(9), Article e13034. doi:10.1111/cogs.13034.

Weiner, I. B. (1999). What the Rorschach can do for you: Incremental validity in clinical applications. *Assessment*, 6(4), 327–339. doi:10.1177/107319119900600404.

Weiner, I. B. (2005). Rorschach assessment in child custody cases. *Journal of Child Custody: Research, Issues, and Practices*, 2(3), 99–119. doi:10.1300/J190v02n03_05.

Wood, J. M., Garb, H. N., Nezworski, M. T., Lilienfeld, S. O., & Duke, M. C. (2015). A second look at the validity of widely used Rorschach indices: Comment on Mihura, Meyer, Dumitrascu, and Bombel (2013). *Psychological Bulletin*, 141(1), 236–249. doi:10.1037/a0036005.

Wood, J. M., Nezworski, M. T., Lilienfeld, S. O., & Garb, H. N. (2003). *What's wrong with the Rorschach? Science confronts the controversial inkblot test.* Jossey-Bass.

Zillmer, E. A. (1994). The brain has a personality of its own. *SPA Exchange*, 6(2), 7–8.

Zillmer, E. A., & Perry, W. (1996). Cognitive-neuropsychological abilities and related psychological disturbance: A factor model of neuropsychological, Rorschach, and MMPI indices. *Assessment*, 3(3), 209–224. doi:10.1177/107319119600300303.

Chapter 2

Rorschach, Piotrowski, and Early Studies on Neurological Populations

The Rorschach stands apart from other widely used psychological assessment tools in that it emerged before the advent of modern neuroimaging technologies. By the late nineteenth century, important discoveries—such as those by Paul Broca and Carl Wernicke on language-related brain areas—had begun to illuminate brain–behavior relationships, though the field of neuropsychology was still in its infancy (for a broad historical review, see Finger, 2001). As the Rorschach gained popularity in the first half of the twentieth century, psychiatric hospitals typically treated patients with a wide range of both psychiatric and neurological conditions—such as schizophrenia, epilepsy, dementia, and traumatic brain injury (TBI)—offering Hermann Rorschach, then a hospital psychiatrist, broad clinical exposure to both populations (Caputo, 1999). It is within this historical context that Rorschach began using his method.

Hermann Rorschach's Seminal Work

Five of the twenty-eight cases Rorschach used as examples in his 1921 monograph *Psychodiagnostics* illustrate the use of the test in assessing "organic psychotic disorders" (Rorschach, 2021, pp. 203–210). These included a case of "depression in arteriosclerotic dementia," a case of "alcoholism with Korsakoff's psychosis," a case of "progressive paralysis," a case of "definite dementia," and a case of "encephalitis lethargica." In the chapter preceding the one where he presents these cases, Rorschach also outlines two protocols for epileptic patients: one defined as "typical epileptic dementia, rapid onset," and the other as "epileptoid" (2021, pp. 198–202).

For these seven cases, Rorschach presents only a few structural findings for the protocols and provides only brief descriptions. His "counts, calculations, and summary scores" section includes a limited set of codes for "whole or parts," "determinants," and "contents." The structural summary findings reported concern the percentage of responses with good form quality (i.e., perceptually accurate responses: *F*+), the percentage of animal content (*A*), the percentage of "original responses," and a

DOI: 10.4324/9781003731894-3

classification of the "visual-grasping type" and "succession"—terms related to the types of location codes used and their sequence. This illustrates how Rorschach was primarily focused on quantifying perceptual accuracy and conventionality as well as qualifying information processing in terms of both location and determinants. Contents were of marginal importance.

As an example, in the case Rorschach labels "definite dementia," which concerns a 78-year-old man who had "shown definite senile dementia for the last three years," Rorschach writes that "the experiment was spread over several days to avoid perseveration" (2021, pp. 208–209). The reasons for this choice remain unclear although he states that "if the whole experiment had been performed in one day, the patient would probably have seen nothing but 'horses' heads' or 'sunshades' (parasols), or perhaps nothing but plants and flowers" (pp. 208–209). This is speculative, although it is true that the protocol consisted of purely formal responses, either with animal content (horses' heads, birds), botanical content (flowers, leaves), or sunshades.

Rorschach adds that the patient "always returned to plants in his responses, as did another respondent with senile dementia" (2021, pp. 208–209). He also notes that, interestingly, "six- to eight-year-old children also appear to prefer plants in their interpretations" (2021, pp. 208–209). Finally, he concludes his commentary by noting that "the intelligence type remains more like that which prevailed when the patient was normal for a longer period in patients with senile dementia than in patients with paresis (progressive paralysis)" (2021, pp. 208–209).[1] This illustrates how Rorschach looked for patterns in responding across conditions and how he considered his test a potentially useful tool for differential diagnosis.

Rorschach's early observations and comments regarding the neuropsychological cases he presented as examples are brief and sometimes speculative given their explorative nature. However, from the outset of his experiment, Rorschach demonstrated that his test could be used for both "organic" and "nonorganic" mental disorders. The fact that a significant proportion of the cases he chose to present in his monograph fall into the "organic" category supports this idea. At the end of the monograph, he concludes by writing that "the experiment has the advantage of almost unlimited applicability, and the findings of the most heterogeneous respondents can easily be compared with each other" (Rorschach, 2021, p. 212).

For Rorschach, his inkblot test was not, strictly speaking, a test but rather an experiment of an eminently empirical nature and an investigation for which the theoretical foundations were largely in their infancy. The formulation of Rorschach responses reflected, for him, a conscious operation in which the subject integrates memory traces with the sensations provoked by the stimulus. He describes a continuum between recognition (e.g., in dementia, other neurocognitive disorders, or schizophrenia, where patients "name" the stimuli as if they were something concrete) and interpretation (i.e., the way the task is perceived by most healthy respondents—with an awareness of the associative effort of integration involved in the task). As Rorschach noted in a 1920 lecture, the experiment represents the *fonction du réel*—that is, the adaptation of the person to external sensations, or external reality. It is not a test of free association (Rorschach, 2021, p. 25).

Finally, Rorschach considered—just as is the case today in leading systems such as the Comprehensive System (CS; Exner, 2003) and the Rorschach Performance Assessment System (R-PAS; Meyer et al., 2011)—that the task constitutes a representative sample of an individual's behavior, collected in a standardized situation and enabling inferences about various aspects of psychological functioning, including the integrity of brain functioning. However, as Piotrowski later pointed out, "Rorschach did not present his ideas about the organic personality in a systematic manner," and "he had not examined all types of organic nervous disorders" (Piotrowski, 1937, pp. 525–526).

Zygmunt Piotrowski's Ten Organic Signs

Emil Oberholzer, a close collaborator of Hermann Rorschach, continued to explore the test's application to neurological cases after Rorschach's death in 1922. In a detailed case study of a patient with a TBI, he observed that such individuals struggled to synthesize details, often interpreted the inkblots as concrete objects they were expected to recognize, and gave poor, uniform responses marked by frequent perseverations and delayed reaction times. Although they produced many original responses, these were typically of poor quality and inadequate. Oberholzer also noted a tendency to give more color-determined responses and fewer human movement (*M*) responses. Nevertheless, their cooperation and interest in the task remained intact (Oberholzer, 1931, as cited in Piotrowski, 1937).

Piotrowski (1937) noted that while not all patients exhibited every characteristic described by Oberholzer, these features were typical of individuals with neurological conditions. He emphasized that no single sign alone indicates psychiatric or organic brain abnormality; rather, it is the accumulation of abnormal signs that suggests dysfunction. He also stressed that such signs offer only part of the picture and must be integrated with broader aspects of the individual's Rorschach performance.

Confirming most of Oberholzer's observations, Piotrowski called for more specific interpretive guidelines. His seminal study compared Rorschach characteristics across three groups: patients with cortical–subcortical conditions (n = 18), those with noncerebral neurological conditions (n = 10), and individuals with conversion hysteria (n = 5). Building on the observations of Rorschach and Oberholzer, reference data from healthy adults, and his own preliminary findings, Piotrowski identified ten Rorschach signs indicative of "organicity." He proposed that the presence of at least five of these signs in an adult's protocol could suggest an organic disorder affecting cortical and/or subcortical brain regions. These ten signs are presented and described in Table 2.1.

Piotrowski's findings supported his hypothesis. In the cortical–subcortical group (n = 18), the average number of organic signs was 6.2, compared to only 1.5 in the noncerebral groups (n = 15). All patients in the cortical–subcortical group had more organic signs than any individual in the other groups, with scores ranging from 4 to 9. Only one patient with cortical brain damage—a 36-year-old woman with a favorable prognosis and residual damage to the left frontal lobe—had fewer than five signs. In contrast, the highest number of signs in the noncerebral groups was three.

As described in more detail below and in later chapters, subsequent research with neurocognitively impaired patients supports the validity of Piotrowski's ten organic signs. However, his administration and scoring methods differ from contemporary systems such as the CS and the R-PAS. For instance, Piotrowski included response time, which is not measured in the CS or the R-PAS. He also reported that adults rarely gave fewer than thirty responses, whereas CS reference data show an average of around twenty-two (Meyer et al., 2007). This discrepancy likely reflects differences in instructions and administration procedures, especially given the consistent average number of responses across CS international samples. In clinical practice using the CS or the R-PAS, protocols with more than thirty responses are uncommon.

Signs unique to the cortical–subcortical group are of particular interest. One of the more specific indicators, according to both Piotrowski and Rorschach, is color-naming (*Cn*). Rorschach observed this in epileptic patients, including a 26-year-old man with epileptic seizures since age thirteen, whose protocol included ten color nominations out of twenty-nine responses, and a 29-year-old "epileptoid" nurse, with two *Cn* responses out of twenty.

Piotrowski describes color-naming as a clear sign of neurocognitive impairment in these patients. It does not reflect the kind of avoidance that can be observed in some neurotic patients, for example. The difference lies in the formulation of *Cn* responses and in the definitive nature of these responses in the neuropsychologically impaired subject. Drohocki (1928; cited by Piotrowski, 1937), in a study of the different states of a group of eighty epileptic patients, noted that the quality of these patients' responses varied according to their condition. In the period following a seizure, there was an increase in the number of *M* responses and especially in the number of color responses, a decrease in the number of responses determined exclusively by form (*F*), a decrease in the formal quality of responses (*F+%*) and an increase in the number of *Cn* responses. The latter

Table 2.1 Piotrowski's ten organic signs (Piotrowski, 1937).

1.	*R*	The total number of responses is less than 15.
2.	*T*	The average time per response is more than one minute.
3.	*M*	The number of movement responses, as defined by Rorschach (meaning only human movement; for more details see Rorschach, 2021, pp. 45–49) is no more than one. Piotrowski adds here that "few normals give less than two (human) movement responses" (1937, p. 527).
4.	*Cn*	The protocol contains at least one color denomination. Piotrowski adds here that "normal subjects give no color denominations at all" (1937, p. 527). He defines these as responses that contain merely the name and description of the stimulus and, if it is considered by the subject as a satisfactory response, calling for no additional explanations. The subject must clearly show that by naming the color they have "settled the matter" to their "satisfaction." Examples from cortical–subcortical organic patients are: "This is red." "These are four daubs of red ink, two of green and two of yellow." "This one has a number of nice colors, particularly the yellow one, the pink, the green and on the top here the gray" (Piotrowski, 1937, p. 527). Piotrowski also mentions that "sometimes neurotics give responses which are similar to those just cited but which really are more than color denominations, and not difficult to recognize" (1937, p. 527). He offers as examples from his material the following: "What the heck is the red going through?" "I cannot guess it, just a mass of colors," and "The green is beyond me, dear, I cannot say anything about it." The phrasing suggests that these subjects do not consider their responses to be satisfactory or adequate. As Piotrowski puts it, "the doubt puts these responses outside the class of color denominations" (1937, p. 527).
5.	*F+%*	The percentage of "good form responses" (i.e., perceptually accurate responses), as defined by Rorschach (see 2021, pp. 43–45), is below 70 percent. Piotrowski mentions here that the average is around 80 percent for normal adults.
6.	*P%*	The percentage of popular responses (i.e., responses given by at least one-third of normal subjects) is less than 25 percent. Piotrowski states that normal subjects give about 30 percent of such responses on average and that "a very small percentage of popular responses points to an inability to adjust to the practical requirements of life, to an insufficient participation in collective common thinking" (1937, p. 527).
7.	*Rpt*	The repetition or the giving of the same response to several inkblots. As Piotrowski specifies further, this "does not imply meaningless and stereotyped perseveration of one idea," although the latter can also occur. Piotrowski gives the example of a patient who gave fourteen responses of which ten expressed the idea: "Decoration on a helmet for high officials" (1937, pp. 527–528). He also adds that usually the first of such repetitive responses is of good formal quality while those that follow are of poorer quality. Normal adults do not perseverate in such a manner.

8.	*Imp*	"Impotence" or giving a response despite recognition of its inadequacy. The patient has realized that at least one of their responses is of poor quality and yet has not withdrawn it. Here Piotrowski adds that "in cortical cases valid self-criticism is disproportionately better than the ability to correct the recognized mistakes" (1937, p. 528). He continues: "Their intellectual impotence appears to be due, on the one hand, to a paucity of ideas, an inability to think of a new and better response, and on the other hand to a strong tendency to give a definite response to any stimulation, to go through with the process that has once been initiated" (1937, p. 528). This does not occur in the absence of *Rpt*: the previous sign and these responses are almost invariably of poor form quality, which distinguishes them from other types of tendencies to hesitate. Apparent impotence in healthy adults is typically prompted by the realization that the inkblots can be interpreted in a variety of ways. In contrast, as Piotrowski describes, "The cortical case does not seem to think in terms of better and worse but merely in terms of yes and no. He prefers clear cut decisions to qualified statements" (1937, p. 528). Piotrowski gives the following examples: "The shape of a butterfly, yet that seems ridiculous to say. I'm afraid I'll be a bad pupil." "If that is a bat, it is a foolish one." "A butterfly perhaps. What is it really, doctor?" "Some kind of animal but I cannot tell what it is" (1937, p. 528).
9.	*Plx*	Perplexity associated with distrust of one's own ability and quest for reassurance. The subject experiences unpleasant doubt and tries to satisfy their mind by pressing the examiner to decide for them whether their responses are adequate. Examples mentioned by Piotrowski are, for example: "I never saw anything like this before. Is it supposed to be an air bird or something? That's where I am puzzled." "Two dogs. I love dogs. I had a dog. It was a brown dog. No, he was yellow. What else can a dog be, doctor? I can't explain myself. Symmetry, two things on both sides. I give up" (1937, pp. 528–529). This type of perplexity is extremely infrequent in normal adults.
10.	*AP*	Automatic phrases or the frequent use of a pet phrase in an indiscriminate fashion. These phrases are used mechanically without troubling to see whether they are appropriate or not. They may be described as stereotyped reactions to new situations taking place or preceding a more specific and better adjusted reaction to the situation. Piotrowksi gives the following examples: "It's some kind of work . . . It's good work . . . This is some work." "Previously I could recognize this but now I cannot say anything." "I don't like it. It is not nice" (1937, p. 529). These types of automatic phrases are extremely infrequent in normal adults.

appeared to be given to locations where, before the seizure, a more articulated response was given. For example, one of Drohocki's patients gave the following response before the seizure episode: "A little frog because it's green." On the day of the episode, the response was transformed into "It's painted green, blue, pink." Drohocki concludes that epileptic seizures inhibit the most phylogenetically recent mental mechanisms, as expressed in the formal quality of responses, and trigger the use of more primitive forms of reaction, such as color responses without regard to form (Drohocki, 1932; cited by Piotrowski, 1937).

Piotrowski argued that, unlike Rorschach's original view, *Cn* responses are not exclusive to epilepsy and can appear even in protocols with a high proportion of perceptually accurate responses. In his sample, three of eight cortical-subcortical patients with *Cn* responses had over 70 percent good form quality. He interpreted *Cn* as a sign of "emotional disintegration," reflecting emotional reactions that lacked strength and persistence. These responses appeared impulsively and dissipated quickly.

In a study of ninety chronic schizophrenia patients, Skalweit (1934, as cited in Piotrowski, 1937) found twenty-eight protocols with *Cn* responses. He considered these responses as indicative of "organic" schizophrenia, particularly when associated with overall low form quality and a predominantly extratensive style with few or no *M* responses.

Another pathognomonic sign of organicity observed by Piotrowski was the inability to respond to the inkblots. Eleven of his eighteen cortical–subcortical patients failed to respond to at least one of the ten cards. These same patients often showed a tendency to respond despite recognizing the inadequacy of their answers ("impotence") along with perplexity and the use of automatic or stereotyped sentences. According to Oberholzer (1931, as cited in Piotrowski, 1937), this may also occur in schizophrenia.

Piotrowski observed, with some surprise, that many patients in the cortical–subcortical group showed a high percentage of responses with good form quality—a finding later echoed in other studies of neuropsychological populations. He also noted a low number of *M* responses and a high number of color-determined responses, which he interpreted as reflecting a poverty of inner life and a strong dependence on environmental stimuli. Additionally, he reported a high frequency of anatomical content and perseverations, particularly in cases then classified as "senile dementia."

Piotrowski's seminal work marked the beginning of a more systematic exploration of neurologically impaired individuals using the Rorschach. His system of administration and scoring became one of the five most widely recognized Rorschach approaches in the USA with the publication of *Perceptanalysis* (Piotrowski, 1957). Alongside the systems developed by other Rorschach pioneers, Piotrowski's approach served as a foundational influence in the development of the CS (for an overview of early Rorschach history, see Exner, 2003, pp. 3–27).

In addition to quantitative findings, Piotrowski also described qualitative features typical of neuropsychological protocols. He noted a pattern of "intellectual passivity," in which patients appeared unaware that multiple interpretations of the inkblots were possible. Rather than selecting among alternatives, they treated the images as if they depicted concrete, recognizable objects, often resisting the idea that no single "correct" answer exists. Piotrowski also observed that these individuals tended to perceive the inkblots vaguely, struggling to localize percepts—a difficulty he attributed to the vagueness of the internal images they attempted to project. Based on these observations, Piotrowski described the personalities of these patients as lacking coherence and stability, which led to a mode of responding that was unpredictable and variable in quality, despite a cooperative attitude and apparent motivation to do well.

Four of Piotrowski's ten organic signs were present in at least two-thirds of his eighteen cortical–subcortical protocols. These signs were, in order of frequency: $M < 2$, the presence of several perseverative responses (*Rpt*), a high average response time ($T > 1$ min), and overall poor form quality ($F+\% < 70$ percent). Piotrowski (1937, p. 536) deduced from this that "the function suffering most is the ability for a well-developed, active and constructive inner life." From Piotrowski's perspective, perseverative responses were the aftereffect of this deficit. They represented a tendency to use old ideas that were adaptive at one time but often inadequate in the present moment rather than not using any at all. This could also be seen as a sign of poverty of associations, which, along with the impoverishment of the subject's inner life and the decline of their cognitive functions, ultimately translates into a progressive increase in response times and a loss of clarity in perception and thinking.

The validity of Piotrowski's signs has been supported by subsequent studies involving diverse groups of neuropsychological patients and healthy controls as well as by research examining their associations with neurodiagnostic methods and patients' response to treatment. In a study by Aita et al. (1947), the Rorschach protocols of sixty patients with TBI were compared to those of 100 control patients to identify features characteristic of cerebral organicity using Piotrowski's ten organic signs. The results indicated that *impotence* (*Imp*), *perplexity* (*Plx*), *automatic phrases* (*AP*), *repetition* (*Rpt*), and *color-naming* (*Cn*) were useful in identifying patients with brain injury. The authors also observed that schizophrenia-like disturbances occasionally appeared in the TBI group. A high frequency of organic signs in TBI patients was later confirmed by studies that also demonstrated their strong diagnostic specificity (Chaudhury et al., 1999; Nedelcu & Zellingher, 1971). Additionally, Piotrowski's signs have been associated with abnormal electroencephalogram (EEG) results and psychotic disorders classified as organic (Vitorović et al., 1975); with performance on the Bender–Gestalt Test—a visual-motor test (Piotrowski, 1995)—in patients with brain lesions (Shukla et al., 1987); with the performance of patients who had undergone commissurotomy (Lewis, 1979); and with poorer response to L-Dopa treatment in patients with Parkinson's disease (Sevilla et al., 1973).

A study of 181 nonclinical subjects aged 18–62 years (Mattlar et al., 1986) found that a score of 5 or more on Piotrowski's ten-sign scale is rare among younger individuals (ages 20–40) but becomes increasingly common from age 48 onward. Analysis of variance revealed a significant association with age but not with intelligence, as measured by IQ scales. Factor analysis identified a three-factor structure: (1) *Disturbance of the speed of percept formation* (*R, T, M*); (2) *Hesitation and rigidity* (*F+%, P, Rpt, Imp*); and (3) *Inability to manage emotions* (*Cn*). *Perplexity* (*Plx*) correlated primarily with the first factor but also with the second. Age was significantly associated with the first two factors. *Cn*, which alone defined the third factor, appeared to have a special status: it was not directly related to age although it did correlate with the first factor. This supports the view that *Cn* may reflect a more specifically organic response pattern, as originally proposed by Piotrowski (1937).

Many of the features described as organic signs on the Rorschach can be generalized to other performance-based or projective personality tests commonly used by psychologists and neuropsychologists. In the fourth edition of *Neuropsychological Assessment*, for example, Lezak et al. (2004, pp. 738–743) describe several characteristics typical of individuals with brain damage on such tests. These include response constriction and simplification as well as *stimulus-boundedness*—a tendency to respond in concrete ways closely tied to the superficial features of the stimulus. For instance, on the Thematic Apperception Test (Murray, 1943), a subject might give a concrete, literal description of a static scene (e.g., "Here's a man with a horse, and here's a woman and a younger woman"), rather than generating a story, as required by standard instructions. On the Wartegg Drawing Completion Test (Crisi & Palm, 2018), a subject might repeatedly copy the original stimulus (a little mark) instead of producing a meaningful drawing. On the Rorschach, this phenomenon might manifest as a response like "It looks like an inkblot," or as a *Cn* response. As Lezak et al. (2004) described, these responses often have a "sticky" quality.

Lezak et al. also describe typical behaviors in brain-damaged individuals such as structure-seeking, response rigidity, and fragmentation. These individuals often feel uncomfortable in unstructured, open-ended, or emotionally arousing situations. They frequently seek guidance from the examiner and tend to get "stuck" in recurring themes or response patterns, indicating impaired cognitive flexibility. Such difficulties are particularly evident in cases of prefrontal damage or executive dysfunction and are reflected in rigid task approaches and perseverative responses. A common difficulty involves organizing stimuli meaningfully, resulting in fragmented perception. For example, a subject might describe "head," "hands," and "feet" on Rorschach Card IV without integrating them into a coherent human or humanlike figure. This lack of synthesis is often striking, particularly in situations where most individuals would integrate elements easily and spontaneously.

Finally, Lezak et al. also report other common features, including conceptual confusion, spatial disorientation, confabulation, and perplexity. These behaviors—observed across both structured and open-ended tasks—reflect disordered thinking, often marked by unrealistic, bizarre, or tangential reasoning, as well as repeated hesitation and difficulty improving the quality of their responses.

Echoing Piotrowski's observations, Lezak et al. emphasize that these response patterns are rare in healthy individuals but can also appear in severe psychopathology (e.g., schizophrenia). They note, however, that it is uncommon to find all these features in a single brain-damaged subject (Lezak et al., 2004, p. 739). As shown in the next section and subsequent chapters, different types of neuropsychological impairment appear to impact Rorschach performance in distinct ways. Recognizing these patterns may assist clinicians with questions of differential diagnosis and deepen our understanding of the perceptual and cognitive effects of different forms of brain damage.

The Long History of Rorschach Research with Neurological Populations

In her review of the literature, Caputo (1999) identified 417 published studies that used the Rorschach to assess neurological populations between the publication of Rorschach's seminal work and the 1990s, with publication activity peaking in the 1940s and 1950s (accounting for 45 percent of the total). As summarized by Caputo, research during that period focused primarily on describing personality functioning in various neurological disorders (e.g., temporal lobe epilepsy, Parkinson's disease); examining the psychological characteristics of individuals with intellectual disabilities or head injuries (particularly in the context of World War II); or assessing individuals who had undergone lobectomies or prefrontal lobotomies for therapeutic purposes. Most studies were aimed at assisting clinicians with the differential diagnosis of brain lesions, assessing perceptual and cognitive processes, describing characteristic personality features in these individuals, or identifying Rorschach signs of "organicity," as discussed in the previous section.

Caputo also highlights the interesting fact that, during a period when prefrontal lobotomies and lobectomies were frequently employed as psychosurgical treatments for a broad range of mental disorders (1936–1955), Rorschach studies on these patients were among the first to identify core neuropsychological characteristics associated with prefrontal lesions—such as impulsivity and a tendency to produce perseverative responses (e.g., McReynolds & Weide, 1959). She notes, however, that these early contributions are rarely cited, recognized, or even known by contemporary neuropsychologists.

With the development of increasingly sophisticated neuroimaging technologies and standardized neurocognitive tests beginning in the mid twentieth century, criticism of the Rorschach's lack of standardization grew, leading to a decline in its use within neuropsychological settings—particularly among younger clinicians. Nonetheless, some prominent neuropsychologists, such as Ralph Reitan, continued to recognize its value within multimethod assessment, and the Rorschach remained in use for both research and clinical purposes during this period (Caputo, 1999). The introduction of Exner's CS (Exner, 2003) in the 1970s—reconceptualizing the test as a perceptual-cognitive problem-solving task—and its broader international adoption by the 1990s, revived interest in applying the Rorschach from both personality assessment and neuropsychological perspectives (e.g., Acklin & Wu-Holt, 1996), a trend described in further detail in the following chapters.

Note

1 Rorschach used the concept of intelligence in a broad sense, encompassing both cognitive skills and cognitive styles or dispositions. He writes: "Certain optimal relationships of the factors of the experiment correspond to certain components of the trait 'intelligence.' In particular, the calculation of the visual-grasping modes allows the establishment of certain 'visual-grasping types' and intelligence types (abstract, theoretical, practical, imaginative, grumbling, pedantic, etc.)" (Rorschach, 2021, p. 211).

References

Acklin, M. W., & Wu-Holt, P. (1996). Contributions of cognitive science to the Rorschach Technique: Cognitive and neuropsychological correlates of the response process. *Journal of Personality Assessment, 67*(1), 169–178. doi:10.1207/s15327752jpa6701_13

Aita, J. A., Reitan, R. M., & Ruth, J. M. (1947). Rorschach's test as a diagnostic aid in brain injury. *American Journal of Psychiatry*, 103, 770–779. doi:10.1176/ajp.103.6.770

Bornstein, R. F., & Masling, J. M. (2005). The Rorschach Oral Dependency scale. In R. F. Bornstein & J. M. Masling (Eds.), *Scoring the Rorschach: Seven validated systems* (pp. 135–157). Erlbaum.

Caputo, J. S. (1999). The Rorschach as a neuropsychological instrument: Historical precedents and future use. Paper presented at the 16th Congress of the Rorschach and Projective Methods, Amsterdam, Netherlands.

Chaudhury, S., John, T. R., Bhatoe, H. S., & Rohatgi, S. (1999). Evaluation of Piotrowski's organic signs of head injury. *Journal of Projective Psychology & Mental Health*, 6(1), 53–57.

Crisi, A., & Palm, J. A. (2018). *The Crisi Wartegg System (CWS): Manual for administration, scoring, and interpretation.* Routledge.

Drohocki, Z. (1928). Psychologiczne badania nad epilepsja przy pomocy metody Rorschacha [Psychological research on epilepsy using the Rorschach method]. *Nowiny Psychjatryczne*, 1, 32–33.

Drohocki, Z. (1932). Znaczenie typologiczne orjentacji przy pomocy barwy lub kształtu [The typological significance of orientation using color or shape]. *Polish Archives of Psychology*, 5, 406–426.

Exner, J. E. (2003). *The Rorschach: A comprehensive system: Volume 1: Basic foundations and principles of interpretation* (4th ed.). Wiley.

Finger, S. (2001). *Origins of neuroscience: A history of explorations into brain function*. Oxford University Press.

Friedman, M., & Rosenman, R. H. (1974). *Type A behavior and your heart*. Fawcett.

Lewis, R. T. (1979). Organic signs, creativity, and personality characteristics of patients following cerebral commissurotomy. *Clinical Neuropsychology*, 1(4), 29–33.

Lezak, M. D., Howieson, D. B., & Loring, D. (2004). *Neuropsychological assessment*. Oxford University Press.

Mattlar, C. E., Knuts, L. R., & Alanen, E. (1986). The Piotrowski sign system: Its association with age and intelligence and the structure of the Piotrowski signs. *British Journal of Projective Psychology & Personality Study*, 31(1), 3–15.

McReynolds, P., & Weide, M. (1959). The prediction and assessment of psychological changes following prefrontal lobotomy. *Journal of Mental Science*, 105, 971–978. doi:10.1192/bjp.105.441.971

Meyer, G. J., Erard, R. E., Erdberg, P., Mihura, J. L., & Viglione, D. J. (2011). *Rorschach Performance Assessment System: Administration, coding, interpretation, and technical manual*. Rorschach Performance Assessment System LLC.

Meyer, G. J., Erdberg, P., & Shaffer, T. W. (2007). Toward international normative reference data for the Comprehensive System. *Journal of Personality Assessment*, 89(S1), S201–S216.

Meyer, G. J., & Friston, K. J. (2022). The active Bayesian brain and the Rorschach task. *Rorschachiana*, 43(2), 128–150. doi:10.1027/1192-5604/a000158

Murray, H. A. (1943). *Thematic Apperception Test manual*. Harvard University Press.

Nedelcu, A., & Zellingher, R. (1971). Comparative results obtained with the test of organic integrity in recent craniocerebral traumas. *Annales Médico-Psychologiques*, 2(4), 521–526.

Oberholzer, E. (1931). Zur Differentialdiagnose psychischer Folgezustande nach Schadeltraumen mittels des Rorschachschen Formdeutversuchs [Toward the differential diagnosis of psychological sequelae following cranial trauma using the Rorschach test]. *Zeitschrift für Neurologie*, 136, 596–629.

Piotrowski, C. (1995). A review of the clinical and research use of the Bender–Gestalt Test. *Perceptual and Motor Skills*, 81(3), Pt 2, 1272–1274. doi:10.2466/pms.1995.81.3f.1272

Piotrowski, Z. (1937). The Rorschach inkblot method in organic disturbances of the central nervous system. *Journal of Nervous and Mental Disease*, 86(5), 525–537. doi:10.1097/00005053-193711000-00002

Piotrowski, Z. (1957). *Perceptanalysis*. Macmillan.

Rorschach, H. (1976). *Psychodiagnostic* (A. Ombredane & A. Landau, Trans., 5th ed.). Presses Universitaires de France. First published 1921.

Rorschach, H. (2021). *Hermann Rorschach's Psychodiagnostics: Newly translated and annotated 100th anniversary edition*. (P. J. Keddy, R. Signer, P. Erdberg & A. Schneider-Stocking, Eds.). Hogrefe Publishing. First published 1921.

Sevilla, M., Vernet, J. P., Becle, J., & Darcourt, G. (1973). The Rorschach test in Parkinsonians: Its evolution in the course of treatment by L-Dopa. Its prognostic value. *Annales Médico-Psychologiques*, 1(5), 577–608.

Shukla, V., Tripathi, R. R., & Dhar, N. K. (1987). Validation of Pitrowski's Rorschach signs of "organicity" against Bender Visual Motor Gestalt test. *Indian Journal of Clinical Psychology*, 14(2), 84–86.

Skalweit, W. (1934). Konstitution und Prozess in der Schizophrenie [Constitution and process in schizophrenia]. *Sammlung psychiatrischer und neurologischer Einzeldarstellungen*, 5, 88.

Vitorović, M., Cvetko, B., Požarnik, H., & Štrus, F. (1975). Relationship between Rorschach test and electroencephalogram: Preliminary remarks. *Neurologija*, 23 (1–4),111–113.

Waxman, S. G., & Geschwind, N. (1975). The interictal behavior syndrome of temporal lobe epilepsy. *Archives of General Psychiatry*, 32(12), 1580–1586. doi:10.1001/archpsyc.1975.01760300118011

Chapter 3

The Rorschach, Intelligence, and Cognitive Functions

The Rorschach is not a measure of intelligence or cognitive ability. However, Hermann Rorschach was the first to observe that intelligent individuals do tend to share certain perceptual–cognitive characteristics such as good perceptual accuracy or the tendency to produce at least a few responses including human movement (*M*; Rorschach, 2021, p. 77).[1] While not all the features Rorschach originally described are coded in contemporary systems such as the Comprehensive System (CS; Exner, 2003) or the Rorschach Performance Assessment System (R-PAS; Meyer et al., 2011), many correspond to variables later confirmed to correlate with cognitive functioning.

In fact, a substantial body of research has demonstrated associations between Rorschach variables and cognitive test performance, including Wechsler intelligence scales and standard neuropsychological measures of attention, memory, and executive functioning. Much of this work has focused on variables from the CS's *Cognitive Triad*, which includes three clusters of variables: *Information Processing, Cognitive Mediation*, and *Ideation*. These clusters reflect the effort and quality of processing, the identification and translation of stimuli, and the conceptualization of input, respectively (Exner, 2003, pp. 335–444). Although often examined sequentially for practical purposes, Exner emphasized that these processes occur in parallel.[2] For instance, while ideation is influenced by perceptual input, conceptual frameworks (e.g., paranoid ideation) can also shape how new information is perceived and processed (e.g., via a hypervigilant style).

Examining the Cognitive Triad is both clinically intuitive and empirically supported when assessing the relationship between Rorschach and cognitive performance. In the R-PAS, relevant variables are primarily found in the *Engagement and Cognitive Processing* and *Perception and Thinking Problems* domains. Other domains or clusters include significantly fewer variables related to cognitive abilities. However, the assignment of variables to domains or clusters is somewhat arbitrary, as many reflect multiple aspects of functioning. For example, *F%* (*Lambda* in the CS) and *Complexity* (R-PAS) relate to information processing but also

DOI: 10.4324/9781003731894-4

represent a broader coping style. High *F%* (*Lambda*) or low *Complexity* indicates a tendency to oversimplify experience—an approach that affects not only cognitive operations but also emotional processing, self-perception, and interpersonal behavior.

The Rorschach is a test of *typical performance* that reveals how people function in more open-ended situations. Responses may reflect, for example, whether a person tends to perceive stimuli accurately and conventionally or to integrate ideas meaningfully. While there are no explicit "correct" answers on the Rorschach, patterns of responses can reflect either psychological strengths or vulnerabilities, with some codes and scores empirically associated with liabilities or impairment (e.g., *X–%* in the CS or *FQ–%* in the R-PAS) and others with resources (e.g., *M*). By contrast, neurocognitive tests like Wechsler's intelligence scales are tests of *maximum performance*, designed to assess what individuals can do when mobilizing all their resources. These tasks typically involve clear performance criteria. Cronbach (1990) articulated this distinction between maximum performance, which reflects what a person *can* do, and typical performance, which reflects what a person *will* do. Thus, an individual may possess high intellectual ability yet struggle to realize their potential due to factors such as passive-dependent attitudes, a perfectionistic processing style, or depressive symptoms.

The distinction between typical and maximum performance helps explain why statistically significant correlations between Rorschach and cognitive performance variables are typically nonlinear with effect sizes rarely beyond $r = .50$. As shown in Figure 3.1, variables like *M* (a psychological resource), for example, show a triangular pattern: lower cognitive performance predicts low *M* scores, but high cognitive performance allows for a wide range of values for *M*. Figure 3.2 illustrates a similar pattern for negative correlations, for example between cognitive scores and *X–%* or *FQ–%,* where lower cognitive ability predicts higher levels of perceptual inaccuracy but higher cognitive ability allows for a wide range of values for *X–% (FQ–%).*

The following sections review Rorschach variables empirically linked to intelligence and cognitive functions. Many have also been shown to be neurocognitively meaningful in studies of patients with neurocognitive or neurodevelopmental disorders, as well as in neuroimaging research (see Chapters 4 and 5).

Adaptive Resources, Mentalization, and the Coping Deficit Index

According to Exner, "the concept of resource refers to the collective of cognitive capabilities that have been developed, including the manner in which feelings are identified and utilized" (2003, p. 232). Exner described

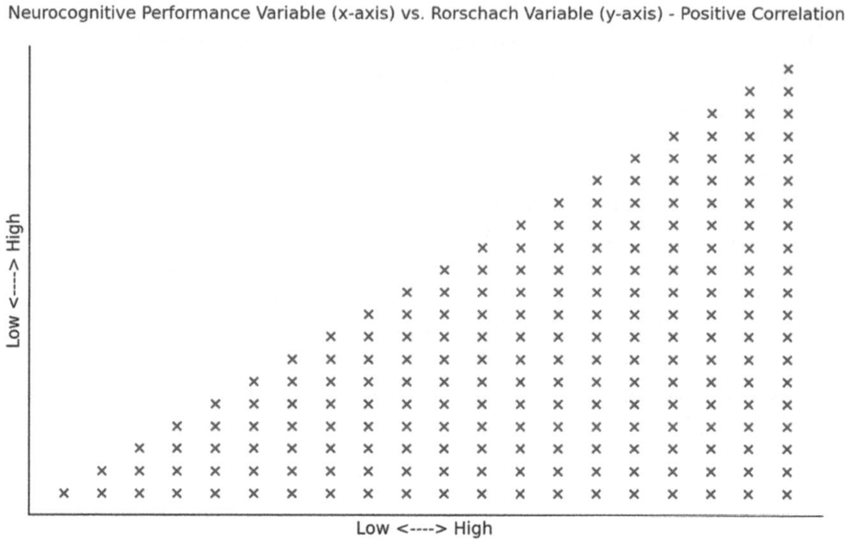

Figure 3.1 Theoretical scatter plot model for significant positive correlations between neurocognitive performance variables and related Rorschach variables representing psychological resources.

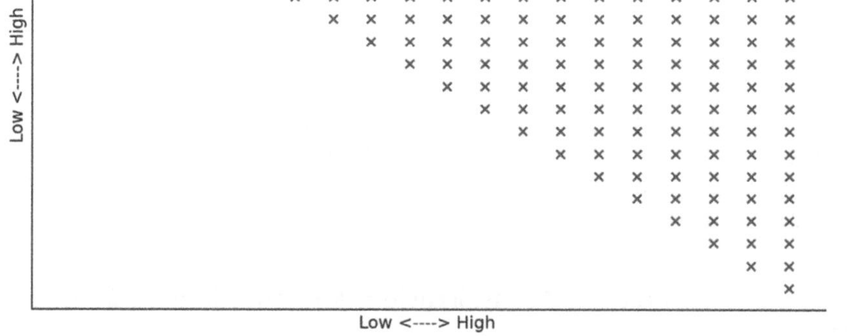

Figure 3.2 Theoretical scatter plot model for significant negative correlations between neurocognitive performance variables and related Rorschach variables representing psychological liabilities.

psychological resources in this sense as being moderately associated with intelligence but as having little to do with psychopathology or ego strength, which he understood as having a direct relationship with the potential for psychopathology.[3] To further articulate this idea, Exner observed that "seriously disturbed people often have a wealth of available resources, and many persons with limited resources are able to adjust to their world quite effectively" (2003, p. 232). He added that "the more resources available, the more likely the person is able to form and direct behaviors, *regardless* (italics in original) of whether or not those behaviors are productive or adaptive" (2003, pp. 232–233). In considering a person's capacity for control and stress tolerance, Exner described how one must weigh a person's resources against the internal and external demands that person is currently experiencing (2003, pp. 232–233). Several Rorschach variables in both the CS and the R-PAS relate to these concepts of resources, stimulus demand and stress tolerance.[4]

Based on observations regarding the protocols of individuals who had completed psychotherapy successfully, it was Beck who suggested that, by summing up the number of human movement responses (*M*) and the weighted sum of color responses (*WSumC*), the result would provide an indication of the extent to which resources are organized and accessible. This variable, referred to as the Experience Actual in the CS (*EA*), appeared therefore to be a measure of the development of ones' inner life and affective experiences (Beck, 1960). Other psychotherapy outcome studies confirmed this idea (e.g., Exner & Andronikof-Sanglade, 1992; Piotrowski & Schreiber, 1952; Weiner & Exner, 1991). Additionally, although *EA* tends to increase over time during treatment, it has been shown to be relatively stable over time in nonpatient adults (e.g., $r = .85$ at a three-year retest; Exner, 2003, p. 179). It therefore appears to reflect a relatively stable personality trait rather than a situationally determined psychological state. Also noteworthy is the fact that *EA* tends to increase each year from ages 5 through 13. As Exner noted, this suggests an association between *EA* and important aspects of psychological development. (For a broader review of this research literature, see Exner, 2003, pp. 244–246.)

In the R-PAS, *EA* was renamed *MC* and described as reflecting "the ability and propensity to populate, animate, and color one's experiential world" or "the ability to mentally engage with the world with vitality, reflective thought, emotion, and psychological activity" (Meyer et al., 2011, p. 354). Like Exner, Meyer et al. note that this ability to engage with the world is not always associated with better adaptation and can indeed even be accompanied by psychopathology. The authors note, based on ideas from Kleiger (1992), that "a high *MC* should be challenged by noting if Movement and Color responses are accompanied by vague or formless percepts (*Pure C, M* with *FQn*), distorted form quality (*FQ–*), or thinking disturbance (Cognitive Codes)" (Meyer et al., 2011, p. 354).

As further elaborated in Chapter 5 with a review of the neuroimaging research on *M* and *WSumC*, these variables appear to be associated with a wide range of psychological characteristics representing adaptive resources, psychological strengths, as well as the capacity to mentalize (e.g., Porcelli, 2025). Mentalization refers to the ability to understand and interpret one's own and others' behavior as driven by internal mental states such as thoughts, feelings, and intentions. It is a deliberate process involving agency and active reflection on mental states, enabling nuanced social interactions, greater self-understanding, and awareness of internal experience (Allen et al., 2008).

As further elaborated in Chapter 5, *M* appears to reflect *embodied mentalization*. It can contribute to empathy and "may involve more awareness, agency, deliberation, and purposefulness, thus seeing the self as the agent or the initiator of the experience" (Meyer et al., 2011, p. 355). Moreover, it is an "indicator of ideation, interpersonal cognition, and related constructs such as imagination, intelligence, reasoning, and thinking before acting" (Meyer et al., 2011, p. 355). The other component of *MC* (or *EA*)—*WSumC*—appears to reflect an "interest in and awareness of stimulating, compelling features in the environment, which may include one's emotional reactions to them" (Meyer et al., 2011, p. 369) but also, as elaborated further in Chapter 5, a capacity and willingness to identify, verbally process, and integrate emotions into problem-solving and decision-making activities.

Exner et al. (1984) found that in individuals with above-average to superior IQs (110 to 140), there was a statistically significant relationship between *EA* and intelligence ($r = .38$). This relationship was not significant when IQ values were within the normal range (80 to 120). Exner concluded that "the most conservative explanation for this finding is that more intelligent people are able to identify and organize resources in ways that make them more easily accessible" (2003, p. 246). In my doctoral dissertation, which examined the relationship between Rorschach variables and cognitive measures in a very heterogeneous geriatric population (N = 102), I found a similar medium-sized correlation between *EA* and cognitive functioning ($r = .36$, $p < .001$; Muzio, 2006). In this study, a scatter plot closely approximating the one presented in Figure 3.1, showed that a low total score on the Batterie d'Évaluation Cognitive 96 (BEC96; Signoret, 1998) predicted a low *EA*, while a high score allowed a significantly broader range of values for *EA* (Muzio, 2006, p. 139).[5]

At first glance, these results might appear to contradict those of Exner et al. (1984), given that in this geriatric population the association with *EA* was most apparent in individuals with severe cognitive deficits. However, a more likely explanation is that individuals with above-average intelligence are better able to organize their psychological resources whereas those with severe neurocognitive deficits tend to lose this capacity systematically.

In other words, severe cognitive deficits predict a broad range of impoverished behavior that consistently extends to tests of typical performance and other open-ended or ambiguous tasks or situations. Conversely, in people of average intelligence who do not show signs of cognitive impairment, the capacity and propensity to mentalize and deliberately animate and color one's experience with a sense of agency can vary greatly. Hence, especially when the overall cognitive performance falls within the normal range, *EA* will give us important incremental information about a person's overall adaptive capacity and stress tolerance, beyond what can be predicted through measures of intelligence or cognitive skills. Specifically, *EA* will give us valuable additional information about a person's overall capacity to sustain goal-directed thinking and to regulate emotions and impulses. For example, a child or adult may score in the high average range on a Wechsler intelligence scale but still struggle to reflect, self-regulate, or maintain goal-directed behavior under stress.

In a clinical sample of children and adolescents referred for assessment in a pediatric neuropsychology laboratory (N = 100), Meyer (2016) found statistically significant correlations between the age-adjusted standard scores for Full-Scale IQ (FSIQ) and Verbal Comprehension (VC) from the Wechsler Intelligence Scale for Children—Revised (WISC-R; Wechsler, 1974) and *EA* (*MC*), with $r = .31$ and $r = .36$, respectively. An even stronger correlation was found in a study conducted by de Araújo et al. (2011) with a group of twenty-one children and adolescents diagnosed with autism—but of approximately average intelligence—between FSIQ and Verbal IQ, and *M*, at $r = .57$ and $r = .54$, respectively ($p < .01$). These findings support the association already noted by Exner between *EA*, its subcomponents (*M* in particular), and key aspects of neurocognitive development and functioning. It also suggests that in children and adolescents, *EA* might be more specifically linked to *crystallized intelligence* (Cattell, 1963), which involves knowledge and skills acquired through experience and education as well as the ability to apply this knowledge in various situations.

When collecting CS adult reference data, Exner (2003, p. 191) found that individuals from the lowest socioeconomic group (SES 9; 7 percent of the nonclinical sample, $N = 600$) had significantly higher *Lambda* and lower *es* and *EA* scores than other SES groups. They also showed lower mean values for key determinants contributing to *EA* and *es* (*M, WSumC*, and shading responses). These findings suggest limited adaptive resources and an avoidant or simplistic coping style, with reduced sensitivity to the subtleties of internal and external stimuli—factors that may impair adaptation to the demands of a complex reality.

Research has consistently shown a strong and complex relationship between general intelligence and socioeconomic status (e.g., Gottfredson, 2011).[6] Given the link between intelligence and the adaptive coping resources reflected in *EA*, it is not surprising that *EA*, experience-based skills, and socioeconomic status are also related. Higher socioeconomic status predicts greater intelligence and adaptive strengths, while intelligence and *EA* can, in turn, predict better socioeconomic outcomes.

In addition to *EA*, an important marker in the assessment of a person's adaptive resources when using the CS is the Coping Deficit Index (*CDI*). As described by Exner (2003, pp. 310–314), the *CDI* was a direct by-product of the research which led to the revision of the Depression Index (*DEPI*), originally designed to identify people with depression. However, false positive and especially false negative rates for the *DEPI* were found to be exceedingly high. Based on these observations, Exner aimed to distinguish between different types of affective disturbance. Of three proposed subtypes, research ultimately showed that only one—marked by helplessness in dealing with societal demands—stood out as a distinct construct. This "helpless" group became the basis for the development of the *CDI*, while the *DEPI* was retained as a broader marker of affective difficulty and later relabeled as the Affective Difficulty Index in the Comprehensive System—Revised (CS-R; Exner et al., 2022). The *CDI* proved particularly useful in identifying a specific profile in patients frequently diagnosed with depression. Exner and his collaborators noted that a large majority (79 percent) of subjects with a diagnosed affective disorder who did not score positive on the *DEPI* (i.e., *DEPI* > 4/7) had a positive *CDI* (i.e., *CDI* > 3/5). They observed that most of the eleven empirically derived variables ultimately included in the *CDI*—and distributed across five criteria—are related to deficits in basic social skills, interpersonal needs, or both. These criteria reflect the presence of the following features:

1 Limited coping resources or poor control capacity (*EA* < 6 or *AdjD* < 0).
2 Difficulties anticipating positive and more assertive interactions with others (*COP* < 2 and *AG* < 2).
3 A limited capacity to process emotional experiences or a tendency to avoid emotionally arousing situations (*WSumC* < 2.5 or *Afr* < .46).
4 A tendency to assume a more passive role in interpersonal relations, a difficulty understanding others, or a lack of interest in others (*p* > *a* + 1 or *Pure H* < 2).
5 A limited capacity to form close attachments, feelings of loneliness, social isolation, or an unusual dependence on others for direction and support (*T* > 1 or *Isolate/R* > .24 or *Fd* > 0).

Individuals meeting four or more of these five criteria are typically seen as having limited coping skills and often appear helpless in managing the demands of daily living. They frequently struggle with relationships due to poor social skills. Exner and colleagues observed that a positive *CDI* was present in 6–24 percent of nonclinical children and adolescents (depending on age), 88 percent of individuals with personality disorders, 74 percent of those with substance-related disorders, and 69 percent of those with personality disorders in forensic settings. Gacono et al. (2008) found positive *CDI*s in nearly half of male psychopaths and pedophiles and in 36 percent of female psychopaths (Cunliffe & Gacono, 2008). These findings highlight that the *CDI* is not a second depression index but rather an index that identifies individuals with significant coping vulnerabilities. About half of those with a positive *CDI* report interpersonal difficulties as a central complaint (Exner, 2003, pp. 310–314). Also notably, most patients with a positive *CDI* no longer show it after 8–14 months of psychotherapy while briefer treatments (2–3 months) show little effect—suggesting the relative stability of these features over time (Exner & Andronikof-Sanglade, 1992; Weiner & Exner, 1991).

Although a positive *CDI* was originally seen as a stable personality marker, Weiner (2003) noted that its meaning varies depending on the value of *EA*. A positive *CDI* with low *EA* (typically < 6) reflects broad-based coping deficits and limited psychological competence, often seen in individuals with poor educational, occupational, and interpersonal outcomes. In children and adolescents, this profile may reflect developmental delay and suggests a need for interventions aimed at building social skills and the capacity to mentalize. In contrast, a positive *CDI* with a normal or high *EA*—though seemingly paradoxical—often occurs in individuals with intact or even above-average functioning who nonetheless struggle with interpersonal relationships specifically (Weiner, 2003, p. 151).

A good example of this second pattern is sexual serial killer Ted Bundy, who had a FSIQ of 122 and an *EA* of 14.5. Despite his substantial psychological resources and superficial charm, along with the ability to convince others he was successful, reliable, and empathic, he had a *CDI* of 5/5 (Muzio, 2018). Consistent with his positive *CDI*, both Bundy and his acquaintances recalled that even in childhood he struggled in loosely structured social situations. He lacked self-confidence, was often excluded from social events, and felt awkward when he did attend them, stating, "I had trouble grasping any of it."

Composite international reference data published by Meyer et al. (2007), based on samples from seventeen countries, showed that positive *CDI* scores are more common than previously indicated by US reference data—particularly scores of 4/5, found in 25 percent of the sample, and 5/5, in 11 percent, totaling 36 percent. These findings, along with evidence linking the *CDI* to education and socioeconomic status, led it to be relabeled as the Coping Vulnerability Index in the CS-R (Exner et al., 2022). Interpretation has shifted from viewing the index as a sign of deficit to one of vulnerability, often shaped by environmental factors. However, it is important to note that in clinical practice, a positive *CDI* is frequently observed alongside cognitive deficits in neurocognitive, neurodevelopmental, and severe psychiatric disorders.

With the objective of providing more direct empirical evidence of a relationship between the *CDI* and neurocognitive functions, Ilonen et al. (2016) examined the relationship between the *CDI* and neurocognitive performance in adolescent psychiatric inpatients (n = 267), adult inpatients with first-episode schizophrenia or severe affective disorders (n = 117), and in healthy adults (n = 94). As expected, a significant association was found between the *CDI* and cognitive deficits.

In inpatient adolescents, elevated *CDI* scores were significantly predicted by impaired verbal abilities—specifically, performance on the Similarities, Vocabulary, Comprehension, and Information subtests of the Wechsler Intelligence Scale for Children (WISC-III; Wechsler, 1992) or the Wechsler Adult Intelligence Scale—Revised (WAIS-R; Wechsler, 1999), as well as, to a lesser extent, FSIQ and Verbal IQ. Lower scores on Delayed Logical Memory from the Wechsler Memory Scale—Revised (WMS-R; Wechsler, 1987) also predicted a positive *CDI*. However, most cognitive measures in Ilonen et al.'s study did not, including executive functioning (e.g., the Wisconsin Card Sorting Test [WCST]; Heaton et al., 1993), Perceptual Organization (PO), and Performance IQ. These findings suggest that, in this group, a positive *CDI* is often linked specifically to deficits in verbal reasoning and knowledge typically acquired through education and experience. A similar result was reported by de Araújo et al. (2011) in the sample of twenty-one autistic children and adolescents with average intelligence mentioned earlier: *CDI* scores correlated significantly with Verbal IQ (r = .54, p = .012) but not with Performance IQ or FSIQ.

Forty percent of adolescent inpatients in Ilonen et al.'s sample had a positive *CDI*, highlighting the prevalence of both social coping and verbal processing deficits in severe adolescent psychopathology. The findings also support the view that, in this population, a positive *CDI* often reflects developmental arrest. Many of these adolescents likely have persistent neurodevelopmental disorders that impair their ability to navigate complex social situations or solve everyday problems. Such vulnerabilities frequently contribute to secondary symptoms, including anxiety, depression, or impulse control problems, especially under stress.

In inpatient adults with first-episode schizophrenia or severe affective disorders, the range of cognitive impairments predicting a positive *CDI* was considerably broader than in inpatient adolescents. Of the thirty-one cognitive measures used by Ilonen et al., only two failed to predict an elevated *CDI*, and effect sizes were generally larger than those observed in the adolescent sample. Eleven measures correlated with the *CDI* at or above r = ±.30, compared to none in the adolescent group. Strongest associations were found for executive functions (via key WCST measures), FSIQ, Verbal IQ, and both General and Delayed Memory from the WMS-R. Thirty-five percent of adults in this group had a positive *CDI*. These findings align with the extensive cognitive deficits commonly seen in adults with severe mental illness and also suggest that a wide range of impairments may contribute to the coping vulnerabilities captured by an elevated *CDI.*

As with adult inpatients, a broad range of cognitive deficits predicted an elevated *CDI* in healthy subjects. Of the twenty-four cognitive tasks used by Ilonen et al., only five did not significantly predict *CDI* elevation, and nine showed at least a moderate effect size ($r = \pm.30$). This also contrasts sharply with the adolescent inpatient group, where no measure reached that threshold. Strongest associations were found in healthy subjects for FSIQ, Verbal IQ, and language skills (especially Vocabulary and Similarities from the WAIS-R), as well as verbal and visual memory (e.g., Logical Memory, Verbal Learning, and Visual Reproduction from the WMS-R). While only 16 percent of this group had a positive *CDI*, the findings suggest that even in healthy individuals, a wide range of cognitive deficits may be linked to the coping vulnerabilities reflected by an elevated *CDI.*

Ilonen et al. conclude that the *CDI* reflects not only developmental arrest but also persistent deterioration linked to neurocognitive dysfunction. They highlight the association between the *CDI* and poor verbal memory, even in healthy individuals, as well as its links to verbal processing, reasoning, and executive function. Deficits in these areas can significantly impair a person's ability to adapt to the demands of daily living and social interactions.

The *CDI* variables significantly associated with neurocognitive function in this study were *EA, WSumC, H,* and *COP,* reflecting adaptive resources such as the capacity to mentalize, verbally process emotions, form integrated views of self and others, and anticipate cooperative social interactions. Ilonen et al. also obtained structural brain data via magnetic resonance imaging for a subsample of adult inpatients ($n = 58$) and found that both *EA* and *WSumC* correlated significantly with relative temporal gray-matter volume ($rs = .30$ and $.29$, respectively; $p < .05$). These findings underscore the particular importance of these two variables in identifying coping deficits associated with neurocognitive impairment.

In contrast, variables in the fifth *CDI* criterion appeared unrelated to neurocognitive function and more tied to interpersonal needs or deficits. As Ilonen et al. note, the traditional recommendation of using social-skills training in treating patients with an elevated *CDI* may be insufficient, especially when the most neurocognitively correlated variables of the index are involved. For instance, if a patient diagnosed with major depression has a profile showing $EA = 2$, $COP = 0$, $WSumC = 1$, and $H = 0$, additional neuropsychological assessment might be warranted. If deficits are identified, it may be advisable to address these first—possibly through neuropsychological rehabilitation or other treatments—before proceeding to social-skills training or psychotherapy if needed.

Perceptual–Cognitive Engagement, Cognitive Sophistication, and Complexity

In clinical practice, a positive *CDI* is often associated with a high *Lambda* (i.e., > .99). This makes clinical sense given that an avoidant coping style shares many features with a positive *CDI*. Probably most notably, both individuals with a high *Lambda* and individuals with an elevated *CDI* are typically superficial or simplistic in their way of dealing with people and situations in their lives. This makes them vulnerable to problems in coping, particularly in more complex or demanding situations. This also makes it more difficult for them to create and sustain meaningful relationships. Their relation to others tends to be superficial or immature. Furthermore, technically a high *Lambda* protocol represents fertile ground for lower values in the kinds of variables included in the *CDI*, particularly *EA* and *WSumC*, but also *COP* or *H*. The *EA* variable and its subcomponents *M* and *WSumC* tend to be lower the higher the value for *Lambda*. Additionally, the higher the value for *Lambda*, the lower the number of *M* and—consequently—*COP* and *H* responses.

Despite these overlaps, high *Lambda* and elevated *CDI* do not consistently cooccur. In a US nonpatient sample with *Lambda* > .99 (*N* = 58), only 10 percent showed an elevated *CDI*, all of the milder variety (*CDI* = 4; Exner, 2001, p. 187). This is not surprising given that *Lambda* and *CDI* differ significantly in content. Supporting this distinction, Ilonen et al. (2016) found that in both inpatient and healthy samples, *Lambda* values were in the average range. Moreover, results remained unchanged when controlling for *Lambda* or education, suggesting the constructs are related but relatively independent.

Although the developers of the R-PAS do consider the *CDI* to be an "index of limited coping resources and general psychological deficits, which may have secondary consequences for interpersonal ineffectiveness" (Meyer et al., 2011, p. 462), the *CDI* was not included in the R-PAS for three reasons. First, despite Exner's idea that it would be "erroneous to assume that the social immaturity indicated by a positive *CDI* in the protocol of an individual with an avoidant style is simply a result of that style" (Exner, 2003, p. 507), the authors of the R-PAS considered that the construct of the *CDI* "adds very little" (Meyer et al., 2011, p. 462) to variables in the Engagement and Cognitive Processing domain. Second, the authors considered that, in terms of assessing interpersonal problems, variables from the Self and Other Representation domain permit "more specific and better validated inferences" (Meyer et al., 2011, p. 462). Third, the *CDI* includes variables that were excluded from the R-PAS due to limited meta-analytic validity support—specifically *Fd* and *Isolate/R* (Mihura et al., 2013).

Although in fact only four of the eleven variables of the *CDI* are covered by the Engagement and Cognitive Processing domain of the R-PAS, the domain does include the two most neurocognitively relevant variables: *MC* (*EA*) and *WSumC*. Additionally, this domain is neurocognitively relevant in a variety of ways as it includes several other variables which have been consistently linked to intelligence and cognitive functions in the research literature. The most important of these variables from a neurocognitive standpoint is *Complexity*.

Unique to the R-PAS, *Complexity* is an aggregate measure involving information from several sections across all the responses in a protocol. Each response is assigned complexity points for three sets of codes: (1) Location, Space, and Object Qualities (*LSO*); (2) Contents (*Cont*); and (3) Determinants (*Det*). In this way, responses can be systematically scored on a continuum ranging from, for example, an animal content (*A*) response given to a *D* location based solely on the outline of the inkblot (*F*), which would receive 1 point, to a response including three different content categories (e.g., *H, Cg, Bl*), covering all parts of the inkblot (*W*), animated with human movement (*M*), including objects seen as meaningfully related (*Sy*), and determined by the chromatic color (e.g., *FC*) as well as the shading qualities (e.g., *Y*) of the inkblot, which would receive 9 points. The latter example is clearly both perceptually and cognitively more complex and sophisticated than the former. The latter response also reflects considerable engagement in the task, as opposed to the avoidance or constriction reflected by the former. To calculate *Complexity*, scores are summed across all the responses to produce the overall protocol-level *Complexity* score. The sum of responses produced (*R*) also impacts this score, given that the more responses one gives, the higher the overall score for *Complexity* will tend to be. (For more details on how responses are scored for complexity, see Meyer et al., 2011, p. 295.)

In the R-PAS, *Complexity* is understood as:

> An overall index of complexity of processing in that it measures differentiation, integration, and productivity at the response level. Associated with age, education, intelligence, and adaptation. Responding to the test with a high *Complexity* score means that the person has brought a considerable amount of psychological activity and effort to bear in coping with the demands of the test. Doing so in real life should be associated with more success and flexibility in coping, and a preference for more cognitive activity and energy when responding to challenges.
>
> (Meyer et al., 2011, p. 349)

As described by Meyer (2023), the roots of *Complexity* as a psychological construct can be traced back to Hermann Rorschach, who distinguished between *coarcted* (i.e., constricted, simplistic) and *dilated* (i.e., rich) types.

Later theorists such as Rapaport et al. (1968) and Schachtel (2001) expanded on this continuum. Rapaport spoke of the qualitative wealth of the record, while Schachtel emphasized the Rorschach as revealing the individual's *experiential field*—their way of perceiving, organizing, and assigning meaning to experience. As these authors described, and as seen in clinical practice, low *Complexity* may be found in a range of conditions, including dementia, severe depression, and schizophrenia with prominent negative symptoms, as well as in individuals with rigid, pedantic, or overly concrete coping styles. At the other end of the continuum, high *Complexity* may be seen in hypomanic states, in individuals under considerable emotional pressure or in those who are exceptionally intelligent, creative, and multitalented. Most individuals fall somewhere between these poles, producing records that reflect varying degrees of complexity. Rorschach and subsequent authors considered this dimension to involve several response features, beginning with human movement (*M*) and chromatic color (*WSumC*) but also including variables related to location, levels of integration, content, and originality.

In the R-PAS, *Complexity* is grounded in conceptual work on guardedness versus richness and factor-analytic research by Meyer (1992), which identified the first unrotated principal component (FUPC) of the Rorschach as a simplicity–complexity dimension. The algorithm developed to calculate *Complexity* within the context of Exner's Rorschach Research Council (RRC) was shown to be the best marker of the FUPC, with loadings on the component or simple correlations of the scale with the component of about $r = .95$ (e.g., RRC, 1999, cited by Meyer, 2023).

Since the publication of the R-PAS manual, several studies have explored associations between *Complexity*, education, and cognitive functioning. One unpublished study found a strong correlation between *Complexity* and education ($r = .44$; Dumitrascu et al., 2011, cited in Meyer et al., 2011, p. 442), suggesting that individuals with higher education tend to produce more complex, integrated, and sophisticated Rorschach responses. Meyer (2016) found that, in children and adolescents, *Complexity* was significantly correlated with raw FSIQ scores on the WISC-R (Wechsler, 1974; $r = .24$). Its subcomponents *LSO* and *Det* were similarly correlated with FSIQ ($r = .25$ for both). Correlations with VC were somewhat higher: $r = .28$ for *Complexity*, $r = .25$ for *LSO*, and $r = .32$ for *Det*. Additionally, both *Complexity* and *LSO* were associated with PO, at $r = .24$ and $r = .29$, respectively. When age-adjusted standard scores were used instead of raw scores, the correlations strengthened—particularly with FSIQ. Specifically, *Complexity, LSO, Cont*, and *Det* correlated with FSIQ at $r = .37$, $r = .31$, $r = .34$, and $r = .37$, respectively. Notably, the *Cont* subcomponent showed no significant correlations with any cognitive measure when only raw scores were considered, suggesting that the multiplicity of contents is probably only weakly associated with cognitive functioning.

Meyer's findings suggest that *Complexity* is linked to both verbal and nonverbal processing abilities, which appear to be prerequisites for producing perceptually sophisticated responses on the Rorschach. One example of such responses is the perception of three-dimensionality, as seen in *V* or *FD* responses—both recently confirmed to be associated with advanced cognitive abilities through systematic reviews, updated meta-analyses, and construct validity studies (Mihura & Görner, 2025). Other examples include responses involving nonhuman movement, shading, or achromatic color. In de Araújo et al.'s study (2011) of twenty-one children and adolescents with autism and average intelligence, *es* (*PPD* in the R-PAS) showed strong correlations with FSIQ (r = .65) and Verbal IQ (r = .56, p <.01). Children or adolescents with verbal deficits are therefore more likely to produce protocols dominated by simple, form-based responses that lack more complex forms of cognitive-perceptual integration. This simplistic approach may extend to social situations, limiting their ability to perceive subtle cues and respond adaptively, as is often observed in neurodevelopmental conditions such as autism spectrum disorder.

Meyer's child and adolescent data (Meyer, 2016) show that several perceptually sophisticated determinants correlate with general intelligence and cognitive functions. In addition to showing how *V* and *FD* correlate with FSIQ, especially when considered together (*VFD*, r = .42), they also found a correlation between FSIQ and reflection responses (r = .27). These variables all showed significant associations with verbal and nonverbal subtests of the WISC-R. Additionally, *F%* and *Blends* also correlated with cognitive performance, particularly with VC (r = –.24 and .32, respectively), underscoring once again the central role of verbal processing. Finally, *F %* correlated with the Judgment of Line Orientation Test (r = .42; Benton et al., 1978).[7]

The important function of verbal processing skills in enabling more complex protocols with a variety of determinants has also been reported in a heterogeneous geriatric population (N = 102; Muzio, 2006; Muzio & Andronikof, 2008). In this group, *F%* was found to correlate significantly with a measure of verbal learning (r = –.24), suggesting that—in this very heterogeneous clinical population of senior adults—deficits in verbal learning tended to be associated with simplistic and constricted Rorschach protocols. The data also showed that the value for *F%* was unrelated to the level of cognitive impairment for a broad range of other cognitive measures in this population, including the Mini-Mental State Exam (MMSE; Folstein et al., 1975).[8] For example, both a low and a high score on the MMSE in this population could be associated with a high *F%* (*Lambda* >.99), and most subjects (62 percent) had indeed a high *Lambda*, regardless of their cognitive status.

While determinant complexity (*Det*) is strongly linked to cognitive functioning—particularly verbal processing and crystallized intelligence—

location, space, and object quality complexity (*LSO*) also shows important associations, especially with nonverbal abilities such as visuospatial skills and problem-solving. The codes and scores comprising *LSO* have been consistently correlated with cognitive functions in the literature. Moreover, perhaps even more than *Det, LSO* appears to reflect not only cognitive capacity but also the person's willingness to engage, differentiate, integrate, and synthesize ideas and percepts—revealing a flexible, creative approach to the task.

One cognitively sophisticated way of approaching the Rorschach task is to incorporate the white space surrounding the inkblots into a response (*S*). Mihura et al. (2018), in discussing the importance of the response processes for construct validity, highlight two R-PAS categories of space use: Space Reversal (*SR*), involving figure–ground reversals, and Space Integration (*SI*), where white space is integrated with parts of the inkblot. These response types show distinct patterns of convergent and discriminant validity: *SR* is uniquely associated with oppositionality, while *SI* relates to cognitive complexity. *SI* reflects a more advanced processing style, involving simultaneous attention to multiple elements in an integrative manner. Both *SR* and *SI* have also been linked to creativity.

An eye-tracking study by Ales et al. (2022), involving seventy-one nonclinical adult volunteers who completed the Rorschach while their eye movements were recorded, confirmed the validity of the two distinct R-PAS interpretations for white space responses. Results showed that (1) *SI*, but not *SR*, was positively associated with the overall number of eye fixations while scanning the inkblots; and (2) *SR*, but not *SI*, was associated with a proportionally greater number and longer duration of fixations on white versus non-white areas of the cards. These findings confirm that *SI* reflects greater cognitive engagement and a tendency to consider and integrate more information when forming responses, whereas *SR*—although it may reflect creativity—appears more related to a deliberate attempt to do something other than what is expected by the examiner.

Even more indicative of cognitive complexity than *SI* are responses of synthesis, where two or more objects are meaningfully related or interacting (coded as *Sy* in R-PAS; *DQ+* or *DQv/+* in the CS). These responses occur more frequently than *S* and have been more extensively studied in relation to intelligence and neurocognitive functioning. Whole inkblot responses (*W*) have also been widely examined, as they often reflect greater cognitive effort and perceptual integration, especially on more complex or fragmented inkblot designs. Some studies have analyzed whole responses that are also syntheses (*W-Sy* or *W+*). In contrast, selecting commonly used smaller areas (*D*) or rarely chosen locations (*Dd*) is seen as a more economical strategy requiring less cognitive effort, particularly on more complex designs.

At the opposite end of the integration spectrum are vague responses, in which perceived objects lack specific form (*e.g., The red looks like blood*). These are coded *Vg* in the R-PAS and *DQv* or *DQv*/+ in the CS. The R-PAS defines *Vg* responses as reflecting "vague, impressionistic, unsophisticated processing" potentially due to cognitive deficits, impulsivity, defensiveness, or style (Meyer et al., 2011, p. 367). In rare cases, a response can be both *Sy* and *Vg* (*DQv*/+). Exner (2003, p. 350) noted that while *DQv*/+ may indicate emerging cognitive complexity in young children, in adolescents or adults it typically reflects flawed or impaired synthesis due to faulty processing.

Building on the work of Kissel (1965) and Friedman (1953), Exner (2003) proposed that perceptual–cognitive activity exists along a developmental continuum—from immature, vague, and concrete processing (*DQv*) to more differentiated and integrated forms (*DQ*+*)*. *DQv* is more typical of children, individuals with intellectual limitations, or those with neurological impairments, while *DQ*+ is more common among highly educated or psychologically complex individuals. Between these two poles is a type of processing Exner described as a "conservative but committed form of cognitive functioning" involving a "straightforward definition of the stimulus field or part of it" (*DQo*; 2003, pp. 349–350). *DQo* responses—simple and precisely defined with minimal integration—are the most common on the Rorschach, which is why Exner labeled them "ordinary."

In a group of 134 middle-class children and adolescents (aged 5 to 16 years), Ridley and Bayton (1983) found that Friedman's developmental level (*DL*) score and Exner's weighted *DQ* scores were highly correlated ($r = .70$), suggesting they reflect a similar construct. Weighted *DQ* scores were also positively correlated with age ($r = .45$) and FSIQ ($r = .34$). The association between *DL* and general intelligence had been previously noted by Kissel (1965) as well as by Greenberg and Cardwell (1978), who looked at the relationship between performance on the WAIS and Rorschach *DL* scores in a group of eighty-six psychiatric inpatients. They found that the relationship between intelligence and *DL* was of a general nature and did not rely specifically on verbal, perceptual, or memory factors. They also found that verbal abilities in particular play a significant role in the quality of Rorschach responses (see, for example, the factor-analytic review by Murstein, 1960).

Allison and Blatt (1964) examined the relationship between *W* responses and intelligence using Friedman's (1953) *DL* score. They analyzed five adults per WAIS IQ band across eight intervals (IQ 60–140). Only *W* responses that were both cognitively complex and accurately perceived showed a significant positive association with FSIQ. The authors emphasized the importance of evaluating qualitative features of Rorschach responses rather than relying solely on scores. Supporting this, Blatt and Allison (1963) found that while *W* and *W%* did not correlate with intelligence, the complexity of *W* responses did. Marsden (1970) later confirmed that only developmentally advanced *W* responses were linked to general intelligence.

Acklin and Fechner-Bates (1989) studied the relationship between *DQ* scores and performance on the WAIS-R in 125 undergraduate volunteers. Consistent with earlier research, *W*+ (whole responses with *DQ*+) was the only variable that reliably predicted FSIQ and cognitive factor scores, especially PO (r = .32, p <.001). In contrast, *Do* scores were inversely related to PO (r = –.34, p <.001). Based on these findings, the authors argued that *DQ* does not reflect a single continuum of perceptual complexity but rather two distinct modes: complex (*W*+) and simple (*Do*). *Ddo* also showed modest negative correlations with Verbal IQ and VC. These were the only *DQ* scores that correlated with measures from the WAIS-R. Interestingly, *DQv*/+ was unrelated to any cognitive variable in this study, suggesting it may not reflect a true or even failed synthesis, as previously proposed by Exner, but rather a qualitatively different phenomenon. Finally, Acklin and Fechner-Bates found a moderate positive correlation between *S*+ (later *SI* in the R-PAS) and both PO and Performance IQ—an expected result, given that these combinatorial responses often cooccur with *W*+ and *Dd*+.

Acklin and Fechner-Bates (1989, p. 542) concluded that "complex whole responses tap an ambitious, combinatorial visual-perceptual operation," consistent with earlier findings. For example, Smith (1981) found that in second- and sixth-graders, Piagetian stage of cognitive development positively correlated with both the number and complexity of *W* responses.[9] This association was strongest for complex or fragmented inkblots, suggesting that producing well-articulated *W* responses requires the abstracting and synthesizing abilities characteristic of formal operational thought.[10]

Zillmer and Perry (1996) conducted a factor analysis with 190 adult psychiatric inpatients, 38 percent of whom had been diagnosed with schizophrenia. The study examined select Rorschach (CS), Minnesota Multiphasic Personality Inventory (MMPI; Hathaway & McKinley, 1943), and Halstead–Reitan Neuropsychological Test Battery (HRNTB; Reitan & Wolfson, 1985) variables to clarify how emotional disturbance and neurocognitive dysfunction are interrelated. Results supported the idea that neuropsychological and personality assessments tap distinct domains. MMPI variables formed two factors: Somatic–Neurotic (Scales 3, 1, 2, 7, 4) and Severe Disturbance (Scales 8, 6, 7, 9, 4, 2). Rorschach variables also yielded two factors: Response Process (*Zf, W, R, M*) and Perceptual Accuracy (*X+%, P, X–%, F+%*).[11] HRNTB measures loaded onto Motor/Visuospatial Learning and Verbal Comprehension factors. The two MMPI factors correlated only with each-other (r = .35), while Rorschach Response Process correlated with both HRNTB factors (r = .39 and .36, respectively). In contrast, Rorschach Perceptual Accuracy did not correlate with other factors, and the two Rorschach factors were almost completely unrelated ($r = -.01$).

Variables loading on the Rorschach Response Process factor—*Zf, W, M,* and *R*—have been widely linked to cognitive effort, complexity, and cognitive functions. *Zf* and *W* reflect cognitive effort and organizational activity, and *M* has been associated with both intelligence and the capacity to mentalize. *R*, although linked to *Complexity* and historically viewed as an "organic" sign when exceptionally low (Piotrowski, 1937), has been found to have only weak associations with cognitive functioning (e.g., $r = .09$ with FSIQ in children [Meyer, 2016]; $r = .06$ with the MMSE in geriatric patients [Muzio, 2006]).

Zillmer and Perry's findings suggest that only a subset of Rorschach variables—those reflecting effortful, integrative processing and mentalization—correlate with neurocognitive performance. In contrast, perceptual accuracy and conventionality variables did not correlate with the MMPI or the HRNTB scores, highlighting the Rorschach's incremental value in assessing psychological functioning, particularly psychotic phenomena, beyond what is captured by self-report or standard neuropsychological measures (Dao et al., 2008; Mihura, 2012; Mihura et al., 2013).

Wood et al. (2003) used factor analysis to examine the relationship between Rorschach (CS) variables and cognitive performance on various Wechsler scales—the WISC-R, WAIS-R, and WISC-III (Wechsler, 1974, 1981, 1991). Their study included 152 adolescents referred for psychological evaluation in inpatient, outpatient, residential, and day treatment settings. Using a set of nineteen Rorschach variables, the authors identified three distinct Rorschach factors:

1 Synthesized Complexity: *Zf, DQ+*, and *F%*.
2 Productivity: *R, D*, and *Dd*.
3 Form Quality: *X+%, F+%*, and *X–%*.

Variables on the Synthesized Complexity and Form Quality factors showed statistically significant correlations ($p < .05$) with FSIQ, Verbal IQ, and Performance IQ. For instance, *DQ+, F%*, and *Zf* correlated with FSIQ at $r = .37$, $r = -.29$, and $r = .25$, respectively. Moreover, *X–%* and *X+%* correlated with FSIQ at $r = -.29$ and $r = .24$, respectively. In contrast, *R* and closely related variables *D* and *Dd,* which tend to covary with *R,* showed no meaningful relationship with intelligence or cognitive functioning.

Wood et al. concluded that the Rorschach variables linked to cognitive functions in adolescents largely replicated findings from adult samples. These results were later confirmed in other child and adolescent samples (e.g., Meyer, 2016). However, variables reflecting perceptual accuracy and conventionality (e.g., *X–%, X+%*)—which correlate with cognitive performance in youth—did not show such associations in adult psychiatric inpatients (Zillmer & Perry, 1996).

As discussed further below, correlations between perceptual accuracy, conventionality, and cognitive functioning tend to weaken in adult and older adult samples. This may reflect both methodological differences and developmental factors. Many Rorschach scores stabilize around age 16 (Exner et al., 1985), and variables like *X+%* and *F%* (*Lambda*) have been shown to follow developmental trends. Notably, these same variables are included in the Developmental Index (*DI*), designed to capture psychological development, growth, and maturity (Stanfill et al., 2013a, 2013b). Given the close relationship between emotional and cognitive development in childhood and adolescence, associations between developmental variables and intelligence or cognitive functioning are more evident in youth. Still, some adult groups—such as violent offenders with psychiatric and cognitive impairments—also show significant correlations between *DI* scores and neurocognitive functioning (Groenewold, 2020).

The *DI* includes a range of variables: *F%, X–%, X+%, m, FD, T, V, An, Art, Sx*, and *Xy*. Stanfill et al. (2013a, 2013b) found that the *DI* was strongly correlated with age in individuals aged 25 and younger ($r = .71$, $p < .0005$) but not in older adults ($r = .11$, $p = .10$). The *DI* also correlated significantly with *Complexity* ($r = .52$), though *Complexity* showed a weaker correlation with age ($r = .37$), suggesting that the *DI* may indeed more closely reflect psychological development and maturity. These findings were supported by Giromini et al. (2015), who showed that the *DI* remained significantly correlated with age even after controlling for *R* and *Complexity* in a cross-cultural sample.

Importantly, the *DI* has been associated with intelligence and cognitive functioning. In a study of 231 children aged 7 to 11, Resende et al. (2019) found an exceptionally strong correlation between the *DI* and nonverbal intelligence as measured by Raven's Colored Progressive Matrices ($r = .83$, $p < .001$).[12] Among *DI* components, *FQ–%* (*X–%* in the CS), *FQo%* (*X+%* in the CS), and *F%* had the strongest correlations with nonverbal intelligence ($p < .001$). Other *DI* variables showed weaker associations, and no significant correlation was found for *FD, Sx*, or *Art*. Findings confirm that the *DI* reflects aspects of perceptual accuracy, conventionality, and information processing linked to intelligence in children. However, some *DI* components—such as *Art*—appear unrelated to cognitive ability ($r = .03$; Resende et al., 2019), likely reflecting other developmental or personality factors. As Exner (2003, p. 440) noted, *Art* content can represent a defensive intellectualization style more common in adults than in younger children.

Overall, a compelling body of research with consistent findings suggests that Rorschach variables related to cognitive effort, engagement in processing, and more complex and sophisticated forms of information processing correlate with intelligence and performance on a broad range of cognitive tasks across different age groups. As noted earlier, many of these variables contribute to the *Complexity* score in the R-PAS and are represented in the Engagement and Cognitive Processing domain (R-PAS) or the Cognitive Triad (CS).

Additionally, as previously described in studies with children and adolescents, variables related to perceptual accuracy and conventionality also show meaningful correlations with cognitive functioning, particularly in a developmental context. Moreover, as discussed in the next section, variables related to the quality of thought processes have also been found to be associated with cognitive functioning. However, as stated at the beginning of the chapter, these are not linear relationships but typically correlations with moderate to large effects, reflecting the tendency of specific or more widespread cognitive deficits to disrupt the psychological functions captured by certain Rorschach variables.

Research has linked several R-PAS variables with eye-tracking measures that reflect increased engagement and effort in visually scanning the inkblot stimuli, providing additional validity evidence for their interpretation. One such study was discussed earlier in relation to *SI* and *SR* (Ales et al., 2022). In another study using the same sample of seventy-one nonclinical adult volunteers, Ales et al. (2020) recorded fixation duration, number of fixations, and other metrics during the response phase of Rorschach administration. As expected, *Complexity* showed a significant correlation with the number of fixations ($r = .53$, $p < .01$), with similarly strong associations for related variables such as *Sy* and *Vg%*. Some eye-tracking variables, however, yielded weak or nonsignificant correlations.

The study of Ales et al. (2020) was successfully replicated by Dauphin et al. (2024) in a separate sample of sixty adults. They also identified new eye-tracking indicators linked to *Complexity* and *Vg%*, showing that higher *Complexity* was associated with scanning more regions of the blot—though at a slower rate. Results were consistent across cultural contexts (Italy and the USA). In contrast, higher *Vg%* values were linked to more superficial search strategies, reinforcing its interpretation as indicative of vague, impressionistic, and unsophisticated processing.

Vitolo et al. (2021) tested the validity of eye-tracking findings by examining fMRI data from twenty-six healthy participants instructed to think of what the Rorschach inkblots might be. They hypothesized that greater cognitive effort during the task would correspond to increased activation in brain regions related to top-down attentional processes. As expected, *Complexity* showed the strongest association with dorsal attention network activation ($d = 0.43$), followed by *Sy* ($d = 0.32$) and *M* ($d = 0.21$). Notably, the correlation between fMRI effect sizes and those from prior eye-tracking data was an impressive $r = .80$.

Perceptual Accuracy, Conventionality, and Thought Organization

As described in Chapter 2, Piotrowski (1937) noted early in the history of the Rorschach that patients with neuropsychological conditions tend to produce fewer perceptually accurate responses than expected. He observed that typical, nonclinical respondents produce approximately 80 percent of responses with good form quality—meaning that about 20 percent are perceptually inaccurate—and suggested that a percentage below 70 percent of perceptually accurate responses should be considered abnormal. These expectations remain virtually unchanged today and are remarkably consistent with Piotrowski's normative expectations from the 1930s, despite the availability of a considerable amount of new reference data. For instance, *X–%* > .29 is one of the criteria in the empirically developed Perceptual-Thinking Index (*PTI*) and signals significant perceptual inaccuracy and impaired reality testing (Exner, 2003, pp. 389–393). This cutoff corresponds roughly to two standard deviations above the mean in US adult reference data from 2007 (Exner et al., 2022, p. 12; Exner, 2007). Composite international reference data for adults across seventeen countries report a mean *X–%* of .19 with a standard deviation of .11 (Meyer et al., 2007). The exact same mean value was found in international reference data for adolescents (Tibon-Czopp & Weiner, 2016) and senior adults (Weiner et al., 2019).

As noted earlier, perceptual accuracy and conventionality—as measured by *X–%* and *X+%*—are linked to psychological development. These variables are significantly associated with cognitive functioning in children and adolescents (Meyer, 2016; Wood et al., 2003) but have shown much weaker associations in adults (e.g., Zillmer & Perry, 1996). In younger individuals, how they perceive themselves and the world develops alongside broader cognitive functions. In adulthood, however, perceptual accuracy and cognitive ability appear to be more independent; an adult may be intelligent yet perceive things inaccurately or present cognitive deficits while maintaining perceptual conventionality. Later in life, this association appears to gain strength again, as cognitive decline in conditions like dementia is frequently accompanied by varying degrees of misperception.

In my doctoral dissertation (Muzio, 2006), I examined correlations between Rorschach variables and cognitive functioning in a sample of 102 geriatric patients (mean age = 80) whose average education corresponded to completion of elementary school.[13] In this group, *X–%* was significantly correlated with the MMSE ($r = -.20$), as was *P* ($r = .21$). Using another cognitive measure—the BEC96 (Signoret, 1998)—*X–%* and *P* showed the strongest correlations with subtests assessing verbal fluency (naming as many animals as possible in one minute) and visual recognition (naming familiar objects).[14] These correlations ranged from $r = .24$ (between *P* and verbal fluency) to $r = .38$ (between *P* and visual recognition). *X–%* also correlated with a visual-constructive task involving copying geometric figures (r = –.26), while *P* correlated with both visual memory and verbal learning (r = .22). Overall, findings suggest that as the ability to recognize familiar objects and retrieve representations from semantic memory declines, so does the capacity to produce perceptually accurate or conventional responses on the Rorschach. Likewise, greater perceptual inaccuracy was associated with weaker visual-spatial processing, and fewer popular responses were observed as memory functions deteriorated.

These associations between Rorschach and neurocognitive variables make sense both in the context of cognitive decline in geriatrics and within a developmental framework. Psychotic symptoms are more common in older adults with dementia or neurocognitive disorders than in cognitively healthy peers (e.g., Ballard et al., 1997a, 1997b; Drevets & Rubin, 1989). Similarly, *X–%* has shown consistent negative correlations with FSIQ in children and adolescents, ranging from r = –.29 (Wood et al., 2003) to r = –.31 (Meyer, 2016).

In line with Kleiger's (2017) approach, I prefer the term *psychotic phenomena* when referring to perceptual inaccuracy and disordered thinking on the Rorschach. While both perceptual inaccuracy and disordered thinking (e.g., incoherence, peculiar logic, bizarre combinatory thinking) are associated with psychotic symptoms and psychotic disorders (Mihura et al., 2013), they are not the equivalent of a diagnosis of psychosis. Only a multimethod assessment can support such a diagnosis. Moreover, clinical experience supports the idea that many psychiatric patients without psychotic symptoms may still present psychotic or psychotic-like phenomena on the Rorschach. In sharp contrast with this, in nonclinical populations Level 2 Cognitive Codes (*Lvl-2*) or other severe cognitive codes such as *ALOG* (*PEC* in the R-PAS) or *CONTAM* are exceptionally rare, and one does not expect high values for *X–%* or *WSum6* (*FQ–%* or *WSumCog* in the R-PAS). As Kleiger (2017, p. 1) describes, the concept of psychotic phenomena refers to a broad range of psychosis-like features that exist along a continuum—a view "consistent with how psychosis is currently regarded, less in terms of discrete categories of disorders and more as a series of symptom dimensions that can be placed along a continuum of severity."

The weighted sum of Cognitive Codes (*WSum6* or *WSumCog*), developed to quantify disordered thinking on the Rorschach, has shown significant correlations with cognitive functioning. In the geriatric sample described earlier (Muzio, 2006), *WSum6* correlated negatively with the MMSE (r = –.30, p < .01). Strongest correlations on the BEC96 subscales were with verbal fluency (r = –.25) and visual recognition (r = –.37), as well as a correlation with orientation to time and place (r = .31). These results suggest that disordered thinking is associated with some of the core symptoms of dementia: impaired semantic memory, visual agnosia, and disorientation. Disorientation, a hallmark of dementia of the Alzheimer's type (DAT), is linked to deficits in memory, visuospatial ability, and attention and reflects dysfunction in a distributed network of association cortices (Mesulam, 1998; Weissberger et al., 2017). In clinical practice, patients with DAT who present with disorientation often also show more disturbed thought processes, including conceptual incoherence and tangentiality. Certain Cognitive Codes—such as ALOG, CONTAM, and possibly DR1 and DR2—may be especially frequent in these cases (Muzio et al., 2001; Muzio & Luperto, 1999).

As summarized by Kleiger (2017), cognitive neuroscience research suggests that disordered thinking arises from dysfunction in neural systems supporting attention, memory, verbal fluency, and executive functioning. For example, McGuire et al. (1998) found that verbal disorganization was associated with reduced activity in brain areas involved in speech monitoring (e.g., inferior frontal, cingulate, and left superior temporal cortex) and increased activity in regions related to the processing of linguistic anomalies (e.g., parahippocampal/anterior fusiform cortex, right caudate).

The *PTI* has robust validity support for assessing psychotic phenomena, symptoms, and disorders (Mihura et al., 2013). It has proven useful for distinguishing psychotic from nonpsychotic inpatients (Benedik et al., 2013) and for identifying adolescents at high risk for psychosis (Ilonen et al., 2010), suggesting it may also signal vulnerability. Some evidence suggests that *X–%* (*FQ–%*) is more related to negative symptoms, *WSum6* (*WSum-Cog*) to positive symptoms and disordered thinking, and *M–* to delusional thinking (Mario et al., 2015). In a study of 211 adult inpatients, Dzamonja-Ignjatovic et al. (2013) found that the R-PAS Thought and Perception Composite (*TP-Comp*) slightly outperformed the *PTI* in identifying schizophrenia. The R-PAS Ego Impairment Index–3 (*EII-3*) also performed slightly better than its predecessor, the *EII-2* (Perry et al., 2003). All four indexes—*PTI, TP-Comp, EII-2*, and *EII-3*—successfully differentiated psychotic from nonpsychotic patients.

In geriatric patients (Muzio, 2006), the *PTI* has been shown to correlate significantly with the MMSE ($r = -.23$) and more specifically with subscales of the BEC96 measuring verbal fluency ($r = -.35$), the visual recognition of familiar objects ($r = -.40$), and visual-constructive abilities ($r = -.30$). It has also been found to correlate—along with *X–%* in particular—with visual-constructive abilities when measured through copy accuracy scores on the Rey-Osterrieth Complex Figure test (ROCF; Osterrieth, 1944) in a sample of adolescents seen in an outpatient setting. In the latter study, the *PTI* and *X–%* remained significant predictors of copy accuracy scores on the ROCF even once general intelligence (FSIQ) was controlled for (McTaggart, 2015). Taken together, these findings suggest several significant relationships between Rorschach variables related to psychotic phenomena and neurocognitive functions.

Additional Rorschach Variables Related to Intelligence and Cognitive Functions

As described in the previous sections, Rorschach variables related to intelligence and cognitive functions reflect an individual's capacity to adapt to the demands of a complex reality and to mentalize. They also reflect the degree to which a person is cognitively engaged when dealing with ambiguity and the level of sophistication demonstrated in their approach to problem-solving. Finally, they involve the capacity to perceive both external and internal stimuli accurately as well as the ability to think logically and coherently.

In addition to these, several Rorschach variables not typically associated with cognitive ability have also shown neurocognitive correlations. One is human content (*SumH*), which correlated with cognitive functioning (MMSE) in geriatric patients (r = .26; Muzio, 2006). Particularly relevant is whole, nonfictional human content (*Pure H*), which has been linked to cognitive functioning in adults and adolescents with severe psychiatric disorders and in healthy adults (Ilonen et al., 2016). *Pure H* also tends to be significantly lower in individuals with neurodevelopmental conditions such as autism spectrum disorders (Holaday et al., 2001) or attention-deficit/hyperactivity disorder (Locke, 1999). These findings suggest that neurocognitive deficits and disorders may reduce *SumH* and *Pure H*, possibly because *M*—which often includes human content and is correlated with cognitive functioning—tends to covary with them. Additionally, the low values for human content variables may reflect reduced interest in others, social withdrawal, or impaired mentalization often seen in severe psychiatric, neurocognitive, or neurodevelopmental disorders.

Another such variable is cooperative movement (*COP*), which has been found to significantly correlate with cognitive functions in adults and adolescents with severe psychiatric disorders, as well as in healthy adults (Ilonen et al., 2016). Like *Pure H*, *COP* responses are significantly lower in individuals with autism spectrum disorders, for example (Holaday et al., 2001). While *COP* often cooccurs with *M*, partially explaining this link, it likely also reflects a core feature of neurodevelopmental disorders—namely, reduced interest in relationships or difficulties in anticipating relationships to be supportive or cooperative.

The variety of different contents in children's and adolescents' Rorschach responses (i.e., content complexity [*Cont*]) is moderately associated with age-adjusted FSIQ (Meyer, 2016). However, specific content categories generally show little association with intelligence. Exceptions may include *Pure H*, as previously discussed, and *Xy* and *An*, which have been linked to nonverbal intelligence in children (Resende et al., 2019). In contrast, *Sx* and *Art* do not correlate with intelligence, although—like *Xy* and *An*—they are rarely seen in young children's protocols. For instance, none of 120 US healthy seven-year-olds produced *Sx* responses, while 7 percent of healthy fifteen-year-olds did (Exner, 2003, pp. 644, 660). Overall, associations between response contents and intelligence appear to be either weak or indirect, likely reflecting broader developmental progress.

Although variables other than those described in this chapter have been given less attention in the research literature in terms of their possible associations with intelligence and cognitive functions, existing evidence, and clinical experience both suggest that many Rorschach variables have little to do with intelligence or neurocognitive performance. For example, *Afr* (*8910%* in the R-PAS), which reflects an individual's level of engagement in emotionally arousing situations, has shown to be unrelated to neurocognitive functioning in a geriatric population as expected (Muzio, 2006). In this same study, the Egocentricity Index (*3r+(2)/R*) used in the CS was also unrelated to cognitive functions. Similar observations have been made repeatedly for variables such as *F%* or *R* which, despite their relationship to *Complexity*, appear to be unrelated to most cognitive functions in both children and adolescents (Meyer, 2016), as well as in senior adults (Muzio, 2006). The only exceptions appear to be a relationship between *F%* and verbal comprehension and processing in children (Meyer, 2016), as well as a relationship between *F%* and verbal learning in senior adults (Muzio, 2006).

Gold (1987) noted that Rorschach theory has often emphasized perceptual and cognitive aspects while overlooking the linguistic demands of the task. However, responding to the Rorschach also requires verbalizing perceptual and cognitive processes, and research has shown that verbal processing deficits can significantly reduce both protocol length and the diversity of response determinants (Meyer, 2016; Muzio, 2006).

Finally, *Zd*—described in the CS as an index of visual scanning efficiency (Exner, 2003)—has shown weak, nonsignificant correlations with cognitive functioning in both children (Meyer et al., 1993) and senior adults (Muzio, 2006). Given concerns about its computation and unclear interpretive value, some authors have questioned its validity (Meyer et al., 2011). While *Zd* may reflect aspects of processing efficiency, it is probably best considered tentatively as an indicator of cognitive style (overinclusiveness versus a tendency to omit relevant details) rather than a marker of neurocognitive functioning.

Notes

1 Hermann Rorschach coded only human movement as a movement response (*M*); animal and inanimate movement were not coded.
2 For a review of how networks of neurons represent and compute information, see Churchland and Sejnowski (1992).
3 According to Exner (2003, p. 232), "ego strength can be thought of as the effectiveness of mental activity (secondary process activity) when mediating between the needs, values, and external realities, while selecting and directing behaviors." When it is weak, "faulty adjustment or pathology can be expected

because of a failure to contend with internal conflict and/or a failure to weigh external reality adequately when selecting behaviors."

4 For a review of variables related to controls and stress tolerance, as well as to situationally related stress, see Exner (2003, pp. 231–279; CS) or Meyer et al. (2011, pp. 353–373; R-PAS).

5 The BEC96 is a brief French neurocognitive screening tool assessing multiple domains (e.g., orientation, memory, visuospatial skills). It correlates strongly with the MMSE (r = .88; Muzio, 2006), indicating they assess a similar construct.

6 The general intelligence (g) factor refers to a common cognitive ability underlying performance across diverse tasks. It was first proposed by Spearman in 1904 (see Spearman, 1961).

7 The Judgment of Line Orientation Test measures the ability to perceive spatial orientation and determine the angular relationships between line segments.

8 The MMSE is a brief neurocognitive test typically used in neurological or geriatric settings. It is designed to assess functions such as orientation to time and place, memory, and visuospatial abilities to screen for cognitive impairment.

9 Piagetian techniques assess cognitive development by evaluating how children solve problems and reason, aligned with Piaget's stages of development: sensorimotor, preoperational, concrete operational, and formal operational (Piaget, 1954).

10 Formal operational thought, as defined by Piaget, is the stage (beginning around age twelve) where individuals develop the ability to think abstractly, logically, and systematically, handling hypothetical and deductive reasoning.

11 As one would expect, *X–%* was the only variable with a negative loading on the Rorschach Perceptual Accuracy factor, as it relates to perceptual inaccuracy.

12 The Raven's Colored Progressive Matrices—Special Scale (often referred to as the Raven's Scale) is a nonverbal test used to measure abstract reasoning and general intelligence. It consists of multiple-choice items where individuals are asked to identify the missing piece of a pattern or matrix, with increasing complexity.

13 Subjects presented a wide range of somatic and neuropsychiatric disorders, and approximately half of them presented some form of cognitive decline (MMSE < 26/30).

14 The BEC96 is a French screening test of cognitive function like the MMSE (Folstein et al., 1975) but including subscales.

References

Acklin, M. W., & Fechner-Bates, S. (1989). Rorschach developmental quality and intelligence factors. *Journal of Personality Assessment*, 53(3), 537–545. doi:10.1207/s15327752jpa5303_10.

Ales, F., Giromini, L., Bosi, J., & Zennaro, A. (2022). White space responses in the Rorschach: Using eye-tracking to further understand the distinction between space reversal and space integration. *Current Psychology: A Journal for Diverse Perspectives on Diverse Psychological Issues.* Advance online publication. doi:10.1007/s12144-021-02632-4.

Ales, F., Giromini, L., & Zennaro, A. (2020). Complexity and cognitive engagement in the Rorschach task: An eye-tracking study. *Journal of Personality Assessment*, 102(4), 538–550. doi:10.1080/00223891.2019.1575227.

Allen, J. G., Fonagy, P., & Bateman, A. W. (2008). *Mentalizing in clinical practice.* American Psychiatric Publishing, Inc.

Allison, J., & Blatt, S. J. (1964). The relationship of Rorschach whole responses to intelligence. *Journal of Projective Techniques & Personality Assessment*, 28(3), 255–260. doi:10.1080/0091651X.1964.10120130.

Angelini, A. L., Alves, I. C. B., Custódio, E. M., Duarte, W. F., & Duarte, J. L. M. (1999). *Matrizes progressivas coloridas de Raven: Escala especial. Manual* [*Raven's colored progressive matrices: Special scale. Manual*]. CETEPP.

Ballard, C., O'Brien, J. T., Coope, B., Fairbairn, A., Abid, F., & Wilcock, G. (1997a). A prospective study of psychotic symptoms in dementia sufferers: Psychosis in dementia. *International Psychogeriatrics*, 9(1), 57–64. doi:10.1017/S1041610297004201.

Ballard, C. G., O'Brien, J. T., Coope, B., & Wilcock, G. (1997b). Psychotic symptoms in dementia and the rate of cognitive decline. *Journal of the American Geriatrics Society*, 45(8), 1032–1033. doi:10.1111/j.1532-5415.1997.tb02980.x.

Beck, S. J. (1960). *The Rorschach experiment: Ventures in blind diagnosis.* Grune & Stratton.

Benedik, E., Čoderl, S., Bon, J., & Smith, B. L. (2013). Differentiation of psychotic from nonpsychotic psychiatric inpatients: The Rorschach Perceptual Thinking Index. *Journal of Personality Assessment*, 95(2), 141–148. doi:10.1080/00223891.2012.753898.

Benton, A. L., Varney, N. R., & de Hamsher, K. S. (1978). Visuospatial judgment: A clinical test. *Archives of Neurology*, 35(6), 364–367.

Blatt, S. J., & Allison, J. (1963). Methodological considerations in Rorschach research: The W response as an expression of abstractive and integrative strivings. *Journal of Projective Techniques & Personality Assessment*, 27(3), 269–278. doi:10.1080/0091651X.1963.10120047.

Cattell, R. B. (1963). Theory of fluid and crystallized intelligence: A critical experiment. *Journal of Educational Psychology*, 54(1), 1–22. doi:10.1037/h0046743.

Churchland, P. S., & Sejnowski, T. J. (1992). *The computational brain*. MIT Press.

Cronbach, L. J. (1990). *Essentials of psychological testing*. Harper & Row.

Cunliffe, T. B., & Gacono, C. B. (2008). A Rorschach understanding of antisocial and psychopathic women. In C. B. Gacono & F. B. Evans (Eds.), *The handbook of forensic Rorschach assessment* (pp. 361–378). Routledge.

Dao, T. K., Prevatt, F., & Horne, H. L. (2008). Differentiating psychotic patients from nonpsychotic patients with the MMPI-2 and Rorschach. *Journal of Personality Assessment*, 90(1), 93–101. doi:10.1080/00223890701693819.

Dauphin, B., Greene, H. H., Juve, M., Boyle, M., Day, E., & Bemis, E. (2024). Expanding the interpretive potential of eye tracking for the Rorschach: Replication and extension of the findings of Ales et al. (2020). *Journal of Personality Assessment*, 106(4), 429–435. doi:10.1080/00223891.2024.2303433.

de Araújo, C. A., do Nascimento, R. S. G. F., & Assumpção Junior, F. B. (2011). Autismo e psicodiagnóstico de Rorschach [Autism and Rorschach test]. *PSICO*, 42(4), 434–441.

Drevets, W. C., & Rubin, E. H. (1989). Psychotic symptoms and the longitudinal course of senile dementia of the Alzheimer type. *Biological Psychiatry*, 25(1), 39–48. doi:10.1016/0006-3223(89)90145-5.

Dumitrascu, N., Mihura, J. L., & Meyer, G. J. (2011, March). *Selected RPAS variables and their relationship to level of education (as a proxy for cognitive sophistication)*. Paper presented at the annual meeting of the Society for Personality Assessment, Boston, MA.

Dzamonja-Ignjatovic, T., Smith, B. L., Jocic, D. D., & Milanovic, M. (2013). A comparison of new and revised Rorschach measures of schizophrenic functioning in a Serbian clinical sample. *Journal of Personality Assessment*, 95(5), 471–478. doi:10.1080/00223891.2013.810153.

Exner, J. E. (2000). *A primer for Rorschach interpretation*. Rorschach Workshops.

Exner, J. E. (2001). *A Rorschach workbook for the Comprehensive System*. Rorschach Workshops.

Exner, J. E. (2003). *The Rorschach: A comprehensive system: Volume 1: Basic foundations and principles of interpretation* (4th ed.). Wiley.

Exner, J. E. (2007). A new US adult nonpatient sample. *Journal of Personality Assessment*, 89(S1), S154–S158.

Exner, J. E., & Andronikof-Sanglade, A. (1992). Rorschach changes following brief and short-term therapy. *Journal of Personality Assessment*, 59(1), 59–71. doi:10.1207/s15327752jpa5901_6.

Exner, J. E., Colligan, S. C., Boll, T. J., Stischer, B., & Hillman, L. (1996). Rorschach findings concerning closed head injury patients. *Assessment*, 3(3), 317–326. doi:10.1177/107319119600300311.

Exner, J. E., Fontan, P., & Andronikof, A. (2022). *The Rorschach: A comprehensive system—revised. Interpretation and technical manual*. Rorschach Workshops.

Exner, J. E., Thomas, E. A., & Mason, B. (1985). Children's Rorschachs: Description and prediction. *Journal of Personality Assessment*, 49(1), 13–20.

Exner, J. E., Viglione, D. J., & Gillespie, R. (1984). Relationships between Rorschach variables as relevant to the interpretation of structural data. *Journal of Personality Assessment*, 48(1), 65–70. doi:10.1207/s15327752jpa4801_11.

Folstein, M. F., Folstein, S. E., & McHugh, P. R. (1975). "Mini-mental state": A practical method for grading the cognitive state of patients for the clinician. *Journal of Psychiatric Research*, 12(3), 189–198.

Friedman, H. (1953). Perceptual regression in schizophrenia: A hypothesis suggested by the use of the Rorschach test. *Journal of Projective Techniques*, 17, 171–185. doi:10.1080/08853126.1953.10380477.

Gacono, C. B., Meloy, J. R., & Bridges, M. R. (2008). A Rorschach understanding of psychopaths, sexual homicide perpetrators, and nonviolent pedophiles. In C. B. Gacono & F. B. Evans (Eds.), *The handbook of forensic Rorschach assessment* (pp. 379–402). Routledge.

Giromini, L., Viglione, D. J., Brusadelli, E., Lang, M., Reese, J. B., & Zennaro, A. (2015). Cross-cultural validation of the Rorschach Developmental Index. *Journal of Personality Assessment*, 97(4), 348–353. doi:10.1080/00223891.2014.960927.

Gold, J. M. (1987). The role of verbalization in the Rorschach response process: A review. *Journal of Personality Assessment*, 51(4), 489–505. doi:10.1207/s15327752jpa5104_1.

Gottfredson, L. S. (2011). Intelligence and social inequality: Why the biological link? In T. Chamorro-Premuzic, S. von Stumm, & A. Furnham (Eds.), *The Wiley-Blackwell handbook of individual differences* (pp. 538–575). Wiley-Blackwell. doi:10.1002/9781444343120.ch20.

Greenberg, R. P., & Cardwell, G. F. (1978). Rorschach developmental level and intelligence factors. *Journal of Consulting and Clinical Psychology*, 46(5), 844–848. doi:10.1037/0022-006X.46.5.844.

Groenewold, S. L. (2020). The relationship between the Rorschach performance assessment system cognitive processing variables and neuropsychological status among conditional release offenders. *Dissertation Abstracts International Section A: Humanities and Social Sciences*, 81(5-A).

Hathaway, S. R., & McKinley, J. C. (1943). *Manual for the Minnesota Multiphasic Personality Inventory*. University of Minnesota Press.

Heaton, R. K., Chelune, G. J., Talley, J. L., Kay, G. G., & Curtiss, G. (1993). *Wisconsin Card Sorting Test Manual: Revised and expanded.* Psychological Assessment Resources.

Holaday, M., Moak, J., & Shipley, M. A. (2001). Rorschach protocols from children and adolescents with Asperger's disorder. *Journal of Personality Assessment*, 76(3), 482–495. doi:10.1207/S15327752JPA7603_09.

Ilonen, T., Heinimaa, M., Korkeila, J., Svirskis, T., & Salokangas, R. K. R. (2010). Differentiating adolescents at clinical high risk for psychosis from psychotic and nonpsychotic patients with the Rorschach. *Psychiatry Research*, 179(2), 151–156. doi:10.1016/j.psychres.2009.04.011.

Ilonen, T., Salokangas, R. K. R., & Turku Study Group. (2016). The Rorschach Coping Deficit Index as an indicator of neurocognitive dysfunction. *Rorschachiana*, 37(1), 28–40. doi:10.1027/1192-5604/a000075.

Kay, S. R., Fiszbein, A., & Opler, L. A. (1987). The Positive and Negative Syndrome Scale (PANSS) for schizophrenia. *Schizophrenia Bulletin*, 13(2), 261–276. doi:10.1093/schbul/13.2.261.

Kissel, S. (1965). A brief note on the relationship between Rorschach Developmental Level and intelligence. *Journal of Projective Techniques & Personality Assessment*, 29(4), 454–455. doi:10.1080/0091651X.1965.10120235.

Kleiger, J. H. (1992). "A conceptual critique of the EA: ES comparison in the Comprehensive Rorschach System": Response. *Psychological Assessment*, 4(3), 301–302. doi:10.1037/1040-3590.4.3.301.

Kleiger, J. H. (2017). *Rorschach assessment of psychotic phenomena: Clinical, conceptual, and empirical developments.* Routledge. doi:10.4324/9781315271385.

Locke, S. R. (1999). Adult attention deficit disorder: Its impact on Rorschach scores. *Dissertation Abstracts International: Section B: The Sciences and Engineering*, 60(2-B), 0850.

Mario, B., Paolo, R., Anna, C., Maria Paola, A., Ileana, D. P., Valentina, C., Martina, C., Grace Allison, M., & Stefano, F. (2015). Relationship between the Rorschach Perceptual Thinking Index (*PTI*) and the Positive and Negative Syndrome Scale (PANSS) in psychotic patients: A validity study. *Psychiatry Research*, 225(3), 315–321. doi:10.1016/j.psychres.2014.12.018.

Marsden, G. (1970). Intelligence and the Rorschach whole response. *Journal of Projective Techniques & Personality Assessment*, 34(6), 470–476. doi:10.1080/0091651X.1970.10380289.

Matsuda, R., Suzuki, C., Takamura, K., & Hatano, Y. (2025). Exploring cognitive processing and neural correlates in Rorschach responses: A reanalysis of two experimental studies. *Rorschachiana*. Advance online publication. doi:10.1027/1192-5604/a000195.

McGuire, P. K., Quested, D. J., Spence, S. A., Murray, R. M., Frith, C. D., & Liddle, P. F. (1998). Pathophysiology of "positive" thought disorder in schizophrenia. *The British Journal of Psychiatry*, 173, 231–235. doi:10.1192/bjp.173.3.231.

McTaggart, S. C. (2015). An exploratory study examining the relationship between the Rey-Osterrieth complex figure and the Rorschach inkblok test. *Dissertation Abstracts International: Section B: The Sciences and Engineering*, 75(10-B(E)).

Mesulam, M.-M. (1998). From sensation to cognition. *Brain: A Journal of Neurology*, 121(6), 1013–1052. doi:10.1093/brain/121.6.1013.

Meyer, G. J. (1992). The Rorschach's factor structure: A contemporary investigation and historical review. *Journal of Personality Assessment*, 59(1), 117–136. doi:10.1207/s15327752jpa5901_10.

Meyer, G. J. (2016). Neuropsychological factors and Rorschach performance in children. *Rorschachiana*, 37(1), 7–27. doi:10.1027/1192-5604/a000074.

Meyer, G. J. (2023). Understanding complexity as a construct and as a formally scored variable. *Rorschachiana*, 44(1), 23–58. doi:10.1027/1192-5604/a000166.

Meyer, G. J., Erard, R. E., Erdberg, P., Mihura, J. L., & Viglione, D. J. (2011). *Rorschach Performance Assessment System: Administration, coding, interpretation, and technical manual.* Rorschach Performance Assessment System LLC.

Meyer, G. J., Erdberg, P., & Shaffer, T. W. (2007). Toward international normative reference data for the Comprehensive System. *Journal of Personality Assessment*, 89(Suppl1), S201–S216. doi:10.1080/00223890701629342.

Meyer, G. J., Murphy, S. G., Kiolbasa, T., Daly, M., Orput, D., Zelko, F. A. J., Remer-Osborn, J., & Zillmer, E. A. (1993, March). Neuropsychological factors and Rorschach performance in children. Paper presented at the Annual Meeting of the Society for Personality Assessment, San Francisco, CA.

Mihura, J. L. (2012). The necessity of Multiple Test Methods in conducting assessments: The role of the Rorschach and self-report. *Psychological Injury and Law*, 5(2), 97–106. doi:10.1007/s12207-012-9132-9.

Mihura, J. L., Dumitrascu, N., Roy, M., & Meyer, G. J. (2018). The centrality of the response process in construct validity: An illustration via the Rorschach space response. *Journal of Personality Assessment*, 100(3), 233–249. doi:10.1080/00223891.2017.1306781.

Mihura, J. L., & Görner, K. J. (2025). Perceptions of three-dimensionality on the Rorschach and experience of the self in the world: Updated systematic reviews. *Rorschachiana*, 46(1), 62–97. doi:10.1027/1192-5604/a000185.

Mihura, J. L., Meyer, G. J., Dumitrascu, N., & Bombel, G. (2013). The validity of individual Rorschach variables: Systematic reviews and meta-analyses of the comprehensive system. *Psychological Bulletin*, 139(3), 548–605. doi:10.1037/a0029406.

Murstein, B. I. (1960). Factor analyses of the Rorschach. *Journal of Consulting Psychology*, 24(3), 262–275. doi:10.1037/h0041619.

Muzio, E. (2006). Vers une approche neuropsychologique intégrée de la personnalité à travers le Rorschach en gériatrie et dans la démence de type Alzheimer [Toward an integrated neuropsychological approach to personality through the Rorschach in geriatrics and dementia of the Alzheimer's type]. Doctoral dissertation. Université Paris X–Nanterre.

Muzio, E. (2018). Understanding the psychology of evil: The Rorschach of serial-killer Ted Bundy. Paper presented at the Annual Convention of the Society for Personality Assessment, Washington, DC.

Muzio, E., & Andronikof, A. (2008, July). Verbal learning ability and performance on the Rorschach Comprehensive System: a neuropsychological approach to personality. Paper presented at the Paper presented at the nineteenth International Congress of the Rorschach and Projective Methods, Leuven, Belgium.

Muzio, E., Andronikof, A., David, J. P., & Di Menza, C. (2001). L'Intérêt du test du Rorschach (Système Intégré) dans l'évaluation psychométrique en gériatrie: Exemple de la démence de type Alzheimer [The usefulness of the Rorschach test (Comprehensive System) in psychometric assessment in geriatrics: The example of dementia of the Alzheimer's type]. *La Revue de Gériatire*, 26(2), 121–130.

Muzio, E., & Luperto, L. (1999). Démence et fonctionnement de la personnalité à travers le Rorschach chez un groupe de femmes âgées hospitalisées [Dementia and personality functioning through the Rorschach in a group of hospitalized elderly women]. *European Review of Applied Psychology/Revue Européenne de Psychologie Appliquée*, 49(3), 227–236.

Osterrieth, P. A. (1944). Le Test de copie d'une figure complexe: Contribution à l'étude de la perception et de la mémoire [The test of copying a complex figure: Contribution to the study of perception and memory]. *Archives de Psychologie*, 30, 206–356.

Perry, W., Minassian, A., Cadenhead, K., Sprock, J., & Braff, D. (2003). The use of the Ego Impairment Index across the schizophrenia spectrum. *Journal of Personality Assessment*, 80(1), 50–57. doi:10.1207/S15327752JPA8001_13.

Piaget, J. (1954). *The construction of reality in the child.* Basic Books. First published 1937. doi:10.1037/11168-000.

Piotrowski, Z. (1937). The Rorschach inkblot method in organic disturbances of the central nervous system. *Journal of Nervous and Mental Disease*, 86(5), 525–537. doi:10.1097/00005053-193711000-00002.

Piotrowski, Z. A., & Schreiber, M. (1952). Rorschach perceptanalytic measurement of personality changes during and after psychoanalytically oriented psychotherapy. *Specialized techniques in psychotherapy.* Basic Books.

Porcelli, P. (2025). Embodied mentalization: The case of human movement in the Rorschach. *Rorschachiana*, 46(1), 3–23. doi:10.1027/1192-5604/a000189.

Rapaport, D., Gill, M. M., & Schafer, R. (1968). *Diagnostic psychological testing* (R. R. Holt, Ed. Revised). International Universities Press.

Reitan, R. M., & Wolfson, D. (1985). *The Halstead–Reitan Neuropsychological Test Battery: Theory and clinical interpretation.* Neuropsychology Press.

Resende, A. C., Viglione, D. J., Martins, L. D., & Yazigi, L. (2019). Criterion validity of the Rorschach Developmental Index with children. *Journal of Personality Assessment*, 101(2), 191–198. doi:10.1080/00223891.2017.1368021.

Ridley, S. E., & Bayton, J. A. (1983). Validity of two scoring systems for measuring cognitive development with the Rorschach. *Journal of Consulting and Clinical Psychology*, 51(3), 470–471. doi:10.1037/0022-006X.51.3.470.

Rorschach, H. (2021). *Hermann Rorschach's psychodiagnostics: Newly translated and annotated 100th anniversary edition* (P. J. Keddy, R. Signer, P. Erdberg & A. Schneider-Stocking, Eds.) Hogrefe Publishing. First published 1921.

Rorschach Research Council. (1999). Notes: Rorschach Research Council meeting, October 9–10, 1999.

Schachtel, E. G. (2001). *Experiential foundations of Rorschach's test.* The Analytic Press. First published 1966.

Signoret, J.-L. (1998). *Évaluation des troubles de mémore et des désordres cognitifs associés.* Laboratoires IPSEN.

Smith, N. M. (1981). The relationship between the Rorschach whole response and level of cognitive functioning. *Journal of Personality Assessment*, 45(1), 13–19. doi:10.1207/s15327752jpa4501_4.

Spearman, C. (1961). "General intelligence" objectively determined and measured. In J. J. Jenkins & D. G. Paterson (Eds.), *Studies in individual differences: The search for intelligence* (pp. 59–73). Appleton-Century-Crofts.

Stanfill, M. L., Viglione, D. J., & Resende, A. C. (2013a). Measuring psychological development with the Rorschach. *Journal of Personality Assessment*, 95(2), 174–186. doi:10.1080/00223891.2012.740538.

Stanfill, M. L., Viglione, D. J., & Resende, A. C. (2013b). Correction to: Measuring psychological development with the Rorschach. *Journal of Personality Assessment*, 95(4), 435. doi:10.1080/00223891.2013.779563.

Tibon-Czopp, S., & Weiner, I. B. (2016). *Rorschach assessment of adolescents.* Springer. doi:10.1007/978-1-4939-3151-4.

Vitolo, E., Giromini, L., Viglione, D. J., Cauda, F., & Zennaro, A. (2021). Complexity and cognitive engagement in the Rorschach task: An fMRI study. *Journal of Personality Assessment*, 103(5), 634–644. doi:10.1080/00223891.2020.1842429.

Wechsler, D. (1974). *Wechsler Intelligence Scale for Children: Revised (WISCR).* Psychological Corporation.

Wechsler, D. (1981). *Wechsler Adult Intelligence Scale: Revised (WAISR) manual.* The Psychological Corporation.

Wechsler, D. (1987). *Wechsler Memory Scale: Revised manual.* The Psychological Corporation.

Wechsler, D. (1991). *Wechsler Intelligence Scale for Children: Third edition (WISCIII) manual.* The Psychological Corporation.

Wechsler, D. (1992). *Wechsler Adult Intelligence Scale—Revised manual.* The Psychological Corporation.

Wechsler, D. (1999). *Wechsler Intelligence Scale for Children (WISCIII).* The Psychological Corporation.

Weiner, I. B. (2003). *Principles of Rorschach interpretation.* Routledge.

Weiner, I. B., Appel, L., & Tibon-Czopp, S. (2019). *Rorschach assessment of senior adults.* Routledge. doi:10.4324/9780429282171.

Weiner, I. B., & Exner, J. E. (1991). Rorschach changes in long-term short-term psychotherapy. *Journal of Personality Assessment*, 56(3), 453–465.

Weissberger, G. H., Melrose, R. J., Fanale, C. M., Veliz, J. V., & Sultzer, D. L. (2017). Cortical metabolic and cognitive correlates of disorientation in Alzheimer's disease. *Journal of Alzheimer's Disease*, 60(2), 707–719. doi:10.3233/JAD-170420.

Wood, J. M., Krishnamurthy, R., & Archer, R. P. (2003). Three factors of the Comprehensive System for the Rorschach and their relationship to Wechsler IQ scores in an adolescent sample. *Assessment*, 10(3), 259–265. doi:10.1177/1073191103255493.

Zillmer, E. A., & Perry, W. (1996). Cognitive-neuropsychological abilities and related psychological disturbance: A factor model of neuropsychological, Rorschach, and MMPI indices. *Assessment*, 3(3), 209–224. doi:10.1177/107319119600300303.

Chapter 4

Rorschach Performance of Patients with Specific Neurocognitive and Neurodevelopmental Disorders

In this chapter, I review some of the central research findings concerning Rorschach response tendencies in different groups of neuropsychologically impaired subjects. In doing so, I focus primarily—though not exclusively—on research using the two most widely used and researched contemporary Rorschach systems and their variables: the Comprehensive System (CS; Exner, 2003) and the Rorschach Performance Assessment System (R-PAS; Meyer et al., 2011). The Comprehensive System—Revised (CS-R; Exner et al., 2022) will not be referred to here as there is no published research that uses it in this area.

It is important to note that covering the full spectrum of published research on neuropsychological and neurodevelopmental disorders using the Rorschach is beyond the scope of this chapter. Instead, selected conditions are presented as illustrative examples. This decision reflects the fact that much of the existing research in this area predates the widespread international adoption of the CS and the R-PAS and often relies on outdated systems or methods lacking strong empirical support. This is particularly true for conditions such as Parkinson's disease and intellectual disability, for which a considerable body of Rorschach research exists, though much of it is based on earlier conceptual and methodological frameworks unaligned with current standards.

For Parkinson's disease, for example, findings suggest a psychological functioning marked by introversion, emotional overcontrol (e.g., elevated Form-Color [*FC*], overall limited use of color determinants) but preserved perceptual accuracy (Ogawa, 1981). Moreover, it has been observed that some patients undergoing deep brain stimulation (DBS) of the subthalamic nucleus (STN) have demonstrated decreased reality testing postoperatively, though related scores remained within normative ranges and did not reflect clinically meaningful personality changes (Castelli et al., 2008).[1]

As to intellectual disability (ID), Rorschach studies have suggested, for example, that individuals diagnosed with this condition often produce few human movement (*M*) responses and may show signs of lower self-esteem, particularly when comorbid psychiatric conditions are present (Cattonaro,

DOI: 10.4324/9781003731894-5

1959; Colucci et al., 1998). Furthermore, earlier research supports the idea that the Rorschach can be particularly useful in capturing aspects of affect regulation, perceptual-cognitive processing, and social adjustment that go beyond what can be obtained from IQ or other tests (Allen, 1975; Brink & Grundlingh, 1976; Sloan, 1948). For example, its potential contribution to complex diagnostic clarifications has been illustrated in situations where masked cognitive strengths were revealed in individuals misdiagnosed with ID due to underlying language impairments (Lovinger, 1981).

Quite unsurprisingly, most of the variables addressed in this chapter are those shown to correlate with intelligence and cognitive functions discussed in Chapter 3. Also unsurprisingly, many of these variables are common across different forms of neuropsychological impairment. This supports an early observation by Piotrowski (1937), who noted that patients with neuropsychological disorders tend to exhibit similar types of deficits and dysfunctions on the Rorschach, regardless of the specific neurological condition involved. However, Piotrowski's organic sign approach overlooked the fact that, despite considerable overlap in response tendencies and processing styles, different neuropsychological conditions are also associated with distinct response patterns. In addition to considering individual differences within each group, such variation underscores the importance of attending to the distinct perceptual and cognitive profiles associated with different forms of neuropsychological impairment.

Dementia of the Alzheimer's Type

Perry et al. (1996) compared Rorschach performance in twenty-two patients with probable dementia of the Alzheimer's type (DAT), diagnosed using National Institute of Neurological and Communicative Disorders and Stroke and the Alzheimer's Disease and Related Disorders Association (NINCDS-ADRDA) criteria (McKhann et al., 1984), to that of nineteen age- and education-matched healthy controls.[2] The mean age of DAT patients was seventy-six, the mean number of years of education was thirteen, and the mean score on the Mini Mental State Exam (MMSE; Folstein et al., 1975) was 20/30 (SD = 5.7), which roughly corresponds to the early to middle stages of DAT.[3] The study aimed to illustrate the utility of the Rorschach (CS) as a neuropsychological tool, particularly through a *process approach* (Kaplan, 1988), which emphasizes how individuals solve tasks rather than focusing solely on quantitative scores. This approach aligns with Exner's (2003) view of the Rorschach as a problem-solving task, offering insight into cognitive processes such as linguistic errors or patterns of perseveration in DAT.

Perry et al. (1996) attempted to align CS Rorschach variables with the five cardinal neuropsychological signs of DAT—for example, by classifying *P* as reflecting amnesia, and *X–%* as apraxia.[4] However, these assignments were somewhat arbitrary; it is unclear why *X–%* would represent apraxia rather than agnosia or why *P* responses would relate more to memory than to perceptual recognition. This variable-to-deficit mapping overlooks the influence of psychological and psychopathological factors, which can also affect Rorschach scores. Importantly, while the Rorschach is not designed to diagnose specific neuropsychological deficits or conditions like DAT, it remains a valuable tool for understanding an individual's perceptual-cognitive functioning and psychological strengths and weaknesses.

Compared to nonpatient controls, DAT patients showed markedly lower perceptual-cognitive complexity, with more simplistic processing and reduced attention to subtlety (*Blends, Lambda*). They were also less productive (*R*) and demonstrated weaker efforts to organize the stimulus field or form meaningful relationships between percepts (*Zf, DQ+%*). In terms of perceptual accuracy, they gave fewer conventional responses (*X+%, P*) and more perceptual distortions (*X–%)*, though the latter reached a lower level of statistical significance ($p < .01$ instead of $p < .001$). The DAT group also produced fewer *M* responses, reflecting diminished psychological resources such as goal-directed thinking, agency, and mentalization (Meyer et al., 2011, p. 355). Interestingly, they showed fewer indicators of internal tension or distraction (*FM, m*) than controls. No significant group differences emerged for disordered thinking (*WSum6), DQo%, DV*, or *PSV*, with both groups showing low values on these indices.

The absence of group differences in *DV* and *PSV* was unexpected given the typical language, memory, and executive impairments associated with DAT. However, using a more refined coding system adapted from prior methodologies (e.g., Barr et al., 1989), the authors identified significant group differences in specific types of linguistic and executive perseveration errors. Among eight linguistic error subtypes, DAT patients more frequently showed wordfinding circumlocution and use of superordinate categories ($p < .001$), as well as semantic paraphasia ($p < .01$). Among five executive error subtypes, they showed more thematic perseveration ($p < .001$), phonemic perseveration ($p < .01$), and stuck-in-set perseveration ($p < .05$). Although not all subtypes differed individually, the total error score was significantly higher in the DAT group ($p < .001$). These findings suggest that while traditional cognitive codes and scores like *DV, PSV*, or *WSum6* may not differentiate DAT patients from healthy senior adults, more specific linguistic and executive error types on the Rorschach may have diagnostic value.[5] Perry later refined his method, introducing more nuanced coding categories such as *organizational perseverations*, further supporting the Rorschach's value in process-oriented neuropsychological assessment (Perry, 2005).

Despite shedding light on response processes in DAT, several methodological issues limit the clinical utility of Perry et al.'s findings. First, standard CS administration procedures were not followed—some protocols included fewer than fourteen responses, and several cards were rejected, undermining test-retest reliability (Exner, 1988). Second, for five DAT patients, inquiry was conducted immediately after each response due to assumed memory deficits, without evidence that this adjustment improves recall. In my clinical experience, even individuals with moderate DAT are typically able to engage meaningfully in standard delayed inquiry, making this deviation unnecessary.

These departures from standard procedure led to fewer responses, more card rejections, and questionable protocol validity. Third, comparisons were made with nonpatients rather than a clinical control group, limiting the findings' value for differential diagnosis. As Mihura et al. (2013) note, using clinical controls enhances diagnostic relevance by reducing inflated effect sizes on Rorschach measures of psychopathology.

In my doctoral dissertation (Muzio, 2006), I compared twenty carefully diagnosed patients with probable DAT (NINCDS-ADRDA criteria; McKhann et al., 1984) to an age- and education-matched clinical control group of forty geriatric patients with a broad variety of somatic (e.g., cardiovascular, rheumatological), neurological, and/or psychopathological conditions but an absence of significant cognitive deficits (MMSE > 25).[6] The mean age of DAT patients was eighty-one, the mean number of years of education was nine, and the average score on the MMSE was 16.5/30 (SD = 3.5). Patients in the DAT group were clinically classified as presenting either mild (n = 9) or moderate (n = 11) levels of functional impairment according to the Clinical Dementia Rating (CDR) scale (Hughes et al., 1982), which roughly corresponds to the early to middle stages of the disorder.[7] The DAT group was relatively homogeneous and resembled Perry et al.'s sample, though the latter had slightly higher average education and MMSE scores. Clinically, patients with this profile often present with severe memory deficits but still manage to make a psychologically healthy first impression—a phenomenon geriatric professionals often describe as a "polished facade."

In this second Rorschach study on DAT, standard CS administration was followed, and invalid protocols were excluded. Notably, most patients were able to indicate where they saw each percept and what made it look like what they saw when asked during the standard inquiry phase. Although Perry et al.'s linguistic and executive perseveration errors were not coded, additional CS variables not included in their study were analyzed, broadening the scope of the study.

As hypothesized, there were several statistically significant differences between the DAT group and the clinical control group. The most significant differences ($p < .001$) with large effect sizes—despite the use of a clinical control group—were found for *EA* ($d = -.99$), *M* ($d = -.94$), and *Blends* ($d = -.93$), followed by statistically significant ($p < .05$) but more moderate effects for *DQ+, DQv, F%, X–%, WSumC, SumH*, and *CDI*, which were all in the expected direction. These results confirm a considerable lack of both cognitive and emotional adaptive resources and stress tolerance in DAT, combined with simplistic, vague, and impressionistic information processing, as well as a tendency to misperceive stimuli and to lose interest in people.

Nonsignificant differences were found for *R* ($d = -.11$), *Afr* ($d = .06$), *Zf, P, FM, m*, and *es*. While *X–%* differed significantly, *WSum6* and *PTI* did not. These findings suggest that, in early-stage DAT, patients generally produce a typical number of responses, remain engaged with emotionally arousing tasks, and exert normal efforts in processing information. This last point may reflect anosognosia, as patients unaware of their deficits may overestimate their cognitive capacity. Similarly, DAT patients do not tend to show difficulties in responding to obvious cues—supporting the idea of a "polished facade"—nor do they show diminished capacity for experiencing internal tension or distress. Although perceptual misinterpretations are relatively common in DAT, other psychotic features—such as disordered thinking—are typically absent. These misperceptions likely result from cognitive deterioration caused by neurodegeneration rather than from true psychotic processes. Clinically, this is often seen when patients misplace belongings and, due to memory loss and lack of awareness of their deficits (anosognosia), come to believe the items were stolen. Such psychotic-like experiences are best understood as secondary manifestations of disease progression rather than as core features of DAT.

In the more recent study (Muzio, 2006), Perry et al.'s statistically significant findings were replicated for *F%, DQ+, M*, and *X–%*, but not *R, FM, m, P*, or *Zf*. Negative findings could be explained, at least in part, by the fact that *R* was controlled in the more recent study, allowing for less variance in *R*-dependent variables such as *FM, m, P*, or *Zf*.

Beyond its value for early and differential diagnosis, the Rorschach provides a more nuanced view of the perceptual and cognitive processes in DAT—insights not easily captured by standard neuropsychological tests. These findings align with prior studies of patients with advanced dementia (e.g., Muzio & Luperto, 1999; Muzio et al., 2001), where markers such as *EA* < 3, *X–%* > .29, and *DQ+* < 3 effectively distinguished DAT and other dementias from cognitively intact geriatric patients. These variables reflect diminished adaptive capacity, reduced perceptual accuracy, and impaired integrative processing. Notably, elevated *WSum6* scores—particularly involving *ALOG* and *CONTAM* codes—also emerged in severe cases, suggesting that disordered thinking may become more prominent as dementia progresses. Such thinking may include peculiar logic, strained reasoning, or a bizarre fusion of percepts and ideas, even if it is not a defining feature in early-stage DAT (Perry et al., 1996; Muzio, 2006).

The importance of *EA*, and especially *M*, as markers of severe neurocognitive impairment has been noted in earlier Rorschach research on dementia (Insua & Loza, 1986). As observed in geriatric neuropsychological assessment and noted by Dörken and Kral (1951), patients with advanced dementia not only show an increased tendency to distort reality but often become unable to generate Rorschach responses altogether. In late-stage DAT, individuals may lose the capacity to make sense of their surroundings as well as the more nuanced aspects of their personality. From a psychoanalytical perspective, this decline reflects a breakdown in mental representations and boundaries, leading to confusion, regression to sensory and motor modes of experiencing, and a narcissistic withdrawal from external reality (Péruchon, 1996, 2020).

As summarized by Perry et al. (1996, p. 359) from a neuropsychological perspective, "substantial cognitive resources must be mobilized in the service of generating novel responses to the Rorschach stimuli." This makes the Rorschach a useful neuropsychological problem-solving task in detecting impaired cognitive processes. Concurrently, as a test of typical performance, it can give us a better sense of the subjective experience of patients with DAT, thus serving as an *empathy magnifier* for healthcare providers or those living with these patients daily (Finn, 2020, 2022).

Dementia with Lewy Bodies

While DAT typically begins with early deficits in episodic memory and progresses to broader neurocognitive impairment, dementia with Lewy bodies (DLB) is characterized by early cognitive fluctuations, recurrent visual hallucinations, and Parkinsonian motor symptoms.[8] In a Rorschach study comparing visuoperceptual functioning, Kimoto et al. (2017) examined thirty-two patients with probable DLB (McKeith et al., 2017), twenty-six with probable DAT (McKhann et al., 2011), and fourteen age-matched controls (MMSE > 26). The mean age across groups was approximately eighty, and mean MMSE scores for the dementia groups were nearly identical (DLB: ~17; DAT: ~18), with standard deviations around 4. Patients with MMSE scores below 9 were excluded. Inquiry was conducted immediately after each response, based on the assumption that delayed recall might be unreliable in this population.

Results showed significant differences between both dementia groups and the control group on variables such as *X–%, S–*, and *W*, indicating reduced perceptual accuracy and problems with higher-order perceptual organization. Additionally, several variables significantly differed for the DLB group compared to controls, but not for the DAT group. Patients with DLB showed more signs of disordered thinking (*Sum6, WSum6*), more severe or potentially delusional thinking (*Lv2, DR2, M–*), and greater executive dysfunction, particularly in shifting attention (*PSV*).

Most notably, the DLB group had a significantly higher mean *PTI* score than the DAT group (2.5 vs. 0.7), indicating a stronger tendency to present perceptual inaccuracy and disordered thinking. Related variables—including *X–%, S–*, and *DV1*—were also elevated, along with *Zd* and *Dd*, suggesting more meticulous scanning and heightened attention to detail in the DLB group.

Kimoto et al. also conducted a qualitative analysis and found that significantly more patients in the DLB group reported seeing an eye in the shaded areas of the inkblots compared to those with DAT (63 percent vs. 39 percent). DLB patients tended to identify the eye first and reason concretely (e.g., "It's an animal because there is an eye"), while DAT patients were more likely to infer the eye afterward (e.g., "It's an animal, so the eyes should be here"). Receiver Operating Characteristic (ROC) curves showed that a *PTI* cutoff of 2/3 yielded 78 percent sensitivity and 81 percent specificity for distinguishing DLB from DAT.[9] Diagnostic accuracy improved further when combining *PTI, Dd,* and the eye response, resulting in 91 percent sensitivity and 73 percent specificity with a cutoff of 4.5/4.6. According to this, a combined score of 5 or higher (*PTI* + *Dd* + eye responses) indicates probable DLB, whereas a score of 4 or lower suggests DAT.

Although sample sizes were small and the groups were not matched for education, the findings support the Rorschach's utility in differentiating DLB from DAT. Consistent with other assessment methods (e.g., Ota et al., 2015), DLB patients showed marked impairments in perceptual accuracy, thinking, and the organization of visual information. These results align with clinical features of DLB, such as visual hallucinations or illusions involving small insects or figures seen in vague settings (Simard et al., 2000). DLB is also associated with pareidolia—the tendency to perceive meaningful patterns in ambiguous stimuli (Uchiyama et al., 2012)—a phenomenon reflected in *FQ–* responses on the Rorschach.

Polycystic Lipomembranous Osteodysplasia with Sclerosing Leukoencephalopathy

Polycystic lipomembranous osteodysplasia with sclerosing leukoencephalopathy (PLOSL), also known as Nasu–Hakola disease, is a rare autosomal recessive disorder characterized by early-onset frontotemporal dementia and cystic bone lesions.[10] The neuropsychological profile affects not only behavior and cognition but also personality structure.

In a study by Ilonen et al. (2012), Rorschach profiles were examined in eight genetically confirmed PLOSL patients aged 28–36. The group showed high *Lambda* values (> .99), prompting comparison with healthy adults with similarly avoidant protocols (Exner, 2001, pp. 185–187; *N* = 58). Significant differences compared to the reference group included low productivity (*R,* M = 17.25), high *Lambda* (M = 2.21), and impairments across multiple domains: simplistic information processing (*DQ+,* M = 3.38), poor cognitive flexibility (*PSV,* M = 1.75), and severely impaired perceptual accuracy (*X–%,* M = 36.12; *P,* M = 3.88). They also showed disordered and pessimistic thinking (*WSum6,* M = 14.62; *Lv2,* M = 0.87; *MOR,* M = 2.25), poor emotional control (*Pure C,* M = 0.88), and a negative self-image (*Ego Index,* M = .33; *MOR*). Half the patients had a positive *CDI,* indicating poor social functioning and the presence of significant coping deficits. While *EA* was also low (M = 4.18), it did not differ significantly compared to the high-*Lambda* reference sample.

As in other neuropsychological groups, Rorschach variables in the PLOSL sample showed high variability, indicating notable individual differences. However, clear trends emerged that align with known neuropsychological features of PLOSL, supporting the Rorschach's validity in this context. Furthermore, as with other neuropsychological disorders, incorporating the Rorschach into a multimethod assessment can meaningfully capture both common and unique features of individuals with this condition.

Traumatic Brain Injury

Traumatic brain injury (TBI) refers to damage to the brain caused by an external force—such as a blow to the head, a fall, or a motor-vehicle accident—that disrupts normal brain function. As Parker (1996) noted in a study of thirty-three individuals with mild TBI from vehicular accidents, emotional disturbance and neuropsychological symptoms often significantly impair postinjury adaptation. For this reason, a broad range of assessment procedures—including interviews, observation, checklists, neurocognitive testing, and the Rorschach—has been recommended to obtain the data needed for diagnosis, prognosis, and treatment planning. Psychological test batteries are typically more sensitive than clinical interviews or ancillary tests like electroencephalograms (EEG) in detecting subtle or persistent brain damage, which may remain long after the acute phase has passed (D'Netto & Kishore, 1976). As de Mol (1990) emphasized, TBI often impacts the totality of personality functioning. Anxieties concerning physical, cognitive, and emotional integrity may evolve into an anxious sense of loss, further complicating the clinical picture and affecting self-perception. While a general post-TBI syndrome can often be identified, its manifestations vary greatly across individuals. The Rorschach can be of great help in assisting clinicians and rehabilitation specialists better understand these differences, by illuminating both the neurocognitive and psychodynamic consequences of injury—thus supporting the individual's psychological and neuropsychological reorganization following the narcissistic wound of trauma.

Neuropsychological assessment of TBI patients typically reveals a combination of pretrauma factors (e.g., personality structure and dynamics, cognitive functioning), injury-related impairments (e.g., diffuse axonal injury, lesion-specific effects), and psychological reactions to neurocognitive disruption. Without pretrauma or longitudinal data, it is often difficult—or impossible—to disentangle these influences. Such data can aid in predicting outcomes and tailoring interventions. Still, even in their absence, a multimethod assessment that includes a typical performance measure like the Rorschach can provide valuable insights for individualized rehabilitation and treatment planning (e.g., Ellis & Zahn, 1985; Exner et al., 1996).

Ellis and Zahn (1985) examined the Rorschach (CS) performance of thirty-five young adults with severe closed head injury (CHI), compared to thirty-six healthy controls matched for age, education (9–16 years), socioeconomic status (mostly middle to upper middle class), marital status (mostly single), and race (predominantly white).[11] Severe CHI was defined as blunt head trauma resulting in coma for at least five days (range: 5–180 days; M = 34). The CHI group had an average Full-Scale IQ (FSIQ) of 87 on the WAIS-R (range: 69–108; Wechsler, 1981). Computed axial tomography scans and EEGs revealed diffuse brain damage with mixed pathology due to tearing and shearing from the trauma.

Compared to healthy controls, the CHI group showed significantly lower *R, Afr, P, X+%, D, WSumC*, and *T*, along with higher *Lambda, DQv*, and *W*. Although Ellis and Zahn (1985) also described confusion, cognitive disarray, and emotional distress in the CHI group, these were not evident in the reported data. Rorschach performance suggested that many patients struggled to process ambiguous, complex, or emotionally arousing stimuli. Their responses were often overly simplistic, vague, and lacked conventionality and emotional integration—pointing to deficits in adaptive resources as well as signs of emotional shutdown. Using a discriminant function analysis, Ellis and Zahn correctly classified 100 percent of their seventy-one participants into the CHI or control group, echoing Piotrowski's (1957) observation that individuals with severe neuropsychological disorders often show difficulties in producing responses or responding in perceptually accurate and conventional ways on the Rorschach.

The impact of severity on Rorschach performance has been emphasized by several authors. In a study of twenty-two adults with severe TBI, Cattelani et al. (1998) confirmed the Rorschach's sensitivity to postinjury cognitive and personality changes but found it added limited value beyond standard neurocognitive measures or commonly used rating scales in more severe cases. This limitation likely reflects the fact that when impairment is pronounced, conventional neuropsychological tests already capture the relevant deficits. In contrast, in the early years of Rorschach research, Aita, Reitan, and Ruth (1947) found that most of Piotrowski's ten organic signs (Piotrowski, 1937) were less useful in identifying individuals with mild or moderate TBI. In this instance, the limitation reflects the opposite issue: the early organic signs were probably not sufficiently sensitive to more subtle injuries. Thus, although both these studies reported limited utility, they did so for different severity-related reasons and the latter study looked specifically at Piotrowski's ten organic signs.[12] Among the original signs, only impotence (*Imp*), perplexity (*Plx*), automatic phrases (*AP*), repetition (*Rpt*), and color-naming (*Cn*) showed diagnostic value. Aita, Reitan, and Ruth also proposed nine new signs based on a qualitative review of the protocols. Anxiety, depression, and hypochondriasis were frequently observed, and psychotic-like symptoms occasionally appeared. These findings underscore the importance of a process-oriented approach that considers both quantitative and qualitative aspects of Rorschach performance, especially given that many response features are not specific to brain injury.

Exner et al. (1996) examined the Rorschach (CS) performance of sixty individuals with mild to moderate CHI, as classified by the Halstead-Reitan Impairment Index (Reitan & Wolfson, 1985). Participants, who were all inpatients or outpatients of a neurology service, had a mean age of thirty-eight years (range = 24–59) and an average of thirteen years of education (range = 7–18). Most had no psychiatric history; only three had been treated for depression or anxiety, and six had received marital therapy. Forty-three had experienced loss of consciousness from a few minutes to 72 hours. Although no control group was used, comparisons were made to US reference data. The study aimed to provide a general description of the Rorschach performance of CHI patients and explore implications for intervention and rehabilitation.

As expected, the Rorschach performance of patients with CHI differed markedly from normative expectations. A total of 73 percent had a high *Lambda* (> .99), over half had a positive *CDI* (53 percent, with 20 percent scoring 5/5), and the mean *EA* was roughly half that of the reference sample. Eight patients gave no *M* responses, and twenty had no chromatic color responses. They were more often ambitent, less often extratensive, and showed a lower mean *Afr, es*, and *Adj es.* Significantly more had an underincorporative style (*Zd* < –3.0), and significantly fewer had an over-incorporative one (*Zd* > +3.0). Notably, 27 percent gave at least one reflection response (*Fr* + *rF*), versus 7 percent in the reference sample.[13] A comparable frequency for the *CDI* (60 percent) was reported in another TBI sample with similar characteristics (Sinacori, 2000).

Interestingly, variables like *X–%* and *WSum6* showed no notable group differences, with similarly low means in both samples. None of the CHI subjects showed elevations on the Schizophrenia Index (*SCZI*) (an earlier version of the *PTI*) or the Depression Index (*DEPI*), and comparable values were also found for *Zf, P, HVI, OBS, SumH, MOR*, and shading-related responses.

Overall, the data suggest that individuals with mild to moderate CHI tend to show reduced adaptive capacity, difficulties attending to thoughts and feelings, a simplistic processing style, and states of emotional shutdown. These features may interfere with problem-solving, emotion regulation, and social functioning, contributing to a vulnerability to emotional flooding and a tendency to withdraw from social interaction.

Despite these cognitive and emotional challenges, CHI patients in this sample did not show signs of more severe psychopathology. Their perceptual accuracy, capacity to think logically and coherently, and reality testing were intact. However, such an absence of psychotic or psychotic-like phenomena in their Rorschach performance may not generalize to more severe forms of TBI, and, as prior research has demonstrated, more severe injuries may produce more frequent signs of misperception and disordered thinking (Aita et al., 1947; Cattelani et al., 1998; Ellis & Zahn, 1985).

Finally, the elevated frequency of reflection responses in the Exner et al. sample is noteworthy, given their association with intelligence and cognitive functioning (Meyer, 2016). This may reflect either an underestimation of base rates in earlier US normative data (Meyer et al., 2007) or premorbid personality traits (e.g., narcissism, sensation-seeking, risk-taking) common in TBI populations. These explanations, while speculative, merit further research. In all cases, the findings underscore once again the need to interpret Rorschach results within a multimethod framework, especially in the absence of preinjury baseline data.

Unilateral Brain Lesions and Hemispheric Asymmetry

Numerous studies using the Rorschach have explored questions related to hemispheric specialization and functional asymmetry. Belyi (1983), for example, conducted a Rorschach study with 140 right-handed patients aged 20–60 who had unilateral benign hemispheric tumors (gliomas and meningiomas). Left-hemisphere tumors were linked to more form-based responses, fewer *M* responses, more perseverations and "I don't know" responses, and a higher frequency of animal content. Moreover, the use of color as a determinant was limited and mostly form-dominated (*FC*), suggesting that left-hemisphere dysfunction leads to simpler, more constricted protocols. In contrast, right-hemisphere tumors were associated with lower perceptual accuracy, fewer popular responses, more *W* responses, and more color responses, which tended to be color-dominated (*CF, C*). While this might seem counterintuitive given the right hemisphere's role in emotional arousal, and as further discussed in Chapter 5, it is the left hemisphere that appeared to play a central role in the verbal–semantic processing and integration of emotion with problem-solving and decision-making activities.

Belyi also found that left frontal tumors were associated with slower response times and fewer responses, while right posterior lesions led to more *Dd* and *S* responses, including integrations of *S* areas. He concluded that the right hemisphere appears to play a key role in visual gestalt formation, whereas the left governs semantic processing. In later work, Belyi (1988) described right hemisphere form perception as hierarchically organized, with visual engrams stored diffusely like a hologram—allowing partial recognition if damaged but with loss of detail.

Several studies using lateralized tachistoscopic presentations have supported Belyi's findings and advanced our understanding of how functional asymmetry affects Rorschach performance.[14] For example, Minor et al. (1989) briefly presented Rorschach cards to either visual field in twenty-eight male undergraduates. In each trial, participants heard two interpretive words—one based on form (e.g., *People*) and one based on color (e.g., *Blood*), or one based on movement (e.g., *Lifting*). They were asked to choose which word better matched the image. Participants made more form-based choices when stimuli were presented to the right hemisphere (left visual field) and more color-based choices when presented to the left hemisphere (right visual field). No hemispheric differences emerged for movement, likely due to its greater neurocognitive complexity. These findings align with dual-code theory (Paivio, 1978), which proposes that the left hemisphere is more engaged in verbal–semantic processing (e.g., color-naming), while the right hemisphere is more engaged in imaginal and spatial processing (e.g., visual form recognition).

Rorschach research directly testing the hypothesis that right-hemispheric perception is global-gestalt in nature and left-hemispheric perception is analytical-sequential in nature has yielded inconclusive results and remains an area in need of further investigation. For example, in a study by Gainotti et al. (1984), the Rorschach was administered to thirty-one patients with unilateral hemispheric lesions. The researchers predicted that patients with right-hemisphere lesions would show fewer global responses (*W*) and more detail responses (*D* and *Dd*), while the opposite pattern was expected for those with left-hemisphere lesions. Contrary to these predictions, no relationship was found between lesion location and response location on the Rorschach.

Berry et al. (2024) investigated how visual attention and hemispheric activation influence neurocognitive performance, including responses on the Rorschach (R-PAS). In one experiment, participants wore glasses that simulated simultanagnosia by narrowing their visual field. This led to more uncommon detail responses (*Dd*), fewer symmetrical (*Pair*) responses, and reduced use of complex visual features—reflected in lower scores for Location, Space integration, and Object Quality complexity (*LSO*).[15] These findings suggest a fragmented, left-hemisphere-biased attentional style. In a second experiment using lateralizing glasses to stimulate each hemisphere, no significant R-PAS changes were found. The study underscores the right hemisphere's role in global integration and symmetry and illustrates how attentional style can influence Rorschach performance—insights relevant to both brain-behavior research and clinical assessment.

Brugger and Regard (1995) explored hemispheric differences by briefly presenting Rorschach inkblots to either the left or right visual field of twenty-four right-handed participants, who were instructed to give a single immediate verbal association. Many gave multiple responses spontaneously. Significantly more varied associations occurred when stimuli were shown to the right hemisphere (left visual field), suggesting a slight right-hemisphere advantage in perceiving meaningful forms in ambiguous stimuli—consistent with earlier findings using random dot patterns (Brugger et al., 1993). The authors also noted that this right-hemisphere bias extends beyond visual stimuli: in word-recognition tasks, the left hemisphere tends to produce closely related responses (e.g., *apple–fruit*), while the right hemisphere makes broader, more associative links (e.g., *apple–Eve* or *diet*; Rodel et al., 1992). This supports the view that the right hemisphere is specialized for looser, more creative associations. Brugger and Regard suggest that such semantic hyperactivation may underlie phenomena like thought disorder in schizophrenia and propose that productive psychotic symptoms may reflect a pathological release of right-hemisphere processing.

Regard and Landis (1997) used lateralized tachistoscopic presentations of inkblots to examine hemispheric differences in perception. Despite the verbal task, participants' responses varied by hemisphere: right-hemisphere stimulation elicited more integrative, imaginative, and affect-laden responses, while left-hemisphere stimulation produced more literal, structured, and emotionally neutral interpretations. Qualitative analyses reinforced these findings, portraying the right hemisphere as intuitive, emotionally responsive, and creative—yet potentially vulnerable to disturbance due to heightened emotional responsiveness—and the left hemisphere as better at grasping essentials but limited in combinatory ability and affective nuance, appearing "tedious, somewhat dry, unstimulating although fairly well adjusted" (Regard and Landis, 1997, p. 115).

These findings align with research showing that developmental trauma disrupts right-hemisphere functions and contributes to various forms of psychopathology. Such trauma impairs emotional learning and the maturation of right-hemisphere-based emotional intelligence, especially when meaningful early emotional connections and complex affective experiences are absent (Schore, 2023). As Finn (2012) notes, performance-based tests like the Rorschach access right-hemisphere and subcortical processes that clients often cannot articulate, offering emotionally meaningful experiences that are often essential for promoting therapeutic change.

As an extension of their research paradigm, Regard and Landis studied split-brain patients with surgically disconnected hemispheres. These individuals showed even more marked hemispheric differences: when inkblots were presented to the right hemisphere and responses were given with the left hand, interpretations were affectively rich and visually imaginative but could not be verbalized due to disrupted interhemispheric communication. In contrast, left-hemisphere responses were more conventional and structured. These findings suggest that standard Rorschach responses may largely reflect left-hemisphere processing, potentially underrepresenting the emotional and imaginal contributions of the right hemisphere.

To further explore affective lateralization, Regard and Landis used a nonverbal forced-choice task with inkblots and emotionally evocative images, asking participants to judge which they liked or disliked more when presented to one hemisphere. Results showed the left hemisphere was more involved in positive judgments ("like") and the right in negative judgments ("dislike"), especially among men. This pattern appeared in both healthy individuals and those with focal or commissurotomy lesions, supporting hemispheric asymmetry in emotional evaluation.

Research has demonstrated that the right hemisphere is more involved in the emotional, associative, and imaginative interpretation of ambiguous stimuli like inkblots, while the left is more analytical, structured, and emotionally neutral. Regard and Landis argue that using the Rorschach in lateralization research offers an ecologically valid way to study how emotional and perceptual processes are distributed across hemispheres. This approach not only enhances our understanding of hemispheric asymmetry but also generates clinically useful hypotheses—for instance, about how lateralized brain damage may affect cognition, perception, and behavior, and how such functions may change over time in individual clients.

Attention-Deficit/Hyperactivity Disorder

The DSM-5-TR (American Psychiatric Association [APA], 2022) outlines three attention-deficit/hyperactivity disorder (ADHD) presentations, which may shift over time: Predominantly Inattentive, Predominantly Hyperactive-Impulsive, and Combined. ADHD often cooccurs with other mental health conditions, with 60–100 percent of affected children exhibiting comorbidities such as anxiety, depression, or conduct disorders—many of which persist into adulthood (Gnanavel et al., 2019). Given this high comorbidity rate, comprehensive ADHD assessment requires a multimethod approach that examines both neurocognitive and personality functioning. In this context, the Rorschach adds valuable performance-based insights into perception, thinking, self-image, interpersonal style, and emotional functioning.

Although no two individuals with ADHD present with identical Rorschach profiles, research and clinical experience suggest that consistent patterns of responding do emerge. Recognizing these trends can benefit clinicians by highlighting atypical features that may indicate comorbidities or alternative diagnoses and by deepening our understanding of the psychological and neurocognitive features commonly associated with ADHD.

Cotugno (1995) compared the Rorschach (CS) performance of forty children with ADHD to a clinical and a nonclinical control group. All children in the ADHD and clinical groups (ages five and six) were referred for evaluation; the clinical group included children who did not meet full ADHD criteria, while the nonclinical group had no history of special education or mental-health referrals. Groups were matched by age and gender (mostly boys). Compared to controls, children with ADHD showed lower *WSumC, Afr, Ego Index, COP, Pure H, P, X+%,* and *WSum6*; and higher *Lambda, X–%, Xu%, CDI*, and *DEPI.*[16] These results indicate reduced integration of emotion in problem-solving, a tendency to avoid emotionally arousing situations, lower self-esteem, and diminished expectations of cooperative interactions. Children with ADHD also showed reduced self-awareness, difficulty recognizing obvious cues, perceptual idiosyncrasy and inaccuracy, and a simplistic, avoidant, and concrete cognitive style. Findings further suggest difficulties adapting to daily demands, interpersonal struggles, and elevated levels of affective disturbance compared to controls.

These findings were largely confirmed by Strickland (2006), who studied boys with ADHD referred for special-education evaluation. Results showed avoidance of complexity (high *Lambda*), limited social coping skills (high *CDI*), low self-esteem (low Ego Index), avoidance of emotionally arousing situations (low *Afr*), and difficulties with interpersonal perception and social interactions (fewer *COP, AG, H, T*). Boys also showed poor reality testing (high *PTI*, low *P*), affective difficulties (high *DEPI*), and an inefficient, neglectful problem-solving style (57 percent had *Zd* < –3.0). Additional support for broad difficulties in affective and social adaptation in ADHD comes from Fouques and Mouren-Simeoni (1998), who studied twenty-five boys aged 6 to 12 with ADHD—fifteen unmedicated and ten on Ritalin. ADHD children showed cognitive, affective, and interpersonal difficulties compared to controls. While Ritalin improved cognitive adaptation and reduced aggressivity, the authors note that it sometimes negatively affected emotional and social functioning.

Locke (1999) recruited twenty-six adult volunteers through public advertisements for a study on adult ADHD. Nineteen were diagnosed with ADHD and assessed using the Rorschach (CS). Due to small, uneven group sizes, comparisons were made using *z*-tests against US reference data. Adults with ADHD showed significantly higher *X–%* and *Lambda* and significantly lower *X+%, EA, M, CF, FC, es, Afr, DQv/+*, and *H.* Most were ambitent, reflecting low production of human movement and color responses. No significant differences were found for *A, Zd, Adj D, F+%, Ego Index, DQv*, or *WSum6*. As in studies with children, adults with ADHD misperceived stimuli, approached complex or emotionally arousing situations in avoidant or overly concrete ways, overlooked obvious cues, and had reduced internal resources for emotion regulation and stress tolerance. They also showed a reduced capacity to view themselves and others holistically as complex and integrated. Importantly, disordered thinking (*WSum6*) was not elevated, consistent with findings from Cotugno (1995) and Ando et al. (2019), suggesting that, despite the high comorbidity of ADHD with other mental disorders, disordered thinking is not a typical feature of ADHD.

In a study on social perception, Kutz (2006) compared nineteen children with ADHD of the inattentive type (ADHD/PI), seventeen with the combined type (ADHD/C), and seventeen healthy controls, all aged 8–14 with at least average intelligence (FSIQs 109–113). Groups did not differ significantly in age, intelligence, or the sum of responses on the Rorschach (*R* ≈ 18–19). No significant group differences were found on four key variables: *F%* (simplicity or avoidance of complexity), *X–%* (perceptual inaccuracy), *Pure H* (integrated view of self/other), or *CDI* (coping vulnerabilities and interpersonal difficulties). All groups showed similarly high *F%* values (46–48 percent). However, Kutz observed clinically relevant differences. In controls, most *Pure F* responses appeared early in the protocol, suggesting situational avoidance. In contrast, ADHD groups showed *Pure F* responses more evenly throughout, indicating a more pervasive avoidant style and insensitivity to subtle cues and nuances. Perceptual inaccuracy *(X–%)* also differed meaningfully: while controls performed within adaptive norms (M = 0.19), both ADHD groups showed elevated mean values (ADHD/PI = 0.27; ADHD/C = 0.24), supporting the idea that perceptual inaccuracy underlies social and functional difficulties in ADHD. Finally, children in the ADHD/PI group had longer response latencies, while those with ADHD/C responded more quickly and impulsively. This suggests different mechanisms for perceptual inaccuracy: impulsivity in ADHD/C, and a more fundamental tendency to misperceive stimuli in ADHD/PI.

ADHD/PI may involve greater perceptual inaccuracy when associated with nonverbal learning disability (NVLD). In fact, these two conditions frequently cooccur. NVLD is marked by difficulties in visual-spatial, tactile-perceptual, psychomotor, social, and nonverbal reasoning skills, alongside relative strengths in verbal abilities (Harnadek & Rourke, 1994). Some experts consider NVLD to be a milder variant of autism spectrum disorder (ASD), in which disordered thinking and atypical sensory experiences are more frequently observed (Frechette et al., 2024).

In a study examining social and self-perception, O'Neal (2006) found that children with both ADHD/PI and NVLD demonstrated significantly higher levels of perceptual inaccuracy (*X–%*, M = .41) than those with only ADHD/PI (M = .26) or the nonclinical control group (M = .21; $p < .05$). This group also showed lower self-esteem (lower *Ego Index*) and a greater level of coping vulnerability (higher *CDI*), suggesting that the combination of ADHD/PI and NVLD is associated with greater impairments in perception, self-image, and social functioning than either condition alone.

In Kutz's (2006) study, children with ADHD/PI, ADHD/C, and healthy controls all showed similar values for *Pure H* responses, within the expected range for their age. Despite reports that children with ADHD/PI are often socially withdrawn or aloof (e.g., Maedgen & Carlson, 2000), their Rorschach results suggest a normative awareness of others and interest in social relationships—possibly helping explain their frequent struggles with anxiety or depression. While no statistically significant group differences were found for *CDI* scores, the frequency of elevated *CDI*s was notably elevated in all three groups, including the control group (35.3 percent). Children with ADHD had even higher frequencies (ADHD/PI = 47.4 percent; ADHD/C = 41.2 percent), reinforcing findings that many children with ADHD experience difficulties coping with everyday demands and navigating social relationships. As Spender et al. (2023) report, children with ADHD typically have fewer friendships, poorer friendship quality, and more difficulties in social interaction. Kutz's findings align with earlier Rorschach studies (e.g., Cotugno, 1995; Bartell & Solanto, 1995), which also observed elevated values for *X–%* and a reduced number of *M* responses, suggesting problems with perceptual accuracy and limited internal resources for reflection, impulse control, and understanding self and others.

Like most Rorschach studies on ADHD, Cotugno (1995) and Kutz (2006) focused on predominantly white, middle- to upper-class children. In contrast, Meehan et al. (2008) studied forty-two children aged 7–10 from more ethnically diverse, lower- to middle-income urban backgrounds. Most were enrolled in public schools and referred for behavioral or reading problems. Children with severe psychiatric, neurological, or cognitive impairments were excluded. Among the twenty-eight children with significant ADHD symptoms, scores on two of seven selected Rorschach variables—*M* and *EA*—were significantly lower than those of the fourteen children without ADHD symptoms ($p < .05$), suggesting reduced internal resources for emotional self-regulation, mentalization and stress tolerance. Lower *M* scores in particular reflected difficulties with impulse control, self-reflection, and internal representations of self and others. No significant differences were found for *R, X+%, Lambda, SumH*, or *D*.

Although broadly consistent with prior findings, Meehan et al. did not replicate Cotugno's significant group differences on *Lambda* and *X+%*. This may be due to greater similarities between groups in Meehan et al.'s sample, where both had psychological difficulties and were matched for cognitive functioning. In contrast, Cotugno included a nonclinical control group, likely amplifying effect sizes (Mihura et al., 2013). For instance, children with reading or behavioral issues may also exhibit an elevated *Lambda*, making group differences less pronounced.

As summarized by Ando et al. (2019), "it appears that hyperactivity and impulsivity are associated with unconventional and sometimes mistaken processing of information especially relevant to people and relationships" (p. 1196). Using archival R-PAS data from fifty-four children and adolescents (ages 7–17) with a primary ADHD diagnosis, Ando et al. compared their average standard scores to international child reference data (Meyer et al., 2011). Statistically significant deviations ($p < .001$) were found using multistage significance testing. Most deviations appeared in the Perception and Thinking Problems domain: elevated *EII-3, TP-Comp, FQ–%, WD–%, FQu%*, and reduced *FQo%* and *P*. Additional but less pronounced deviations appeared in the Engagement and Cognitive Processing domain (*MC, M* both low); the Self and Other Representation domain (elevated *PHR/GPHR*, low *H*); and the Stress and Distress domain (elevated *SC-Comp*). Contrary to some earlier suggestions that ADHD is linked to a visuospatial bias (more *D*, fewer *W* responses; Cohen & Kalanthroff, 2019), Ando et al. did not find such a pattern.

Given the high comorbidity of ADHD with other mental-health problems, it is unsurprising that Rorschach findings often reflect issues across multiple areas of personality functioning. However, individuals with ADHD, both children and adults, show wide variation in personality structure and dynamics, resulting in diverse Rorschach profiles. A multimethod assessment that includes both self-report and performance-based measures can offer valuable insights for tailoring interventions. Furthermore, because ADHD is frequently accompanied by emotional and interpersonal difficulties—and arises in specific referral contexts—integrating a psychodynamic perspective can help move beyond purely neuropsychological considerations, enriching the diagnostic process and guiding more targeted and sophisticated treatment planning (Leak, 2021).

Autism Spectrum Disorders

The DSM-5-TR (APA, 2022) incorporates Asperger's Disorder (AD) into the broader category of ASD while acknowledging the distinct profile of individuals with average or above-average intelligence and preserved language skills. As with ADHD, ASD frequently cooccurs with other neurodevelopmental or psychiatric conditions—such as ADHD, learning disabilities, anxiety, and mood disorders—complicating diagnosis and treatment (Lai et al., 2019). Moreover, ASD shares clinical and neuropsychological features with nonverbal learning disorder (NVLD), including deficits in nonverbal reasoning, emotion regulation, social cognition, and social skills—often associated with right-hemisphere dysfunction (Yalof, 2006). Given the heterogeneity of ASD, a multimethod assessment that integrates cognitive and personality measures can clarify individual strengths and weaknesses. As with other neuropsychological and neurodevelopmental disorders, performance-based tests like the Rorschach can offer valuable insights into perceptual and cognitive functioning, self and other representation, and emotional processing.

Holaday et al. (2001) compared the Rorschach (CS) protocols of twenty-four boys with AD (DSM-IV criteria; APA, 1994) to twenty-four age-matched boys with other emotional or behavioral disorders and to US reference data. Participants were aged seven to eighteen (M ≈ 12–13). As hypothesized, the AD group differed significantly from clinical controls on five variables ($p < .001$), showing lower *COP*, *H*, *M*, and *EA*, and a higher *CDI*. Compared to reference data, both clinical groups also had significantly lower *T* and *WSumC*, and higher *PSV*, reflecting cognitive rigidity. These findings were interpreted as reflecting core AD features such as poor social reciprocity, social ineptness, a failure to develop a theory of mind, and limited adaptive resources. The authors proposed tentative Rorschach indicators for identifying AD: *COP* = 0, *CDI* > 3, *H* < 2, *M* < 2, *EA* < 4, half the value expected for *WSumC* based on age, and *T* = 0. While *WSumC* and *T* signaled difficulties mentalizing emotions and establishing closeness, they were not specific to AD. Holaday et al. (2001) conclude that, although the Rorschach cannot diagnose AD, translating diagnostic criteria into Rorschach variables can support the diagnostic process.

De Araújo et al. (2011) used the Rorschach (CS) to examine cognitive and affective characteristics in twenty-one boys aged 6 to 16 diagnosed with autism (DSM-IV-TR; APA, 2000) and with average intelligence. Findings suggested that these boys did not exhibit the kind of disordered perception and thinking commonly associated with psychotic disorders. None of the participants scored above 3/5 on the *PTI*, which had a mean value of 1.71. The authors noted that this supports the view that autism should not be classified as a psychotic disorder. However, 38 percent of participants had a *PTI* of 3/5—significantly more than is typically found in nonclinical populations—indicating the presence of moderate disturbances in perception and/or thinking. *PTI* scores did not correlate with Verbal, Performance, or Full-Scale IQ, suggesting that these disturbances were unrelated to general cognitive ability. The authors concluded that while some children with autism may show moderate impairments in perception and/or thinking, they typically do not exhibit the full range of psychotic phenomena seen in psychotic conditions like schizophrenia.

Consistent with the findings of Holaday et al., 85.7 percent of De Araújo et al.'s sample had a positive *CDI*, reflecting marked difficulties in managing social interactions and environmental demands. Although profiles varied, some common patterns were noted. Many participants exhibited a low *WSumC*, low levels of engagement with emotionally arousing stimuli (*Afr*), and human content responses frequently involved fantasy or mythological figures rather than nonfictional representations, suggesting distortions in self-perception and social cognition. The authors emphasized the value of the Rorschach for assessing relational and affective functioning in autism and for highlighting individual differences within this population.

As described by Keller et al. (2018), patients with high-functioning ASD (DSM-5; APA, 2013) are often not recognized in childhood, with diagnosis commonly occurring in adolescence or adulthood—frequently in general psychiatric settings due to comorbid symptoms like anxiety, depression, or somatic complaints. In a pilot study, Keller et al. used the

Rorschach to assess forty adults with Level 1 ASD.[17] Participants were either self-referred to an adult autism center or brought by family for psychological evaluation. The Rorschach was administered using the method of the French School, which emphasizes psychoanalytic, qualitative interpretation focused on self-representation, identity, and inner conflict (Verdon & Azoulay, 2019). While not an evidence-based system, the authors reported some clinically relevant findings. For example, they noted that patients generally approached the test with interest and cooperation, and nearly half gave over twenty responses—suggesting strong engagement with the task. Despite social challenges, about two-thirds gave a typical number of human content responses, indicating an interest in others. Just over half were classified as extratensive, suggesting relatively few *M* responses compared to color responses. The authors conclude that the Rorschach offers useful insights for better understanding individuals with ASD, especially as it avoids difficulties often encountered in this population with self-report measures, such as the literal interpretation of questions, poor attentional focus, or discomfort with self-report formats.

Yalof (2006) presented the case of "Allen," a latency-age boy referred for assessment of a possible NVLD and concerns about social-emotional functioning. Previous diagnoses had included ADHD (mixed subtype) and anxiety; OCD had also been considered and ruled out. Drawing on prior assessments, clinical observations, rating scales, and a posttest consultation with a fellow neuropsychologist, Yalof concluded that Allen met criteria for NVLD with features of AD. On the Rorschach, Allen did not meet the a priori variables identified by Holaday et al. (2001) as reflective of AD, except for $T = 0$, which Yalof noted has limited diagnostic value. Allen's protocol showed signs of disordered thinking (*WSum6* = 56; *FAB2* = 4; *INC2* = 1) without perceptual inaccuracy (*X–%* = .15), resulting in a *PTI* of 3/5. In accordance with the findings of Araújo et al. (2011) and Yalof's diagnostic formulation, Allen did not present the full range of impairment in perception and thinking typically seen in psychotic disorders such as schizophrenia. Additionally, although significant overlap between the clinical presentation of ASD and schizophrenia is frequently observed, Allen's clinical presentation did not appear to suggest the latter. In fact, Allen's Rorschach profile serves as a good example of a profile one might consider to be closer to ASD than to schizophrenia.

In a study of eleven high-functioning autistic adolescents and adults (DSM-III-R; APA, 1987; ages 16–38, M IQ = 83, SD = 17.63), Dykens et al. (1991) compared results from the Thought, Language and Communication (TLC) Disorder Scale (Andreasen, 1979) and the Rorschach (CS) to reference groups with schizophrenia.[18] On the TLC, autistic participants showed significantly more poverty of speech but less illogicality. On the Rorschach, however, they exhibited features of disordered thinking also seen in schizophrenia, including a high *X–%* (M = .47, SD = .14) and an elevated *WSum6* (M = 42.64, SD = 63.69), indicating a trend toward perceptual inaccuracy and thought disturbance despite significant individual variability.

Kishimoto et al. (2016) compared the Rorschach (CS) performance of twenty young adults with ASD to twenty with schizophrenia (DSM-IV-TR; APA, 2000), matched for age, sex, general assessment of functioning, and FSIQ (ASD group: M = 91.90, SD = 13.81; IQ ≥ 70). Compared to the ASD group, the schizophrenia group showed higher *D, Adj D, DQo*, and *FQ–* values, and lower *DQ+* and active movement responses (all $p < .05$), suggesting less integrative processing and more perceptual distortions. No significant group differences were found for *R* or *WSum6*, which was exceptionally low in both groups. Both groups also had high values for *Lambda*, indicating avoidant and overly simplistic processing. Overall, schizophrenia patients showed more perceptual inaccuracy and less sophisticated processing than those with ASD but lower levels of stress and distress.

Interestingly, Rorschach findings on perceptual inaccuracy and disordered thinking diverged between the studies by Dykens et al. (1991) and Kishimoto et al. (2016). While Dykens et al. found autistic individuals to show more signs of perceptual inaccuracy and disordered thinking than those typically reported for schizophrenia, Kishimoto et al. reported the opposite pattern. Several factors may account for this inconsistency. First, Dykens et al. had a small sample size (N = 11), increasing the likelihood of sampling bias. Second, they used DSM-III-R criteria, which tend to identify more severe forms of autism, emphasizing deficits in social interaction, communication, and behavior. In contrast, Kishimoto et al. used more inclusive DSM-IV-TR criteria, likely capturing higher-functioning individuals. This difference is reflected in the higher mean FSIQ in the Kishimoto study (92 vs. 83), which may help explain the lower frequency of psychotic-like features on the Rorschach in their ASD sample.

In line with findings for ASD in the Kishimoto et al. study, Yalof's (2006) patient, Allen, was experiencing significant stress and distress at the time of assessment (*D* = –1, *Adj D* = 0). His information-processing was exceptionally integrative and sophisticated (*DQ+* = 17), and although some of this activity led to bizarre combinatory thinking (*FAB2, INC2*), he did not tend to misperceive visual stimuli (*X–%* = .15).

Although cognitive-behavioral therapy is commonly recommended for children and adults with AD, Ramires et al. (2015) presented a case study of "Peter," an eight-year-old boy with AD who underwent psychodynamic psychotherapy, with the Rorschach used as the outcome measure. His initial protocol showed several findings often seen in boys with AD (e.g., Holaday et al., 2001), including *CDI* > 3, *H* < 2, *Lambda* >.99, and *WSumC* < 2.5—suggesting social immaturity, a concrete and avoidant processing style, and difficulties integrating emotions into thought and behavior. As therapy progressed toward a mentalizing and affect-focused approach, Peter became more expressive and socially engaged, and his Rorschach scores reflected these changes. Most notably, his *CDI* decreased from 5/5 to 3/5 after 12 months and remained stable at the 24-month follow-up. This case illustrates how psychodynamic therapy can foster emotional growth and relational connectedness in children with AD—and how the Rorschach remains a powerful tool for tracking therapeutic change in personality functioning (Exner & Andronikof-Sanglade, 1992), with promising applications even in the context of neuropsychological and neurodevelopmental disorders.

Notes

1 DBS-STN involves surgically implanting electrodes into the STN to deliver electrical impulses that help regulate abnormal motor circuitry in Parkinson's disease, reducing symptoms such as tremor, rigidity, and bradykinesia.
2 According to NINCDS-ADRDA criteria, a diagnosis of definite DAT can only be established on autopsy.
3 The MMSE is a brief cognitive screening tool assessing orientation, memory, attention, language, and visuospatial skills, commonly used to detect and monitor cognitive impairment in geriatric settings. Scores range from 0 to 30 with MMSE < 26 typically signaling the presence of significant cognitive deficits.
4 The cardinal neuropsychological signs of DAT include amnesia, apraxia, agnosia, and aphasia, as well as impaired abstract thinking and executive functions.
5 For a more detailed description of the different kinds of linguistic and executive perseveration errors considered in this study see Perry et al. (1996, Appendix A).
6 As part of another research project on the biology of aging, DAT patients received more thorough differential diagnostics than is typical in routine clinical practice.
7 The CDR rates the level of a patient's functioning in six categories: Memory, Orientation, Judgment/Problem-Solving, Home and Hobbies, Community Affairs, and Personal Care.
8 Lewy bodies are clumps of misfolded proteins in neurons that disrupt neural networks, especially in dopamine and acetylcholine systems, primarily affecting the cortex and brainstem.
9 The purpose of the ROC curve is to determine the optimal balance between sensitivity and specificity.
10 An autosomal recessive disorder is a genetic condition that occurs only when a person inherits two copies of a faulty gene, one from each parent.
11 CHI is a type of TBI in which the brain is damaged without penetration of the skull.
12 For a detailed description of Piotrowski's ten organic signs see Chapter 2.
13 Although substantial differences were found for these variables when comparing patients to the US reference sample for adults, some of these findings represent marginal differences or even an absence of differences when compared with international reference data (Meyer et al., 2007). Most notably, 25 percent of adults in the international sample presented reflection responses, and 29 percent of adults in the international sample had an underincorporative processing style ($Zd < -3.0$), compared to only 5 percent in the US sample used in the Exner et al. (1996) study.

14 Tachistoscopy is a technique used in research and experimental psychology which consists in presenting a visual stimulus for a very brief and controlled duration, typically only for a few milliseconds. This brief exposure ensures that the participant's response is based on an immediate perception, minimizing the influence of conscious analysis or reflection.
15 *LSO* variables in the R-PAS reflect how actively a person engages with the inkblot and how well they organize and integrate visual information.
16 Note that there was great variability in the values for *WSum6* in this group, with M = 7.78 and SD = 8.61.
17 The DSM-5 defines three levels of severity for ASD: requiring support (Level 1), requiring substantial support (Level 2), and requiring very substantial support (Level 3).
18 The TLC is designed to assess formal thought disorders, such as incoherence or tangentiality, commonly observed in psychiatric populations, particularly in schizophrenia.

References

Aita, J. A., Reitan, R. M., & Ruth, J. M. (1947). Rorschach's test as a diagnostic aid in brain injury. *American Journal of Psychiatry*, 103, 770–779. doi:10.1176/ajp.103.6.770.

Allen, R. M. (1975). There is no alternative to the IQ. *Journal of Personality Assessment*, 39(4), 377–380. doi:10.1207/s15327752jpa3904_8.

American Psychiatric Association. (1987). *Diagnostic and statistical manual of mental disorders* (3rd ed., rev.). American Psychiatric Association.

American Psychiatric Association. (1994). *Diagnostic and statistical manual of mental disorders* (4th ed.). American Psychiatric Association.

American Psychiatric Association. (2000). *Diagnostic and statistical manual of mental disorders* (4th ed., text rev.). American Psychiatric Publishing.

American Psychiatric Association. (2013). *Diagnostic and statistical manual of mental disorders* (5th ed.). American Psychiatric Publishing.

American Psychiatric Association. (2022). *Diagnostic and statistical manual of mental disorders* (5th ed., text rev.). American Psychiatric Association. doi:10.1176/appi.books.9780890425787.

Ando, A., Pignolo, C., Viglione, D. J., Zennaro, A., Cristofanelli, S., & Ferro, L. (2019). Assessing the personality profile with ADHD characteristics using the Rorschach Performance Assessment System (R-PAS). *Journal of Child and Family Studies*, 28(5), 1196–1206. doi:10.1007/s10826-019-01359-y.

Andreasen, N. C. (1979). Thought, language, and communication disorders: II. Diagnostic significance. *Archives of General Psychiatry*, 36(12), 1325–1330. doi:10.1001/archpsyc.1979.01780120055007.

Banich, M. T., & Compton, R. J. (2018). *Cognitive neuroscience* (4th ed.). Cambridge University Press.

Barr, W. B., Bilder, R. M., Goldberg, E., Kaplan, E., & Mukherjee, S. (1989). The neuropsychology of schizophrenic speech. *Journal of Communication Disorders*, 22(5), 327–349. doi:10.1016/0021-9924(89)90009-9.

Bartell, S. S., & Solanto, M. V. (1995). Usefulness of the Rorschach inkblot test in assessment of attention deficit hyperactivity disorder. *Perceptual and Motor Skills*, 80(2), 531–541. doi:10.2466/pms.1995.80.2.531.

Beck, S. J., Beck, A. G., Levitt, E. E., & Molish, H. B. (1961). *Rorschach's test: Basic processes* (3rd ed. rev.). Grune and Stratton.

Belyi, B. I. (1983). Reflection of functional hemispheric asymmetry in some phenomena of visual perception. *Human Physiology*, 8(6), 410–417.

Belyi, B. I. (1988). The role of the right hemisphere in form perception and visual gnosis organization. *International Journal of Neuroscience*, 40(3–4), 167–180.

Benton, A. L. (1956). Current status of the Rorschach test: Symposium, 1955: 2. The Rorschach test and the diagnosis of cerebral pathology in children. *American Journal of Orthopsychiatry*, 26(4), 783–791. doi:10.1111/j.1939-0025.1956.tb06222.x.

Berry, B. A., Meyer, G. J., O'Gorman, E. T., Roy, M., Sholander, L. E., & Mihura, J. L. (2024). Simulating local biases in visual attention in neurocognitive performance. *Perceptual and Motor Skills*, 131(1), 135–160. doi:10.1177/00315125241228128.

Bigler, E. D. (2013). Traumatic brain injury, neuroimaging, and neurodegeneration. *Frontiers in Human Neuroscience*, 7(395), 1–14. doi:10.3389/fnhum.2013.00395.

Brink, M., & Grundlingh, E. M. (1976). Performance of persons with Down's syndrome on two projective techniques. *American Journal of Mental Deficiency*, 81(3), 265–270.

Brugger, P., & Regard, M. (1995). Rorschach inkblots in the peripheral visual fields: Enhanced associative quality to the left of fixation. *Journal of Genetic Psychology: Research and Theory on Human Development*, 156(3), 385–387. doi:10.1080/00221325.1995.9914831.

Brugger, P., Regard, M., Landis, T., Cook, N., Krebs, D., & Niederberger, J. (1993). "Meaningful" patterns in visual noise: Effects of lateral stimulation and the observer's belief in ESP. *Psychopathology*, 26(5–6), 261–265. doi:10.1159/000284831.

Castelli, L., Perozzo, P., Caglio, M., Rizzi, L., Zibetti, M., Lanotte, M., & Lopiano, L. (2008). Does subthalamic stimulation induce personality modifications in Parkinson's disease? A Rorschach test explorative study. *Acta Neurologica Belgica*, 108(1), 5–8.

Cattelani, R., Patruno, M., Catellani, A., Cesana, L., Lombardi, F., & Mazzucchi, A. (1998). Il metodo Rorschach in soggetti traumatizzati cranici [The Rorschach inkblot method in traumatic brain injured subjects]. *Archivio di Psicologia, Neurologia e Psichiatria*, 59(3–4), 314–326.

Cattonaro, E. (1959). Le interpretazioni kinestetiche nel Rorschach di fanciulli deboli mentali [Kinesthetic interpretations in the Rorschach of mentally defective children]. *Archivio di Psicologia, Neurologia e Psichiatria*, 20, 309–323.

Cohen, E., & Kalanthroff, E. (2019). Visuospatial processing bias in ADHD: A potential artifact in the Wechsler Adult Intelligence Scale and the Rorschach Inkblots Test. *Psychological Assessment*, 31(5), 699–706. doi:10.1037/pas0000687.

Colucci, G., Pellicciotta, A., Buono, S., & Di Nuovo, S. F. (1998). The Rorschach Egocentricity Index in subjects with intellectual disability: A study on the incidence of different psychological pathologies. *Journal of Intellectual Disability Research*, 42(5), 354–359. doi:10.1046/j.1365-2788.1998.00137.x.

Cotugno, A. J. (1995). Personality attributes of attention deficit hyperactivity disorder (ADHD) using the Rorschach Inkblot Test. *Journal of Clinical Psychology*, 51(4), 554–562. doi:10.1002/1097-4679(199507)51:4-554:AID-JCLP2270510415-3.0.CO;2-Y.

De Araújo, C. A., do Nascimento, R. S. G. F., & Assumpção Junior, F. B. (2011). Autismo e psicodiagnóstico de Rorschach [Autism and Rorschach psychodiagnosis]. *PSICO*, 42(4), 434–441.

de Mol, J. (1990). Les modifications post-traumatiques de la représentation de soi au Test du Rorschach [Posttraumatic changes in self-representation in the Rorschach test]. *Bulletin de la Société du Rorschach et des Méthodes Projectives de Langue Française*, 34, 77–84.

D'Netto, T. B., & Kishore, R. (1976). The psychometric assessment of head injury. *Indian Journal of Clinical Psychology*, 3(1), 23–28.

Di Nuovo, S. F., Colucci, G., Pellicciotta, A., & Buono, S. (1997). Rorschach cognitive developmental indices of mentally retarded persons: A comparison with scores on Wechsler Intelligence Scale for Children–Revised. *Psychological Reports*, 81(1), 139–145. doi:10.2466/PR0.81.5.139-145.

Dörken, H., & Kral, V. A. (1951). Psychological investigation of senile dementia. *Geriatrics*, 6, 151–163.

Dykens, E., Volkmar, F., & Glick, M. (1991). Thought disorder in high-functioning autistic adults. *Journal of Autism and Developmental Disorders*, 21(3), 291–301. doi:10.1007/BF02207326.

Ellis, D. W., & Zahn, B. S. (1985). Psychological functioning after severe closed head injury. *Journal of Personality Assessment*, 49(2), 125–128. doi:10.1207/s15327752jpa4902_3.

Exner, J. E. (1988). Problems with brief Rorschach protocols. *Journal of Personality Assessment*, 52, 640–647.

Exner, J. E. (2001). *A Rorschach workbook for the Comprehensive System* (5th ed.). Rorschach Workshops.

Exner, J. E. (2003). *The Rorschach: A comprehensive system: Volume 1: Basic foundations and principles of interpretation* (4th ed.). Wiley.

Exner, J. E., & Andronikof-Sanglade, A. (1992). Rorschach changes following brief and short-term therapy. *Journal of Personality Assessment*, 59(1), 59–71. doi:10.1207/s15327752jpa5901_6.

Exner, J. E., Fontan, P., & Andronikof, A. (2022). *The Rorschach: A comprehensive system—revised. Interpretation and technical manual.* Rorschach Workshops.

Exner, J. E., Jr., Colligan, S. C., Boll, T. J., Stischer, B., & Hillman, L. (1996). Rorschach findings concerning closed head injury patients. *Assessment*, 3(3), 317–326. doi:10.1177/107319119600300311.

Finn, S. E. (2003). Therapeutic assessment of a man with "ADD." *Journal of Personality Assessment*, 80(2), 115–129. doi:10.1207/S15327752JPA8002_01.

Finn, S. E. (2012). Implications of recent research in neurobiology for psychological assessment. *Journal of Personality Assessment*, 94(5), 440–449. doi:10.1080/00223891.2012.700665.

Finn, S. E. (2020). *In our clients' shoes: Theory and techniques of therapeutic assessment.* Routledge.

Finn, S. E. (2022). The development of therapeutic assessment: From shame and isolation to connection and love. In C. J. Hopwood (Ed.), *The evolution of personality assessment in the 21st century: Understanding the people who understand people* (pp. 12–39). Routledge. doi:10.4324/9781003036302-2.

Folstein, M. F., Folstein, S. E., McHugh, P. R. (1975). Mini-mental state exam. *Journal of Psychiatric Research*, 12, 189–198.

Fouques, D., & Mouren-Simeoni, M.-C. (1998). Contribution du Rorschach (Système Intégré) à la compréhension de l'hyperactivité avec déficit de l'attention et à la mesure des effets psychologiques du traitement par psychostimulants (Ritaline®) chez des garçons de 6 à 12 ans. (Étude de 25 protocoles) [Contribution of the Rorschach (integrated system) to the understanding of hyperactivity with attention deficit and to the measurement of the psychological effects of psychostimulant (Ritalin®) treatment in 6–12 yr old boys: A study of 25 protocols]. *Pratiques Psychologiques*, 2, 67–74.

Frechette, J. D., Murphy, L., Castro, R., & Boyle, K. (2024). Differential diagnosis: Understanding nonverbal learning disorder and autism spectrum disorder. *Applied Neuropsychology: Child*. Advance online publication. doi:10.1080/21622965.2024.2425363.

Gainotti, G., de Rosa, E., & Fischetti, C. (1984). Spécialisation hémisphérique et traitement analytique et gestaltique des informations. Une recherche avec le test de Rorschach [Hemispheric specialization and analytical and Gestalt treatment of information: Research with the Rorschach test]. *Revue de Psychologie Appliquée*, 34(1), 89–98.

Gnanavel, S., Sharma, P., Kaushal, P., & Hussain, S. (2019). Attention deficit hyperactivity disorder and comorbidity: A review of literature. *World Journal of Clinical Cases*, 7(17), 2420–2426. doi:10.12998/wjcc.v7.i17.2420.

Harnadek, M. C. S., & Rourke, B. P. (1994). Principal identifying features of the syndrome of nonverbal learning disabilities in children. *Journal of Learning Disabilities*, 27(3), 144–154. doi:10.1177/002221949402700303.

Holaday, M., Moak, J., & Shipley, M. A. (2001). Rorschach protocols from children and adolescents with Asperger's disorder. *Journal of Personality Assessment*, 76(3), 482–495. doi:10.1207/S15327752JPA7603_09.

Horiuchi, H. (1961). A study of perceptual process of Rorschach cards by tachistoscopic method on movement and shading responses. *Journal of Projective Techniques*, 25, 44–53. doi:10.1080/08853126.1961.10381006.

Hughes, C. P., Berg, L., Danziger, W. L., Coben, L. A., & Martin, R. L. (1982). A new clinical scale for the staging of dementia. *The British Journal of Psychiatry*, 140, 566–572. doi:10.1192/bjp.140.6.566.

Ilonen, T., Hakola, P., Vanhanen, M., & Tiihonen, J. (2012). Rorschach assessment of personality functioning in patients with polycystic lipomembranous osteodysplasia with sclerosing leukoencephalopathy. *Acta Neuropsychiatrica*, 24(4), 236–244. doi:10.1111/j.1601-5215.2011.00626.x.

Insua, A. M., & Loza, S. M. (1986). Psychometric patterns on the Rorschach of healthy elderly persons and patients with suspected dementia. *Perceptual and Motor Skills*, 63(2, Pt 2), 931–936. doi:10.2466/pms.1986.63.2.931.

Kaplan, E. (1988). A process approach to neuropsychological assessment. In T. Boll & B. K. Bryant (Eds.), *Clinical neuropsychology and brain function: Research, measurement, and practice* (pp. 127–167). American Psychological Association. doi:10.1037/10063-004.

Kaplan, S., Abbott, J. A., Hincks, E. M., & Waldfogel, S. (1948). Feeblemindedness or pseudoretardation? *American Journal of Medicine*, 5, 891–897. doi:10.1016/0002-9343(48)90168-5.

Keller, R., Bari, S., Fratianni, B., Piedimonte, A., & Freilone, F. (2018). Response to Rorschach test in autism spectrum disorders in adulthood: A pilot study. *Journal of Psychopathology*, 24(4), 224–229.

Kimoto, A., Iseki, E., Ota, K., Murayama, N., Sato, K., Ogura, N., & Arai, H. (2017). Differences in responses to the Rorschach test between patients with dementia with Lewy bodies and Alzheimer's disease: From the perspective of visuoperceptual impairment. *Psychiatry Research*, 257, 456–461. doi:10.1016/j.psychres.2017.08.038.

Kishimoto, N., Yamamuro, K., Iida, J., Ota, T., Tanaka, S., Kyo, M., Kimoto, S., & Kishimoto, T. (2016). Distinctive Rorschach profiles of young adults with schizophrenia and autism spectrum disorder. *Neuropsychiatric Disease and Treatment*, 12, 2403–2410.

Kutz, A. S. (2006). Social perception in children with attention deficit/hyperactivity disorder: A Rorschach study. Doctoral dissertation. The University of Texas at Austin.

Lai, M.-C., Kassee, C., Besney, R., Bonato, S., Hull, L., Mandy, W., Szatmari, P., & Ameis, S. H. (2019). Prevalence of cooccurring mental health diagnoses in the autism population: A systematic review and meta-analysis. *The Lancet Psychiatry*, 6(10), 819–829. doi:10.1016/S2215-0366(19)30289-5.

Leak, S. (2021). Through a psychoanalytic lens: A sharpened view of neuropsychological assessment. In J. A. Yalof & A. D. Bram (Eds.), *Psychoanalytic assessment applications for different settings* (pp. 28–57). Routledge.

Locke, S. R. (1999). Adult attention deficit disorder: Its impact on Rorschach scores (Publication No. 0850). Doctoral dissertation. University of Windsor.

Lovinger, S. L. (1981). Language handicaps can masquerade as mental retardation. *Academic Therapy*, 17(1), 29–33.

Maedgen, J. W., & Carlson, C. L. (2000). Social functioning and emotional regulation in the attention deficit hyperactivity disorder subtypes. *Journal of Clinical Child Psychology*, 29(1), 30–42. doi:10.1207/S15374424jccp2901_4.

McKahnn, G., Drachman, D., & Folstein, M. (1984). Clinical diagnosis of Alzheimer's disease: Report of the NINCDSADRDA Work Group under the auspices of Department of Health and Human Services Task Force on Alzheimer's Disease. *Neurology*, 34, 939–944.

McKeith, I. G. (2017). Clinical diagnostic criteria for dementia with Lewy bodies. In K. Kosaka (Ed.), *Dementia with Lewy bodies: Clinical and biological aspects* (pp. 59–71). Springer Science + Business Media. doi:10.1007/978-4-431-55948-1_5.

McKhann, G., Drachman, D., Folstein, M., Katzman, R., Price, D., & Stadlan, E. M. (1984). Clinical diagnosis of Alzheimer's disease: Report of the NINCDS-ADRDA Work Group* under the auspices of Department of Health and Human Services Task Force on Alzheimer's Disease. *Neurology*, 34(7), 939.

McKhann, G. M., Knopman, D. S., Chertkow, H., Hyman, B. T., Jack, C. R., Jr., Kawas, C. H., Klunk, W. E., Koroshetz, W. J., Manly, J. J., Mayeux, R., Mohs, R. C., Morris, J. C., Rossor, M. N., Scheltens, P., Carrillo, M. C., Thies, B., Weintraub, S., & Phelps, C. H. (2011). The diagnosis of dementia due to Alzheimer's disease: Recommendations from the National Institute on Aging-Alzheimer's Association workgroups on diagnostic guidelines for Alzheimer's disease. *Alzheimer's & Dementia: The Journal of the Alzheimer's Association*, 7 (3), 263–269. doi:10.1016/j.jalz.2011.03.005.

Meehan, K. B., Ueng-McHale, J. Y., Reynoso, J. S., Harris, B. H., Wolfson, V. M., Gomes, H., & Tuber, S. B. (2008). Self-regulation and internal resources in school-aged children with ADHD symptomatology: An investigation using the Rorschach inkblot method. *Bulletin of the Menninger Clinic*, 72(4), 259–282. doi:10.1521/bumc.2008.72.4.259.

Meyer, G. J. (2016). Neuropsychological factors and Rorschach performance in children. *Rorschachiana*, 37(1), 7–27. doi:10.1027/1192-5604/a000074.

Meyer, G. J., Erard, R. E., Erdberg, P., Mihura, J. L., & Viglione, D. J. (2011). *Rorschach Performance Assessment System: Administration, coding, interpretation, and technical manual.* Rorschach Performance Assessment System LLC.

Meyer, G. J., Erdberg, P., & Shaffer, T. W. (2007). Toward international normative reference data for the Comprehensive System. *Journal of Personality Assessment*, 89(Suppl1), S201–S216. doi:10.1080/00223890701629342.

Mihura, J. L., Meyer, G. J., Dumitrascu, N., & Bombel, G. (2013). The validity of individual Rorschach variables: Systematic reviews and meta-analyses of the comprehensive system. *Psychological Bulletin*, 139, 548–605. doi:10.1037/a0029406.

Minor, S. W., White, H., & Owings, E. P. (1989). Hemispheric asymmetries in interpreting forms vs colors in ambiguous patterns. *Brain and Cognition*, 9(1), 123–135. doi:10.1016/0278-2626(89)90048-1.

Muzio, E. (2006). Vers une approche neuropsychologique intégrée de la personnalité à travers le Rorschach en gériatrie et dans la démence de type Alzheimer [Toward an integrated neuropsychological approach to personality through the Rorschach in geriatrics and Dementia of the Alzheimer's Type]. Doctoral dissertation. Université Paris X–Nanterre.

Muzio, E., & Luperto, L. (1999). Démence et fonctionnement de la personnalité à travers le Rorschach chez un groupe de femmes âgées hospitalisées [Dementia and personality functioning through the Rorschach in a group of hospitalized elderly women]. *European Review of Applied Psychology/Revue Européenne de Psychologie Appliquée*, 49(3), 227–236.

Muzio, E., Andronikof, A., David, J. P., & Di Menza, C. (2001). L'intérêt du test du Rorschach (Système Intégré) dans l'évaluation psychométrique en gériatrie: exemple de la démence de type Alzheimer [Contribution of the Rorschach test (Comprehensive System) to psychometric assessment in geriatrics: The example of Dementia of the Alzheimer's Type]. *La Revue de Gériatrie*, 26(2), 121–130.

Ogawa, T. (1981). Personality characteristics of Parkinson's disease. *Perceptual and Motor Skills*, 52(2), 375–378. doi:10.2466/pms.1981.52.2.375.

O'Neal, C. C. (2006). Social and self-perception in children with nonverbal learning disabilities (NVLD). Doctoral dissertation. The University of Texas at Austin.

Ota, K., Murayama, N., Kasanuki, K., Kondo, D., Fujishiro, H., Arai, H., Sato, K., & Iseki, E. (2015). Visuoperceptual assessments for differentiating dementia with Lewy bodies and Alzheimer's disease: Illusory contours and other neuropsychological examinations. *Archives of Clinical Neuropsychology*, 30(3), 256–263. doi:10.1093/arclin/acv016

Paivio, A. (1978). Mental comparisons involving abstract attributes. *Memory & Cognition*, 6(3), 199–208. doi:10.3758/BF03197447.

Parker, R. S. (1996). The spectrum of emotional distress and personality changes after minor head injury incurred in a motor vehicle accident. *Brain Injury*, 10(4), 287–302. doi:10.1080/026990596124467.

Perry, W. (2005, July 25). The use of the Rorschach as a neuropsychological instrument [Workshop]. International Congress of the Rorschach and Projective Methods, Barcelona, Spain.

Perry, W., Potterat, E., Auslander, L., Kaplan, E., & Jeste, D. (1996). A neuropsychological approach to the Rorschach in patients with dementia of the Alzheimer type. *Assessment*, 3(3), 351–363.

Péruchon, M. (1996). Le déclin de la vie psychique à travers le Rorschach [The decline of psychic life as seen through Rorschach]. *Psychologie Clinique et Projective*, 2(2), 279–291.

Péruchon, M. (2020). Maladie d'Alzheimer et autisme infantile: Repères métapsychologiques pour une comparaison [Alzheimer's disease and infantile autism: Metapsychological landmarks for a comparison]. *NPG Neurologie—Psychiatrie—Gériatrie*, 20(117), 152–158. doi:10.1016/j.npg.2019.12.006

Piotrowski, Z. (1937). The Rorschach inkblot method in organic disturbances of the central nervous system. *Journal of Nervous and Mental Disease*, 86(5), 525–537. doi:10.1097/00005053-193711000-00002

Ramires, V. R. R., Carvalho, C., Schmidt, F. M. D., Fiorini, G. P., & Goodman, G. (2015). Interaction structures in the psychodynamic therapy of a boy diagnosed with Asperger's disorder: A single-case study. *Research in Psychotherapy: Psychopathology, Process and Outcome*, 18(2), 129–140.

Rapaport, D., Gill, M. M., & Schafer, R. (1968). *Diagnostic psychological testing* (2 vols.). International Universities Press.

Regard, M., & Landis, T. (1997). Hemispheric differences in the processing of ambiguity: Tachistoscopic studies with inkblots. *Rorschachiana*, 22(1), 114–129. doi:10.1027/1192-5604.22.1.114.

Reitan, R. M., & Wolfson, D. (1985). *The Halstead-Reitan neuropsychological test battery: Theory and clinical interpretation*. Neuropsychology Press.

Rodel, M., Cook, N. D., Regard, M., & Landis, T. (1992). Hemispheric dissociation in judging semantic relations: Complementarity for close and distant associates. *Brain and Language*, 43(3), 448–459. doi:10.1016/0093-934X(92)90111-Q.

Schore, A. N. (2023). Attachment trauma and the developing right brain: Origins of pathological dissociation and some implications for psychotherapy. In M. J. Dorahy, S. N. Gold, & J. A. O'Neil (Eds.), *Dissociation and the dissociative disorders: Past, present, future* (2nd ed., pp. 177–208). Routledge.

Simard, M., van Reekum, R., & Cohen, T. (2000). A review of the cognitive and behavioral symptoms in dementia with Lewy bodies. *Journal of Neuropsychiatry and Clinical Neurosciences*, 12(4), 425–450. doi:10.1176/appi.neuropsych.12.4.425.

Sinacori, D. R. (2000). Depression in a brain-injured sample: An investigation of indicators on the Rorschach and MMPI-2. *Dissertation Abstracts International: Section B: The Sciences and Engineering*, 60(8-B), 4251.

Sloan, W. (1948). Prediction of extramural adjustment of mental defectives by use of the Rorschach test. *Journal of Consulting Psychology*, 12(5), 303–309. doi:10.1037/h0060787.

Spender, K., Chen, Y.-W. R., Wilkes-Gillan, S., Parsons, L., Cantrill, A., Simon, M., Garcia, A., & Cordier, R. (2023). The friendships of children and youth with attention-deficit hyperactivity disorder: A systematic review. *PLoS ONE*, 18(8), e0289539. doi:10.1371/journal.pone.0289539.

Spitzer, M., Braun, U., Hermle, L., & Maier, S. (1993). Associative semantic network dysfunction in thought-disordered schizophrenic patients: Direct evidence from indirect semantic priming. *Biological Psychiatry*, 34(12), 864–877. doi:10.1016/0006-3223(93)90054-H.

Strickland, V. L. (2006). A descriptive study of boys with AD/HD referred for special education evaluation (Publication No. 3207939). Doctoral dissertation. Wright Institute Graduate School of Psychology.

Uchiyama, M., Nishio, Y., Yokoi, K., Hirayama, K., Imamura, T., Shimomura, T., & Mori, E. (2012). Pareidolias: Complex visual illusions in dementia with Lewy bodies. *Brain: A Journal of Neurology*, 135(8), 2458–2469. doi:10.1093/brain/aws126.

Verdon, B., & Azoulay, C. (Eds.). (2019). *Psychoanalysis and projective methods in personality assessment: The French school*. Hogrefe Publishing.

Wechsler, D. (1981). *Wechsler Adult Intelligence Scale—Revised (WAISR) manual*. The Psychological Corporation.

Yalof, J. (2006). Case illustration of a boy with nonverbal learning disorder and Asperger's features: Neuropsychological and personality assessment. *Journal of Personality Assessment*, 87(1), 15–34. doi:10.1207/s15327752jpa8701_02.

Chapter 5

Neuroimaging Studies of Specific Rorschach Variables

John Exner's Comprehensive System (CS; Exner, 2003) defines the Rorschach as a *perceptual-cognitive problem-solving task*, while the Rorschach Performance Assessment System (R-PAS; Meyer et al., 2011) emphasizes its *performance-based* nature and the interpretive value of the *response process.* Both frameworks align with Hermann Rorschach's original conception of the test as an empirical experiment on perception and apperception (Rorschach, 2021), and both have contributed to its growing neuropsychological conceptualization. As noted in Chapter 1, this neuropsychological perspective became especially prominent in the 1990s, with the Rorschach increasingly viewed as engaging widespread neural networks involved in visual attention, object recognition, memory, language, and executive function (Acklin & Wu-Holt, 1996). Functional magnetic resonance imaging (fMRI) was later used to identify the neural correlates of the task. In a study of twenty-six healthy participants, for example, Giromini et al. (2017) found that viewing Rorschach inkblots and thinking about what they might look like activated temporooccipital and frontoparietal regions bilaterally, as well as subcortical structures that are part of the limbic system. These results support traditional views of the test, indicating the involvement of high-level visual processing, top-down and bottom-up attentional processes, and the perception and processing of emotions and emotional memories.

In a recent review of thirteen studies using fMRI, electroencephalography (EEG), and functional near-infrared spectroscopy (fNIRS) with healthy participants, Vecchio et al. (2023) concluded that the Rorschach engages psychological processes typically inaccessible through self-report.[1] Investigating brain activity during the Rorschach task appears promising in two key areas: identifying the neural correlates of perceptual-cognitive processing and detecting neuroimaging markers of psychopathology or personality functioning. For example, preliminary data suggest that oral content responses from the Oral Dependent Language variable included in the R-PAS are linked to motor and premotor activity, while dependency-related responses engage the brain's reward system (Giromini et al., 2019). Vecchio et al. note,

DOI: 10.4324/9781003731894-6

however, that the field faces important limitations given that most studies involve small samples, a narrow range of Rorschach variables, and are largely limited to research laboratories in Japan, Italy, and the USA.

Neuroimaging Rorschach research has thus far focused primarily on three variables: *FQu* and *FQ–* (perceptually unusual or inaccurate responses, also referred to as unique responses), *M* (responses of human movement), and *WSumC* (chromatic color-determinants). Studies have used EEG, MRI, fMRI, and, in some cases, fMRI combined with repetitive transcranial magnetic stimulation (rTMS) to explore their neural underpinnings.[2] Each section of this chapter introduces the psychological relevance of the variable, reviews the related neuroimaging findings, and discusses implications for interpretation.

Unique Perception, Emotional Interference, and Amygdalar Structure and Function

Rorschach variables that assess the accuracy and conventionality of perception are among the test's most well validated and researched components. Moreover, the Rorschach remains the only psychological test that directly measures these aspects. Of particular importance is the percentage of responses reflecting perceptual distortions (*X–%* in the CS; *FQ–%* in the R-PAS)—responses in which individuals fail to adequately integrate the most common and defining features of the stimulus, or *distal properties* (e.g., the legs, seat, and back of a chair; Exner, 2003, p. 167). Such *FQ–* responses, often referred to as "minus responses," indicate a disregard for these critical stimulus features and reflect a distortion of reality. Consistent with their underlying response process, *FQ–* scores have shown strong meta-analytic support as markers of impaired reality testing, psychotic symptoms, and overall severity of psychopathology—especially in studies comparing psychotic and nonpsychotic groups or correlating scores with observer ratings and structured interviews (Mihura et al., 2013).[3]

The percentage of *FQ–* responses significantly influences scores on the Perceptual-Thinking Index (*PTI*; Exner, 2003, pp. 390–393) and the various forms of the Ego Impairment Index (*EII*; Perry & Viglione, 1991; Viglione et al., 2003, 2011).[4] Both indices have strong validity support for assessing perceptual and thinking disturbances, as well as the overall severity of psychopathology (Diener et al., 2011; Mihura et al., 2013; Stenius et al., 2018; Valkonen et al., 2012). As the R-PAS manual summarizes, a high *FQ–%* is "strongly associated with reality disturbance and psychopathology" (Meyer et al., 2011, p. 359).

As described in Chapters 2–4, *X–%* has long been linked to neurocognitive disorders and cognitive functioning. Rorschach (2021) considered it to be a part of intelligence, specifically reflecting the clarity of form perception.[5]

Piotrowski (1937) later included *F+%* < 70 among his ten organic signs indicating possible neuropsychological impairment.[6] Research and clinical practice both support that elevated *FQ–%* or *X–%* is often observed in individuals with neurocognitive (e.g., dementia), psychiatric (e.g., schizophrenia), or personality disorders (e.g., borderline personality disorder [BPD]) that involve distorted or idiosyncratic interpretations of reality.

Emotional interference is widely recognized as a key factor in distorted perception. This is supported by studies on stress in extreme survival situations (Ross & Murphy, 2017), minor daily stresses triggering subtle increases in psychotic symptoms among individuals with schizophrenia (Myin-Germeys et al., 2005), and the presence of psychotic symptoms in severe personality disorders. For example, a focused review of auditory verbal hallucinations (AVH) in BPD found that AVHs in BPD are phenomenologically similar to those in schizophrenia, are highly stress-related, and are strongly linked to dissociation and childhood trauma (Beatson et al., 2019). These findings suggest that emotionally arousing situations tend to disrupt higher-level cognitive processes and judgment, leading to misinterpretations or hallucinatory experiences.

Functional neuroimaging studies show that the amygdala—a key limbic structure involved in emotion and fear processing—significantly influences perception. For instance, individuals with higher negative affect show greater amygdala activation to fear stimuli, as measured by fMRI and experience sampling, in which participants report their emotional state at regular daily intervals (Anderson, 2007). Amygdala activation also correlates with increased fusiform gyrus activity, suggesting enhanced perceptual encoding of emotional faces in anxious individuals (Barrett et al., 2007).[7] As Anderson (2007) concludes, the amygdala enhances attention and perceptual encoding of emotional events, increasing their subjective salience.

Contemporary neuroscientific theories emphasize the amygdala's central role in emotion, including evaluating sensory input, assigning emotional value (e.g., valence, intensity), regulating autonomic and endocrine functions, supporting implicit learning, guiding adaptive behavior, and activating the fight-or-flight response through widespread cortical and subcortical projections (Šimić et al., 2021). Moreover, neurophysiological and neuroimaging studies have shown that the amygdala influences perceptual processing, with more frequent activation increasing the likelihood of emotional bias (e.g., Kilpatrick & Cahill, 2003; Phelps & LeDoux, 2005). Additionally, repeated activation can enlarge brain structures, a phenomenon linked to the "bigger is better" hypothesis (Clark et al., 2020; Yuan & Raz, 2014). However, excessive amygdalar enlargement has also been associated with dysfunction, as seen in affective psychosis (Velakoulis et al., 2006) or temporal lobe epilepsy with psychosis (Tebartz Van Elst et al., 2002).

Drawing on prior research, a Japanese team investigated whether emotional signals—particularly amygdalar activity—interfere with perception as reflected on the Rorschach. Their studies linked amygdalar enlargement with unique perception (Asari et al., 2010a) and explored how temporopolar and amygdalar activation modulate the neocortical interpretation of ambiguous stimuli (Asari et al., 2008, 2010b). In a structural MRI study, they examined whether amygdala volume in healthy individuals correlated with a tendency to produce unique responses. This was measured using the Unique Response Ratio (URR), defined as the proportion of responses not found in a matched Japanese control sample. While the URR is not directly comparable to CS or R-PAS FQ variables due to differing coding criteria, it roughly corresponds to a combination of *X–%* or *FQ–%* and *Xu%* or *FQu%*, capturing both infrequent perceptual distortions and infrequent but accurate perceptions.

In the structural study, Rorschach inkblots were projected on a screen while sixty-eight healthy participants lay in an MRI scanner and described what they saw using an MRI-compatible microphone. A control group of 217 healthy individuals matched for age and education completed the same task outside the scanner to create the URR reference database. Post-experimental inquiry followed standard procedures.

Voxel-based morphometry revealed a significant positive correlation between URR scores and bilateral amygdala volume ($p < .05$), as well as other limbic and associative areas, including the bilateral cingulate gyri, left lateral temporal regions, right inferior occipital cortex, right precentral gyrus, right paracentral lobule, and left caudate.[8] To further examine these findings, participants were grouped by URR quartiles. Comparing the highest and lowest quartiles, *t*-tests showed significantly greater gray matter volume in the right amygdala ($p < .01$), left amygdala ($p < .05$), and cingulate gyri ($p < .01$), with medium to large effect sizes (Cohen's d ≈.70, .51, .78). A one-way ANOVA confirmed significant volume differences across all four quartiles.

Asari et al. (2010a) emphasized the strong anatomical connections between the amygdala and cingulate gyri (e.g., Pandya et al., 1973), noting that both structures appear to support the production of unique responses on the Rorschach (*FQ–* or *FQu*). Their findings support the hypothesis that key limbic structures contribute to the generation of unique perception. Additional correlations with visual recognition areas (temporal and occipital regions) suggest these regions may also be more developed in individuals producing more unique responses. Although original responses are more frequent among artists (e.g., Ramachandra, 1994; Rorschach, 2021; Satterlee, 2006), highly idiosyncratic or unrecognizable responses (*FQ–*) are common in psychotic patients and those with severe psychopathology.[9]

Interestingly, while schizophrenia spectrum disorders are marked by an elevated frequency of *FQ–* responses, they also show gray-matter deficits in key areas such as the amygdala (Honea et al., 2005; Wright et al., 1999). Earlier-onset psychosis is linked to widespread gray-matter loss (Tordesillas-Gutierrez et al., 2015), and delayed treatment correlates with volume reduction in regions like the inferior-orbital cortex (Malla et al., 2011). These findings suggest that both hyperdevelopment and hypodevelopment of emotion-regulating structures can lead to unique perception. On the healthy end, amygdala and cingulate enlargement may foster creative or original perception (*FQu*). On the pathological end, gray-matter deficits may underlie perceptual distortions (*FQ–*) tied to psychotic disorders. Since Asari et al.'s (2010a) participants were neurologically and psychiatrically healthy, their findings likely reflect normative individual variation rather than psychosis. The authors conclude that frequent activation of emotion-related circuits may drive both artistic originality and psychotic phenomena, depending on the broader context.

Future studies comparing standard Rorschach scores like *Xu%* (*FQu%*) and *X–%* (*FQ–%*) to URR findings could help clarify which process—unusual but accurate or truly distorted perception—is more closely tied to amygdala volume. As always, no single Rorschach variable should be interpreted in isolation; all data must be integrated with other test findings and clinical observations.

In a parallel fMRI study, Asari et al. (2010b) investigated how amygdalar activity modulates top-down and recognition processes during Rorschach performance. Two brain regions were targeted: the left anterior frontal cortex, associated with top-down control (Petrides, 2005), and the right temporopolar cortex, linked to integrating recognition processes (Martin & Chao, 2001). Using psychophysiological interaction (PPI) analysis, the authors assessed functional connectivity in forty-one healthy females (aged 20–36), who viewed Rorschach cards in an MRI scanner and vocalized their responses.[10] Responses were categorized as frequent, infrequent, or unique using an age- and gender-matched Japanese reference sample (Asari et al., 2008). URR and *WSumC* were computed. Brain activity was compared across response types using statistical parametric mapping (SPM).[11]

Findings support the amygdala's modulatory role in perceptual-cognitive processing. Building on prior structural and event-related studies, the authors showed that amygdalar activity positively modulated prefrontal-to-temporopolar connectivity and negatively modulated temporopolar-to-occipitotemporal connectivity. This suggests that heightened amygdalar activation may interfere with cognitive control and visual integration, disrupting accurate perception. The right temporal pole appeared to serve as a critical relay linking emotional modulation and perceptual integration.

These findings illuminate how emotional interference—via the amygdala—can influence reality testing, defined as the matching of internal images to external stimuli. The observed increases in frontal control signals may reflect compensatory mechanisms in response to emotional intrusion. Conversely, disruptions in anterior-to-posterior temporal connectivity may impair precise recognition (Bar et al., 2001; Wheeler & Buckner, 2003). Overall, the study reinforces the hypothesis that emotional modulation or interference can distort perceptual accuracy on the Rorschach.

Asari et al. (2010b) also suggested that different aspects of Rorschach responding may relate to differential hemispheric activation, as discussed in Chapter 4. Frequent responses—linked to more accurate, conventional perception—were associated with left prefrontal activity, often involved in executive and verbal functions (Golby et al., 2001; Yuan & Raz, 2014). In contrast, unique responses—typically more personal and emotionally influenced—were associated with the right temporopolar region, a hub linking the frontotemporal and anterior-posterior temporal networks through amygdalar modulation. This region has been implicated in emotional memory (Dolan et al., 2000), name–face recall (Tsukiura et al., 2006), mentalizing (Fletcher et al., 1995; Spunt et al., 2011), and the storage/reactivation of perception–emotion linkages (Olson et al., 2007). According to Asari et al., the right temporal pole helps integrate bottom-up visual signals from the occipitotemporal cortex, top-down control from left anterior temporal regions, and amygdalar emotional input. Supporting this, the study found a significant positive correlation between *WSumC* and URR ($r = .41$, $p < .001$), suggesting an association between emotionally determined responses (via color determinants) and unique perception.

These findings reinforce the widely accepted view among Rorschach experts that the test is emotionally arousing and that emotion plays a central role in response production. Patients with borderline personality organization (BPO) or BPD, for example, are often emotionally activated by the task and tend to produce disturbed protocols, including many unusual responses, perceptual distortions, and signs of disordered thinking, although these disturbances are typically less severe than in psychotic disorders such as schizophrenia (Kleiger, 2017, pp. 227–235).[12] This mirrors the clinical observation that borderline patients often experience distorted perception and thought processes in emotionally charged situations, especially in attachment or relational contexts.

A similar pattern of moderate disturbance is seen in individuals with trauma histories, dissociation, or post-traumatic stress disorder, who may become emotionally flooded and lose regulatory control in emotionally evocative situations. As has been demonstrated in the research literature, the Rorschach can trigger trauma flashbacks, especially in those with trauma histories, due to its use of dark shading, vivid color, and content evocative of threat or harm (Kaser-Boyd & Evans, 2008; Kleiger, 2017, pp. 235–240). As Kleiger (2017, p. 236) summarizes, elevated indicators of disorganization or illogicality in responses containing trauma-related content (e.g., blood, sex, aggressive movement) may reflect encapsulated psychotic-like phenomena on the Rorschach.

Recent neuroimaging findings also support the link between emotional interference and perceptual disturbance. Mitolo et al. (2024), using resting-state fMRI, found structural and functional abnormalities in the amygdala and insula of BPD patients. These abnormalities were associated with emotion dysregulation, anger, and depressive rumination—consistent with the idea that amygdalar dysfunction plays a central modulatory role in emotional interference and distorted perception.

The Human Movement Response, Embodied Mentalization, and the Mirror Neuron System

The human movement response (*M*) is one of the most neurocognitively meaningful Rorschach variables, as outlined in Chapters 2–4. From Rorschach's early insights and Piotrowski's organic signs to recent empirical studies, *M* has consistently been linked to neurocognitive functioning as well as neurocognitive and neurodevelopmental disorders. Additionally, research shows that the average number of *M* responses increases with age from childhood through adolescence (e.g., Ames et al., 1971; Exner, 2003, pp. 427–428; Exner & Weiner, 1982; Kallstedt, 1952; Meyer et al., 2007), then declines in older adulthood (Ames, 1960). As Exner (2003, p. 428) notes, aging adults vary widely in cognitive capacity, consistent with both the rising incidence of neurocognitive disorders (e.g., dementia) and the preservation of normal or above-average cognitive functioning in many senior adults (e.g., Moorman et al., 2021). Drawing on this body of research, it is now clear that individuals with significant cognitive impairment may still produce a normal number of responses on the Rorschach but rarely more than one *M*.

In contrast to contemporary Rorschach practice, Hermann Rorschach coded movement only when responses involved human activity, including animals engaged in humanlike actions—a convention retained in the CS and the R-PAS (e.g., *Two bears playing cards*). Rorschach considered nonhuman movement responses (i.e., animal or inanimate) as form-based rather than what he referred to as "felt movement." He noted: "These are form responses, solely denoting the form of the picture, and the indication of movement is often only a rhetorical embellishment . . . a *secondary* association" (Rorschach, 2021, p. 45, italics in original). By contrast, *M* responses reflected "form perception plus kinesthetic factors," often observable in respondents' bodily movements or involuntary innervations during testing.

Like Rorschach, later pioneers and systematizers agreed that *M* responses—and their frequency—reflect various higher mental functions. They emphasized that *M* involves adding something to the stimulus, drawing on the respondent's internal representations, emotions, and thoughts. Unlike properties such as form, color, or shading, *M* is not inherent to the stimulus and is often accompanied by a subjective sense of movement. However, authors highlighted different aspects of *M* (for a summary, see Porcelli et al., 2013). Piotrowski (1977) described *M*s as incipient actions with minimal intensity and awareness. Beck (1944) viewed them as expressions of strong emotions that are internally contained and channeled into creative, adaptive processes. Klopfer and Kelley (1942) associated *M*s with creative capacity. Rapaport et al. (1946) emphasized their link to emotional delay, anticipation, and flexible perception and association. Overall, these theorists agreed that *M* is an indicator of cognitive sophistication and is typical of well-functioning, mentally resourceful individuals.

As summarized by Porcelli et al. (2013), *M* responses are empirically linked to a cognitive style marked by field independence—the capacity to focus on internal referents while filtering out distractions (Witkin & Goodenough, 1981). They are also associated with emotion processing, as individuals with alexithymia show significantly fewer *M*s (Porcelli & Meyer, 2002; Porcelli & Mihura, 2010), as well as with creative thinking (Ferracuti et al., 1999), dream recall (Orlinsky, 1966), and symptom improvement after psychotherapy (Exner & Andronikof-Sanglade, 1992; Weiner & Exner, 1991). As Exner (2003, p. 429) wrote:

> Any attempt to summarize the full psychological meaning of *M* responses will probably fall short of describing the extremely complex activities to which they relate. Clearly, they involve the elements of reasoning, imagination, and a higher form of conceptualization. They are also contingent on a form of delay from yielding to more spontaneous translations of the stimulus field, during which time an active and deliberate form of ideation occurs. This deliberate directing of one's inner life breeds images and/or fantasies that become the basis of decision making concerning the formation of responses to a given constellation of distal features in a field.

As noted by Porcelli et al. (2013), Exner emphasized the cognitive aspects of *M* more than its social-cognitive dimensions, though he acknowledged the role of identification in its formation. He also criticized early research for neglecting the context of *M* responses, highlighting the importance of both qualitative factors (e.g., perceptual accuracy, conventionality) and quantitative variables, including the ratio of *M* to *WSumC* (*EB* or *M*/*MC* in the R-PAS). Building on this, the R-PAS manual describes *M* as reflecting the imaginative capacity to envision human experiences and activities (Meyer et al., 2011, p. 340):

> *M* is therefore a type of mentalization that contributes to the capacity of identification with others and empathy. The cognitive abilities associated with giving an *M* response include the ability to imagine and to envision action or emotion, some capacity to reflect on life experience, and a degree of developmental maturity. Based on the implicit identification of the self with human action and experience, *M* (relative to *FM* and *m*) may involve more awareness, agency, deliberation, and purposefulness, thus seeing the self as the agent or the initiator of the experience.

The mirror neuron system (MNS) consists of neurons activated both when performing and observing actions. First identified in macaques' premotor cortex (Gallese et al., 1996), the MNS is implicated in social cognition and empathy in humans. Initially linked to the inferior frontal gyrus, it is now known to involve a broader network, including the inferior parietal lobule, superior temporal sulcus, sensorimotor cortex, and parts of the limbic system. This suggests the MNS supports not only action recognition but also understanding others' intentions and emotions—underpinning empathy, theory of mind, and social functioning. Research using transcranial magnetic stimulation (TMS), positron emission tomography (PET), fMRI, and EEG (e.g., Gallese, 2007a, 2007b; Giromini et al., 2010) fueled a surge of interest peaking over a decade ago.[13] Since then, skepticism has grown regarding its role in high-level functions (Heyes & Catmur, 2022), with evidence suggesting MNS involvement in low-level action perception but not intention inference.

Giromini et al. (2010), referencing Kourtzi and Kanwisher (2000), proposed that the MNS may also respond to internally generated feelings of motion, even when triggered by static, ambiguous stimuli such as Rorschach inkblots. Prior to 2010, no empirical studies addressed the topic, but, historically, *M* responses were thought to reflect the ability to internally evoke and integrate movement experiences when interpreting ambiguous stimuli (e.g., Porcelli & Meyer, 2002). Both *M* and the MNS are linked to empathy, mentalizing, and *embodied simulation*—the prerational capacity to understand others' actions, emotions, and sensations. Embodied simulation enables social stimuli to activate internal body-state representations, as if one were experiencing them firsthand (Freeberg & Gallese, 2007).

To test early hypotheses linking *M* responses, MNS activation, and embodied simulation, a team of Italian and US researchers initiated a series of empirical studies. In the first, Giromini et al. (2010) used EEG to record mu suppression—a marker of sensorimotor activation—from students during four conditions: baseline (fixating a white screen), experimental (attributing human movement), contrast (responding to verbally suggested interpretations), and control (viewing inkblot-like drawings).[14]

The experimental condition used four Rorschach cards: two high-*M* (III, VII) and two low-*M* (V, VI). Participants viewed the cards, thought about what they saw, and then gave verbal responses, following standard CS procedures (Exner, 2003). Mu suppression, calculated as the reduction in power relative to baseline, was analyzed using a three-way repeated measures ANOVA. Results showed significantly greater mu suppression for high-*M* stimuli, confirming that static, ambiguous images like Rorschach inkblots can evoke mirroring activity. This suggests that internally generated movement representations may be enough to activate the MNS.

A follow-up study by Pineda et al. (2011) addressed limitations of the initial research by using a larger sample, improved baseline control, longer EEG recording, and a procedure more aligned with standard CS administration (Exner, 2003). All ten Rorschach cards were shown, with participants silently considering their responses before verbalizing them. Attention was monitored through a performance task, and the sequence was repeated to collect additional data. Responses were transcribed and coded using the CS. Results showed a mean of 4.3 *M* responses (SD = 2.2), consistent with normative adult data. Mu suppression was significantly greater for *M* than non-*M* responses and strongest at the beginning of exposure. These findings support the embodied simulation hypothesis, suggesting that internal representations of movement can activate MNS-related processes even with minimal external input.

In a third study with the same sample, Porcelli et al. (2013) tested two hypotheses. First, mu suppression over the sensorimotor cortex would occur only with *M* responses—due to their link to social cognition—and *not* with other determinants (e.g., animal/inanimate movement, shading, color). Second, *M* responses most associated with social cognition and competence (e.g., active movement [*Ma*], conventional form [*FQo*], and whole/nonfictional human content [*H*]) would show the strongest mu suppression. Results supported the first hypothesis: only *M* responses elicited significant mu suppression over the sensorimotor cortex. Other determinants and nonhuman movements did not, though human content without *M* approached statistical significance ($p = .055$). For the second hypothesis, only *Ma* responses showed stronger mu suppression than *Mp*, with a medium to large effect. No differences emerged for form quality or human content type.[15]

Despite the small sample size (N = 24), Porcelli et al. were the first to show that mu suppression over the sensorimotor cortex occurs *only* with *M* responses—not with animal or inanimate movement or other determinants. It also confirmed that *Ma* responses, linked to active engagement and social competence, elicit stronger MNS activity and are more desirable than passive forms of human movement (*Mp*), as demonstrated in the research literature. Notably, a finding such as *Mp* > *Ma* is rare and associated with what Exner (2003) referred to as the Snow White syndrome—a passive, fantasy-prone interpersonal coping style. As Porcelli et al. concluded, *Ma* responses in particular may serve as markers of empathy and social cognition through their capacity to trigger mirroring activity.

The case of Ted Bundy, a notorious sexual serial killer with narcissistic and psychopathic traits, previously discussed in Chapter 3, can serve here again as an illustrative example. Bundy's Rorschach, administered in the mid-1970s using the CS, yielded a notably long protocol with forty-nine responses. Despite being assessed as having high average to superior intelligence, he produced only three *M* responses, all of which were passive. An R-PAS version of the protocol presented at the Annual Convention of the Society for Personality Assessment in Washington, DC (Muzio, 2018), showed that although *M* = 3 is within normal limits for an average-length protocol, when adjusted for *Complexity*, it fell down to the fourth percentile—an exceptionally low value. Additionally, and in light of the findings of Porcelli et al. (2013), the fact that all three *M*s were passive could be seen as further confirming the presence of significant deficits in terms of empathy, social cognition, and the commonly shared experience of embodied simulation represented by MNS activation. Other notable findings included the presence of food content, an active-to-passive movement ratio of 5 to 15, the presence of a Snow White syndrome, three *T* responses, and a Coping Deficit Index (*CDI*) of 5/5—together pointing to interpersonal difficulties, emotional dependency, a marked tendency to substitute fantasy for reality in stressful situations, feelings of loneliness, and social immaturity. As Exner observed, fantasy can offer not only escape from reality but also a sense of control, however illusory. In this light, an *Mp* > *Ma* pattern may not only reflect detachment from reality, but also from the experience of shared humanity—as dramatically exemplified by Bundy.

As Porcelli et al. noted, future studies should contrast *M*– responses with *Mu* and *Mo* responses. Their study could not do so due to the limited number of *M*– responses and EEG data. Such comparisons would isolate perceptually inaccurate responses from accurate ones, rather than mixing perceptually inaccurate with unusual but accurate responses. Of the three types, *M*– is most strongly linked—both theoretically and empirically—to pathological features such as disordered thinking, impaired empathy, and poor social perception (Weiner, 2003, p. 182). Producing *M*– responses, especially when *M*– > 1, suggests difficulties in realistic social cognition and is associated with indexes of psychosis (e.g., Schizophrenia Index [*SCZI*] and *PTI*; Exner, 2003, pp. 390–393, 524–525) and ego impairment (*EII, EII-2, EII-3*; Perry & Viglione, 1991; Viglione et al., 2003, 2011).[16]

Porcelli et al. also emphasized the need for further research into the relationship between different types of *M* responses, particularly those associated with psychopathology, and MNS activation. Furthermore, while *M* responses are known to evoke embodied simulation, their findings suggest that human content alone may not significantly influence MNS activity. This distinction supports the idea that *M* responses and human content reflect different underlying neurobiological and psychological processes: the former associated more closely with mentalization and empathy, the latter with self-representation and identity.

Additionally, recent developments have proposed that some *M* responses may be related to trauma. Miron (2025), for instance, introduced a new variable: traumatic human movement (*trauM*), defined as *M* responses that include trauma-related content (e.g., *CritCont* in the R-PAS), aggressive content (*AGC*), and/or specific cognitive codes. This new construct is thought to be linked to disturbed or traumatic forms of mentalization and represents a promising avenue for future research.

Summarizing the three EEG studies described above, Porcelli and Kleiger (2016a) suggest that the Rorschach evokes embodied simulation almost immediately after stimulus exposure, generating a preconscious "feeling of movement" before any verbal response. They note that premotor areas involved in *M* responses are strongly connected to limbic and somatosensory regions, indicating that mirroring activity supports deliberate behavioral readiness rather than mere action recognition. Low *M* levels in individuals with neurocognitive dysfunction (e.g., Alzheimer's disease) align with their reduced capacity for agency, decision-making, and mentalization.

According to Porcelli and Kleiger, the MNS is engaged when individuals interpret others' behavior and prepare for deliberate action by activating relevant motor systems. For instance, the sensorimotor cortex is involved in action execution, prefrontal and premotor areas in action encoding, and subcortical structures in processing emotionally salient stimuli (Keysers et al., 2010; Rizzolatti et al., 2001). Based on this, they propose that *M* responses reflect both embodied self-awareness (the *body that I am*) and the neural processes underlying empathy and mentalization. This hypothesis is supported by two lines of evidence: (1) meta-analytic findings linking *M* to advanced psychological functions such as self-awareness, impulse control, and empathic identification; and (2) research connecting *M* responses to MNS activity through integration of Rorschach variables and neuroscience.

Porcelli and Kleiger suggest that the *M* response may be the Rorschach's most distinctive proxy for mentalization. Conklin et al. (2012) similarly argue that the Rorschach is a powerful tool for studying mentalization, given its access to largely unconscious processes. They outline how *M*, the quality of *M* responses, and human representations relate to empathy, social understanding, and boundary formation. Still, as Porcelli and Kleiger caution, *M* alone does not fully capture the complexity of mentalization. Allen et al. (2008) define mentalization as attending to mental states in oneself and others and interpreting behavior in terms of these mental states. It is about keeping (or holding) the mind in mind. We mentalize when we are aware of mental states in ourselves or others, like when we think about feelings or about what might have motivated us or another person to do something, for example. As Allen et al. describe, there are many facets to mentalizing, or concepts related to or overlapping with the concept of mentalizing, such as theory of mind, metacognition, emotional intelligence, or insight. The key brain structures involved in mentalizing are the superior temporal sulcus for perceiving agency and intentionality in behavior; the amygdala for assigning emotional meaning to behavior; the temporal poles for generating semantic contexts for behavior; and mirror neurons for resonating with observed actions and emotions, just to name a few (Allen et al., 2008, p. 118).

Two rTMS studies confirmed the role of the left inferior frontal gyrus (LIFG) in mirroring activity by showing that its disruption reduces the number of *M* responses.[17] In the first, Ando et al. (2015) exposed participants to the Rorschach twice: once at baseline and once after inhibitory rTMS. Half (n = 18) received stimulation over the LIFG, the other half over the Vertex (control site). Only LIFG stimulation led to a significant reduction in *M* responses (mean = 1.33 vs. 3.39; median = 1.00 vs. 3.50), with a large effect size. Notably, no participant in the control group had a protocol without *M* responses, while this was common in the experimental group. These results suggest that inhibiting the LIFG impairs the ability to produce human movement responses.

In a second study, Ando et al. (2018) examined the effects of rTMS over the LIFG on both Rorschach responses and EEG mu suppression. Participants were again shown Rorschach stimuli twice—once at baseline and once after rTMS. The experimental group (n = 15) received stimulation over the LIFG, and the control group (n = 13) over the Vertex. Consistent with the 2015 study, *M* responses significantly decreased in the LIFG group compared to controls (d = 1.47, $p < .001$). The replication across different languages and cultural contexts (Italy vs. USA) supports the cross-cultural validity of the findings. In contrast, EEG mu suppression showed no significant group differences. The authors attributed this null result to small sample sizes, variability in EEG data, and limited statistical power. They recommended further research using larger samples, alternative control sites, and more comprehensive EEG protocols. They also acknowledged that mirroring likely involves additional brain regions beyond the core frontoparietal MNS (Molenberghs et al., 2009).

Giromini et al. (2019) used fMRI to further examine the relationship between *M* and MNS activity in twenty-six healthy adults. Participants viewed each Rorschach card twice in the scanner and were instructed to think of one response per card. Only responses recalled with full certainty (92.5 percent) were analyzed and coded using standard procedures (Exner, 2003; Meyer et al., 2011). *M* responses were associated with significantly greater activation in MNS-related regions (d = .45, $p < .001$), as well as in motion-sensitive visual areas (MT+) and MNS regions excluding MT+ ($p < .01$).[18] In contrast, form-only (*F*) responses were linked to decreased activity in all three regions of interest ($p < .03$), likely due to the overlap of non-*F* responses with movement content. Nonhuman movement (*m, FM*) showed marginal activation in MT+ ($p = .05$), but not in MNS regions.

At the cluster level, sixteen of seventeen MNS clusters showed greater activation for *M* than non-*M* responses—a result unlikely due to chance (binomial $p < .001$).[19] However, only five clusters reached conventional significance ($p < .05$), including areas in the right temporal lobe, left temporal lobe, LIFG, and right superior parietal lobule. Effect sizes across the seventeen clusters ranged from $d = -.13$ to .48, with seven clusters exceeding the small-effect threshold ($d > .20$; Cohen, 1988).

In a related study, Giromini et al. (2016) tested whether MNS priming influences *M* production. Thirty participants viewed one of three videos designed to elicit low to high MNS activation before responding to Cards II, III, and VII. Although *M* responses followed a linear trend, increasing with MNS activation, the result was not statistically significant ($p = .107$), suggesting a possible, but inconclusive, effect of neurological priming.

To summarize, research findings appear to confirm the existence of a relationship between *M* and MNS activation. Although sample sizes have been small, findings have consistently yielded similar results regardless of the method used (EEG, rTMS, and fMRI). Furthermore, research has demonstrated the specificity of the *M* response compared to other Rorschach codes in its association to MNS activity. No significant association was found between MNS activity and other determinants, including animal and inanimate movement responses, or human content on its own. Perhaps most importantly, these findings have provided additional support and a biological basis for ideas articulated in the Rorschach literature beginning with the seminal work of Hermann Rorschach himself. According to the literature, the *M* response has been understood as a cognitive resource related to a complex process involving identification, embodied simulation, empathy, social cognition, and the "mentalization of one's own and others' experiences and actions" (Meyer et al., 2011, p. 445). Moreover, a recent study by Porcelli et al. (2024) suggests that the number of *M* responses produced by patients in psychotherapy can predict the degree of emotional engagement experienced by the therapist. Specifically, a lower number of *M* responses was linked to therapists feeling more disengaged, while a higher number was associated with greater involvement. These findings indicate that *M* responses may not only contribute to the development of a stronger therapeutic alliance but may also influence the cognitive and emotional engagement of other individuals interacting with the patient. Higher values appear more likely to foster interpersonal engagement, affecting both the individual producing the *M* responses and those around them.

Color-Determinants, Affect Mentalization, and Functions of the Left Hemisphere

Although Rorschach did not fully explain the link between color and affect, he believed that color responses were emotionally driven. He observed that melancholic patients often reported seeing everything in gray, while manic patients perceived colors as unusually bright (Rorschach, 1976, pp. 101–102). He also noted cultural associations between mood and color—such as seeing the world "in black" when depressed or "through rose-colored glasses" when euphoric—and believed color responses reflected emotional excitability, whereas achromatic colors had a different significance (Rorschach, 1976, p. 19). De Villemor-Amaral and Yazigi (2022) highlight that the connection between color and affect dates back to early civilizations. Finn (2012) emphasizes that Rorschach responding involves right-hemisphere and subcortical activation, in contrast to the more left-hemisphere dominated responding in self-report measures, probably due—at least in part—to the inkblots' emotionally arousing, compelling and colorful features. Supporting this, fMRI data has shown that viewing Rorschach stimuli activates both cortical and subcortical (limbic) regions (Giromini et al., 2017).

Rorschach proposed that the balance between the use of color and the use of form reflects affective control. He observed that pure color responses (*C*), lacking form, were common in individuals prone to emotional outbursts or impulsivity (Rorschach, 1976, p. 21). He conceptualized *FC* as reflecting well-regulated affect, *CF* as indicating partial control with some degree of emotional discharge, and *C* as suggesting emotional lability and little willingness to adapt and modulate emotional displays. Like modern systems (e.g., Mihura et al., 2013), Rorschach viewed the *FC:CF + C* ratio as an index of affective control.

Other early authors supported this view, proposing that color perception is more immediate and affect-driven (Schachtel, 1943) and that *CF* and *C* responses reflect diminished cognitive delay functions under emotional pressure (Rapaport et al., 1946; Shapiro, 1956; cited in Exner, 2003). Piotrowski (1937) found that *FC* responses require greater cognitive complexity and integration of contour and color. Finally, several empirical studies have linked $FC < CF + C$ patterns to impulsive and aggressive behavior (Townsend, 1967; Mihura et al., 2003).

In his review of the literature, Exner concludes that research supports Rorschach's core ideas about color responses. He notes that in US adult normative data, *FC:CF + C* ratios show high test–retest stability, with non-patients typically producing at least as many *FC* responses as *CF + C*. This ratio remains stable over time, including in outpatients (Exner & Andronikof-Sanglade, 1992; Weiner & Exner, 1991) and inpatients with schizophrenia or depression (Exner, 1983). In contrast, children tend to produce more *CF + C* than *FC* into mid-adolescence (Exner, 2003, pp. 639–665).

Exner emphasized that chromatic responses reflect the modulation of emotional expression. At the extreme, *Pure C*—rare in adults (about 10 percent; Exner, 2001)—signals emotional lability, reflecting either overwhelming affect or a decision to yield to impulse without cognitive regulation (Exner, 2003, p. 323). More broadly, when *CF* + *C* clearly exceeds *FC*, it typically indicates a situation where

> reactions to emotionally-toned stimuli in one's external or internal environment tend to be direct, spontaneous, immediate, and absorbing. These reactions are accompanied by relatively little cognitive control, mental filtering, intellectual processing, or restraint. In healthy individuals, and in responses with pleasant content, high scores suggest receptivity to pleasant or positive emotions that allow one to enjoy life. At the extreme end, emotional reactions may be overly intense, and dramatic responses to emotional situations. The research literature suggests this interpretation may be true more for the modulation of negative emotions rather than for general emotional control.
>
> (Meyer et al., 2011, p. 357)

A study by Steinert et al., (2021) using structural MRI provides further evidence supporting the validity of these color-related variables as behavioral measures of emotional control.

In the CS, the EB ratio (relation of *M* responses to *WSumC*) reflects a person's coping style.[20] *WSumC* is interpreted—by both Rorschach and contemporary systems—as indicating a more intuitive, affect-driven approach to decision-making, often involving trial-and-error strategies (Exner, 2003, p. 286). A *WSumC* of 0 is extremely rare in both nonpatient and most psychiatric samples and is associated with marked affective constriction (Exner, 2003, p. 287).[21] In contrast, individuals with high *WSumC* relative to *M* responses (the *extratensive* type) can be described as individuals who "cope by spontaneously reacting to and interacting with the world. A trial-and-error or give-and-take approach is more prominent in guiding action. Gut reactions, inspirations, and emotions, rather than thinking things through and playing events out on a mental stage, influence how one views events, oneself, and the world" (Meyer et al., 2011, p. 356).

The research literature has also found *WSumC* to be related to being more easily hypnotized (Brennen & Richard, 1943), being more prone to alter judgments in accord with the suggestions of an examiner (Linton, 1954; Steisel, 1952), sensation-seeking (Exner & Armbruster, 1979) as well as panic disorder and agoraphobia when the value is low (de Ruiter & Cohen, 1992).

Early authors proposed that the proportion of responses to the last three pastel-colored cards reflects affective responsiveness (Beck et al., 1961; Klopfer & Kelley, 1942). Exner formalized this as the Affective Ratio (*Afr*), comparing the number of responses to Cards VIII–X to the number of responses to Cards I–VII, and defined it as a measure of receptivity to emotional stimuli.[22] *Afr* shows strong test–retest reliability in adults and age-related differences in children, indicating greater affective excitability in younger ages (Exner, 2003, pp. 320–322). R-PAS authors similarly view their version of this variable as reflecting responsiveness to emotionally salient stimuli but recommend also considering the qualitative features of responses due to limited research (Meyer et al., 2011, p. 369).

Validity evidence for color-related variables is strong. *WSumC*, the *FC:CF + C* ratio, and *Afr* have "good" support, relating respectively to affective and trial-and-error-based decision-making, modulation of emotional expression, and engagement with emotionally salient stimuli (Mihura et al., 2013). Additionally, *EA* (CS; Exner, 2003) and *MC* (R-PAS; Meyer et al., 2011), which include *WSumC,* have "excellent" support, largely due to the strong validity of *M*, which correlates, as we have seen, with adaptive resources, embodied mentalization, and neurocognitive functioning. Even shading and achromatic color responses, though less face-valid, show excellent empirical support as indicators of implicit distress. Overall, color-related variables appear to work well in terms of validity—but the deeper question remains: why do they work?

A useful starting point in attempting to answer this question is to take a closer look at the response process for *WSumC*, for example, as emphasized in the R-PAS with the following tentative explanation:

> The response process suggests this variable is related to an interest in and awareness of stimulating, compelling features of the environment, which *may* include one's emotional reactions to them. It can be viewed as a gross measure of reactivity, vitality, and liveliness, and *perhaps* a willingness to process and respond to emotion. As a component of *MC*, it is also globally associated with adaptation and psychological strength.
>
> (Meyer et al., 2011, p. 369; emphasis added)

As with Vista (*V*) responses, which in R-PAS are primarily interpreted as indicators of cognitive sophistication though they may also reflect depressive processes and negative self-evaluation (Meyer et al., 2011, p. 368), the relationship between color and affect may also be more complex. Rather than a direct link, it possibly involves additional contributing factors.

Neuropsychological studies have made important contributions to understanding the relationship between color-determined responses and neurocognitive function. Of particular interest are the studies concerning color responses and hemispheric functional lateralization, such as those reviewed in Chapter 4. In one such study (Belyi, 1983), results showed that subjects with tumors located in the right hemisphere tended to give more color-determined responses. Subjects with tumors located in the left hemisphere tended to give comparatively fewer color-determined responses and color responses tended to be form-dominated (mostly *FC*). A longitudinal study involving twenty-five epilepsy patients undergoing neurosurgery (left or right temporal lobectomy or commissurotomy) later confirmed that the left hemisphere appeared to be more involved in the production of color-determined responses (Yazigi, 1997). Additionally, a number of studies using tachistoscopic procedures (reviewed in Chapter 4) were also consistent with these findings (e.g., Brugger & Regard, 1995; Minor et al., 1989).

In a special issue of *Rorschachiana*, Ishibashi et al. (2016) used fMRI to examine brain responses to chromatic and achromatic Rorschach cards in forty healthy adults. Participants viewed all ten cards in the scanner and were asked to think of as many responses as possible. Achromatic cards activated bilateral visual areas V2 and V3, parietooccipital junctions, pulvinars, the right superior temporal gyrus, and the left premotor cortex ($p < .001$). Chromatic cards activated left visual area V4 and the left orbitofrontal cortex ($p < .001$), which is involved in decision-making and intuitive judgment. Notably, chromatic stimuli elicited stronger left-hemisphere activation, despite the right hemisphere's general role in emotion processing. These results align with earlier work by Acklin and Wu-Holt (1996) and Giromini et al. (2017), who found that Rorschach responding engages both cortical and subcortical regions bilaterally. However, specific response features (e.g., *M*) and stimulus properties (e.g., color) show differential associations with distinct brain areas.

At first glance, neuropsychological findings on color-determined Rorschach responses may seem counterintuitive. Emotion processing—especially for negative emotions—is strongly linked to the right hemisphere and its connections to limbic and subcortical regions.[23] Yet Rorschach research suggests that generating color responses is primarily mediated by the left hemisphere. This is supported by findings showing that right-hemisphere lesions do not impair color responses and that color responses increase when stimuli are presented to the left hemisphere (Regard & Landis, 1997).[24] The left hemisphere is dominant in verbal-semantic processing and deliberate, goal-directed decision-making, while the right integrates sensory and emotional experiences, supports intuition, and processes information holistically (McGilchrist, 2019). As Larsen et al. (2003) note, verbal and conscious processing is typically left-lateralized while nonverbal and emotional processing is primarily right-lateralized.

While not representative of most views in neuropsychoanalysis (see e.g., Turnbull & Solms, 2007), some authors in this field have proposed that the right hemisphere may serve as the neural basis of Freud's unconscious. Schore (2001, 2008) describes a right-hemisphere-based *implicit self* that continuously interprets experience and supports nonverbal, affective communication between individuals—a concept he links to a *relational unconscious*. Schore argues that psychoanalysis is shifting toward a focus on affect and right-brain emotional processes over left-brain verbal, rational ones. Supporting this view, Rorschach shading responses, for example, which have been associated with the right hemisphere, appear to reflect basic mood and implicit distress (Yazigi, 1997). Further supporting this view, Perry et al. (1995) found that amphetamine-induced physiological stress (e.g., elevated blood pressure and pulse) was linked to an increase in *m* responses and especially diffuse shading (*Y*), the latter reflecting implicit distress. Other Rorschach variables, including other shading variables, achromatic color (*C'*), and *WSumC*, were unaffected, as were self-reported mood states—underscoring the implicit, nonverbal nature of these emotion-related responses.

Overall, research suggests that *WSumC* does not reflect emotion itself or any specific emotional state. Individuals may experience significant distress, for example, without producing responses determined by chromatic color; in such cases, the distress may instead manifest itself through a constricted protocol or an increased use of shading or achromatic color. Additionally, *color shock*—understood as a startle response to chromatically colored cards (e.g., Card II or Card VIII)—can be observed through behaviors such as card rejections, long response times, or reduced perceptual accuracy, even when few responses determined by chromatic color are given (Exner, 2003, pp. 323–326). Emotional engagement with color is therefore often present in Rorschach responding but not always expressed through the use of color as a *determinant* (e.g., *The red makes it look like blood*).

Color-determined responses and *WSumC* do not reflect any specific emotional state but instead represent higher-level cognitive processing of emotion. This may correspond to what Damasio (1999) describes as *feeling*, as opposed to *emotion*, or what Fonagy et al. (2002) describe as *affect*, as opposed to *emotion*. Emotion refers to lower-level, automatic, and implicit physiological responses to salient internal or external stimuli, whereas feeling or affect involves the mental experience that emerges when meaning is attributed to these responses and these states of emotional arousal are interpreted and integrated into higher-order processes such as conscious reflection, verbal-semantic processing, or deliberate decision-making.

The Rorschach assesses only the highest level of emotion processing—cognitive or top-down—not the physiological or neural activation involved in bottom-up processes.[25] Feelings or affect emerge from the integration of autonomic responses, brain mapping of stimuli, and cognitive processing at both implicit and explicit levels. It is important to note that the Rorschach offers only an indirect view of neurocognitive functioning and captures only selected aspects of emotion regulation, without measuring autonomic or central nervous system activity. While emotions prepare the body for immediate action, feelings enable reflection and nuanced understanding. Damasio's work also highlights how feelings integrate bodily states and mental processes to support consciousness and a coherent sense of self. Though neither Damasio nor Fonagy and colleagues are Rorschach experts, their conceptual models help better understand *WSumC* as a marker of higher-level neurocognitive processing and mentalization.

As Schachtel (2013) noted, the perception of color on the Rorschach is immediate and passive, as is emotional experience. When color becomes a determinant, however, the individual chooses to integrate it into a meaningful response, indicating higher-order processing involving semantic, executive, and deliberate problem-solving functions. Unlike shading, which reflects more implicit and right-hemisphere mediated affect, chromatic color responses suggest mentalization—linking emotion to thoughts, memories, or symbolic meaning. As discussed in Chapter 2, Piotrowski (1937) described color-naming (*Cn*) as a key sign of neurocognitive dysfunction: the subject identifies the color but fails to use it meaningfully. This stimulus-bounded style reflects a limited capacity to integrate and mentalize emotions. As noted in Chapter 4, such limitations are often observed in neurocognitive disorders, where *WSumC* tends to be exceptionally low. At the opposite end of the spectrum, high *WSumC* scores often reflect strengths in affective-cognitive integration. This aligns with Damasio's (1994) notion of *somatic markers* as signals that help guide decisions, especially in complex personal situations (e.g., choosing a partner or a job). A high *WSumC* might reflect this same capacity to integrate somatic-emotional signals into adaptive decision-making. At times, however, one may experience a strong emotional reaction but fail to use it in guiding decisions—just as color perception does not always translate into a color-determined response.

Interestingly, although *WSumC* is considered an adaptive resource, its weighting system (*C* = 1.5, *CF* = 1.0, *FC* = 0.5) favors less well-modulated responses.[26] Given that *FC* is more typical of mature emotional functioning, an inverted weighting scheme might better reflect developmental trends. To explore this, I tested three versions of the variable—the original *WSumC*, a revised reversed weighted version (*WSumC-R*), and *SumC*—in a geriatric sample (N = 60; Muzio, 2019). All versions correlated significantly and similarly with cognitive performance, suggesting that how color codes are weighted has limited impact on their relationship with neurocognitive resources. These findings support the view that *WSumC* primarily reflects verbal-semantic emotion processing as a neuropsychological resource, distinct from the emotion regulation measured by the *FC:CF + C* ratio (Mihura et al., 2013). For example, a person may meaningfully integrate emotional experiences into thought and problem-solving without necessarily regulating those emotions effectively.

In conclusion, *WSumC,* like *M,* reflects a higher-level adaptive capacity grounded in cognitive-affective integration and embodied mentalization.

Rorschach research highlights how these responses involve the deliberate use of emotion within left-hemisphere-mediated verbal-semantic processing, offering insights not easily captured by standard neuropsychological measures.

Notes

1 fMRI measures brain activity by detecting changes in blood flow, providing high spatial resolution images of brain regions involved in specific tasks. EEG records electrical activity of the brain via electrodes placed on the scalp, offering high temporal resolution for tracking neural responses. fNIRS uses near-infrared light to measure changes in blood oxygenation and volume, providing insights into brain function.

2 MRI produces detailed images of brain structures using magnetic fields and radio waves. rTMS noninvasively stimulates brain areas using repeated magnetic pulses.

3 Impaired reality testing is understood here as an impairment of the capacity to differentiate between self-generated stimuli and attributions (e.g., thoughts, emotions, and imagery) and the objective properties of external (or internal) stimuli.

4 A dimensional version of the *PTI*; the Thought & Perception Composite (*PT-Comp*), is included in the R-PAS (Meyer et al., 2011).

5 Hermann Rorschach originally used two Form Quality codes: *F+* (frequent) and *F–* (less clearly seen) (Rorschach, 2021). Mayman (1970) later expanded this to seven levels (cited in Exner, 1974), which were reduced to four in the CS for reliability. Both the CS (Exner, 2003) and the R-PAS (Meyer et al., 2011) classify responses by frequency and fit, but differ in criteria and norms: for example, *FQ–* in the R-PAS requires both inaccuracy and infrequency, while the CS uses a broader definition. The R-PAS uses international data for determining FQ; the CS relies on US data.

6 Like Rorschach, Piotrowski used only two codes for Form Quality: *F+* (frequently recurring responses) and *F–* (responses less clearly seen). Interestingly, the interpretive cut-off used as one of Piotrowski's organic signs implied *F–%* > 30, which is almost identical to the one empirically shown to be typical of psychotic levels of perceptual inaccuracy in the CS (*X–%* > .29).

7 The fusiform gyrus, located in the temporal lobe, plays a crucial role in various visual processes, including face perception and recognition.

8 Voxel-based morphometry is a neuroimaging analysis technique used primarily to study differences in brain anatomy between groups of subjects.

9 Note that none of the subjects in Asari et al.'s (2010a) experimental group had formal art education, nor was there any evidence of them being psychotic. Hence, the URR (i.e., *X–%* and *Xu%* together) is best understood as a ratio related to an idiosyncratic (i.e., infrequent, unconventional, and personal) way of seeing the world. It does not tell us directly whether this feature is related to originality/creativity, psychotic phenomena, or both.

10 PPI analysis examines how functional connectivity between brain regions varies depending on task conditions or psychological context.

11 SPM is a sophisticated statistical technique used in neuroimaging to detect, analyze, and compare brain activity between different experimental conditions or groups.

12 Although the two concepts overlap, the concept of BPO is based on psychodynamic theory (e.g., Kernberg, 1985) and is a broader concept than that of BPD, which comes from a tradition of descriptive psychiatry (e.g., DSM-5-TR; American Psychiatric Association, 2022).

13 TMS is a noninvasive method that uses magnetic fields to stimulate nerve cells in the brain. PET is a neuroimaging technique that measures metabolic activity in the brain by detecting radioactive tracers.
14 Mu suppression refers to a decrease in the 8–13 Hz mu rhythm over the sensorimotor cortex, indicating motor system activation during movement, motor imagery, or observed action.
15 Note that Porcelli et al. (2013) made the decision to compare *M* with *FQo* (*Mo*) to *M* with *FQu* (*Mu*) and *M* with *FQ–* (*M-*), instead of comparing *Mo* and *Mu* to *M–*. This decision was based on the exceptionally low base rate of *M–* responses in this sample, as would be expected in a healthy population.
16 In the R-PAS (Meyer et al., 2011), a dimensional version of this variable, based on the *PTI* is used: the Thought & Perception Composite (*TP-Comp*).
17 rTMS is a noninvasive technique that uses magnetic pulses to modulate neural activity in targeted brain regions.
18 MT+ regions are typically triggered by both MNS and non-MNS motion-related tasks, such as observing moving dots or lines.
19 The binomial theorem is a formula for finding any power of a binomial without multiplying at length.
20 Calculated as *M*/*M* + *WSumC* and referred to as *M*/*MC* in the R-PAS.
21 Note that only one of the 600 individuals included in the US reference sample, and only about 6 percent of 193 inpatient depressives with Rorschach protocols of otherwise normal complexity (i.e., *Lambda* < 1.0) present a finding of *WSumC* = 0 (Exner, 2001, p. 231).
22 The *Afr* is calculated in the R-PAS as *R8910%*; i.e., the percentage of responses to the last three pastel-colored cards.
23 See Borod (2000) for a review of traditional neuropsychology of emotion. While earlier literature emphasized hemispheric lateralization, more recent research highlights the involvement of broader, bilateral networks (e.g., Suchy, 2011).
24 For a broader review of the literature on the Rorschach and hemispheric specialization see Chapter 4.
25 Top-down processing originates in the cortex and influences lower-level sensory or motor systems (e.g., from expectations, predictions, and goals to perception). Bottom-up processing refers to information processing that originates in sensory input and moves upward toward higher cognitive functions (e.g., from visual input to object recognition and verbal-semantic processing).
26 Rorschach developed a weighting system to balance the typically higher number of color responses relative to *M* responses when calculating the Erlebnistypos ratio (i.e., *EB* in the CS or *M*/*MC* in the R-PAS). He emphasized the interpretive value of their relationship and proposed that responses with stronger color-determinants should carry greater weight (Rorschach, 2021).

References

Acklin, M. W., & Wu-Holt, P. (1996). Contributions of cognitive science to the Rorschach technique: Cognitive and neuropsychological correlates of the response process. *Journal of Personality Assessment*, 67(1), 169–178.

Allen, J. G., Fonagy, P., & Bateman, A. W. (2008). *Mentalization in clinical practice*. American Psychiatric Association.

American Psychiatric Association. (2022). *Diagnostic and statistical manual of mental disorders* (5th ed., text rev.). American Psychiatric Association.

Ames, L. B. (1960). Specific stability of cognitive functioning in the aged. *Journal of Genetic Psychology*, 96, 185–193.

Ames, L. B., Metraux, R. W., & Walker, R. N. (1971). Discriminative validity of the Rorschach test in children. *Journal of Projective Techniques and Personality Assessment*, 35(3), 278–285.

Anderson, A. K. (2007). Feeling emotional: The amygdala links emotional perception and experience. *Social Cognitive and Affective Neuroscience*, 2(2), 71–72.

Ando, A., Pineda, J. A., Giromini, L., Soghoyan, G., Bohm, M., Maryanovsky, D., & Zennaro, A. (2018). Effects of repetitive transcranial magnetic stimulation (rTMS) on attribution of movement to ambiguous stimuli and EEG mu suppression. *Brain Research*, 1680, 69–76.

Ando, A., Salatino, A., Giromini, L., Ricci, R., Pignolo, C., Cristofanelli, S., Ferro, L., Viglione, D. J., & Zennaro, A. (2015). Embodied simulation and ambiguous stimuli: The role of the mirror neuron system. *Brain Research*, 1629, 135–142.

Asari, T., Konishi, S., Jimura, K., Chikazoe, J., Nakamura, N., & Miyashita, Y. (2008). Right temporopolar activation associated with unique perception. *NeuroImage*, 41(1), 145–152.

Asari, T., Konishi, S., Jimura, K., Chikazoe, J., Nakamura, N., & Miyashita, Y. (2010a). Amygdalar enlargement associated with unique perception. *Cortex*, 46 (1), 94–99.

Asari, T., Konishi, S., Jimura, K., Chikazoe, J., Nakamura, N., & Miyashita, Y. (2010b). Amygdalar modulation of frontotemporal connectivity during the inkblot test. *Psychiatry Research: Neuroimaging*, 182(2), 103–110.

Bar, M., Tootell, R. B., Schacter, D. L., Greve, D. N., Fischl, B., Mendola, J. D., Rosen, B. R., & Dale, A. M. (2001). Cortical mechanisms specific to explicit visual object recognition. *Neuron*, 29(2), 529–535.

Barrett, L. F., Bliss-Moreau, E., Duncan, S. L., Rauch, S. L., & Wright, C. I. (2007). The amygdala and the experience of affect. *Social Cognitive and Affective Neuroscience*, 2(2), 73–83.

Beatson, J. A., Broadbear, J. H., Duncan, C., Bourton, D., & Rao, S. (2019). Avoiding misdiagnosis when auditory verbal hallucinations are present in borderline personality disorder. *The Journal of Nervous and Mental Disease*, 207 (12), 1048–1055.

Beck, S. J. (1944). *The relationship between three measures of L (No. 3)*. National Research Council Committee on Selection and Training of Aircraft Pilots.

Beck, S. J., Beck, A., Levitt, E. E., & Molish, H. B. (1961). *Rorschach's test. I: Basic processes* (3rd ed.). Grune & Stratton.

Belyi, B. I. (1983). Reflection of functional hemispheric asymmetry in some phenomena of visual perception. *Human Physiology*, 8(6), 410–417.

Borod, J. C. (Ed.). (2000). *The neuropsychology of emotion*. Oxford University Press.

Brennen, M., & Richard, S. (1943). Use of the Rorschach test in predicting hypnotizability. *Bulletin of the Menninger Clinic*, 7, 183–187.

Brugger, P., & Regard, M. (1995). Rorschach inkblots in the peripheral visual fields: Enhanced associative quality to the left of fixation. *Journal of Genetic Psychology*, 156(3), 385–387.

Clark, I. A., Monk, A. M., Hotchin, V., Pizzamiglio, G., Liefgreen, A., Callaghan, M. F., & Maguire, E. A. (2020). Does hippocampal volume explain performance differences on hippocampal-dependant tasks? *NeuroImage*, 221, 117211.

Cohen, J. (1988). *Statistical power analysis for the behavioral sciences* (2nd ed.). Lawrence Erlbaum Associates.

Conklin, A. C., Malone, J. C., & Fowler, J. T. (2012). Mentalization and the Rorschach. *Rorschachiana*, 33(2), 189–213. doi:10.1027/1192-5604/a000035.

Damasio, A. R. (1994). *Descartes' error: emotions, reason, and the human brain.* Avon Books.

Damasio, A. R. (1999). *The feeling of what happens: Body and emotion in the making of consciousness.* Harcourt Brace.

de Ruiter, C., & Cohen, L. (1992). Personality in panic disorder with agoraphobia: A Rorschach study. *Journal of Personality Assessment*, 59(2), 304–316.

de Villemor-Amaral, A. E., & Yazigi, L. (2022). Color and affect: A long, never-ending history. *Rorschachiana*, 43(1), 70–88. doi:10.1027/1192-5604/a000156.

Diener, M. J., Hilsenroth, M. J., Shaffer, S. A., & Sexton, J. E. (2011). A meta-analysis of the relationship between the Rorschach Ego Impairment Endex (EII) and psychiatric severity. *Clinical Psychology & Psychotherapy*, 18(6), 464–485. doi:10.1002/cpp.725.

Dolan, R. J., Lane, R., Chua, P., & Fletcher, P. (2000). Dissociable temporal lobe activations during emotional episodic memory retrieval. *Neuroimage*, 11(3), 203–209.

Exner, J. E. (1974). *The Rorschach: A comprehensive system. Volume 1: Basic foundations.* Wiley.

Exner, J. E. (1983). Rorschach assessment. In I. B. Weiner (Ed.), *Clinical methods in psychology* (2nd ed.). Wiley.

Exner, J. E. (1993). *The Rorschach: A comprehensive system—Basic foundations* (3rd ed.). John Wiley & Sons.

Exner, J. E. (2001). *A Rorschach workbook for the Comprehensive System.* Rorschach Workshops.

Exner, J. E. (2003). *The Rorschach: A comprehensive system—Volume 1: Basic foundations and principles of interpretation* (4th ed.). Wiley.

Exner, J. E., & Andronikof-Sanglade, A. (1992). Rorschach changes in long-term and short-term psychotherapy. *Journal of Personality Assessment*, 58(3), 449–461.

Exner, J. E., & Armbruster, G. L. (1979). *Correlations between some Rorschach variables and Zuckerman sensation seeking scores* (Study No. 252, unpublished). Rorschach Workshops.

Exner, J. E., & Weiner, I. B. (1982). *The Rorschach: A comprehensive system—vol. 3: Assessment of children and adolescents.* Wiley.

Ferracuti, S., Cannoni, E., Burla, F., & Lazzari, R. (1999). Correlations for the Rorschach with the Torrance Tests of Creative Thinking. *Perceptual and Motor Skills*, 89(3), 863–870.

Finn, S. (2012). Implications of recent research in neurobiology for psychological assessment. *Journal of Personality Assessment*, 94(5), 440–449. doi:10.1080/00223891.2012.700665.

Fletcher, P. C., Happe, F., Frith, U., Baker, S. C., Dolan, R. J., Frackowiak, R. S., & Frith, C. D. (1995). Other minds in the brain: A functional imaging study of "theory of mind" in story comprehension. *Cognition*, 57(2), 109–128.

Fonagy, P., Gergely, G., Jurist, E. L., & Target, M. (2002). *Affect regulation, mentalization, and the development of the self.* Other Press.

Freeberg, D., & Gallese, V. (2007). Motion, emotion and empathy in esthetic experience. *Trends in Cognitive Sciences*, 11, 197–203.

Gallese, V. (2007a). Before and below "theory of mind": Embodied simulation and the neural correlates of social cognition. *Philosophical Transactions of the Royal Society of London. Series B, Biological Sciences*, 362(1480), 659–669. doi:10.1098/rstb.2006.2002.

Gallese, V. (2007b). The mirror neuron system and the consequences of its dysfunction. *Nature Reviews Neuroscience*, 8(4), 221–229.

Gallese, V., Fadiga, L., Fogassi, L., & Rizzolatti G. (1996). Action recognition in the premotor cortex. *Brain*, 119, 593–609.

Giromini, L., Porcelli, P., Viglione, D. J., Parolin, L., & Pineda, J. A. (2010). The feeling of movement: EEG evidence for mirroring activity during the observations of static, ambiguous stimuli in the Rorschach cards. *Biological Psychology*, 85(2), 233–241.

Giromini, L., Viglione, D. J., Brusadelli, E., Zennaro, A., Di Girolamo, M., & Porcelli, P. (2016). The effects of neurological priming on the Rorschach. *Rorschachiana*, 37(1), 58–73.

Giromini, L., Viglione, D. J., Pineda, J. A., Porcelli, P., Hubbard, D., Zennaro, A., & Cauda, F. (2019). Human movement responses to the Rorschach and mirroring activity: An fMRI study. *Assessment*, 26(1), 56–69.

Giromini, L., Viglione, D. J., Vitolo, E., Cauda, F., & Zennaro, A. (2019). Introducing the concept of neurobiological foundation of Rorschach responses using the example of Oral Dependent Language. *Scandinavian Journal of Psychology*, 60(6), 528–538. doi:10.1111/sjop.12585.

Giromini, L., Viglione, D. J., Zennaro, A., & Cauda, F. (2017). Neural activity during production of Rorschach responses: An fMRI study. *Psychiatry Research: Neuroimaging*, 262, 25–31.

Golby, A. J., Poldrack, R. A., Brewer, J. B., Spencer, D., Desmond, J. E., Aron, A. P., & Gabrieli, J. D. (2001). Material-specific lateralization in the medial temporal lobe and prefrontal cortex during memory encoding. *Brain*, 124(9), 1841–1854.

Heyes, C., & Catmur, C. (2022). What happened to mirror neurons? *Perspectives on Psychological Science*, 17(1), 153–168. doi:10.1177/1745691621990638.

Honea, R., Crow, T. J., Passingham, D., & Mackay, C. E. (2005). Regional deficits in brain volume in schizophrenia: A meta-analysis of voxel-based morphometry studies. *American Journal of Psychiatry*, 162(12), 2233–2245.

Ishibashi, M., Uchiumi, C., Jung, M., Aizawa, N., Makita, K., Nakamura, Y., & Saito, D. N. (2016). Differences in brain hemodynamics in response to achromatic and chromatic cards of the Rorschach: A fMRI study. *Rorschachiana*, 37 (1), 41–57.

Kallstedt, F. E. (1952). A Rorschach study of sixty-six adolescents. *Journal of Clinical Psychology*, 8(2), 129–132.

Kaser-Boyd, N., & Evans, F. B. (2008). Rorschach assessment of psychological trauma. In C. B. Gacono, F. B. Evans (Eds.) & N. Kaser-Boyd, L. A. Gacono (Collaborators), *The handbook of forensic Rorschach assessment* (pp. 255–277). Routledge.

Kernberg, O. F. (1985). *Borderline conditions and pathological narcissism*. Rowman & Littlefield.

Keysers, C., Kaas, J. H., & Gazzola, V. (2010). Somatosensation in social perception. *Nature Reviews Neuroscience*, 11(6), 417–428.

Kilpatrick, L., & Cahill, L. (2003). Amygdala modulation of parahippocampal and frontal regions during emotionally influenced memory storage. *NeuroImage*, 20(4), 2091–2099. doi:10.1016/j.neuroimage.2003.08.006.

Kleiger, J. H. (2017). *Rorschach assessment of psychotic phenomena: Clinical, conceptual, and empirical developments.* Taylor & Francis.

Klopfer, B., & Kelley, D. (1942). *The Rorschach technique.* World Books.

Kourtzi, Z., & Kanwisher, N. (2000). Cortical regions involved in perceiving object shape. *Journal of Neuroscience*, 20(9), 3310–3318.

Larsen, J. K., Brand, N., Bermond, B., & Hijman, R. (2003). Cognitive and emotional characteristics of alexithymia: A review of neurobiological studies. *Journal of Psychosomatic Research*, 54(6), 533–541.

Linton, H. B. (1954). Rorschach correlates of response to suggestion. *Journal of Abnormal and Social Psychology*, 49(1), 75.

Malla, A. K., Bodnar, M., Joober, R., & Lepage, M. (2011). Duration of untreated psychosis is associated with orbital–frontal grey matter volume reductions in first episode psychosis. *Schizophrenia research*, 125(1), 13–20.

Martin, A., & Chao, L. L. (2001). Semantic memory and the brain: Structure and processes. *Current Opinion in Neurobiology*, 11(2), 194–201.

Mayman, M. (1970). Reality contact, defense effectiveness, and psychopathology in Rorschach form-level scores. In B. Klopfer, M. Meyer, & F. Brawer (Eds.), *Developments in Rorschach technique* (Vol. 3, pp. 11–44). Harcourt, Brace & Jovanovich.

McGilchrist, I. (2019). *The master and his emissary: The divided brain and the making of the western world.* Yale University Press.

Meyer, G. J., Erard, R. E., Erdberg, P., Mihura, J. L., & Viglione, D. J. (2011). *Rorschach Performance Assessment System: Administration, coding, interpretation, and technical manual.* Rorschach Performance Assessment System LLC.

Meyer, G. J., Erdberg, P., & Shaffer, T. W. (2007). Toward international normative reference data for the Comprehensive System. *Journal of Personality Assessment*, 89(S1), S201–S216.

Mihura, J. L., Meyer, G. J., Dumitrascu, N., & Bombel, G. (2013). The validity of individual Rorschach variables: Systematic reviews and meta-analyses of the comprehensive system. *Psychological Bulletin*, 139(3), 548–605. doi:10.1037/a0029406.

Mihura, J. L., Nathan-Montano, E., & Alperin, R. J. (2003). Rorschach measures of aggressive drive derivatives: A college student sample. *Journal of Personality Assessment*, 80(1), 41–49. doi:10.1207/S15327752JPA8001_12.

Minor, S. W., White, H., & Owings, E. P. (1989). Hemispheric asymmetries in interpreting forms vs colors in ambiguous patterns. *Brain and Cognition*, 9(1), 123–135.

Miron, T. (2025). Traumatic human movement in the Rorschach and the assessment of disturbed mentalization. *Rorschachiana*. Advance online publication. doi:10.1027/1192-5604/a000183.

Mitolo, M., D'Adda, F., Evangelisti, S., Pellegrini, L., Gramegna, L. L., Bianchini, C., Talozzi, L., Manners, D. N., Testa, C., Berardi, D., Lodi, R., Menchetti, M., & Tonon, C. (2024). Emotion dysregulation, impulsivity and anger rumination in borderline personality disorder: The role of amygdala and insula. *European Archives of Psychiatry and Clinical Neuroscience*, 274(1), 109–116. doi:10.1007/s00406-023-01597-8.

Molenberghs, P., Cunnington, R., & Mattingley, J. (2009). Is the mirror neuron system involved in imitation? A short review and meta-analysis. *Neuroscience and Biobehavioral Reviews*, 33, 975–980. doi:10.1016/j.neubiorev.2009.03.010.

Moorman, S. M., Greenfield, E. A., & Carr, K. (2021). Using mixture modeling to construct subgroups of cognitive aging in the Wisconsin Longitudinal Study. *The Journals of Gerontology: Series B—Psychological Sciences and Social Sciences*, 76(8), 1512–1522. doi:10.1093/geronb/gbaa191.

Muzio, E. (2018). Understanding the psychology of evil: The Rorschach of serial-killer Ted Bundy. Paper presented at the Annual Convention of the Society for Personality Assessment, Washington, DC.

Muzio, E. (2019). Understanding the neuroscience of the color-determined response on the Rorschach. Paper presented at the Annual Convention of the Society for Personality Assessment, New Orleans, LA.

Myin-Germeys, I., Delespaul, P. H., & Van Os, J. (2005). Behavioural sensitization to daily life stress in psychosis. *Psychological Medicine*, 35(5), 733–741.

Olson, I. R., Plotzker, A., & Ezzyat, Y. (2007). The enigmatic temporal pole: A review of findings on social and emotional processing. *Brain*, 130(7), 1718–1731.

Orlinsky, D. E. (1966). Rorschach test correlates of dreaming and dream recall. *Journal of Projective Techniques and Personality Assessment*, 30(3), 250–253.

Pandya, D. N., Van Hoesen, G. W., & Domesick, V. B. (1973). A cingulo-amygdaloid projection in the rhesus monkey. *Brain Research*, 61, 369–373. doi:10.1016/0006-8993(73)90540-4.

Perry, W., Sprock, J., Schaible, D., McDougall, A., Minassian, A., Jenkins, M., & Braff, D. (1995). Amphetamine on Rorschach measures in normal subjects. *Journal of Personality Assessment*, 64(3), 456–465. doi:10.1207/s15327752jpa6403_5.

Perry, W., & Viglione, D. (1991). The Ego Impairment Index as a predictor of outcome in melancholic depressed patients treated with tricyclic antidepressants. *Journal of Personality Assessment*, 56(3), 487–501. doi:10.1207/s15327752jpa5603_10.

Petrides, M. (2005). Lateral prefrontal cortex: Architectonic and functional organization. *Philosophical Transactions of the Royal Society B: Biological Sciences*, 360(1456), 781–795.

Phelps, E. A., & LeDoux, J. E. (2005). Contributions of the amygdala to emotion processing: From animal models to human behavior. *Neuron*, 48(2), 175–187. doi:10.1016/j.neuron.2005.09.025.

Pineda, J. A., Giromini, L., Porcelli, P., Parolin, L., & Viglione, D. J. (2011). Mu suppression and human movement responses to the Rorschach test. *Neuroreport*, 22(5), 223–226.

Piotrowski, Z. A. (1937). The Rorschach inkblot method in organic disturbances of the central nervous system. *Journal of Nervous and Mental Disease*, 86(5), 525–537.

Piotrowski, Z. A. (1977). The movement response. In M. A. Rickers-Ovsiankina (Ed.), *Rorschach psychology* (2nd ed., pp. 189–227). Krieger.

Porcelli, P., Giromini, L., Parolin, L., Pineda, J. A., & Viglione, D. J. (2013). Mirroring activity in the brain and movement determinant in the Rorschach test. *Journal of Personality Assessment*, 95(5), 444–456.

Porcelli, P., Giromini, L., & Zennaro, A. (2024). Rorschach human movement and psychotherapy: Relationship with the therapist's emotional responses. *Journal of Personality Assessment*, 106(4), 436–447. doi:10.1080/00223891.2024.2303443.

Porcelli, P., & Kleiger, J. H. (2016a). The "feeling of movement": Notes on the Rorschach human movement response. *Journal of Personality Assessment*, 98(2), 124–134.

Porcelli, P., & Kleiger, J. H. (2016b). The Rorschach in the context of performance-based personality assessment. In R. P. Archer (Ed.), *Forensic uses of clinical assessment instruments* (2nd ed., pp. 119–158). Routledge.

Porcelli, P., & Meyer, G. J. (2002). Construct validity of Rorschach variables for alexithymia. *Psychosomatics*, 43(5), 360–369.

Porcelli, P., & Mihura, J. L. (2010). Assessment of alexithymia with the Rorschach comprehensive system: The Rorschach Alexithymia Scale (RAS). *Journal of Personality Assessment*, 92(2), 128–136.

Ramachandra, S. (1994). Rorschach and the creative artists. *SIS Journal of Projective Psychology & Mental Health*, 1(1), 38.

Rapaport, D., Gill, M., & Schafer, R. (1946). *Diagnostic psychological testing: The theory, statistical evaluation, and diagnostic application of a battery of tests: Volume II*. The Year Book Publishers.

Regard, M., & Landis, T. (1997). Hemispheric differences in the processing of ambiguity: Tachistoscopic studies with inkblots. *Rorschachiana*, 22(1), 114–129. doi:10.1027/1192-5604.22.1.114.

Rizzolatti, G., Fogassi, L., & Gallese, V. (2001). Neurophysiological mechanisms underlying the understanding and imitation of action. *Nature Reviews Neuroscience*, 2(9), 661–670.

Rorschach, H. (1976). *Psychodiagnostic* (5th ed.). French translation by André Ombredane and Augustine Landau. Presses Universitaires de France. First published 1921.

Rorschach, H. (2021). *Hermann Rorschach's Psychodiagnostics: Newly translated and annotated 100th anniversary edition* (P. J. Keddy, R. Signer, P. Erdberg & A. Schneider-Stocking, Eds.). Hogrefe Publishing. First published 1921.

Ross, D. L., & Murphy, R. L. (2017). Stress, perceptual distortions, and human performance. In *Guidelines for investigating officer-involved shootings, arrest-related deaths, and deaths in custody* (pp. 68–95). Routledge.

Satterlee, S. (2006). *The Rorschach and musical artistry: An exploratory study*. Alliant International University.

Schachtel, E. G. (1943). On color and affect: Contributions to an understanding of Rorschach's test. II. *Psychiatry*, 6(4), 393–409.

Schachtel, E. G. (2013). *Experiential foundations of Rorschach's test*. Routledge. First published 1966.

Schore, A. N. (2001). The effects of early relational trauma on right brain development, affect regulation, and infant mental health. *Infant Mental Health Journal*, 22(1–2), 201–269. doi:10.1002/1097-0355(200101/04)22:1-201:AID-IMHJ8-3.0.CO;2-9.

Schore, A. N. (2008). Paradigm shift: The right brain and the relational unconscious. *Psychologist–Psychoanalyst*, 28(3), 20–25.

Shapiro, D. (1956). Color-response and perceptual passivity. *Journal of Projective Techniques*, 20(1), 52–69.

Šimić, G., Tkalčić, M., Vukić, V., Mulc, D., Španić, E., Šagud, M., Olucha-Bordonau, F. E., Vukšić, M., & Hof, P. R. (2021). Understanding emotions: Origins and roles of the amygdala. *Biomolecules*, 11(6), 823. doi:10.3390/biom11060823.

Spunt, R. P., Satpute, A. B., & Lieberman, M. D. (2011). Identifying the what, why, and how of an observed action: An fMRI study of mentalizing and mechanizing during action observation. *Journal of Cognitive Neuroscience*, 23(1), 63–74.

Steinert, S. W., Daugherty, A. M., Shankar, S., Schwarb, H., Cerjanic, A., Sutton, B. P., & Arble, E. P. (2021). A performance-based measure of emotion response control: A preliminary MRI study. *Scandinavian Journal of Psychology*, 62(3), 321–327. doi:10.1111/sjop.12705.

Steisel, I. M. (1952). The Rorschach test and suggestibility. *Journal of Abnormal and Social Psychology*, 47(3), 607.

Stenius, J., Lindfors, O., Antikainen, R., Wahlström, J., Sares-Jäske, L., & Knekt, P. (2018). Associations between the Rorschach Ego Impairment Index and Measures on Intrapsychic and Interpersonal Functioning. *Open Journal of Psychiatry*, 8(1), 1–19. doi:10.4236/ojpsych.2018.81001.

Suchy, Y. (2011). *Clinical neuropsychology of emotion*. Guilford Press.

Tebartz Van Elst, L., Baeumer, D., Lemieux, L., Woermann, F. G., Koepp, M., Krishnamoorthy, S., Thompson, P. J., Ebert, D., & Trimble, M. R. (2002). Amygdala pathology in psychosis of epilepsy: A magnetic resonance imaging study in patients with temporal lobe epilepsy. *Brain: A Journal of Neurology*, 125(Pt 1), 140–149. doi:10.1093/brain/awf008.

Tordesillas-Gutierrez, D., Koutsouleris, N., Roiz-Santiañez, R., Meisenzahl, E., Ayesa-Arriola, R., de Lucas, E. M., Soriano-Mas, C., Suarez-Pinilla, P., & Crespo-Facorro, B. (2015). Grey matter volume differences in nonaffective psychosis and the effects of age of onset on grey matter volumes: A voxelwise study. *Schizophrenia Research*, 164(1–3), 74–82.

Townsend, J. K. (1967). The relation between Rorschach signs of aggression and behavioral aggression in emotionally disturbed boys. *Journal of Projective Techniques and Personality Assessment*, 31(6), 13–21.

Tsukiura, T., Mochizuki-Kawai, H., & Fujii, T. (2006). Dissociable roles of the bilateral anterior temporal lobe in face−name associations: An event-related fMRI study. *Neuroimage*, 30(2), 617–626.

Turnbull, O. H., & Solms, M. (2007). Awareness, desire, and false beliefs: Freud in the light of modern neuropsychology. *Cortex: A Journal Devoted to the Study of the Nervous System and Behavior*, 43(8), 1083–1090. doi:10.1016/S0010-9452(08)70706-8.

Valkonen, H., Lindfors, O., & Knekt, P. (2012). Association between the Rorschach Ego Impairment Index and the Level of Personality Organization interview assessment in depressive and anxiety disorder patients. *Psychiatry Research*, 200(2–3), 849–856. doi:10.1016/j.psychres.2012.05.012.

Vecchio, A., Roberti, E., Pulido, S. G., Orlandi, M., Provenzi, L., & Mensi, M. (2023). Only an inkblot? A literature review of the neural correlates of the Rorschach inkblot test. *Neuroscience and Biobehavioral Reviews*, 152, 105281. doi:10.1016/j.neubiorev.2023.105281.

Velakoulis, D., Wood, S. J., Wong, M. T., McGorry, P. D., Yung, A., Phillips, L., Smith, D., Brewer, W., Proffitt, T., Desmond, P., & Pantelis, C. (2006). Hippocampal and amygdala volumes according to psychosis stage and diagnosis: A magnetic resonance imaging study of chronic schizophrenia, first-episode psychosis, and ultrahigh-risk individuals. *Archives of General Psychiatry*, 63(2), 139–149. doi:10.1001/archpsyc.63.2.139.

Viglione, D. J., Perry, W., Giromini, L., & Meyer, G. J. (2011). Revising the Rorschach Ego Impairment Index to accommodate recent recommendations about improving Rorschach validity. *International Journal of Testing*, 11(4), 349–364. doi:10.1080/15305058.2011.589019.

Viglione, D. J., Perry, W., & Meyer, G. (2003). Refinements in the Rorschach Ego Impairment Index incorporating the human representational variable. *Journal of Personality Assessment*, 81(2), 149–156. doi:10.1207/S15327752JPA8102_06.

Weiner, I. B. (2003). *Principles of Rorschach interpretation*. Routledge.

Weiner, I. B., & Exner, J. E. (1991). Rorschach changes in long-term short-term psychotherapy. *Journal of Personality Assessment*, 56(3), 453–465.

Wheeler, M. E., & Buckner, R. L. (2003). Functional dissociation among components of remembering: Control, perceived oldness, and content. *Journal of Neuroscience*, 23(9), 3869–3880.

Witkin, H. A., & Goodenough, D. R. (1981). *Cognitive styles: Essence and origins: Field dependence and field independence*. Psychological Issues.

Wright, I. C., Ellison, Z. R., Sharma, T., Friston, K. J., Murray, R. M., & McGuire, P. K. (1999). Mapping of grey matter changes in schizophrenia. *Schizophrenia Research*, 35(1), 1–14.

Yazigi, L. (1997). Rorschach and hemispheric specialization. *Rorschachiana*, 22(1), 92–113.

Yuan, P., & Raz, N. (2014). Prefrontal cortex and executive functions in healthy adults: A meta-analysis of structural neuroimaging studies. *Neuroscience & Biobehavioral Reviews*, 42, 180–192.

Chapter 6

Practical Guidelines for Using the Rorschach from a Neuropsychological Perspective

Like for any test of typical performance, there is no direct link between Rorschach codes, scores, or indexes and specific cognitive functions or neurocognitive disorders. As described in more detail in Chapters 3 and 4, statistically significant correlations or mean comparisons between neuropsychologically impaired and control groups in this field of research typically yield moderate to large effect sizes. However, the relationship between Rorschach and neurocognitive variables is not linear, and there is considerable overlap between the results of individuals with neurocognitive disorders and healthy or clinical control groups. For example, although the number of human movement responses (*M*) tends to be low in individuals with below average intelligence or cognitive deficits, intelligent individuals might also present a low value for *M*. Therefore, in addition to intelligence-related factors, other factors are also involved in the production of *M* responses and the variance of *M* as a score. Similarly, although geriatric patients with dementia of the Alzheimer's type (DAT) tend to consistently present an extremely low value for *M*, this can also happen among geriatric patients with preserved cognitive functions (Muzio, 2006). This is because, as is the case for any psychological test or neurological exam (e.g., electroencephalogram [EEG]), the Rorschach is not a stand-alone diagnostic tool and will always only tell part of the story. Rorschach findings should therefore not only be interpreted in light of other Rorschach findings—as is the standard in clinical practice—but also in light of background information, history, interviews, clinical observations, and other tests to contextualize the data and enhance interpretive accuracy. As is the case for EEG findings, for example, when taken out of their broader context, Rorschach findings or findings from other tests of typical performance become insubstantial and unreliable (Lezak et al., 2004, pp. 738–739).

Historically, assessing emotional and personality functioning has not been emphasized by neuropsychologists. The focus has been almost exclusively on cognitive functioning. Currently, however, most neuropsychologists would agree that, although often challenging, going

DOI: 10.4324/9781003731894-7

beyond the assessment of cognitive functions is an essential part of any thorough neuropsychological assessment (Priluck & Fedio, 2022). A systematic review of the research literature has recently confirmed once again the utility of the Rorschach in neuropsychology (Mento et al., 2025), and—as described in Chapter 1—surveys on test usage show that neuropsychologists tend to present the same patterns of test usage as do clinical psychologists when assessing personality. The assessment methods used by neuropsychologists will typically include not only self-report measures (e.g., different versions of the Minnesota Multiphasic Personality Inventory [MMPI]) but also informant rating scales and tests of typical performance like the Rorschach. Findings from the latter types of measures are often invaluable given the limitations of self-report measures when used in assessing neuropsychologically impaired individuals. These limitations include—but are not limited to—these patients' frequent lack of self-awareness and the lack of sensitivity and specificity of these instruments when assessing neuropsychological conditions (Priluck & Fedio, 2022). In the early 1990s, one such survey on test usage showed that one neuropsychologist out of four used the Rorschach at least occasionally in their practice (Zillmer, 1994). A more recent survey by Smith et al. (2010) indicated that personality tests in general still tend to be infrequently used in neuropsychological practice. Although typically not considered a test of personality, Beck depression inventories were listed as the most used instruments in this area, followed by behavior rating scales and the MMPI-2. While the Rorschach test did not appear to be widely used in neuropsychological assessments, the authors note that it did remain a subject of research interest and may offer valuable insights in specific clinical contexts.

Although the popularity of the Rorschach among neuropsychologists has varied over time in different settings and in different countries, most of those familiar with or specialized in the Rorschach or other tests of typical performance (e.g., the Wartegg Drawing Completion Test [WDCT]; Crisi & Palm, 2018) will agree that such tests can offer rich complementary data when used alongside traditional neuropsychological tests. The Rorschach in particular, because of its long history and impressive body of research, and because of its contemporary conceptualization as a perceptual–cognitive problem-solving task or a test of typical performance, is an invaluable tool for gaining insights into personality functioning that cannot be obtained through other methods. The areas (domains) of personality functioning covered by the Rorschach include performance-based aspects of information processing and cognitive engagement; perception; perception of self and others; thinking; the capacity for control and stress tolerance; and important aspects of emotional functioning.

While neuropsychological or intelligence tests typically measure an individual's maximum performance and self-report measures aspects of an individual's explicit self-representation, the Rorschach will measure more implicit (i.e., outside the individual's awareness) aspects of an individual's personality functioning: their "personality in action" (Meyer et al., 2011, p. 1). Furthermore, framing the Rorschach as a visuo-perceptual and organizational task supports the view that beyond looking at the structure and dynamics of personality functioning, the Rorschach also taps into underlying neurocognitive functions, such as visual integration, perceptual accuracy, and executive organization (Smith et al., 2007).

There are two broad areas of assessment practice where the Rorschach can be put to good use when considered from a neuropsychological perspective. First, in contexts where neuropsychological assessment is conducted to evaluate suspected neurocognitive disorders (e.g., dementia, traumatic brain injury [TBI], attention-deficit/hyperactivity disorder [ADHD], autism spectrum disorder [ASD]), the Rorschach may serve as a valuable adjunct by expanding the scope of the assessment. Specifically, the Rorschach can contribute to differential diagnosis, the identification of comorbid conditions, the formulation of rehabilitation strategies, the delineation of psychological strengths and weaknesses, and the monitoring of changes in neuropsychological functioning over time.

Second, in clinical settings where the primary emphasis lies on the assessment of psychological issues or mental disorders—such as anxiety disorders, mood disorders, personality disorders, or psychotic disorders—the Rorschach can provide a detailed, performance-based profile of psychological functioning. In carrying out this kind of comprehensive assessment, features may emerge that overlap with patterns typically observed in individuals with cognitive deficits or neurocognitive disorders. When such indicators are present, the clinician is better positioned to consider the possibility of underlying neurocognitive dysfunction and, if warranted, to pursue or recommend a more comprehensive neuropsychological and/or neurological evaluation. In both cases, it can be of great use to know which Rorschach variables have been empirically shown to be related to cognitive functions, specific brain structures and functions or specific neurocognitive and neurodevelopmental disorders.

Finally, when using the Rorschach, it is important to keep in mind that, although the method has primarily been approached as a perceptual-cognitive task, it is also a verbal task. As highlighted by Gold (1987), traditional Rorschach theory has typically overlooked this linguistic aspect of the response process by focusing more on the perceptual and cognitive aspects of the test. Differentiating between perception-related and language-related impairment can indeed be challenging given the demand of the test, which requires the articulation of percepts through verbal expression.

When using the Rorschach from a neuropsychological perspective, the clinician must therefore always interpret Rorschach findings within the broader context of the individual's performance on verbal tasks, visuospatial tasks, and other tasks aimed at assessing an individual's maximum performance (i.e., their potential) in different areas (domains) of neurocognitive functioning. For example, when an individual tends to simplify Rorschach stimuli by focusing mostly on the outlines of the inkblots at the expense of other features (e.g., color and shading), there are three interpretive hypotheses which need to be confirmed in light of other test data and clinical observations. First, it is possible that the individual's verbal abilities are intact but that there is a tendency to approach complex perceptual stimuli in overly simplistic and avoidant ways. Second, it is possible that the individual does not tend to approach complex stimuli in overly simplistic and avoidant ways but has trouble verbally articulating more complex percepts (e.g., percepts integrating color, shading or three-dimensionality). Third, it is possible that both abovementioned scenarios hold true to varying degrees.

Table 6.1 summarizes findings concerning both Comprehensive System (CS; Exner, 2003) and Rorschach Performance Assessment System (R-PAS; Meyer et al., 2011) Rorschach variables with neuropsychological correlations, accompanied by general guidelines for interpretation. Observations concerning developmental trends are also considered where relevant. The purpose of this table is to serve as a practical guide for the clinician using the Rorschach in the context of neuropsychological assessment and from a neuropsychological perspective. Beginning with variables with the strongest neuropsychological correlations such as *M* and *EA*, this table serves as a brief overview with examples intended to help clinicians navigate the Rorschach Structural Summary (CS) or Profile Pages (R-PAS) with a neuropsychological framework in mind. For more detailed sources, references, and empirical evidence, the reader is referred to Chapters 2–5.

In the following chapters, I present four clinical cases that illustrate how the Rorschach can contribute to assessment practice when used from a neuropsychological perspective. All are adult cases selected from different points in time throughout my career as a clinician working in various settings. These cases helped me—and I believe they will help the reader—better understand the many ways in which an individual's Rorschach performance can be shaped by different forms of neuropsychological impairment. Their purpose is also to demonstrate how the Rorschach can meaningfully broaden the scope of assessment, deepen our understanding of clients, and lay the foundation for more patient-centered, empathetic, collaborative, and therapeutic neuropsychological assessment, as described by Gorske and Smith (2009).

For each case, I begin by presenting background information and relevant test findings, followed by a focused discussion of the Rorschach's contributions. Each Rorschach section begins with a consideration of protocol validity, followed by an overview of key variables and indexes, as well as other relevant findings. While the emphasis is primarily on quantitative data, qualitative features are also considered throughout.

Table 6.1 Rorschach variables (CS and R-PAS) with neuropsychological correlates and guidelines for interpretation.*

Rorschach variable (CS/R-PAS)	*Examples of neuropsychological correlates*	*Guidelines for interpretation*
Human Movement *[M]*†	Intelligence and a very wide range of cognitive functions and neurocognitive disorders (e.g., dementia of the Alzheimer's type [DAT], closed head injury [CHI], attention-deficit/hyperactivity disorder [ADHD], autism spectrum disorder [ASD], intellectual disability); mirror neuron system activation and embodied simulation/mentalization; dorsal attention network activation. Some preliminary evidence suggests that correlations with the mirror neuron system might be stronger for *Ma*.	$M < 2$ or a significantly low value compared to reference data, with adjustment for *Complexity* if necessary (R-PAS), should alert to the possibility of some form of neurocognitive impairment or deficits in mirror neuron system activation, embodied simulation and mentalization (i.e., understanding by experiencing) or dorsal attention network activation. Also note that this variable has developmental aspects and will tend to be lower in children between the ages of 5 to 10. However, $M = 0$ is extremely rare even in young children and almost always suggests some form of neuropsychological impairment or developmental arrest.
The sum of *M* and the weighted sum of color responses [*WSumC*] (*EA/MC*)	Intelligence and a very wide range of cognitive functions and neurocognitive disorders (e.g., DAT; closed head injury, ADHD, ASD); relative temporal gray matter volume.	$EA < 4$ or a significantly low value compared to reference data, with adjustment for *Complexity* if necessary, should alert to the possibility of some form of neurocognitive impairment and/or mentalization deficits or reduced relative temporal gray matter volume. Also note that this variable has developmental aspects and will tend to be lower in children between the ages of 5 and 6. However, $EA < 3$ is extremely rare even in very young children and almost always suggests neuropsychological impairment. This is also a useful cutoff in identifying patients in the early stages of DAT.

Rorschach variable (CS/R-PAS)	*Examples of neuropsychological correlates*	*Guidelines for interpretation*
WSumC	Intelligence and a wide range of cognitive functions and neurocognitive disorders (e.g., DAT, closed head injury, ADHD, ASD), although correlations consistently weaker than for *M* or *EA*; mentalization and verbal-semantic processing of emotional experience; functions of the left hemisphere; relative temporal gray matter volume. Also note that, in a heterogeneous geriatric population, subjects with *WSumC* < 2.5 tended to have, on average, higher values for *WSum6* (*WSumCog*).	*WSumC* < 2.5 or a significantly low value compared to reference data, with adjustment for *Complexity* if necessary, should alert to the possibility of some form of neurocognitive impairment; deficits in the mentalization and verbal-semantic processing of emotional experience; deficits in left-hemisphere function; reduced relative temporal gray matter volume and higher levels of disordered thinking. Unlike the other component of *EA* (human movement), values of zero are occasionally found in individuals without neuropsychological impairment and are then typically related to a state of emotional shutdown.
Color nomination [*Cn*] †(not considered to be a response in the R-PAS)	Very rare, but relatively specific to severe neurocognitive disorders.	*Cn* > 0 should alert to the possibility of more severe forms of neurocognitive impairment. *Cn* is a good example of stimulus-boundedness (severe executive dysfunction) and a breakdown in the mentalization of emotional experience, especially when unambiguously delivered as a response.
Developmental Quality Plus/Synthesis (*DQ+/Sy*)	Intelligence, particularly verbal processing, as well as a range of cognitive functions and neurocognitive disorders (e.g., DAT, polycystic lipomembranous osteodysplasia with sclerosing leukoencephalopathy); dorsal attention network engagement and particularly dorsomedial frontal cortex activation. Of particular importance in terms of cognitive engagement and dorsal attention network activation might be those responses which are also *W* responses on structurally "broken" cards; number of eye fixations occurring during the response phase of the Rorschach. Note also that frequently within the normal range or higher in ASD.	*DQ+* < 3 (sometimes also *DQ+* < 4; especially if *DQ+* on cards II, III, VII, VIII, and X) or a significantly low value for *Sy* compared to reference data, with adjustment for *Complexity* if necessary, should alert to the possibility of some form of neurocognitive impairment and impairment of the capacity to integrate ideas and percepts. This profile should also alert to the possibility of low levels of dorsomedial frontal activation and related deficits, signaling a lack of volitional visual attention and scanning or a lack of top-down attentional control. A low number of responses of synthesis also signals a low number of eye fixations during the response phase of the test. Although *DQ+* has developmental aspects and tends to be lower in children below the age of 10 years, the same cutoffs can be used in this age group as indicators of possible neuropsychological impairment.

Rorschach variable (CS/R-PAS)	*Examples of neuropsychological correlates*	*Guidelines for interpretation*
Developmental Quality Vague/Vague percent (*DQv*/*Vg%*)	Higher values for *Vg%* are associated with measures indicating shallower and more superficial search strategies (inversely associated with average number of eye fixations and eye fixation duration during the response phase).	Recent findings are consistent with the original interpretation of vague responses as indicative of a vague, impressionistic, and unsophisticated cognitive style.
Perseveration [*PSV*][†] (no R-PAS equivalent)	Tends to be higher in dementia with Lewy bodies (DLB), but not in DAT compared to healthy controls.	Although values of *PSV* > 1 in particular should alert to the possibility of some form of neurocognitive impairment, particularly of the kind including executive dysfunction and problems with attention shifting, this code has been criticized both for its heterogeneity and for its overly narrow definition of perseveration. For a more sophisticated way of identifying perseverations and executive dysfunction on the Rorschach, see the section on DAT in Chapter 4.
Z score frequency [*Zf*] (no R-PAS equivalent)	Intelligence and a wide range of cognitive functions (e.g., verbal processing and learning, visual recognition and memory, perceptual organization). Also associated with cognitive effort. Note that *Zf* tends to remain in the normal range in certain neurocognitive disorders (e.g., the early stages of DAT, CHI).	*Zf* < 6 with *Lambda* >.99 or *Zf* < 8 if *Lambda* < 1.0 should alert to the possibility of some form of neurocognitive impairment. In some cases *Zf* remains in the normal range or above despite the presence of significant cognitive deficits, suggesting that the individual might be attempting to function at a level beyond what their neurocognitive resources allow (e.g., normal to high number of *W* responses or normal to high *W%*). Although *Zf* has developmental aspects with children under the age of ten tending to have lower values and older children including adolescents tending to have higher values compared to adults, the same cutoffs can be used as rough indicators of possible neuropsychological impairment in all age groups.

Rorschach variable (CS/R-PAS)	*Examples of neuropsychological correlates*	*Guidelines for interpretation*
Whole responses/ Whole response percent (*W*/*W%*)	Intelligence, but specifically more cognitively complex (*W*+ or *W-Sy*) and accurately perceived *W* responses—especially on more fragmented inkblots—and a wide range of cognitive functions and neurocognitive disorders, although effect sizes generally lower than for *DQ*+ or *Zf*. More robust neurocognitive correlations for *W* than for *W%*.	Although this variable is often more related to ambition and effort in processing, *W* < 5 (especially if *W* on cards I, IV, and V) or—to a lesser degree—a significantly low value for *W%* compared to reference data, with adjustment for *Complexity* if necessary, should alert to the possibility of some form of neurocognitive impairment. Like for *Zf*, *W* might, in some cases (e.g., DAT), remain in the normal range or above despite the presence of significant cognitive deficits, suggesting that the individual might be attempting to function at a level beyond what their neurocognitive resources allow.
Space responses/ Space Integration and Space Reversal (*S*/*SI* and *SR*)	*SI* is moderately correlated with perceptual organization and Performance IQ; *SI*, but not *SR*, is associated with the overall number of eye fixations recorded while scanning the inkblots; *SR*, but not *SI*, is associated with a proportionally greater number of fixations and longer duration of fixations on white compared to non-white areas.	*SI* is related to greater cognitive engagement in the task, and to a tendency to consider and integrate a greater amount of information when articulating responses. Both kinds of *S* responses can represent a form of creativity, but *SR* is also an implicit measure of independence strivings and the tendency to do something other than what is requested by the examiner (oppositionality).
Lambda/Form percent (*Lambda*/*F%*)	Verbal processing and learning, but also visuoconstructive abilities and visuospatial perception. *F%* is frequently elevated in certain neurocognitive disorders (e.g., DAT, CHI, ADHD, ASD, polycystic lipomembranous osteodysplasia with sclerosing leukoencephalopathy); inferior parietal lobule activation and dorsomedial frontal cortex deactivation when producing *F* responses, which represents lower levels of cognitive engagement.	Signals the possible presence of an avoidant or overly simplistic problem-solving style that may *or may not* be associated with cognitive deficits (e.g., insignificant correlation with the Mini Mental State Exam in hospitalized senior adults). *Lambda* > .99 or a high *F%* compared to reference data, with adjustment for *Complexity* if necessary, should alert to the *possibility* of some form of impairment in verbal processing and learning, visuo-constructive abilities, and visuospatial perception. Deactivation of the dorsomedial frontal cortex and activation of the inferior parietal lobule associated with *F* responses might further indicate lower levels of activation of the dorsal attention network and related deficits. Both *Lambda* and *F%* have developmental aspects with children and adolescents tending to have higher values compared to adults.

Rorschach variable (CS/R-PAS)	*Examples of neuropsychological correlates*	*Guidelines for interpretation*
Coping Deficit Index [*CDI*] (no R-PAS equivalent)	Verbal processing and memory, but also a wide range of other cognitive functions (e.g., executive functions) and neurocognitive disorders (e.g., DAT, CHI, ADHD, nonverbal learning disorder, ASD). The *CDI* variables most significantly associated with neurocognitive functions are *EA, WSumC, COP*, and *H*.	*CDI* > 3, particularly with low values for *EA* (< 4) and its subcomponents *M* (< 2) and *WSumC* (< 2.5), should alert to the possibility of some form of impairment in verbal processing and memory, a reduction in temporal gray matter volume, or other forms of neurocognitive impairment. If, additionally, *COP* < 2 and *H* < 2, this scenario becomes even more likely. However, if a positive *CDI* does not include a low *EA* or a low value for at least one of its subcomponents, the *CDI* is probably more indicative of interpersonal ineffectiveness in the absence of significant cognitive deficits. The *CDI* also has developmental aspects with *CDI* = 4 being more frequently found in early adolescence, as well as—to a lesser degree—in younger age groups, compared to adults. A value of *CDI* = 5 is significantly less frequent in all age groups and should always alert to the possibility of some form of neuropsychological impairment.
Complexity (no equivalent in the CS)	Intelligence and verbal processing (in the case of levels of integration—Location, Space and Object complexity [*LSO*]—and determinant complexity [*Det*]) and perceptual organization (in the case of *LSO*); deep attentional engagement and dorsal attention network activation; medial parietal cortex and dorsomedial frontal cortex activation, suggesting the active integration of perception and memory as well as the active exploration of the inkblots with goal-directed eye movements; inferior parietal lobule deactivation, suggesting a cognitive shift to top-down cognitive control; number of eye fixations occurring during the response phase of the Rorschach; scanning more regions of the inkblot overall, albeit at a slower rate.	Measures overall complexity of processing, levels of differentiation, integration and productivity. Low values compared to reference data should alert to the possibility of an impaired capacity to perceptually organize more complex responses (especially if LSO is low), impaired verbal processing abilities, and an impaired capacity to verbally articulate more complex responses (especially if LSO and/or determinant complexity—e.g., the number of *Blends*—is low). Higher values suggest greater attention network activation (medial parietal cortex and dorsomedial frontal cortex activation) and inferior parietal lobule deactivation, suggesting an increase in self-relevant associations, active and intentional scanning, and a shift from bottom-up sensory reactivity to top-down cognitive control using internally guided processing. Higher *Complexity* therefore typically suggests that the individual is not just reacting to the obvious formal features of the inkblots, but is also providing a more internally driven interpretation of the stimuli.

Rorschach variable (CS/R-PAS)	*Examples of neuropsychological correlates*	*Guidelines for interpretation*
	Note also that content complexity (also a part of *Complexity* in the R-PAS) does not appear to be significantly associated with neurocognitive functions.	
Blend(s)	Verbal processing abilities, intelligence, and neurocognitive disorders (e.g., DAT).	*Blends* < 2 or a significantly low value compared to reference data, with adjustment for *Complexity* if necessary, should alert to the possibility of difficulties in identifying and articulating multiple features in the environment. Like *Lambda* (or *F%*), a lack of *Blends* in a protocol can also be a sign of avoidance, cognitive rigidity or a lack of cognitive sophistication in the absence of neuropsychological impairment. Although *Blends* has developmental aspects, with five and six-year-olds tending to have lower values compared to other age groups, the cutoff of *Blends* < 2 is still a useful indicator of possible neuropsychological impairment in all age groups.
Form Dimension and Vista Shading [*FD* & *V*]	Intelligence and a broad range of cognitive functions and neurocognitive disorders. *FD* has the strongest and broadest range of correlations. Combining both (*VFD*) tends to produce the strongest and broadest range of cognitive correlations.	These responses are perceptually sophisticated and can be challenging to articulate verbally. Although their absence is a common finding, it might also signal limited perceptual-cognitive abilities and should be considered in the broader context of the protocol and other data. Conversely, *FD* > 1 and *V* > 0 might signal normal to above average intelligence or at least some degree of perceptual-cognitive sophistication. Both variables have developmental aspects, with children below the age of twelve being typically incapable of producing *V* responses and adolescents producing them approximately half as often as adults. *FD* responses are significantly more frequent overall, with adolescents producing them almost as often as adults and children under the age of ten producing them significantly less frequently.

Rorschach variable (CS/R-PAS)	*Examples of neuropsychological correlates*	*Guidelines for interpretation*
Reflection responses (*Fr* + *rF*/*r*)	Intelligence and a wide range of cognitive functions, yet unusually frequent in individuals with closed head injury (CHI) when compared to US reference data for adults. However, it is also important to note that, according to international reference data for adults, the frequency of these responses is probably higher than what were expected when only US reference data for adults were available. International reference data suggests that approximately one-fourth of adults produce reflection responses. This is similar to the frequency that has been reported for individuals with CHI.	Like for *FD* and *V*, the absence of reflection responses in a protocol is a common finding. Traditionally associated with the presence of narcissistic features, the presence of reflection responses in a protocol might also signal normal to above average intelligence or some degree of perceptual-cognitive sophistication. However, US reference data suggests that children and adolescents tend to produce reflection responses consistently more frequently than adults, while adolescent international data suggests adolescents present reflection responses about as frequently as adults. In any case, if a developmental trend exists, it has not appeared to be following the expected developmental trajectory considering the positive correlations of reflection responses with measures of intelligence. One would expect frequency to increase as age and intelligence increases, but this is not the case. Additionally, the reason why reflection responses have been found to remain frequent in individuals with CHI remains unexplained given their cognitive correlations. It seems therefore that, overall, additional research is needed to better understand the neurocognitive correlations of this variable.
Cooperative Movement [*COP*]	A wide range of cognitive functions and neurocognitive disorders (e.g., ASD, ADHD).	*COP* = 0 should alert to the possibility of some form of neurocognitive impairment, particularly of the kind including discomfort in interpersonal situations and an inability to anticipate positive interactions between people, but this association should be considered with caution and in light of other sources of information. Although average values are typically between 1 and 2 in all nonclinical age groups, *COP* = 0 is a relatively common finding, even in nonclinical reference samples. It also appears to follow a developmental trend, with the average number of *COP* responses rising between ages five to nine, at which age the average is the same as for adults; declining between ages ten and twelve; and stabilizing between ages thirteen to sixteen at levels below the adult level (US references samples). It is important to note that, for example, 70 percent of adolescents in the international adolescent reference sample (ages eleven to eighteen) have *COP* = 0, so this is certainly not always a sign of neuropsychological impairment.

Rorschach variable (CS/R-PAS)	*Examples of neuropsychological correlates*	*Guidelines for interpretation*
Whole and non-fictional human content [*Pure H*]	A wide range of cognitive functions (e.g., verbal processing and memory) and neuro-cognitive disorders (e.g., ASD, ADHD).	$H < 2$ should alert to the possibility of some form of neurocognitive impairment (e.g., impairment of verbal processing and memory), as well as the kind of neuropsychological impairment that includes difficulties perceiving others and oneself realistically and as complex and integrated, as opposed to fragmented or reduced to single properties or to objects of fantasy and fiction (e.g., being a provider, an individual with extraordinary abilities or an object of sexual desire). The average number of *Pure H* responses in a protocol in different age groups follows a clear developmental trajectory, starting at about two such responses at age five, rising progressively to about three such responses by age twelve, and staying around that level throughout adolescence and adulthood. For this reason, a value of $H = 0$ might be a better indicator of possible neuropsychological impairment, particularly in younger children.
Sum of human content responses [*SumH*]	A wide range of cognitive functions (e.g., verbal processing and memory) and neuro-cognitive disorders (e.g., DAT). Also note an absence of association with CHI or ADHD.	$SumH < 3$ should alert to the possibility of an unusually limited interest in people often found in individuals with severe neurocognitive impairment such as in DAT, for example. However, a low *SumH* is not particularly frequent in CHI or ADHD, for example, suggesting individuals with these disorders do tend to be interested in others, despite their adaptive and interpersonal challenges or inefficiency, as might be illustrated by findings such as $COP = 0$, $Pure\ H < 2$ or $CDI > 3$. Like for *H*, the average *SumH* follows a clear developmental trajectory, with children from ages five to eight producing significantly less human content than older age groups (mean of about four). From age nine onward there is a marked increase, with values generally aligning with or exceeding the adult mean of about six. For this reason, a cutoff of $SumH < 2$ might be a better indicator of possible neuropsychological impairment for children under the age of nine.

Rorschach variable (CS/R-PAS)	*Examples of neuropsychological correlates*	*Guidelines for interpretation*
Percentage of perceptually inaccurate responses (*X–%/FQ–%*)[†]	Intelligence and a very wide range of cognitive functions and neurocognitive disorders (e.g., DLB, DAT, and ADHD, particularly when associated with nonverbal learning disorder); functions of the right hemisphere and the limbic system, particularly amygdalar structure and function. Note that very high values are particularly common in DLB and uncommon in CHI.	*X–%* > .29 or a significantly high *FQ–%* compared to reference data, with adjustment for *Complexity* if necessary, should alert to the possibility of a deficit in cognitive functions or some form of neurocognitive disorder. It should also alert to the possibility of right hemisphere dysfunction or dysfunction of the limbic system, particularly with regard to amygdalar structure (amygdalar enlargement) and function (amygdalar modulatory hyperactivity and increased right temporopolar activation affecting the emotional-perceptual integration process and producing more "unique" [*FQ–* and *FQu*] responses). Although *X–%* does appear to have some developmental aspects, with young children presenting slightly higher average values in some reference samples, *X–%* > .29 works well as an indicator of possible neuropsychological impairment in all age groups.
Percentage of perceptually unusual responses (*Xu%/FQu%*)	ADHD and functions of the right hemisphere and the limbic system, particularly amygdalar structure and function. Tends to be low in patients with DLB.	Approximately *Xu%* > .40 or a significantly high *FQu%* compared to reference data, with adjustment for *Complexity* if necessary, should alert to the possible presence of ADHD or to the possibility of right hemisphere dysfunction or dysfunction of the limbic system, particularly with regard to amygdalar structure (amygdalar enlargement) and function (amygdalar modulatory hyperactivity and increased right temporopolar activation affecting the emotional-perceptual integration process and producing more "unique" [*FQ–* and *FQu*] responses). Although *Xu%* appears to present some developmental aspects, with younger children (ages five to seven) presenting significantly higher average values, stabilization begins at around age eight, with values hovering remarkably close to adult levels. This tendency to present more unusual forms of perception in younger children should be considered when interpreting this variable.

Rorschach variable (CS/R-PAS)	*Examples of neuropsychological correlates*	*Guidelines for interpretation*
Popular responses [*P*][†]	Perceptual organization and visual recognition (naming of common objects); visual memory; verbal learning and fluency (e.g., naming animals) or executive functions; certain neurocognitive or neurodevelopmental disorders (e.g., ADHD). Note also that *P* tends to remain within the normal range in certain neurocognitive disorders (e.g., the early stages of DAT, CHI).	$P < 4$ should alert to the possibility of specific kinds of cognitive deficits involving visual recognition and memory as well as verbal fluency and executive functions. It is also important to note that normal values (4–7) are common in certain neurocognitive disorders, suggesting that these patients tend to succeed in maintaining some degree of appropriate and conventional behavior, despite their cognitive deficits. This ability to produce a conventional response when cues are obvious might in some cases—at least at first—mask the severity of cognitive impairment. *P* shows a clear developmental trend with lower average levels in early childhood (ages five to eight), levels approximating adult levels at around age ten, and levels almost matching adult levels in adolescence. This developmental trajectory reflects the progressive integration of conventional perception and also suggests that a cutoff of $P < 3$ might be a more appropriate indicator of possible neuropsychological impairment in younger children.
Weighted sum of Cognitive (Critical) Special Codes (*WSum6*/*WSumCog*)	General level of neurocognitive functioning, as measured with neurocognitive screening tests such as the Mini Mental State Exam (MMSE), and a range of cognitive functions, such as the capacity to visually recognize common objects, orientation to time and place, and verbal fluency; certain neurocognitive disorders, particularly DLB, but also, for example, patients with polycystic lipomembranous osteodysplasia with sclerosing leukoencephalopathy. In geriatric patients, individuals with $WSumC < 2.5$ have also tended to have higher average values for *WSum6*.	$WSum6 > 17$ or a significantly high *WSumCog* compared to reference data, with adjustment for *Complexity* if necessary, should alert to the possibility of general neurocognitive impairment or more specific cognitive impairment involving visual recognition, disorientation to time and place, and deficits in verbal fluency. These may relate to deficits in semantic memory and/or frontal-executive functions. Higher values might also be related to deficits in the verbal-semantic processing of emotion (mentalization of emotion) or other functions of the left hemisphere. It is important to note that, although a high *WSum6* is common in some neurocognitive disorders, it is also generally not expected in others, and might alert to the possibility of unusual associated symptoms or disorders.

Rorschach variable (CS/R-PAS)	*Examples of neuropsychological correlates*	*Guidelines for interpretation*
	Extremely high values have been observed in DLB when compared to healthy subjects or patients with DAT. DLB patients tend to present more severe forms of disordered or potentially delusional thinking (e.g., Level 2 Special Scores, *DR2, M–*), and more signs of difficulties in shifting attention (*PSV*). Although patients at the early stages of DAT tend to present significantly higher values than healthy adults for *WSum6*, these do not always significantly differ from those of geriatric patients with preserved cognitive functions. However, there does appear to be an increased potential for patients with DAT to present more severe forms of disordered thinking as cognitive deterioration progresses. These might include strained reasoning or a fluid form of perception and conceptualization involving a bizarre merger of percepts and ideas (e.g., *ALOG/PEC, CON*). Dysfunction in association cortices typically affected in DAT, such as regions in the temporal, parietal, and posterior medial cortices. Average values for *WSum6* are not significantly higher than for healthy subjects in individuals with CHI, ADHD or ASD, although values can vary considerably in the latter two groups.	*WSum6* has clear developmental aspects with young children (ages five to nine) showing significantly elevated values (with a peak at ages eight and nine) which are often more than double the adult average. A notable drop begins at around age ten, which continues steadily through adolescence and lands at levels closely matching adult levels by age fifteen and sixteen. This pattern supports the idea that disorganized thought processes diminish with age as executive functions and formal reasoning skills develop. For this reason and, as suggested in the CS, it is important to consider higher cutoffs (e.g., *WSum6* > 20 in children ages five to seven), as well as whether or not severe cognitive codes are present in the protocol (*Lvl-2, ALOG/PEC, CON*), when considering the possibility of neuropsychological impairment. In all age groups, it is extremely rare to have severe (critical) cognitive codes in a nonclinical protocol, and even rarer to have more than one such code in a protocol.

Rorschach variable (CS/R-PAS)	*Examples of neuropsychological correlates*	*Guidelines for interpretation*
Perceptual-Thinking Index/Thought & Perception Composite (*PTI/TP-Comp*)	General level of neurocognitive functioning (e.g., MMSE score), but more specifically verbal fluency, the visual recognition of familiar objects, and visuo-constructive abilities; a range of neurocognitive disorders, particularly DLB, which typically shows extreme elevations. DAT patients also tend to have mildly elevated scores but not significantly more elevated than what is typically found in geriatric patients with mostly well-preserved cognitive functions. Individuals with ASD also tend to have moderate elevations, but typically below what can be observed in psychotic disorders. The *PTI* was also shown not to correlate with measures of intelligence in ASD. In general, children and adults with ADHD do not consistently present high *PTI* scores. However, the *TP-Comp* has been shown to present elevated values in ADHD and might be more sensitive than the *PTI* in detecting issues with perceptual accuracy in particular, given that *WSum-Cog* has not been shown to be elevated in this population.	*PTI* > 2 or a significantly high *TP-Comp* compared to reference data, with adjustment for *Complexity* if necessary, should alert to the possibility of general neurocognitive impairment or more specific cognitive impairment involving verbal fluency, visual recognition, or visuo-constructive abilities. In certain disorders, such as DLB, values have been shown to be consistently and substantially elevated and appear to be an integral part of the disorder. However, in most neurocognitive disorders (e.g., DAT, ADHD), average values are only mildly to moderately elevated. In these cases, elevations should not be equated with primary psychotic-level disordered perception and thinking. They are typically secondary to processing inefficiencies or impulsive information processing styles. The *PTI* has developmental aspects and tends to diminish with age, reflecting a progressive reduction in problems with perception and thinking as children mature cognitively and neurologically. Although not as rare as *PTI* > 3, *PTI* > 2 is rare in all age groups and can serve as an indicator of possible neuropsychological impairment. Whatever the score, its content should systematically be reviewed to determine whether the elevation is due to problems with perceptual accuracy, thinking, or both. Finally, the degree of severity of these problems should always be assessed, as well as the context in which related codes (*FQ–*, Cognitive Codes) appear in the protocol.

Rorschach variable (CS/R-PAS)	*Examples of neuropsychological correlates*	*Guidelines for interpretation*
Ego Impairment Index [*EII-3*]	Tends to be elevated in children and adolescents with ADHD.	Given its tendency to be elevated in ADHD, a significantly elevated value for *EII-3*, with adjustment for *Complexity* if necessary, should alert to this possibility. Given the high degree of comorbidity between ADHD and other mental health problems, the *EII-3* in the context of ADHD can also serve as a useful indicator of the severity of associated psychopathology.

Notes: * For detailed references, sources, and empirical support, see Chapters 2–5. Comments concerning developmental trends are based on normative reference data from multiple sources: US reference data for children, adolescents and adults using the CS (Exner, 2001, pp. 173–215); international reference data for children and adults (Meyer et al., 2007); and international reference data for adolescents (Tibon-Czopp & Weiner, 2016). † Variable of which at least some version was originally identified by Piotrowski (1937) as one of the ten organic signs associated with neuropsychological impairment.

Although all the cases in this book were assessed using the CS, this should not be interpreted as a statement of preference. Rather, it reflects the fact that the R-PAS manual had not yet been published at the time these assessments were conducted. Both the CS and the R-PAS offer empirically grounded, standardized approaches to Rorschach administration, coding, and interpretation. In the hands of the duly trained examiner, either system can yield meaningful data from a neuropsychological perspective.

References

Crisi, A., & Palm, J. A. (2018). *The Crisi Wartegg System (CWS): Manual for administration, scoring, and interpretation.* Routledge.

Exner, J. E. (2001). *A Rorschach workbook for the Comprehensive System* (5th ed.). Rorschach Workshops.

Exner, J. E. (2003). *The Rorschach: A comprehensive system—Volume 1: Basic foundations and principles of interpretation* (4th ed.). Wiley.

Gold, J. M. (1987). The role of verbalization in the Rorschach response process: A review. *Journal of Personality Assessment*, 51(4), 489–505. doi:10.1207/s15327752jpa5104_1.

Gorske, T. T., & Smith, S. R. (2009). *Collaborative therapeutic neuropsychological assessment.* Springer. doi:10.1007/978-0-387-75426-0.

Lezak, M. D., Howieson, D. B., & Loring, D. (2004). *Neuropsychological assessment.* Oxford University Press.

Mento, C., Silvestri, M. C., La Versa, M., Lombardo, C., & Piotrowski, C. (2025). The Rorschach in the assessment of neurocognitive functions: Applications in the clinical neurosciences. *Journal of Projective Psychology & Mental Health*, 32(1), 14–22.

Meyer, G. J., Erard, R. E., Erdberg, P., Mihura, J. L., & Viglione, D. J. (2011). *Rorschach Performance Assessment System: Administration, coding, interpretation, and technical manual.* Rorschach Performance Assessment System LLC.

Meyer, G. J., Erdberg, P., & Shaffer, T. W. (2007). Toward international normative reference data for the Comprehensive System. *Journal of Personality Assessment*, 89(Suppl1), S201–S216. doi:10.1080/00223890701629342.

Muzio, E. (2006). Vers une approche neuropsychologique intégrée de la personnalité à travers le Rorschach en gériatrie et dans la démence de type Alzheimer [Toward an integrated neuropsychological approach to personality through the Rorschach in geriatrics and dementia of the Alzheimer's type]. Doctoral dissertation. Université Paris X–Nanterre.

Piotrowski, Z. (1937). The Rorschach inkblot method in organic disturbances of the central nervous system. *Journal of Nervous and Mental Disease*, 86(5), 525–537. doi:10.1097/00005053-193711000-00002.

Priluck, J., & Fedio, A. (2022). Factors associated with utilization of emotion and personality instruments among neuropsychologists. *Applied Neuropsychology: Adult*, 29(5), 1112–1121. doi:10.1080/23279095.2020.1852238.

Smith, S. R., Bistis, K., & Zahka, N. E. (2007). Perceptual-organizational characteristics of the Rorschach task. *The Clinical Neuropsychologist*, 21(5), 789–799. doi:10.1080/13854040600800995.

Smith, S. R., Gorske, T. T., Wiggins, C. M., & Little, J. A. (2010). Personality assessment use by clinical neuropsychologists. *International Journal of Testing*, 10(4), 274–286. doi:10.1080/15305050903534787.

Tibon-Czopp, S., & Weiner, I. B. (2016). *Rorschach assessment of adolescents: Theory, research, and practice*. Springer. doi:10.1007/978-1-4939-3151-4.

Zillmer, E. A. (1994). The brain has a personality of its own. *SPA Exchange*, fall/winter, 7–8.

Part II

Clinical Case Illustrations

Chapter 7

"It Looks Like an Island"

A Rapidly Progressing Case of Early-Onset Dementia of the Alzheimer's Type

"Catherine" was a 49-year-old French woman referred by her family doctor to the outpatient clinical gerontology department of a Parisian hospital I was working in as a psychologist at the time, due to concerns about her memory.[1] Although younger than the typical clientele, the department specialized in neurocognitive disorders common in senior adults and was deemed appropriate for her evaluation. Her husband and family also suspected depression, noting that she appeared tense, absent-minded, and increasingly self-critical. She would sometimes cry without clear reason or while struggling with routine tasks. The purpose of the assessment was to clarify the nature of her symptoms by conducting a comprehensive somatic, neurological, and neuropsychological evaluation, establishing a diagnosis, and planning appropriate treatment, rehabilitation, or support.

Catherine had not graduated from high school but was considered an above-average student. She had worked primarily part-time in administrative roles, including as a secretary at an elementary school. About a year before the assessment, she began finding her job too demanding—particularly struggling to adapt to new computer software—and chose to retire. Catherine had always been family-oriented and enjoyed reading novels and outdoor activities such as long walks, jogging, and tennis. She and her husband reported a happy marriage of twenty-five years. They had two adult sons: one studying abroad and the other unemployed and living at home. While she reported no personal history of mental or significant physical illness, there was some family history of medical concerns. Her maternal grandmother had reportedly died from complications related to dementia, and her father, a former construction worker, had silicosis and lung cancer. Catherine was an only child, and both parents were alive at the time of the assessment.

The family met regularly, and over the past year, several members had expressed concern about Catherine's memory. She frequently misplaced objects or forgot plans and conversations, requiring frequent reminders about recent events or names. According to her husband and others, her long-term memory seemed relatively intact.

DOI: 10.4324/9781003731894-9

Together with a geriatrician, we conducted the initial interview with Catherine, her husband, and their younger son. Her husband took the lead in describing the situation, with occasional input from the son, both expressing concern about her symptoms. Catherine spoke little, letting her husband take the lead, but was cooperative, smiled frequently, and responded appropriately when prompted. Her speech was coherent, and her behavior socially appropriate, though she appeared tense and uneasy. She acknowledged memory difficulties, describing herself as feeling "stupid," and expressed shame and concern but struggled to elaborate on the nature of her experience. At times, she became tearful, prompting her husband to comfort her.

Catherine's initial assessment included a medical and neurological examination, semi-structured interviews, routine blood tests, and brain magnetic resonance imaging (MRI). Neuropsychological assessment involved interviews, clinical observation, and neurocognitive screening (Mini Mental State Exam [MMSE]; Folstein et al., 1975; Batterie d'Évaluation Cognitive 96 [BEC96]; Signoret et al., 1989), followed by tests of executive function (Wisconsin Card Sorting Test [WCST]; Heaton et al., 1993) and memory (Grober & Buschke, 1987).[2] Depressive symptoms were assessed using the Montgomery and Åsberg Depression Rating Scale (MADRS; Montgomery & Åsberg, 1979). The Rorschach, administered and scored according to the Comprehensive System (CS; Exner, 2003), was used to examine personality structure and dynamics, identify strengths and weaknesses, and explore patterns typically seen in neurocognitive and other mental disorders. Follow-up assessments using selected methods were conducted at six, fourteen, and twenty-six months to monitor symptom progression, cognitive changes, and treatment response. In the sections that follow, I will present the initial assessment results, followed by the follow-up findings and a final discussion of Catherine's multimethod assessment and changes observed over time.

Initial Assessment: Medical and Neuropsychological Assessment Findings

A geriatrician conducted the medical and neurological examination and found Catherine to be in generally good physical health. Aside from memory difficulties reported by others and observed during interviews, no significant neurological abnormalities were noted. MRI revealed medial temporal lobe atrophy, particularly in the hippocampus and entorhinal cortex. Hachinski's Ischemic Score (Hachinski et al., 2012) suggested low likelihood of vascular etiology, as signs such as abrupt onset, fluctuating course, stroke history, or focal deficits were absent. These findings pointed to a probable diagnosis of primary degenerative dementia of the Alzheimer's type (DAT). The results of the neuropsychological assessment—essential for establishing an early diagnosis of DAT—further confirmed this hypothesis.

Catherine was cooperative throughout the neuropsychological testing. However, she also seemed anxious and tense, was extremely critical of herself and her performance, and cried on several occasions throughout the testing. She often expressed the need to be reassured and seemed perplexed and uncertain about her performance. When asked to write down a sentence of her choice on a piece of paper as part of the MMSE, she wrote, "I regret being so negative."

Catherine's performance on neurocognitive screening tests indicated an overall moderate level of impairment, with pronounced deficits in visual memory and significant but milder impairments in verbal memory and learning (MMSE = 20/30; BEC96 = 68/96). She was unable to recall or recognize recently encoded visual stimuli, while verbal learning was moderately impaired, with marked difficulties in cued recall. She also showed disorientation to time and place, poor verbal fluency (e.g., naming only seven animals in one minute with repetitions), impaired abstract reasoning and arithmetic, and visual-constructional dyspraxia. In contrast, functions such as the capacity to recognize and name familiar objects or the capacity to carry out simple motor tasks on demand appeared to be relatively preserved.

The Grober and Buschke test (Grober & Buschke, 1987) assesses various aspects of verbal memory, including immediate and delayed free recall, semantically cued recall, verbal learning, and visual recognition. Catherine showed severe impairment across all components except for visual recognition, where deficits were moderate. Notably, semantic cuing had minimal impact: on her best trial, she freely recalled only two of sixteen words, with cuing raising the total to just five. Her learning curve was flat (5/16 → 4/16 → 4/16; 6/16 on delayed recall), indicating near-total inability to retain new information. Although she could recall some words immediately and recognize some previously presented ones, she frequently endorsed semantically related distractors. This profile was consistent with the hippocampal atrophy observed on her MRI.[3]

In contrast to her severe memory deficits, Catherine's performance on the WCST was generally in the low average range for her age and education (Total Errors Standard Score [SS] = 82; Conceptual Level Responses SS = 83). She completed three categories, completed the first (color) in only eleven trials, and failed to maintain set only twice—all performances within the average range. However, her high rate of perseverative responses and errors (SS = 72 and 76) indicated below-average cognitive flexibility. Notably, 88 percent of her perseverative errors occurred in the second half of the 128-trial test, suggesting that her performance tended to decline over time. Her awareness of the decline was reflected in her self-critical and emotional reactions. After a string of errors, she said, "I think I'm going to lose it," and later, in tears, "I feel like I'm good for nothing." Results indicate executive dysfunction, particularly in situations requiring sustained attention and performance stability.

The MADRS, which is based on clinical observation and interview, indicated a moderate level of depression (19/60), with symptoms including depressed mood, tension, anxiety, attentional difficulties, and self-critical, pessimistic attitudes. A mild loss of appetite was also noted. The nature and severity of Catherine's cognitive deficits, symptom history, and Catherine's behavior during the testing all suggested that depressive symptoms were likely secondary to her cognitive decline.

Initial Assessment: Contributions of the Rorschach

Catherine's complete Rorschach protocol—including verbatim responses, location data, Sequence of Codes, and Structural Summary—is presented in Appendix A at the end of the book. Administered and scored according to the CS (Exner, 2003), the protocol was valid with an average number of responses (*R* = 20), suggesting adequate engagement. However, the record was unusually constricted, reflecting an avoidant coping style, simplistic processing (*Lambda* = 4.00; *Blends* = 0; *DQ*+ = 1), and limited adaptive resources, suggesting the possible presence of an underlying neurocognitive disorder (*EA* = 3.0; *CDI* = 5). This pattern suggests a tendency to rely on quick, concrete solutions even in complex situations requiring more integrative and nuanced processing. Simultaneously, her record indicated that she was striving to accomplish more than was reasonable considering her functional limitations (*W:M* = 8:2). This was likely contributing to repeated failures and emotional distress—reflected, for instance, in her reactions to her deteriorating WCST performance. Although no codable perseverations (*PSV*) were noted, semantic perseverations involving anatomy and "islands" pointed to attentional rigidity as well as to the possible presence of overwhelming concerns. Her information-processing was often vague and impressionistic, including when she attempted to grasp the "big picture" (*DQv* = 6; four of eight *W* responses were *DQv*).

Catherine's social skills were limited, her relationships superficial (*CDI* = 5), and she frequently misunderstood others (*H*:[*H*] + *Hd* + [*Hd*] = 1:2; *H* = 1). Her profile was that of a person with significant difficulties in interacting with her environment and with others. Additionally, Catherine did not appear to anticipate any form of interaction with people (*COP* = 0; *AG* = 0). She had trouble mentalizing emotions or integrating them into her problem-solving activities (*WSumC* = 1.0), and she tended to avoid emotionally arousing situations altogether (*Afr* = 0.33). She assumed a more passive role in her interactions (*a:p* = 0:3), was reluctant to becoming involved in social interactions (*Isolate*/*R* = 0.30), and had probably lost some interest in others (*SumH* = 3).

Catherine's three "island" responses (Isolation Index content) conveyed not only her impressionistic and avoidant processing style but also something about her subjective experience. Metaphorically, they appeared to capture a sense of social isolation but also perhaps the possibility of being "able to escape," as suggested in the verbalization of the inquiry for her second response on Card I. Beginning with a "pelvis," the opening sequence of the protocol suggests that concerns about her own integrity might have triggered a wish to escape a situation where things were falling apart. For Catherine, the vagueness of processing (neurological issue) and the experience of social isolation (psychological issue) seemed to go hand in hand, as further confirmed by the fact that all her *DQv* responses were associated with Isolation Index content.

In addition to a sense of isolation, Catherine exhibited considerable rumination about her health, integrity, and body image, likely accompanied by a disconcerting sense of vulnerability. This was evidenced by her numerous anatomy responses (*An* = 6), including the sign-in response previously mentioned. Also noteworthy was the fact that half of these responses were perceptually inaccurate (*FQ–*), highlighting the overwhelming nature of these concerns and their association with a tendency to distort her perception of herself and her environment.

Furthermore, the elevated number of *An* responses might have suggested that Catherine was experiencing some form of dissociation related to trauma, as indicated by a significant elevation in her Trauma Content Index (*TCI* = 0.30; Armstrong, 2002). In the absence of other trauma-related codes (*AG, MOR, Bl*, and *Sx*), and considering Catherine's sense of bodily and cognitive failure, it was most likely that these issues were related to her neurocognitive condition.

Catherine appeared largely disconnected from the subtle nuances of her emotional life and needs (*WSumC* = 1.0; *Blends* = 0; es = 1; *Lambda* = 4.00; *FM* = 1). Her Card X sign-off (*FM–*) suggested that emerging internal needs may trigger inner tension, distress, and perceptual distortions, reflecting her limited adaptive resources.

Despite the cognitive decline, Catherine maintained her daily routines but showed difficulty shifting attention, adapting to new situations, and integrating key pieces of information when making decisions (*Zd* = –3.5). Her perceptions were vague, simplistic, and lacked integration (*DQv* = 6; *Lambda* = 4.0; *DQ+* = 1), and there appeared to be some mild impairment of reality testing, though not at psychotic levels (*PTI* = 1; *X–%* = 0.25). Catherine appeared to struggle particularly with making sense of complex situations, especially those involving her health and personal integrity (all *FQ–* on more complex or fragmented cards; three out of 5 *FQ–* associated with *An*).

Catherine's thinking, however, did present a level of disturbance like what is typically observed in actively psychotic conditions (*WSum6* = 45; *Lvl-2* = 4). More specifically, Catherine's thinking tended to be tangential, derailed, or circumstantial. She had trouble keeping her focus on target and filtering out irrelevant thoughts or ideas (*DR1* = 5; *DR2* = 4).

Additionally, she tended to have a distorted perception of relationships of causality (*ALOG* = 1). Interestingly, responses including a more severe loss of clarity and coherence began to appear on Card III and were then spread out across the rest of the protocol, appearing mostly during the inquiry and in association with anatomy responses but also with inappropriately self-referential responses (three out of four *DR2*s were also *An* and *PER*). Perceptually inaccurate responses also began to appear on Card III. These observations seem to confirm that, particularly in unfamiliar, emotionally charged, or complex situations, Catherine could initially maintain outwardly normal behavior—but only for brief periods. Over time, the quality of her perception and thinking would decline, eventually giving way to disorganized speech and behavior, and a general loss of control.

Despite the severity of Catherine's cognitive deficits, she retained some ability to pick up on obvious cues and maintain conventional behavior, at least superficially, and in familiar, structured situations (*P* = 5). Additionally, the good quality of her human representations (*GHR:PHR* = 2:1) suggested some degree of well-preserved interpersonal functioning. These features may have led some observers to underestimate her cognitive impairment—for example, attributing her difficulties to depression rather than dementia. Notably, all her popular responses occurred on the first seven cards, while 60 percent of her perceptually inaccurate responses (*FQ–*) came after that. As observed on the WCST or regarding the organization of her thinking on the Rorschach, Catherine's performance tended to deteriorate over time across a wide range of tasks and perspectives. Particularly in new situations, she would tend to find it increasingly difficult to maintain cognitive flexibility, stay focused, or perceive things conventionally over time. In social interactions, she may have initially made a good first impression, but as situations progressed she would tend to struggle to interpret what was happening, process new information, and respond appropriately. This pattern of fatigue—manifesting as mental exhaustion or reduced ability to maintain focus—is common in neurodegenerative diseases such as Alzheimer's disease and often emerges early, possibly involving neural systems also linked to cognitive decline (Angioni et al., 2023).

Overall, Catherine's performance on the Rorschach was very consistent with what one would expect to see in a neurocognitive disorder in general (Ilonen et al., 2016; Piotrowski, 1937), and in dementia or DAT in particular (Muzio, 2006; Muzio et al., 2001; Muzio & Luperto, 1999; Perry et al., 1996). What seemed a little unusual in this context, however, was the fact that Catherine had apparently maintained some capacity to reflect, to think things through and to mentalize (*M* = 2), as well as some capacity to avoid being overly engaged in the processing of new, complex, and emotionally arousing or potentially exhausting stimuli (*Zf* = 4; *Afr* = 0.33; *DQv* = 6).

A common feature in the early stages of DAT is anosognosia, often reflected in limited capacity for reflection and mentalization (*M* typically = 0 or 1) as well as in an overestimation of one's functional abilities, typically resulting in normal values for *Zf*. In contrast, Catherine's performance suggested that she retained some painful awareness of her cognitive decline. This likely contributed to her self-critical attitudes, depressive symptoms, and emotional distress.

Diagnoses, Summary/Discussion Session, and Treatment Plan

Based on the multidisciplinary and multimethod assessment, a diagnosis of DAT according to DSM-IV criteria (American Psychiatric Association, 1994), as well as a diagnosis of probable Alzheimer's disease, according to National Institute of Neurological and Communicative Disorders and Stroke and the Alzheimer's Disease and Related Disorders Association criteria (McKhann et al., 1984) were established. Additionally, it was considered that Catherine was suffering from a chronic adjustment disorder with depressed mood (DSM-IV criteria) in reaction to the severe and progressive decline of her cognitive functions.

The results of the assessment were discussed very openly and in detail with Catherine and her husband. Although Catherine appeared to be a little more surprised by the diagnoses than her husband, both Catherine and her husband had considered the decline in memory functions to be mild to moderate rather than severe in nature. We discussed how this was probably because many of Catherine's cognitive functions were still preserved at this early stage of the disease, which allowed her to adapt to certain situations in her everyday life, particularly those that were familiar and precisely defined. Catherine's cognitive impairment probably became more apparent in unfamiliar situations which required learning new information, synthesizing ideas, or engaging in more complex forms of problem-solving. Furthermore, the severity of her impairment would tend to become more apparent in situations that required sustained attention over longer periods.

In agreement with Catherine and her husband, a cholinesterase inhibitor (Aricept) was prescribed, in hope that it would improve cognitive performance or, at least, slow down the decline in cognitive performance.[4] The importance of emotional support, reasonable levels of cognitive stimulation, as well as regular exercise were discussed, with a particular emphasis on the importance of rest to avoid mental exhaustion. It was also agreed that Catherine would come back for follow-up assessments, which would allow us to monitor treatment outcome. Additionally, it was agreed that the couple as well as the geriatrician and I would later meet with the department's social worker to discuss possible practical next steps to support both Catherine and her immediate family, based on Catherine's and her family's situation and wishes.

Follow-up Assessment at Six Months

At her six-month follow-up, Catherine arrived with her husband and appeared largely unchanged at first glance. She initially reported feeling well, but a more detailed interview revealed she was still moderately depressed (MADRS = 20/60). Her husband was unsure—at times he felt Catherine's condition had remained stable, but at other times he believed her cognitive capacity might have deteriorated further.

Catherine's neurocognitive screening results indicated significant deterioration since the initial assessment (MMSE = 17/30; BEC96 = 50.5/96). BEC96 subtests showed that impairment had progressed beyond memory, orientation, and executive functions to include broader deficits, with worsening visual-constructional dyspraxia. Only a few abilities—such as object recognition and execution of simple motor tasks—remained relatively intact. Her performance on the Grober and Buschke memory test remained severely impaired but now included a marked increase in false recognitions, as she tended to endorse nearly all distractors, regardless of categorical similarity. This pattern suggested the adoption of a new compensatory strategy: answering "yes" to every recognition item to increase the chance of being correct at least some of the time.

Catherine's WCST performance had deteriorated markedly since the initial assessment. Total Errors declined from low average (SS = 82) to extremely low (SS = 63), and Conceptual Level Responses dropped from SS = 83 to SS = 60, indicating a loss of strategic problem-solving and conceptual understanding of the task. When asked what she understood about the task, she replied, "For me it's difficult . . . you have to put them all together," reflecting confusion and random responding. Her execution was slower, marked by hesitation and repeated placement of cards on top of key cards despite repeated reminders—a severe form of stimulus-boundedness and frontal-executive dysfunction not previously observed. Perseverative errors increased (SS = 66), and she also made numerous nonperseverative errors (SS = 71), now distributed throughout the test, suggesting global executive decline rather than fatigue. She failed to complete a single category over 128 trials, indicating significant deterioration in executive functioning.

Follow-up Assessment at Fourteen Months

Fourteen months after the initial assessment, Catherine's neuropsychological profile had deteriorated further, though some functions remained stable (MMSE = 13/30; BEC96 = 52.5/96). Her memory performance declined again on the Grober and Buschke test, with only immediate recall remaining stable. WCST administration was discontinued after thirty-two trials due to severely impaired performance. As before, she was slow, confused, and repeatedly placed cards incorrectly despite reminders. When asked about the task, her response—"It's actually difficult"—was even more vague than before. Clinically, she now appeared severely depressed (MADRS = 30/60), with pronounced depressed mood, tension, agitation, poor appetite, anhedonia, and marked self-criticism. She appeared to be easily overwhelmed, showed little initiative, and, according to her husband, had occasionally expressed suicidal thoughts. When asked to write a sentence of her choice as part of the MMSE, she wrote: "I feel more like going to the grave."

Follow-up Assessment at Twenty-Six Months

More than two years after the initial evaluation, Catherine showed substantial cognitive decline. She appeared more detached than tense or sad, though some depressive features persisted (MADRS = 17/60), including some tearfulness and self-criticism during the testing. However, her appetite had returned, she was less self-critical than before and had not recently expressed suicidal thoughts. As she put it: "I'm trying to get back on my feet, to fight, to do what's necessary, because I want to stay without . . ." and, regarding negative thoughts, "Yes, before, but now I avoid it."

Her husband reported a marked loss of autonomy, even in basic tasks. During the interview, Catherine often gave vague or brief answers (e.g., "I don't know") but could still produce coherent sentences, such as: "Since I can't manage to do anything, it frustrates me, and that's it." Screening tests revealed severe, global impairment (MMSE = 10/30; BEC96 = 23/96). Given the level of deterioration, the Grober and Buschke test and WCST were not readministered.

Signs of stimulus-bound behavior and frontal-executive dysfunction were widespread. For example, when asked to perform Luria's motor sequences, she would repeatedly put her hand next to mine or on top of it, instead of keeping it at a distance, as required by the task. On the BEC96 visual-constructive cube-copying task, she extended the model by attaching her drawing to it, instead of copying the model right below it at a distance, as required by the task. Still, some abilities were relatively well preserved, including object recognition, verbal communication, and reading. Despite the progressive and severe deterioration of her cognitive functioning—particularly her ability to conceptualize and integrate complex information—my clinical impression was that Catherine had retained some degree of insight into her condition. She did not appear to exhibit the level of anosognosia typically expected in a patient with DAT at this stage. Instead, she seemed at least partly aware of her decline, and her depressed mood appeared to reflect the painful reality of what she was experiencing.

Follow-up Assessment at Twenty-Six Months: Contributions of the Rorschach

The Rorschach was readministered in this final assessment to better understand Catherine's experience of herself and the world beyond what could be gathered through interviews, observation, or standard neuropsychological tests. Her follow-up protocol, presented in Appendix B at the end of the book, was psychometrically invalid due to an extremely low number of responses (R = 11), indicating the severity of her widespread cognitive decline and the loss of her ability to associate unfamiliar stimuli with internal representations.[5] As Meyer et al. (2011, p. 1) note, "the behavioral expressions of Rorschach assessed characteristics are most likely to emerge spontaneously over time and to be expressed in relatively unfamiliar and unstructured situations in which individuals must rely on themselves for direction." Catherine's constricted performance reflected both her significant loss of autonomy and severe impairments across the multiple cognitive domains engaged by the Rorschach task—attention, scanning, pattern recognition, executive function, and semantic/conceptual processing—as described by Acklin and Wu-Holt (1996). Notably, fMRI findings by Giromini et al. (2017) demonstrate that the Rorschach activates temporooccipital and frontoparietal regions, as well as limbic structures—all areas affected in dementia of the Alzheimer's type—highlighting the test's relevance for detecting neurodegenerative changes.

Though her Rorschach was psychometrically unreliable and invalid, several qualitative observations were clinically meaningful. Catherine now showed a significant number (> 4) of Piotrowski's organic signs (1937), which was not the case in her initial protocol. She struggled to respond despite repeated encouragements and frequently said, "I don't remember anymore," or "I don't know," treating the task more like a memory test than a test of interpretation.[6] This loss of the interpretive stance became clear on Card VIII: "Here there are two little mice, right?" followed by, "And here . . . what is that then?" On Card IX, after a long series of encouragements, she hesitantly said "the lower back," laughed, then withdrew the response without offering a new one—a classic Piotrowskian sign of "impotence."[7] When asked to locate the image on the card, she first pointed to her own body. This confusion between the external stimulus and her own body continued on Card X, where she asked, "What is this?" and then guessed, "Something on the lower back?" while seeking confirmation. Her world appeared to have become concrete and undifferentiated, marked by a collapse of interpretive distance or what Winnicott (1971) referred to as *potential space*—an intermediate area of experiencing between the subjective and the objective, where inner and external reality meet.

Her responses also showed semantic perseveration, revolving around animals, islands, and body parts—especially "the lower back," reflecting cognitive rigidity, social detachment and vulnerability. "A small island" was her sign-in response this time, reinforcing the centrality of her experience of isolation accompanied by low-quality, vague processing. Yet she also produced two unspecified human responses ("two characters") on Cards III and VII, showing some preserved awareness of others when actively supported and encouraged.

Cognitive disintegration was perhaps most evident in what followed her sign-in "A small island" response: "What else can I say: 'See you soon'? Ah, that's a bit . . . (looks to the side) . . . No, it can't be an island?" These comments convey a severe loss of focus and context, as well as a sense of perplexity and discomfort. The second island response was the first response to Card VII, where one of her two *M* responses had been given in the initial administration. This time the island preceded the popular human response, confirming again the increased centrality of Catherine's experience of social isolation and detachment.

Although the protocol was too brief for quantitative scoring, several other qualitative observations stood out: (1) all responses were form-based; (2) perceptual inaccuracy increased in the latter half of the test (*FQ–* on Cards V, VI, IX, and X); (3) two of these were semantic perseverations; and (4) despite brevity, she succeeded in producing a normal number of popular responses ($P = 4$). These findings reflected a rigid, concrete, and simplistic processing style, a decline in perceptual accuracy related to fatigue, an incapacity to sustain focus over time, and limited cognitive flexibility. Yet she could still behave conventionally when cues were obvious—masking the depth of her impairment during brief and familiar social interactions.

In Conclusion

Catherine was referred to an outpatient clinical gerontology department for memory problems and suspected depression. The initial assessment included interviews with her and her family, a physical and neurological exam by a geriatrician, blood tests, brain MRI, and a multimethod neuropsychological evaluation including the Rorschach CS. Findings supported a diagnosis of DAT and probable Alzheimer's disease, along with a chronic adjustment disorder with depressed mood in response to her cognitive decline. A cholinesterase inhibitor (Aricept) was prescribed in hopes of slowing the progression. Cognitive deficits included severe memory impairment and moderate deficits in attention and executive functions, which worsened as Catherine became overburdened by more demanding, novel or complex situations. Other cognitive domains were largely preserved or only mildly affected.

Catherine's Rorschach performance reflected many features typical of DAT: markedly reduced adaptive coping abilities; impaired capacity to integrate information and make syntheses; a rigid, concrete, and avoidant perceptual-cognitive style; difficulty shifting attention; and perceptual disorganization under emotional stress or cognitive overload. Yet, as often seen in the early stages of DAT, she retained the ability to connect stimuli to representations in long-term memory (*R*) and to behave conventionally in familiar, well-defined contexts (*P*). In clinical gerontology settings, such patients are often described as having a "good veneer"—a seemingly intact facade masking severe impairment.[8] As Barry Ritzler has said (personal communication, October 4, 2008), popular responses can be seen as reflecting a person's "capacity to talk about the weather"—a fitting metaphor for the ability to engage in superficial and expected social exchanges, which Catherine had preserved despite significant decline.[9]

In addition to typical DAT features, Catherine's Rorschach showed patterns not commonly seen in early-stage cases, likely reflecting unique aspects of her experience and psychological makeup. Most notably, she appeared to retain some capacity to mentalize, reflect, and empathize, as indicated by two *M* responses. As Meyer et al. (2011, p. 355) noted, *M* reflects "awareness, agency, deliberation, and purposefulness . . . seeing the self as the agent or the initiator of the experience." Catherine also showed greater avoidance and less effortful processing than is typical at this stage (*Zf* = 4; *Afr* = .33; *DQv* = 6), alongside pronounced self-criticism during task failures. These findings suggest an unusual degree of insight into her decline. She also seemed to maintain some interest in others (*SumH* = 3), which may have intensified her sense of isolation (*Isolate/R* = .30) and concerns with self-image (*An* + *Xy* = 6). Finally, her thinking appeared more disorganized than typically observed in early-stage DAT, particularly in novel or demanding situations requiring sustained focus.

Follow-up neuropsychological assessments at six, fourteen, and twenty-six months confirmed a rapid and progressive cognitive decline. This pattern is common in early-onset Alzheimer's disease (under age sixty-five), where nonmemory domains—especially visual perception, praxis, and executive functions—decline more steeply than in late-onset cases, typically after severe memory deterioration has occurred (Tort-Merino et al., 2022). Catherine's profile exemplified this progression: by the final assessment, her cognitive deterioration was extremely severe and had generalized across most domains.

As part of the final assessment, the Rorschach was readministered. Catherine's performance had deteriorated significantly, mirroring her cognitive decline, and was now extremely impoverished and psychometrically invalid. Despite repeated encouragement, she produced only eleven responses. From a qualitative perspective, her processing and coping style appeared increasingly rigid and simplistic, with perceptual accuracy worsening over time—likely due to difficulty shifting attention and integrating multiple perspectives, as demonstrated earlier. Still, she retained some capacity to behave appropriately in familiar, well-structured situations over brief periods, which may have—at times—masked the severity of her condition. When sufficiently supported and encouraged, brief signs of preserved self-awareness and interest in others could still emerge.

Catherine was experiencing a rapidly progressing form of early-onset Alzheimer's disease, both in expected and uniquely personal ways that the Rorschach helped illuminate. Her experience appeared to involve elements of trauma, dissociation, distress, helplessness, social isolation, and vulnerability. Although anosognosia is common even in the early stages of DAT, Catherine seemed to retain a painful awareness of her decline—a double-edged experience that likely contributed to fluctuations in her depression and anxiety. Her depression worsened by the fourteen-month follow-up but returned to moderate levels by the final assessment, as her cognitive deterioration deepened and her capacity to mentalize, sustain self-awareness, and connect with others began to fade—though stimulation and support could still revive these capacities to some extent.

Summary and discussion sessions were conducted on three separate occasions throughout the follow-up period. These sessions aimed to help Catherine and her family gain a deeper understanding of Catherine's condition and to discuss practical considerations for the immediate future. During these sessions, the metaphor of the island played a significant role in providing Catherine, Catherine's husband and their younger son with a window into Catherine's experience of being in a very lonely place, which she sometimes felt the need to escape to in an attempt to recuperate from the demands of even the most ordinary daily tasks. These sessions turned out to be emotionally meaningful, bringing Catherine, her husband, and her younger son even closer together as a family living with Alzheimer's. In her tragic and irreversible descent into nonexistence, Catherine was not alone.

Notes

1 Personal details and background information have been altered or withheld to protect the patient's identity and ensure confidentiality.
2 The MMSE is a brief neurocognitive screening tool assessing orientation, memory, attention, language, and visual-spatial skills, commonly used to detect and monitor cognitive impairment in geriatric settings. Scores range from 0 to 30. The BEC96 is a brief French neurocognitive screening tool that assesses multiple cognitive domains (e.g., orientation, memory, reasoning, visual-spatial skills) and has the advantage of including subscales, unlike the MMSE. Scores range from 0 to 96.
3 The hippocampus plays a critical role in the consolidation of information from short-term memory to long-term memory.
4 Aricept (donepezil) is an acetylcholinesterase inhibitor that increases acetylcholine levels to support memory and learning. It may improve or slow cognitive decline in some patients with Alzheimer's disease.

5 Given that R < 14, the reliability and validity of quantitative data was considered insufficient (Exner, 1988). For this reason, the protocol was not coded and values for the Structural Summary were not computed.
6 I deviated from standard CS administration by encouraging Catherine to take her time and respond to each card, as it became clear the protocol would otherwise be excessively brief.
7 Catherine used the French term *les reins*, which can mean either kidneys or lower back. Given her gestures and comments, "lower back" is likely the intended meaning, making *Hd* (human detail) a more appropriate code than *An* (anatomy).
8 In French: *Avoir un bon vernis.*
9 Autumn Seminar of the Finnish Rorschach Association, Helsinki, October 4–5, 2008.

References

Acklin, M. W., & Wu-Holt, P. (1996). Contributions of cognitive science to the Rorschach technique: Cognitive and neuropsychological correlates of the response process. *Journal of Personality Assessment*, 67(1), 169–178. doi:10.1207/s15327752jpa6701_13.

American Psychiatric Association. (1994). *Diagnostic and statistical manual of mental disorders* (4th ed.). doi:10.1176/appi.books.9780890423349

Angioni, D., Raffin, J., Ousset, P. J., Delrieu, J., & de Souto Barreto, P. (2023). Fatigue in Alzheimer's disease: Biological basis and clinical management—a narrative review. *Aging Clinical and Experimental Research*, 35(10), 1981–1989. doi:10.1007/s40520-023-02482-z.

Armstrong, J. G. (2002). Deciphering the broken narrative of trauma: Signs of traumatic dissociation on the Rorschach. *Rorschachiana*, 25(1), 11–27.

Exner, J. E. (1988). Problems with brief Rorschach protocols. *Journal of Personality Assessment*, 52(4), 640–647. doi:10.1207/s15327752jpa5204_4.

Exner, J. E. (2003). *The Rorschach: A comprehensive system: Volume 1: Basic foundations and principles of interpretation* (4th ed.). Wiley.

Folstein, M. F., Folstein, S. E., & McHugh, P. R. (1975). Mini-mental state: A practical method for grading the cognitive state of patients for the clinician. *Journal of Psychiatric Research*, 12(3), 189–198. doi:10.1016/0022-3956(75)90026-6.

Giromini, L., Viglione, D. J., Zennaro, A., & Cauda, F. (2017). Neural activity during production of Rorschach responses: An fMRI study. *Psychiatry Research: Neuroimaging*, 262, 25–31.

Grober, E., & Buschke, H. (1987). Genuine memory deficits in dementia. *Developmental Neuropsychology*, 3(1), 13–36. doi:10.1080/87565648709540361.

Hachinski, V., Oveisgharan, S., Romney, A. K., & Shankle, W. R. (2012). Optimizing the Hachinski Ischemic Scale. *Archives of Neurology*, 69(2), 169–175. doi:10.1001/archneur01.2011.1698.

Heaton, R. K., Chelune, G. J., Talley, J. L., Kay, G. G., & Curtiss, G. (1993). *Wisconsin Card Sorting Test Manual: Revised and expanded.* Psychological Assessment Resources.

Ilonen, T., Salokangas, R. K. R., & Turku Study Group. (2016). The Rorschach Coping Deficit Index as an indicator of neurocognitive dysfunction. *Rorschachiana*, 37(1), 28–40. doi:10.1027/1192-5604/a000075.

McKhann, G., Drachman, D., Folstein, M., Katzman, R., Price, D., & Stadlan, E. M. (1984). Clinical diagnosis of Alzheimer's disease: Report of the NINCD-SADRDA Work Group under the auspices of Department of Health and Human Services Task Force on Alzheimer's Disease. *Neurology*, 34(7), 939–944. doi:10.1212/WNL.34.7.939.

Meyer, G. J., Erard, R. E., Erdberg, P., Mihura, J. L., & Viglione, D. J. (2011). *Rorschach Performance Assessment System: Administration coding interpretation and technical manual*. Rorschach Performance Assessment System LLC.

Montgomery, S. A., & Åsberg, M. (1979). A new depression scale designed to be sensitive to change. *The British Journal of Psychiatry*, 134(4), 382–389. doi:10.1192/bjp.134.4.382.

Muzio, E. (2006). Vers une approche neuropsychologique intégrée de la personnalité à travers le Rorschach en gériatrie et dans la démence de type Alzheimer [Toward an integrated neuropsychological approach of personality through the Rorschach in geriatrics and dementia of the Alzheimer's type]. Doctoral dissertation. University of Paris X–Nanterre.

Muzio, E., Andronikof, A., David, J. P., & Di Menza, C. (2001). L'intérêt du test du Rorschach (Système Intégré) dans l'évaluation psychométrique en gériatrie: exemple de la démence de type Alzheimer [Contribution of the Rorschach test (Comprehensive System) to psychometric assessment in geriatrics: The example of dementia of the Alzheimer's type]. *Revue de Gériatrie*, 26(2), 121–130.

Muzio, E., & Luperto, L. (1999). Démence et fonctionnement de la personnalité à travers le Rorschach chez un groupe de femmes âgées hospitalisées [Dementia and personality functioning through the Rorschach in a group of hospitalized elderly women]. *European Review of Applied Psychology/Revue Européenne de Psychologie Appliquée*, 49(3), 227–236.

Perry, W., Potterat, E., Auslander, L., Kaplan, E., & Jeste, D. (1996). A neuropsychological approach to the Rorschach in patients with dementia of the Alzheimer type. *Assessment*, 3(3), 351–363. doi:10.1177/107319119600300314.

Piotrowski, Z. (1937). The Rorschach inkblot method in organic disturbances of the central nervous system. *The Journal of Nervous and Mental Disease*, 86(5), 525–537. doi:10.1097/00005053-193711000-00002.

Signoret, J. L., Allard, M., Benoit, N., Bolgert, F., Bonvarlet, M., & Eustache, F. (1989). *Evaluation des troubles de mémoire et des désordres cognitifs associés: BEC 96 [Evaluation of memory disorders and associated cognitive disorders: BEC 96]*. Ipsen.

Tort-Merino, A., Falgas, N., Allen, I. E., Balasa, M., Olives, J., Contador, J., Castellví, M., Juncà-Parella, J., Guillén, N., Borrego-Écija, S., Bosch, B., Fernández-Villullas, G., Ramos-Campoy, O., Antonell, A., Rami, L., Sánchez-Valle, R., & Lladó, A. (2022). Early-onset Alzheimer's disease shows a distinct neuropsychological profile and more aggressive trajectories of cognitive decline than late-onset. *Annals of Clinical and Translational Neurology*, 9(12), 1962–1973. doi:10.1002/acn3.51689.

Winnicott, D. W. (1971). *Playing and reality*. Tavistock.

Chapter 8

"A Middle Finger"

A Case of Attention-Deficit/Hyperactivity Disorder, Personality Disorder, and Traumatic Brain Injury

"Ville" was a 21-year-old Finnish man undergoing comprehensive medical, neurological, psychosocial, and neuropsychological follow-up at a specialized multidisciplinary rehabilitation center for spinal cord and traumatic brain injury (TBI) where I was working as a psychologist at the time.[1] Two years earlier, he had been involved in a motor-vehicle accident that resulted in diffuse axonal injury and spinal-cord damage causing tetraplegia. Since then, Ville had used a wheelchair.

Records indicated a long-standing history of academic and behavioral difficulties beginning in early childhood. These included poor school performance, temper outbursts, unstable interpersonal relationships, impulsive and violent behavior (frequent fighting), substance abuse (alcohol, cannabis, amphetamines), and depressive symptoms, which intensified in adolescence.

Ville was the eldest of three brothers. His father, who struggled with depression and alcohol abuse, was emotionally abusive and violent toward the family. After his parents separated when Ville was five, he lived with his mother and her new partner. At sixteen, he moved into a shared apartment and enrolled in a vocational program to become an electrician but dropped out due to depression and substance abuse. With support from his mother and psychiatric outpatient care, he later enrolled in culinary school, which he also discontinued due to mental-health issues. Months later, he was in a serious car accident when a friend, under the influence of drugs and alcohol, lost control and crashed the vehicle.

A year before the current assessment, Ville completed a similar multidisciplinary rehabilitation program, including a neuropsychological evaluation. That assessment revealed neurocognitive sequelae of TBI—especially deficits in executive functioning (notably impulsivity), attention, working memory, and processing speed—as well as probable attention-deficit/hyperactivity disorder (ADHD) based on Ville's developmental history. Although some improvement had occurred, significant impairments remained in driving, occupational, and academic functioning.

The current assessment, conducted two years post-injury, aimed to reevaluate Ville's cognitive status and functional abilities. Given the

DOI: 10.4324/9781003731894-10

complexity of his emotional and cognitive presentation, a multi-method approach for assessing personality and psychopathology was also employed, including the Rorschach, to better understand Ville's strengths and vulnerabilities for purposes of identifying relevant treatment targets and methods if deemed necessary. At the time, Ville lived alone with support from a personal assistant and was active in wheelchair athletics. He moved independently and rapidly using his wheelchair.

Ville was cooperative but often passive and tense in assessment sessions. He frequently responded with "I don't know" and rarely elaborated his responses. He appeared agitated, irritable, and impulsive, and expressed frustration about his condition. He believed his disability warranted permanent retirement. He moved swiftly between sessions, sometimes bumping into walls or corners, and occasionally asked for tranquilizers, which I encouraged him to discuss with his physician. Despite his guardedness, Ville showed strong social skills in peer interactions—frequently seen joking and socializing with other young wheelchair users in the facility's courtyard.

Neuropsychological and Self-Report-Based Assessment Findings

On the Wechsler Adult Intelligence Scale—Revised (WAIS-R; Wechsler, 1992), Ville showed average verbal abilities (VIQ = 96) with minimal scatter among subtests. His lowest score was on Comprehension (Standard Score [SS] = 7), suggesting slightly simplistic and immature thinking, though no major issues in verbal reasoning or expression were observed. In contrast, his visual-motor performance was in the high average to superior range (PIQ = 119), with no subtest falling below average (SS = 10). Strengths included spatial processing, visual-construction, and the rapid perception of key details. Ville appeared to be particularly good at evaluating social situations (Picture Completion SS = 16; Picture Arrangement SS = 15). Compared to the previous year, his processing speed and visual-spatial processing and vigilance had notably improved, indicating that difficulties at school had probably not been due to limited intellectual capacity.

On the Wechsler Memory Scale—Revised (WMS-R; Wechsler, 1997), verbal memory was in the low average range (VEM = 88), largely due to impulsive responding on the verbal learning subtest. Visual memory was in the high average range (VIM = 115). Attention and working memory were also low average (ATT/C = 88). Performances on the Rey-Osterrieth Complex Figure Test (Meyers & Meyers, 1995), Trail Making Test A and B (TMT-A and TMT-B; Reitan, 1958), and the Wisconsin Card Sorting Test (WCST; Heaton et al., 1993) were generally average. However, Ville showed an above-average number of failures to maintain set on the WCST, reflecting nonperseverative and impulsive errors. Across tasks, a consistent pattern of hastiness and impulsivity was evident, often undermining performance on tasks requiring sustained focus and self-regulation.

In addition to the neurocognitive testing and given the fact that Ville had previously been diagnosed with depression, I asked him to complete the Beck Depression Inventory (BDI-II; Beck et al., 2004). His score was 20/63, suggesting moderate depression. The highest ratings were for items concerning the feeling that the future has nothing to offer, a sense of dissatisfaction and lack of fulfillment in life in general, a lack of feelings toward other people, and a sense of having lost all occupational capacity.

Contributions of the Rorschach

Ville's complete Rorschach protocol transcribed verbatim and including documentation on response locations, the Sequence of Codes, and the Structural Summary are all presented in Appendix C at the end of the book. The Rorschach was administered and scored according to the Comprehensive System (CS; Exner, 2003).

Ville was clearly engaged in the task and produced a valid protocol with an above-average number of responses (*R* = 26). However, his coping and problem-solving orientation appeared to be overly simplistic and concrete, suggesting a tendency to seek out quick and straightforward solutions even to complex problems (*Lambda* = 1.60; *Blends* = 2). He also appeared to rely almost exclusively on thinking and inner deliberation processes when making decisions, almost completely bypassing the verbal-semantic processing and integration of emotions, or the possibility of using more intuitive, trial-and-error approaches when appropriate (*EB* = 7:0.5). His thinking was superficial, oversimplistic, and inflexible (*a:p* = 7:2; *PSV* = 1), leaving him vulnerable to emotional intrusions when confronted with complexity or ambiguity. This rigid coping style allowed him to be at his best only in straightforward, familiar or unambiguous situations.

Although Ville appeared to have an average level of adaptive resources (*EA* = 7.5) and was inclined to spontaneously integrate ideas and percepts (*DQ+* = 9), these resources were being significantly undermined by three factors. First, they were being undermined by Ville's tendency to ignore important aspects of his emotional life, needs, as well as environmental cues, subtleties and feedback (*WSumC* = 0.5; *FM* = 2; *Lambda* = 1.60; *Zd* = –6.5; *es* = 2). This was impoverishing the quality and depth of his relationship to himself and to others, as well as his efficiency in solving complex emotional or interpersonal problems. Second, his potential in terms of mentalization was being significantly undermined by a pervasive tendency to misperceive things and to misinterpret what people say and do (*M–* = 3; *X–%* = 0.46). These factors significantly reduced Ville's stress tolerance and helped better understand his tendency to turn to drugs and alcohol as a way of coping with emotional discomfort. Third, he sometimes integrated ideas and percepts in ways that were unusual or bizarre (*FAB2* = 2).

Another key feature of Ville's Rorschach was the presence of a positive Hyper-Vigilance Index (*HVI*). A positive *HVI* typically suggests some degree of preoccupation with vulnerability, a mistrusting attitude toward the environment, a constant state of alertness, and a suspicious attitude toward gestures of closeness by others. Especially in the presence of a tendency to distort information to the degree that Ville did, hypervigilance constitutes fertile ground for the emergence of paranoid or paranoid-like features. This helped better understand Ville's history of unstable relationships, frequent fighting, and violent behavior.

Based on Ville's history and clinical presentation there was no reason to believe he was or had previously been actively psychotic. However, as already mentioned, the Rorschach did suggest that he tended to misperceive and misinterpret situations on a regular basis (*X–%* = 0.46). Additionally, his performance on the Rorschach suggested that at times his thinking was seriously disturbed by a tendency to connect ideas or percepts in inappropriate ways (*WSum6* = 17; *FAB2* = 2). Taken together, these two features created a Rorschach profile including significantly more signs of severe psychopathology and psychotic phenomena than what is typically found in people (Ego Impairment Index [*EII-2*] = 2.23; Viglione et al., 2003; Perceptual-Thinking Index [*PTI*] = 3). His perceptual inaccuracy appeared to be associated with concerns about his bodily integrity and body image (all three *An* responses were *FQ–*), as well as oppositional tendencies and paranoid concerns (e.g., R12: "A middle finger"; R21: "A creature with a hanging trunk . . . peaking from behind a bush"; or R25: "Eyes . . ."). In terms of the clarity and coherence of his thinking, it was important to note that, although cognitive codes were sparse in his protocol and mostly of the milder variety, suggesting immaturity or playfulness, Ville did give three responses which indicated instances of disordered thinking. First, Ville gave a response that approached a contamination (*CON*) on Card I where the head of a bat was seen where people usually see a whole bat (R2), leaving the impression of a possible fusion or overlap between the percept of the frequently seen head and the percept of the popular bat. This appeared to underscore how more open-ended, complex, and potentially emotionally arousing situations might be confusing for Ville. Second, and most notably, Ville gave two consecutive responses to Card III where he combined or integrated separate objects in ways that were unusual or bizarre (*FAB2*). The first was a response where two women in high heels were seen carrying a cockroach's or a grasshopper's head (R8), and the second was one where Ville suggested it "could also be birds carrying a cockroach's head, wearing high heels" (R9), which prompted him to laugh. Although both responses represented bizarre combinatory thinking, the way Ville appeared to be delivering them and relating to them also included a humoristic and playful quality. Given the aspects of card pull generally attributed to Card III as evoking associations to interpersonal relationships, it is easy to speculate that both these facets—the bizarreness and the playfulness—characterized the way Ville approached social situations. Both responses could also be characterized as "spoiled" *COP*s in that they included an element of cooperative social interaction accompanied by perceptual inaccuracy, bizarre combinatory thinking and distorted mentalizing (both were *M* with *FQ*–).

Ville's tendency to distort information or to integrate concepts or percepts unrealistically might have been a consequence of his impulsive and hasty processing style, as well as his tendency to oversimplify things and jump to conclusions (*Zd* = –6.5; *Lambda* = 1.60; *FM* = 2). In this sense, at least some of his more severe psychopathology might have been a consequence of ADHD. Indeed, although Ville presented hypervigilant and paranoid-like features, the quality of his attention and information processing was poor.

Ville's performance on the Rorschach also suggested a marked tendency to avoid emotionally arousing stimuli (*Afr* = 0.37). He felt uncomfortable when dealing with emotions, presented a strong tendency to suppress emotional expression, and appeared detached from the subtle nuances of his inner life (*WSumC* = 0.5, *es* = 2; *Lambda* = 1.60). This made him particularly vulnerable to impulsive and intense emotional outbursts when experiencing stress or distress. Furthermore, he appeared to deal with need states and more complicated or frustrating situations by seeking immediate and concrete forms of gratification (*FM* = 2; *Lambda* = 1.60). These findings helped better understand Ville's history of alcohol and drug abuse, as well as his history of impulsive and violent behavior.

Ville's performance on the Rorschach suggested that his relationships were marked by ambivalence. He was interested in others (*SumH* = 9), but also tended to be interpersonally dependent, in need for support and guidance, and markedly sensitive to rejection. This was suggested by his use of oral dependent language (*ODL*) in 23 percent of his response phase verbalizations (Meyer et al., 2011, p. 362). Concurrently, his interest in others and dependent behaviors were accompanied by social hypervigilance, mistrust in others and paranoid preoccupations (positive *HVI*). He was uncomfortable around people (*H*:[*H*] + *Hd* + [*Hd*] = 3:6; *M*– = 2), his representations of others were markedly disturbed, and his social interactions for the most part maladaptive (*GHR:PHR* = 3:7). Although there were suggestions that he could be cooperative and playful, as well as an appreciated member of the social groups with which he interacted (*COP* = 3), these apparent social skills were accompanied by distorted perception and bizarre combinatory thinking, as previously described. These findings regarding the interpersonal domain were consistent with the development of an unresolved attachment style (e.g., Cassidy & Shaver, 2016) which typically develops through a history of insecure attachment relationships in early childhood. Ville's two *ODL*-coded responses on Card VII, which some refer to as the "mother card," probably best capture this ambivalence, as well as the mechanism of splitting from a qualitative perspective.[2] On this card, Ville first sees "two Indians kissing again" (R18; note that he had not seen two Indians kissing earlier in the protocol), and then "a strange-looking monster, the mouth right there . . . very angry . . . it's angry" (R19). This form of attachment and underlying anger rendered Ville particularly vulnerable to ruptures in his relationships or in the therapeutic alliance in treatment, for example. Additionally, the presence of extended aggression codes in the protocol (*AgC* in R2, R19 and R22; *AgPast* in R16) suggested that Ville considered aggression as a natural part of human interaction (Gacono & Smith, 2022).

The way Ville saw himself was both simplistic (*Lambda* = 1.60) and distorted (*X–%* = 0.46). He was preoccupied by a sense of vulnerability, which made him tend to attribute the causes for difficulties or failures to external forces (positive *HVI*). His hypervigilant and avoidant (high *Lambda*) style made it unlikely that he would engage in therapy, although there was some evidence of a capacity to engage in self-inspecting behaviors (*FD* = 2). Unfortunately, however, when Ville engaged in introspection, his perceptions would tend to be inaccurate (both *FD* responses were *FQ–*).

In Conclusion

Ville was a 21-year-old man who was assessed in a rehabilitation facility as part of a global multidisciplinary and multimethod assessment carried out two years after a motor-vehicle accident that left him with a spinal-cord injury and the neuropsychological sequelae of TBI (diffuse axonal injury). The assessment aimed at reevaluating his neuropsychological functioning, as well as his capacity to drive, study, and work. It also aimed at better understanding Ville's current neuropsychological strengths and vulnerabilities, as well as his psychopathology for purposes of identifying relevant treatment targets, as well as appropriate methods for further treatment and rehabilitation.

The clinical picture observed might be best described as a complex interplay between neurodevelopmental and neurocognitive issues, including not only probable ADHD and the neuropsychological sequelae of TBI but also symptoms of depression, as well as a mixed personality disorder, including borderline, paranoid, and dependent features.

In comparison to the assessment carried out one year after the accident, which described the persistence of some of the neuropsychological sequelae of TBI, the assessment described here suggested that the cognitive and functional impairment noted after the accident was in almost full remission. In addition to significant improvement on the neurocognitive testing, Ville's Rorschach profile did not look like what one would expect to see in the context of TBI. Although it is noteworthy that Ville had an avoidant coping style, particularly regarding emotional processing or engaging in emotionally arousing situations (*Lambda* = 1.60; *WSumC* = 0.5; *Afr* = 0.37), he also appeared to have numerous cognitive resources and the capacity to mentalize (*M* = 7; *EA* = 7.5). Unfortunately, however, his mentalization efforts were accompanied by significant levels of perceptual inaccuracy (*M–* = 3).

Ville's hypervigilant information processing style (*HVI*), as well as his problems with reality testing and thinking (*PTI* = 3), were also highly unusual findings in the context of TBI. In one important study mentioned in Chapter 4 (Exner et al., 1996), none of the sixty subjects with TBI (closed head injury) had a positive Schizophrenia Index (*SCZI* > 3)—an earlier and less specific version of the *PTI.* [3]

Research suggests that a high *Lambda* profile (*Lambda* > .99) is common among children and adults with ADHD (Kutz, 2006; Locke, 1998). This was also the case for Ville. Another common finding among children and adults with ADHD is significant problems with perceptual accuracy (Ando et al., 2019; Kutz, 2006; Locke, 1998). This was also the case for Ville. Although there is no single Rorschach profile that is typical of patients with ADHD, we do know that comorbidity with other mental disorders reported for patients with ADHD is common. Hence, it was not particularly surprising to find that Ville also presented features of a mixed personality disorder, as well as a history of substance abuse and depression.

Based on the information derived from the Rorschach and standard neuropsychological tests, it appeared that primary rehabilitation and treatment targets should no longer be those typically recommended for the rehabilitation of clients presenting the neuropsychological sequalae of TBI. Instead, it was suggested that rehabilitation and treatment targets should include focusing on Ville's long-standing problems with attention, impulsivity, as well as features of a mixed personality disorder, associated substance abuse and depression. It was also suggested that addressing Ville's unacknowledged (implicit) emotional and dependency needs could ultimately be of great benefit to him (Bornstein, 1998). In addition to recommending a specialized individual or group rehabilitation program for patients with ADHD, individual psychotherapy or neuropsychotherapy over a period of at least two to three years with a frequency of one or two sessions a week was recommended.[4] The idea was that this might help Ville work through some of the psychological issues which the Rorschach helped highlight. It was also suggested that treatment targets in psychotherapy for Ville might include developing anger-management strategies; learning to identify, reflect upon, and use emotions constructively; developing strategies to diminish impulsive behavior and the tendency to jump to conclusions; social-skills training; and finding ways to improve reality testing (e.g., by learning to consider situations from multiple perspectives before acting or making decisions).

Based on the Rorschach and other sources of information, major challenges in psychotherapy for Ville were likely to include a lack of engagement in treatment, an increased risk of avoidant and confrontational ruptures in the therapeutic alliance, and significant ambivalence in the therapeutic relationship. The high level of psychopathology noted in Ville's Rorschach (*EII-2* = 2.23) is typically a predictor of poorer treatment outcomes (Stenius et al., 2022), suggesting that the process was not likely to be easy. Therefore, it was recommended that considerable attention be given to building a strong therapeutic alliance from the very beginning of psychotherapy. This would involve collaboratively creating a space where Ville could feel safe, comfortable, and accepted. Given his hypervigilant style, maintaining a transparent, candid, and validating approach would be paramount.

Additionally, it was recommended that, at least in the early stages of therapy, therapeutic objectives and methods be within Ville's "comfort zone." This would mean prioritizing concrete and pragmatic approaches (e.g., cognitive-behavioral therapy) focused on Ville's problems in everyday living, problem-solving, social interactions, and coping. More psychodynamic or emotion-focused approaches addressing his inner struggles and implicit tendencies were better deferred until Ville felt ready and secure enough to address them.

Ville's cognitive functioning appeared to have returned to pre-TBI levels, and his capacity to study, work, and drive were considered to have been reestablished. This recovery was likely due to factors involving neuroplasticity, the severity and type of injury, as well as the known positive outcomes of neuropsychological rehabilitation (Cicerone et al., 2011). However, Ville's Rorschach profile suggested that much of the psychopathology observed in his childhood, adolescence, and early adulthood was still present. If left untreated, these issues could make him vulnerable to similar problems in the future. These potential problems included unstable relationships, difficulties with emotion regulation and anger management, impulsive and violent behavior, substance abuse, features of a mixed personality disorder, and feelings of hopelessness and depression.

Following my summary/discussion session with Ville, which was dedicated to collaboratively going through all the results and observations described above, we agreed that psychotherapy might prove helpful to him. We also agreed that, to help things move forward, I would contact a psychiatrist in his hometown who would write a report and assist him in finding an available psychotherapist in his area. Ville agreed that he would contact the psychiatrist and psychotherapist(s) himself whenever he felt ready to do so. Although Ville made very few comments about the results, he expressed that they made sense to him and aligned with his own understanding of the progress he had made since the accident. He seemed to appreciate that the findings also matched his impressions concerning the issues he might still need to work on in the future. While we both recognized that the treatment ahead would be challenging, this mutual understanding gave us a sense of optimism and a shared commitment to Ville's continued growth and healing.

Notes

1 Personal details and background information have been altered or withheld to protect the client's identity and ensure confidentiality.

2 A consensual definition of the defense mechanism of splitting could be the following: "The individual deals with emotional conflict or internal or external stressors by compartmentalizing opposite affect states and failing to integrate the positive and negative qualities of the self or others into cohesive images. Because ambivalent affects cannot be experienced simultaneously, more balanced views and expectations of self or others are excluded from emotional awareness. Self and object images tend to alternate between polar opposites: exclusively loving, poweful, worthy, nurturant, and kind—or exclusively bad, hateful, angry, destructive, rejecting, or worthless" (American Psychiatric Association, 1994, p. 757).

3 The *SCZI* and *PTI* are both indices designed to quantify the presence of psychotic phenomena on the Rorschach, specifically problems with perceptual accuracy and thinking. However, the *PTI* has a lower false positive rate compared to the *SCZI*. It is rarely elevated in nonpatient populations and was designed to replace the *SCZI*, addressing its often misleading diagnostic implications (Exner, 2003, pp. 390–393, 524–525).

4 Neuropsychotherapy is a form of rehabilitation that combines theoretical and clinical aspects of neuroscience, neuropsychology, and psychotherapy. In Finland, neuropsychotherapists are typically psychologists specialized in neuropsychology who work in the field of rehabilitation and who have been further trained to apply methods of psychotherapy in neuropsychological rehabilitation for various neurological and neuropsychiatric disorders (Laaksonen & Ranta, 2013).

References

American Psychiatric Association. (1994). *Diagnostic and statistical manual of mental disorders* (4th ed.). American Psychiatric Association.doi:10.1176/appi.books.9780890423349.

Ando, A., Pignolo, C., Viglione, D. J., Zennaro, A., Cristofanelli, S., & Ferro, L. (2019). Assessing the personality profile with ADHD characteristics using the Rorschach Performance Assessment System (R-PAS). *Journal of Child and Family Studies*, 28, 1196–1206. doi:10.1007/s10826-019-01359-y.

Beck, A. T., Steer, R. A., & Brown, G. K. (2004). *BDI-II: Beckin depressioasteikko, käsikirja* [*BDI–II: Beck Depression Inventory manual*] (S. A. Hautala & K. Alanne, Trans.). Psykologien Kustannus Oy.

Bornstein, R. F. (1998). Implicit and self-attributed dependency needs in dependent and histrionic personality disorders. *Journal of Personality Assessment*, 71(1), 1–14. doi:10.1207/s15327752jpa7101_1.

Cassidy, J., & Shaver, P. R. (Eds.). (2016). *Handbook of attachment: Theory, research, and clinical applications* (3rd ed.). Guilford Press.

Cicerone, K. D., Langenbahn, D. M., Braden, C., Malec, J. F., Kalmar, K., Fraas, M., Felicetti, T., Laatsch, L., Harley, J. P., Bergquist, T., Azulay, J., Cantor, J., & Ashman, T. (2011). Evidence-based cognitive rehabilitation: Updated review of the literature from 2003 through 2008. *Archives of Physical Medicine and Rehabilitation*, 92(4), 519–530. doi:10.1016/j.apmr.2010.11.015.

Exner, J. E. (2003). *The Rorschach: A comprehensive system—volume 1: Basic foundations and principles of interpretation* (4th ed.). Wiley.

Exner, J. E., Colligan, S. C., Boll, T. J., Stischer, B., & Hillman, L. (1996). Rorschach findings concerning closed head injury patients. *Assessment*, 3(3), 317–326. doi:10.1177/107319119600300301l.

Gacono, C. B., & Smith, J. M. (2022). The extended aggression scores: Assessing aggressivity with Comprehensive System-Revised. In J. M. Smith, Y. Weinberger-Katzav, & P. Fontan (Eds.), *The Rorschach: A comprehensive system—revised. Supplementary scales handbook* (pp. 22–36). Rorschach Workshops.

Heaton, R. K., Chelune, G. J., Talley, J. L., Kay, G. G., & Curtiss, G. (1993). *Wisconsin Card Sorting Test manual: Revised and expanded.* Psychological Assessment Resources.

Kutz, A. S. (2006). Social perception in children with Attention Deficit/Hyperactivity Disorder: A Rorschach study. Doctoral dissertation. University of Texas at Austin.

Laaksonen, R., & Ranta, M. (Eds.). (2013). *Introduction to neuropsychotherapy: Guidelines for rehabilitation of neurological and neuropsychiatric patients throughout the lifespan*. Psychology Press.

Locke, S. R. (1998). Adult attention deficit disorder: Its impact on Rorschach scores. Doctoral dissertation. Oklahoma State University.

Meyer, G. J., Erard, R. E., Erdberg, P., Mihura, J. L., & Viglione, D. J. (2011). *Rorschach Performance Assessment System: Administration, coding, interpretation, and technical manual.* Rorschach Performance Assessment System LLC.

Meyers, J. E., & Meyers, K. R. (1995). *Rey Complex Figure Test and Recognition Trial: Professional manual.* Psychological Assessment Resources.

Reitan, R. M. (1958). Validity of the Trail Making Test as an indicator of organic brain damage. *Perceptual and Motor Skills*, 8(3), 271–276. doi:10.2466/pms.1958.8.3.271.

Stenius, J., Heinonen, E., Lindfors, O., Holma, J., & Knekt, P. (2022). Ego Impairment Index (EII-2) as a predictor of outcome in short-and long-term psychotherapy during a 5-year follow-up. *Journal of Clinical Psychology*, 78(9), 1739–1751.doi:10.1002/jclp.23332.

Viglione, D. J., Perry, W., & Meyer, G. (2003). Refinements in the Rorschach Ego Impairment Index incorporating the Human Representational variable. *Journal of Personality Assessment*, 81(2), 149–156. doi:10.1207/S15327752JPA8102_06.

Wechsler, D. (1992). *WAIS-R Wechslerin aikuisälykkyysasteikko: Käsikirja* [*WAIS-R Wechsler Adult Intelligence Scale: Manual*] (T. Järvinen & J. Häkkinen, Trans.) Psykologien Kustannus Oy.

Wechsler, D. (1997). *Wechsler Memory Scale—Revised (WMS-R): Käsikirja* [*Wechsler Memory Scale: Revised manual*]. (M. Ruoppila, T. Era, & K. Heikkinen, Trans.) Psykologien Kustannus Oy.

Chapter 9

"I'm Having Trouble Digesting"

Grieving in a Case of Autism Spectrum Disorder

"Pekka" was a 48-year-old Finnish man who had been referred by a psychiatrist in his occupational health-care service for a comprehensive assessment in the psychiatric day hospital where I was working as a psychologist at the time.[1] The goal of the assessment was to better understand the enigmatic somatic symptoms he presented, to establish an appropriate diagnosis, to determine whether Pekka was occupationally impaired, and to develop a tailored treatment plan. In addition to allowing multiple opportunities to observe Pekka's behavior in various situations over a period of several weeks, it was thought that the day hospital setting might enhance Pekka's social support network and help with the treatment of any underlying mood, anxiety, psychotic, or other disorder that may have been contributing to his clinical presentation and symptoms.

At the time of the assessment at the day hospital, Pekka had been employed as a librarian for twenty-five years, and, for the past two years, he had had several ongoing somatic complaints. These included the experience of having trouble digesting, tiredness, dizziness, stomach pains, and clammy hands. Additionally, Pekka was worried about the possibility of having diabetes. His symptoms prompted numerous medical referrals and exams to help determine their etiology (e.g., blood glucose tests, food allergy and intolerance tests, gastrointestinal examinations, and a cardiac evaluation). No somatic etiology was found, which prompted the referral to a psychiatrist. The diagnosis established by the psychiatrist, based on a single interview, was that of an unspecified nonorganic psychotic disorder. According to the referral letter sent by the psychiatrist to the day hospital, Pekka conveyed his personal history during this session in a confused manner, exhibiting ideas of reference and incoherent thought processes. The psychiatrist also judged that Pekka's case necessitated a more comprehensive psychological and psychiatric assessment to answer the referral questions.

Until the age of thirty-six, Pekka lived with his mother. Although this might be a common occurrence in countries like Italy, for example, this is very unusual for a Finn. Subsequently, Pekka lived alone in a very modest

DOI: 10.4324/9781003731894-11

studio apartment, where he was still living at the time of the assessment. In interviews at the day hospital, he reported a long-established pattern of solitary living, with an absence of intimate relationships. He said he was "used to being alone" and comfortable with this because he had a "rich inner life." However, he did mention one long-lasting relationship with a woman also working at the library. He described this relationship as "platonic." He also described that they did have "deep conversations" but were never more intimately involved.

Pekka was the youngest sibling in a family of five children, with a family history of mental illness. Two of his brothers were identical twins and had been diagnosed with schizophrenia, the symptoms of which included somatic delusions (e.g., one of them believed that he had two hearts), and Pekka's older sister had been struggling with depression for many years. Pekka's early developmental history was complicated by his parents' divorce when Pekka was three, and his father had not been actively involved in his life after that.

Two years prior to his assessment and treatment at the psychiatric day hospital, and shortly before the onset of his numerous somatic symptoms and concerns, Pekka's mother passed away because of "complications due to high blood pressure." Toward the end of her life, she presented some degree of cognitive impairment, possibly due to the early stages of vascular dementia, although this was never confirmed. She had also been diagnosed with Type II diabetes. When questioned about his mother's passing and the significance of that event to him, Pekka responded quite matter-of-factly, stating that he was feeling "okay" and had not experienced significant difficulty in accepting it.

Pekka completed high school with commendable grades, although he mentioned experiencing challenges with subjects that required abstract reasoning, such as advanced mathematics and physics. He described getting along well with his peers and even having had a few friends at school. However, he also said he had always been rather passive in terms of engaging in and maintaining relationships. His hobbies included going to museums or exhibitions and reading (e.g., history books).

During interviews and his stay at the day hospital, Pekka exhibited some behaviors that one might qualify as unusual. These included reduced eye contact, a rigid posture, a tendency to check the time obsessively and repeatedly from a clock on the wall during interviews, and a habit of walking with a fast pace to the door of my office ahead of me every time I went to let him know it was time for our session. During interviews he spoke mostly about his multiple somatic concerns. He did not report feeling anxious, depressed, or struggling with any other psychological issue. Pekka did, however, mention having trouble dealing with difficult or demanding clients at the library where he worked. He often felt overwhelmed in these situations and preferred tasks that did not involve direct client contact.

During his six-week assessment and treatment at the day hospital, Pekka's behavior was—aside from the abovementioned idiosyncrasies—socially appropriate and mostly conventional. Along with the psychiatrist on our team, we found no clear evidence, based on clinical observation and interviews, of the presence of psychotic symptoms (e.g., delusions or hallucinations). Observations made by other staff members regarding Pekka's behavior in the common areas of the day hospital, in therapeutic groups (e.g., discussion groups, art therapy, field trips, or outdoor activities), or while carrying out various tasks (e.g., hosting the morning meetings dedicated to outlining planned activities for the day) also corroborated the idea that Pekka was not psychotic. However, we did find that Pekka's thinking took unusual turns when discussing topics related to his somatic concerns or when potentially emotionally charged issues came up. For instance, Pekka often elaborated on how he believed certain foods triggered specific somatic symptoms, making connections, and interpreting causal relationships in ways that seemed somewhat far-fetched. Moreover, these beliefs led him to continuously expand his list of foods to avoid, resulting in significant dietary restrictions and weight loss. This was particularly concerning for us, considering that Pekka was already quite thin.

Neuropsychological Assessment Findings

Results from the Weschler Adult Intelligence Scale—Revised (WAIS-R; Wechsler, 1992) indicated a high average Full-Scale IQ (FSIQ = 114), with significant scatter among subtests, particularly between verbal and visual-spatial tasks. Pekka's Verbal IQ was well above average (VIQ = 121), with little scatter across subtests. Results for VIQ subtests ranged, for the most part, between high average and well above average standard scores. The only exception to this was the standard score for Comprehension, which fell right in the middle of the average range (Standard Score [SS] = 10). When qualitatively reviewed, this appeared to suggest that, as Pekka himself had mentioned, understanding abstract concepts was not one of his strengths. The highest score for verbal tasks was obtained for the Information subtest, which was well above average (SS = 16). Taken together, results suggested that Pekka knew a lot about the world and was verbally competent. Additionally, his performance on the Digit Span and Arithmetic subscales were, respectively, high average and well above average (SS = 14 and 15, respectively), suggesting that his attention and working memory were intact.

In contrast with his verbal abilities, Pekka's Performance IQ was only average (PIQ = 100), with some scatter among subtests. While his performance on Picture Arrangement and Picture Completion, as well as Object Assembly, were all in the average range (SS = 11, 9 and 8, respectively), his performance for Block Design and Digit Symbol were in the low average range (SS = 6). These last two, and to a lesser extent Object Assembly, were in sharp contrast with Pekka's best performances for the verbal subtests and suggested specific neurocognitive deficits in visual-spatial processing, processing speed, as well as problem-solving and visual organization (e.g., the ability to understand how parts make up a whole). These tasks are commonly considered to be reflective of fluid intelligence, which involves the capacity to solve problems in unfamiliar situations, independent of acquired knowledge. Fluid intelligence is typically thought to encompass the ability to analyze new situations, to integrate new pieces of information rapidly and efficiently, and to identify patterns in novel stimuli (Cattell, 1963).

Self-Report-Based and Other Assessment Findings

In addition to the cognitive testing, I asked Pekka to complete two self-report inventories: the Beck Depression Inventory (BDI-II; Beck et al., 2004) and the Minnesota Multiphasic Personality Inventory (MMPI; Greene, 2011; Hathaway & McKinley, 1943).[2] These were used to help capture the possible presence of psychopathology and to better understand Pekka's personality structure, based on self-report.

The BDI-II measures mostly the cognitive, but also, to a lesser degree, the emotional and somatic symptoms of depression. Pekka's score was 4/63, which typically suggests the absence of depression. Additionally, a qualitative review of the potentially depression-related items endorsed showed that Pekka was in fact reporting mild anhedonia, a lack of initiative, tiredness, as well as his tendency to focus on physical symptoms.

The MMPI drew a quite different picture. Validity scales suggested a valid protocol, including a willingness to report some unusual experiences (F T-Score = 65). However, they also suggested that Pekka often used repression and denial regarding common flaws, put effort into being excessively conventional and controlled, and lacked emotional insight. Results indicated that he might be seen by others as self-centered and inflexible and that, concurrently, he might be uncertain about the effectiveness of his own rigid principles. His validity profile suggested he was defensive, tended to consider psychological problems as weaknesses, and put great effort into maintaining and projecting a sense of control (L T-Score = 63; K T-Score = 70). The profile also suggested a poor prognosis for any psychological intervention, given his lack of insight into psychological issues.

Despite Pekka's defensive attitude and lack of insight, clinical scales on the MMPI showed multiple elevations which, when combined, are typical of people with physical complaints such as abdominal-visceral pain, weakness and fatigue, and a history of hypochondriasis reflecting underlying anxiety. These individuals are often socially introverted (in Pekka's case Scale 0 T-Score = 63), passive-dependent, conforming, naive, and generally apathetic, lacking in assertiveness, and unlikely to take risks (code-type 123 with Scale 1 T-Score = 90, Scale 2 T-Score = 84, Scale 3 T-Score = 74). Individuals with this profile are also often depressed, although they usually do not report this, as appeared to be the case with Pekka. Pekka's profile also suggested a low energy level, a lack of ambition, as well as a strong tendency to spend a significant amount of time lying down or in bed (Scale 9 T-Score = 40). Although a code-type of 123 has been historically described in the literature as the "neurotic triad," and the elevation of its scales shown to predict the clinical severity of depression (Talarowska et al., 2011), there is also evidence that it can be related to neurocognitive impairment or neurodevelopmental disorders. In fact, patients with neurocognitive disorders frequently present symptoms and features such as multiple somatic complaints, a lack of insight, fatigue, and weakness, as well as passivity and apathy, for example. Cerebrovascular disease (e.g., Gass & Lawhorn, 1991; Scales 1 and 3 in particular), traumatic brain injury (e.g., Gass et al., 2017; Scales 1 and 3 in particular), or autism spectrum disorders (e.g., Ozonoff et al., 2005; Scale 2 and 0 in particular), for example, are conditions in which frequent elevations on these scales have been reported in the literature. Finally, although Scale 8 of the MMPI, which was originally developed to diagnose schizophrenia, has been shown to be only modestly associated with observer-rated psychotic symptoms (Carter et al., 2019), it is noteworthy that Pekka's profile did not present a clinically significant elevation on this scale.

At the very end of my battery of tests, a couple of days after the Rorschach, I administered Pekka the Thematic Apperception Test (TAT; Shentoub, 1998), using a qualitative approach to further explore his relation to others, to the world and to himself, as well as the quality of his perception, thinking, and defensive operations. Pekka's narratives to the several cards I chose to present were coherent yet often concrete, with a tendency to stick closely to the superficial characteristics of the stimuli, to gravitate toward popular and conventional themes, and to actively avoid more elaborated, abstract, or emotionally arousing themes. He rarely elaborated on the relationship between people in the cards with two or more people and was reticent to elaborate on what the people in the cards were thinking and feeling, as required by standard instructions. Instead, his tendency was to avoid and distance himself from potentially emotionally arousing stimuli. These tendencies were probably best illustrated by the story he told to go with card 6BM. This card depicts an indoor scene with two people; a young man in the first plan with a concerned expression on his face and an older woman, often identified as a housekeeper due to her outfit, looking away, out the window. Given the generational difference between the characters, this card often pulls for themes revolving around, or potentially related to, the mother–son relationship. Pekka looked at the card and said:

> One could think that this is a housekeeper, this woman here . . . yes, and it becomes more credible if she is being questioned by a detective, perhaps investigating a criminal case or inspecting a crime that happened in this house. The attitude of the woman suggests she is a housekeeper, someone who cleans the house. It doesn't look like the two are related.

Furthermore, what one could characterize as organizational perseverations emerged throughout the cards, with a recurring focus on themes of cessation and departure. Pekka repeatedly ended his stories with phrases such as "He leaves everything," "He's just about to leave this situation," or "It's dark and soon time to go to sleep," evidencing a pattern of preoccupation with endings or transitions, as well as a lack of cognitive flexibility. These repetitive phrases about leaving also conveyed a sense of discomfort with the ongoing assessment situation, as well as a pressing need to have it come to an end reminiscent of Pekka's need to repeatedly check the time during interviews. Finally, there were no clear signs of the emergence of primary processes such as problems with reality testing or disordered thinking.

Upon concluding the TAT, I asked Pekka to comment on what it felt like to do the test. Pekka acknowledged the interpretive challenges he encountered with images that were straightforward or laden with emotion, citing the difficulty with the portrayal of a woman in tears after a confrontation on card 3GF, or the starkness of an "autopsy" on card 8BM, which are both common themes to these cards. Moreover, he described experiencing a sense of detachment when looking at the cards, especially when looking at more simple scenes, perceiving them with a dispassionate objectivity akin to viewing still photographs.

Contributions of the Rorschach

Pekka's complete Rorschach protocol, transcribed verbatim and including documentation on response locations, the Sequence of Codes and the Structural Summary are all presented in Appendix D at the end of the book. The Rorschach was administered and scored according to the Comprehensive System (Exner, 2003).

Pekka produced a valid Rorschach with an average number of responses (R = 20), which suggested he was sufficiently engaged in the task. However, his protocol was unusually constricted in other ways, suggesting a pervasively avoidant coping style and extremely simplistic information processing (*Lambda* = 3.00; *Blends* = 0), a significant lack of adaptive coping resources (*EA* = 3.0), and a severe state of emotional shutdown (*EB* = 3:0). Findings like these are typically associated with a long-standing tendency to seek fast, concrete, and simplistic solutions to problems, even in complex situations where a more nuanced, holistic, and inclusive approach would be more effective. A more integrated approach would include, for instance, analyzing situations from various perspectives, as well as integrating the verbal-semantic processing of emotional information into problem-solving and decision-making activities.

Pekka invested a normative amount of effort into processing (*R* = 20; *Zf* = 8; *W:D:Dd* = 7:11:2; *W:M* = 7:3) but also showed a tendency to miss important cues and to jump to conclusions (*Zd* = –5.0). He failed to make syntheses, typically leaving ideas and percepts disconnected from each other (*DQ+* = 1); his way of seeing things tended to be vague and impressionistic (*DQv* = 2 and the repeated use of the word "vague"); and he appeared to have some trouble shifting his attention from one thing to the next (*PSV* = 1 and a tendency to present semantic perseverations throughout the protocol: animal heads). The quality of his processing was therefore poor and inefficient in a variety of ways. His response to Card III, for example, probably best conveys this simplistic and fragmented approach. Where people often see two people and a separate object in the middle, his response was: "Two. A pot in the middle." In the inquiry he specifies: "The body, the hands, the pot in the middle," and when questioned further about the pot in the middle: "Here. They're cooking something there." Although the whole human content and the integration of the different percepts could be coded, because at the end Pekka gave us all the elements required, at no point did Pekka spontaneously formulate his response as "two people" and the integration occurred only at the very end of the inquiry. Also note that this was his only *DQ+* response.

Despite the overly simplistic and poor quality of processing, Pekka's Rorschach did not suggest significant problems with perceptual accuracy, reality testing, or disordered thinking (*PTI* = 0). However, the conditions under which perceptual distortions or phenomena potentially associated with disordered thinking occurred were of interest. First, of the three perceptual distortions (*FQ–*) in the protocol, the first was of the more benign variety and occurred as the initial response to Card VII, often referred to as the "mother card" (R12: "A face"). This was followed by an unusual (*FQu*) "clenched fist with the thumbs upwards" (R13), confirming a sense of fragmentation. The other two more severe perceptual distortions were given on the last three pastel-colored cards. These included a potentially threatening bear rising (R14; the first response to Card VIII) and heads of hairy dogs (R18; the last response to Card IX). The first of these two *FQ–* responses was an *FM*, and the second an *FT*.

These associations suggested that perceptual distortions might be linked not only to emotionally arousing situations but also to primitive need states (e.g., Pekka's idiosyncratic perception and interpretation of digestive problems). Additionally, most of Pekka's *FQu* responses appeared on the last three cards, further highlighting a pattern of oddness. During the final part of the response phase of the testing, Pekka began turning the cards, even flipping Card IX to look at its back, and both of his *DQv* responses were recorded at the very end of the protocol, indicating both avoidance and a further decline in the quality of information processing.

Taken together, these qualitative observations conveyed a sense of discomfort, a need to process and look at things from different perspectives, but also a tendency to distort things in emotionally arousing situations. It was as if Pekka was trying to see what was behind things in a very concrete way but was unable to give meaningful form to his experiences, particularly in relation to the death of his mother.

Furthermore, the clearly distorted bear response (*FQ–*) on Card VIII was also an *INC*, or possibly a *DV*, due to the "hands" and "feet," which increased its level of disturbance. Finally, a tendency to use peculiar logic (*ALOG*) was noted on Card IV with the response "Some old man . . . Maybe because he's lying down on his back" (R6). Although this comment came later in the inquiry and included some hesitation (use of the word "maybe"), it did suggest some form of peculiar thinking, possibly related to Pekka's perception of himself as old and tired.

Although quantitatively the perception and thinking related phenomena described above remained within normal limits, and Pekka's responses very frequently conveyed conventional perception (P = 7, of which six appeared on the first six cards), their context was indeed noteworthy. They suggested that more emotionally arousing or cognitively demanding situations tended to be psychologically disorganizing and might have felt more threatening to Pekka. Moreover, perceptual inaccuracy might have been related to attachment needs, which helped better understand how Pekka's mother's passing might have triggered Pekka's symptoms. In fact, the death of one's mother is typically an emotionally arousing life event which can also be emotionally demanding. Additionally, it is a primary attachment related event. Based on his performance on the Rorschach, it looked like Pekka was trying to cope with this life-changing event in his personal life in excessively avoidant and concrete ways, as one would have expected him to given his unusual personality structure (most notably *Lambda, EB, WSumC, DQ+, DQv*). One might say he was implicitly trying to grieve the death of his mother by using only his "head," but failing to do so. In fact, a loss of this magnitude would typically require active verbal-semantic processing, the identification and mentalization of emotions, and an explicit cognitive-emotional integration process. Interestingly, although Pekka was significantly disconnected from his emotions and emotions were potentially destabilizing and frightening to him, he did not seem to be actively avoiding emotionally arousing situations (*Afr* = .54). Hence, it was as if he was still attempting to process his mother's death, even with the limited adaptive resources available to him in this situation.

Pekka perceived himself in ways that reflected the way he perceived the world. It was a concrete, simplistic, conventional, yet in some ways idiosyncratic and emotionally detached perspective. One might say he identified primarily as a "head"—a rational and thinking entity—detached from basic bodily needs (*FM* = 1) and emotions (*WSumC* = 0). There was, however, some evidence that his self-image was based on identifications with real people in his life rather than on imagination or partial representations that coincided less with reality (*H*:[*H*] + *Hd* + [*Hd*] = 3:3). Some of the features described here might have therefore been characteristics of people who played an important role in his life, such as his mother, father, siblings, or other important people in his life.

Finally, Pekka's Rorschach performance suggested that he was interested in people and did not have a disturbed or distorted representation of others (*SumH* = 6; *GHR:PHR* = 4:2; *Pure H* = 3). Although there was emotional detachment in the way he related to others, as evidenced qualitatively through the narratives of his TAT, for example, there also seemed to be some inclination to expect cooperative interactions with others when stimulated (*COP* = 1, which appeared at the very end of the inquiry on R4). As Pekka described in interviews, he was "used to being alone." This suggests his socially isolated lifestyle was not a matter of choice but rather something related to long-standing limitations in his capacity to form deeper and more emotionally meaningful relationships with others.

In Conclusion

Pekka was a 48-year-old man assessed in a psychiatric day hospital to better understand his puzzling somatic symptoms, to determine whether he was occupationally impaired, and to develop a tailored treatment plan. The multimethod assessment included interviews, which were carried out by the psychiatrist of the day hospital and myself, behavioral observations carried out by the entire multidisciplinary team during Pekka's six-week assessment and treatment at the day hospital, and psychological tests, including cognitive and self-report methods, the Rorschach, and the TAT.

Cognitive testing using the WAIS-R revealed a considerable degree of heterogeneity in Pekka's performance. Although he showed cognitive strengths on verbal tasks and was very cultivated, moderate impairment was noted in the cognitive domains of processing speed and visuospatial abilities. This was unrelated to attention and working memory, both of which appeared to be intact. Although there were hints to this in Pekka's description of his performance at school, as well as on certain verbal tasks of the WAIS-R, Pekka's tendency to process information in overly simplistic, rigid, vague, and fragmented ways was most evident in his performance on the Rorschach. Furthermore, Pekka's performance on the Rorschach suggested a state of total emotional shutdown and, in large part because of this, an exceptionally low stress tolerance and a vulnerability to widespread coping difficulties. Emotionally arousing situations or situations related to primitive needs tended to be cognitively disorganizing for Pekka and interfered with his otherwise intact reality testing. This helped understand how his first meeting with a psychiatrist might have been somewhat overwhelming and caused him to behave and communicate in ways that made him look odd or even psychotic. However, this first assessment turned out to be a misinterpretation. During Pekka's six-week assessment at the day hospital, we found no clinical or psychometric evidence suggesting a psychotic disorder. On the Rorschach, for example, there was no clear evidence of pervasive problems with perceptual accuracy and thinking (*PTI* = 0).

Pekka appeared unable to identify and process emotions verbally and semantically, which hindered his ability to integrate emotional information into problem-solving. This helped explain why an emotionally arousing life event like the death of his mother did not trigger a normal grieving reaction in him. Although the process of grieving can take many different forms, a normal reaction might have included some form of emotional working through and attending to thoughts, feelings, and memories (i.e., mentalizing). Instead, for Pekka it triggered significant somatic symptoms, accompanied by a total lack of insight as to their possible affective implications. Pekka was not connecting his symptoms with the death of his mother, and he seemed to have little to say when asked about his reactions to her passing away. For Pekka, his mother's death appeared to be primarily a matter of fact.

Pekka's deficit in the mentalization of emotion further manifested itself in the form of social ineptness and withdrawal, as illustrated by his somewhat awkward and rigid interpersonal behavior, his ascetic lifestyle, or his struggles in dealing with difficult clients at the library where he worked. Additionally, Pekka's Rorschach performance confirmed that, despite his difficulties in interacting with others, he was interested in people, and his representation of others was adequate and reality based. Also interestingly, Pekka's Rorschach performance suggested that, although he was struggling with the effective processing of emotional stimuli, he was not actively avoiding such stimuli. These findings suggested two things. First, they suggested that Pekka's somatic concerns and symptoms represented his adaptive efforts and implicit attempts to work through his experience, albeit in exceptionally idiosyncratic and concrete ways. Second, they suggested the presence of an internal conflict between a desire for social interaction and a practical disengagement from it.

Pekka's TAT performance underscored his social-emotional difficulties. He focused on superficial aspects of the images and favored conventional, emotionally neutral narratives, avoiding deeper or affectively charged content. On Card 6BM, which typically evokes mother–son themes, he described the figures as unrelated and framed their interaction in a detached way. However, he did allude to an ongoing investigation into "something bad," subtly echoing both the psychological assessment context and his recent loss.

His stories frequently ended with themes of departure or finality, reflecting both organizational perseveration and a focus on closure. This recurring pattern, along with his compulsive checking of the wall clock during interviews, suggested cognitive rigidity and a possible struggle between avoidance, the need for resolution, and feeling stuck in an unresolved experience.

Depression—which typically includes somatic, affective, and cognitive facets—manifested in Pekka almost exclusively through his somatic concerns and symptoms, as suggested by his MMPI profile. In other words, his inability to emotionally process the loss of his mother left him grappling with the cognitive and somatic components of depression, along with the tension and anxiety implicit in his somatic complaints.

Pekka's focus was on complaining about digestive problems, including queries about possible diabetes, a condition reminiscent of his mother's health challenges. Additionally, Pekka's somatic symptoms might have been the manifestation of what normally should have been a mentalized struggle to "digest" the reality and finality of his loss. His idiosyncratic interpretation and confusion surrounding these symptoms highlighted a complex interplay between his physical sensations and the implicit unresolved emotional turmoil within him. It was a turmoil he was incapable of attending to through mentalizing and the working through typically involved in grieving.

Taken together, the results of the multimethod assessment suggested that, because of what appeared to reflect an underlying neurodevelopmental disorder, Pekka's mind was unable to process the experience of loss and emotions that typically accompany grieving, nor was he able to integrate them into his experience and thinking. After discussions with the psychiatrist of our team, we agreed that Pekka's symptoms were probably associated with an autism spectrum disorder (Asperger's disorder), which accounted for his lack of insight, his concrete thinking, his mentalization deficits, his relative social isolation, and his detached way of interacting with others. The Rorschach significantly contributed to the formulation of this diagnosis and included many of the features typically associated with the performance of individuals with autism spectrum disorders (e.g., Holaday et al., 2001; Kleiger & Weiner, 2019). The death of Pekka's mother had probably served as an emotional stressor and trigger that both exacerbated and brought these issues more into focus, ultimately causing the emergence of symptoms, a decline in occupational functioning, and the necessity to turn to mental health services for help.

From a diagnostic perspective, the diagnoses established according to the International Classification of Diseases (ICD-10; World Health

Organization, 1993) were the following: F84.5 Asperger's Syndrome, F45.2 Hypochondriacal Disorder, F41.3 Other Mixed Anxiety Disorder, and F50.1 Atypical Anorexia Nervosa. The last three accounted for the repeated somatic complaints, the underlying anxiety they were accompanied by, as well as Pekka's restrictive eating and weight loss in a context inconsistent with a typical picture of anorexia.

Given Pekka's psychological profile, we agreed that the treatment plan should prioritize the alleviation of symptoms that were the focus of Pekka's attention, and that adversely affected his social interactions and occupational capacity. These symptoms were his somatic concerns, as well as his restrictive dietary habits and related weight loss. Understanding Pekka's condition through the lens of an autism spectrum disorder and the framework of a complicated or idiosyncratic grieving process was instrumental in contextualizing Pekka's symptoms and understanding their psychological underpinnings.

Given Pekka's primary disorder and unique personality structure and dynamics, we agreed that traditional insight-oriented (e.g., psychodynamic, psychoanalytical) psychotherapies would probably not prove to be effective. Furthermore, they would considerably distance Pekka from his (high *Lambda*) "comfort zone." Instead, supportive, and more concrete and pragmatic forms of therapy, such as cognitive-behavioral therapies, were ultimately recommended, with a focus on symptom management, as well as on fostering self-management and coping skills in a stressful life situation. Regular meetings with a mental health professional in an outpatient clinic were considered for this purpose. Furthermore, it was suggested that occupational therapy might also prove to be beneficial in addressing Pekka's practical difficulties in the workplace.

To create a supportive work environment, and with Pekka's consent, active collaboration with Pekka's employer was undergone toward the last couple of weeks of his assessment and treatment at the day hospital. This involved discussions with Pekka's employer which led to concrete adjustments to minimize social stressors in the workplace (e.g., allowing him to do fewer hours of direct customer service), as well as to modifications in Pekka's working hours to better accommodate his needs and fragile functional capacity.

Together with Pekka we also agreed that regular medical follow-ups should be included in Pekka's comprehensive treatment plan, ensuring that his physical health was monitored alongside his mental health treatment. This multidisciplinary approach aimed to foster Pekka's well-being, enhance his functional capacity both socially and occupationally, and help him find new ways to "digest" the death of his mother.

Notes

1 Personal details and background information have been altered or withheld to protect the patient's identity and ensure confidentiality.
2 In Finland, only the original version of the MMPI has been translated into Finnish. Although reference data for Finland has never been collected, US reference data for the original MMPI was collected in areas of the Midwest with a significant Nordic and Finnish cultural heritage, and many clinicians in Finland find it to be both useful and justified in clinical practice.

References

Beck, A. T., Steer, R. A., & Brown, G. K. (2004). *BDI-II: Beckin depressioasteikko käsikirja* [*BDI–II: Beck Depression Inventory manual*]. (S. A. Hautala & K. Alanne, Trans.) Psykologien Kustannus Oy.

Carter, J. W., Nordgaard, J., & Parnas, J. (2019). Identifying nonaffective psychosis in first admission patients: MMPI-2 structured diagnostic interview and consensus lifetime best estimate. *Psychiatry Research*, 279, 71–76. doi:10.1016/j.psychres.2019.07.010.

Cattell, R. B. (1963). Theory of fluid and crystallized intelligence: A critical experiment. *Journal of Educational Psychology*, 54(1), 1–22. doi:10.1037/h0046743.

Exner, J. E. (2003). *The Rorschach: A comprehensive system—volume 1: Basic foundations and principles of interpretation* (4th ed.). Wiley.

Gass, C. S., & Lawhorn, L. (1991). Psychological adjustment following stroke: An MMPI study. *Psychological Assessment: A Journal of Consulting and Clinical Psychology*, 3(4), 628. doi:10.1037/1040-3590.3.4.628.

Gass, C. S., Rogers, D., & Kinne, E. (2017). Psychological characteristics in acute mild traumatic brain injury: An MMPI-2 study. *Applied Neuropsychology: Adult*, 24(2), 108–115. doi:10.1080/23279095.2015.1107563.

Hathaway, S. R., & McKinley, J. C. (1943). *The Minnesota Multiphasic Personality Inventory*. University of Minnesota Press.

Hathaway, S. R., & McKinley, J. C. (n.d.). Finnish translation of *The Minnesota Multiphasic Personality Inventory*. Psykologien Kustannus Oy.

Holaday, M., Moak, J., & Shipley, M. A. (2001). Rorschach protocols from children and adolescents with Asperger's disorder. *Journal of Personality Assessment*, 76 (3), 482–495. doi:10.1207/S15327752JPA7603_09.

Kleiger, J. H., & Weiner, I. B. (2019). Autistic thinking: Conceptual understanding and Rorschach assessment. *Rorschachiana*, 40(2), 131–150. doi:10.1027/1192-5604/a000117.

Laaksonen, R., & Ranta, M. (Eds.). (2013). *Introduction to neuropsychotherapy: Guidelines for rehabilitation of neurological and neuropsychiatric patients throughout the lifespan*. Psychology Press.

Ozonoff, S., Garcia, N., Clark, E., & Lainhart, J. E. (2005). MMPI-2 personality profiles of high-functioning adults with autism spectrum disorders. *Assessment*, 12(1), 86–95. doi:10.1177/1073191104273132.

Shentoub, V. (1998). *Manuel d'utilisation du TAT (approche psychanalytique)* [*Manual for using the TAT (psychoanalytical approach)*]. Dunod.

Talarowska, M., Zboralski, K., Chamielec, M., & Galecki, P. (2011). The MMPI-2 neurotic triad subscales and depression levels after pharmacological treatment in patients with depressive disorders: Clinical study. *Psychiatria Danubina, 23*(4), 347–354.

Wechsler, D. (1992). *WAIS-R Wechslerin aikuisälykkyysasteikko: Käsikirja* [*WAIS-R Wechsler Adult Intelligence Scale: Manual*] (T. Järvinen & J. Häkkinen, Trans.). Psykologien Kustannus Oy.

World Health Organization. (1993). *The ICD-10 classification of mental and behavioural disorders.* World Health Organization.

Chapter 10

"I'm Feeling Great!"

Cognitive Deterioration in a Woman with a History of Alcoholism and Psychotic Depression

"Tuula", a 43-year-old Finnish general practitioner in private practice, faced multiple complaints to the Finnish National Supervisory Authority for Welfare and Health (Valvira) over suspected workplace alcohol use and professional misconduct.[1] Reports described signs of intoxication and repeated Monday absences, with Tuula often unreachable or sounding severely inebriated on the phone. However, two surprise inspections by Valvira over a two-year period revealed no immediate concerns; she appeared sober, professionally capable, and denied any workplace alcohol use.

Following ongoing complaints, Valvira ordered a psychiatric evaluation to determine possible occupational impairment. At a psychiatric outpatient clinic, Tuula was diagnosed with an unspecified recurrent depressive disorder and referred for assessment and treatment at a clinic specializing in addictions—a plan she initially accepted. She acknowledged a history of alcohol abuse but denied significant ongoing problems. Despite her initial cooperation, Tuula's engagement with the treatment program faltered, leading to its discontinuation after she missed appointments, attributing her absence to illness. The outpatient clinic then resumed follow-up sessions and treatment.

Given ongoing concerns about her mental health and alcohol use, her psychiatrist at the clinic decided that meeting with Tuula a couple of times a month was insufficient to assess her occupational capacity reliably and referred her to a psychiatric day hospital—where I was working as a psychologist at the time—for a more comprehensive assessment. The advantage of a psychiatric day hospital in cases like Tuula's is that it enables a multidisciplinary mental health care team to observe patients over periods of several weeks daily (Monday to Friday from 8:00 to 14:00). Furthermore, a psychological assessment in this setting allows a multimethod approach, which can be of great use in cases that pose challenges to reliably assessing mental health status, the extent of possible problems with substance abuse, as well as functional and occupational capacity. Tuula agreed to this plan and was cooperative but insisted that her occupational capacity was intact.

DOI: 10.4324/9781003731894-12

Tuula had a younger sister. Her parents separated when she was ten, and she described her childhood as "normal." On further inquiry, however, she revealed that her father drank heavily, especially on weekends, and had a violent temper. Tuula was closer to her mother and remains in contact with her and her sister. She described herself as a lively child, successful at school, and later completed her medical studies with good results. She worked for many years in general medicine, primarily in private practice.

Tuula married in her mid-twenties and had two daughters. Though initially happy, the marriage soon became "stormy." Tuula began drinking regularly and became severely depressed, requiring inpatient care for psychotic depression. After recovering, she separated from her spouse, with the divorce finalized about a year later. During this period, she experienced another depressive episode and became involved in a custody dispute. The court ruled that the children, then aged five and seven, would live with their father.

Tuula reported being deeply depressed at the time, though she did not require hospitalization and was treated by a private psychiatrist. In her mid-thirties, she entered a relationship with a heavy drinker. They moved in together and remained a couple at the time of her assessment at the day hospital. She described the relationship as unstable, marked by daily alcohol use for over a decade and incidents of her partner's violent temper, including occasions when she feared for her safety and called the police. In response to Valvira's workplace inspections, Tuula later claimed that her alcohol use had decreased, denied drinking at work, and stated she always canceled appointments when unfit to practice. She also described her relationship as more stable than it had been in the past.

The following sections describe the results of Tuula's initial multimethod assessment at the psychiatric day hospital, which revealed significant mental health and behavioral issues, including alcohol dependence and mild to moderate cognitive decline in specific domains. Emotional and interpersonal problems underlying her alcohol use are also addressed. Based on this assessment, Valvira authorized her to resume work on the condition that she first undergo treatment at a specialized addiction clinic, which she completed. She was eventually cleared to return to practice but reduced her workload to part-time due to increasing strain.

A follow-up occupational assessment two years later led Valvira to authorize her to continue working but only under supervision in the public sector. Over the next three years, she worked intermittently while also receiving treatment for depression. During this period, her relationship deteriorated, and she again found work too demanding, even with professional support and supervision.

Five years after the initial assessment, at age forty-eight, Tuula was referred for a second follow-up multimethod assessment at the same day hospital. By then, her situation had deteriorated significantly, and she sought early retirement for mental health reasons. The findings of this second assessment are also presented. For both the initial and second day hospital assessment five years later, special attention is given to how the Rorschach contributed uniquely to understanding Tuula's psychological and neuropsychological functioning and to the significant changes that occurred over a five-year period.

The First Assessment: Self-Report and Neuropsychological Assessment Findings

As mentioned earlier, Tuula was very cooperative throughout her first assessment at the day hospital, which was carried out by the head psychiatrist, myself, and a multidisciplinary psychiatric team. She smiled a lot but seemed tense and rigid. Her responses to questions were brief and unelaborated. When asked about how she was feeling, she assured us with a big smile that she was "feeling great." She also assured us that she understood the reasons for the assessment and was prepared to cooperate fully. When asked about her drinking, she stated that although she did have a few drinks occasionally, she was drinking significantly less than she used to and had always gone to work sober and in good condition. It was therefore of little surprise that her results on the Minnesota Multiphasic Personality Inventory (MMPI; Greene, 2011; Hathaway & McKinley, 1943) were within normal limits for all clinical scales, suggesting a total absence of self-reported psychological problems and symptoms.[2] Her highest (very mild) elevation was on Scale 5 (T Score = 58), suggesting that she might sometimes be seen by others as dominating, competitive, or manipulative. There were also no significant elevations in validity scales L, F and K, although values suggested the possibility of some rigidity in thinking, as well as concerns with self-control or an attempt to control the outcome of the test. Her profile also indicated the possibility of her being skilled at denying and hiding unacceptable impulses or problems, given her history of mental health issues, as well as the situation that brought her to be assessed at the day hospital.

Tuula appeared to do her best on cognitive tests of maximum performance, although she seemed tense and nervous throughout the testing. Her Full-Scale IQ (FSIQ) was 111 (WAIS-R; Wechsler, 1992), placing her in the higher average range for her age group, with little scatter between subtests. A clear outlier however was her performance on the Picture Completion subtest (Standard Score [SS] = 5), where she showed significant deficits in her ability to recognize the essential features of visual stimuli. On this subtest, Tuula would tend to focus excessively on irrelevant details, especially in relation to drawings of people, which suggested some degree of impaired judgment and problem-solving skills, as well as possible issues with interpersonal perception. The score on this subtest was well below average and explained the slight discrepancy between her Verbal and Performance IQ, which were respectively 113 and 108. Additionally, although her results on the Digit Span, Block Design, and Digit Symbol-Coding subtests were all in the average range for her age group (SSs respectively 10, 10 and 9), her performance seemed weak considering her profession and level of education. Her digit span forward was 7 and digit span backward was 5, which was still in the average range, but her processing speed seemed slow. This suggested problems with attention and working memory, which were later confirmed through other tests.

Tuula's performance on the Rey–Osterreith Complex Figure (ROCF; Meyers & Meyers, 1995) was almost flawless for both copy and delayed recall (after five minutes). This confirmed that she paid sufficient attention to detail and had good visuospatial processing and organizational abilities when it came to more neutral stimuli. However, her performance on the Stroop Test (Stroop, 1935), as well as on Trail Making Tests A and B (TMT-A and TMT-B; Reitan, 1958) was weak in terms of processing speed (approximately two standard deviations [SD] from the mean). She also made a couple of mistakes of negligence on the TMT-B. As to her performance on the Wechsler Memory Scale (WMS-R; Wechsler, 1997), it was well above average for her age group for Verbal Memory (VEM), Visual Memory (VIM), which confirmed what had been noted on the ROCF, General Memory (GEM) and Delayed Recall (DEL), ranging from SS = 122 to 126. In sharp contrast to these excellent scores on both verbal and visual memory tasks, her performance for Attention/Concentration was only average (ATT/C SS = 97).

Despite a FSIQ in the high average range and well above average performances in the domains of visuospatial organization, visual memory, and verbal memory, consistent with her level of education, Tuula's performance suggested lower-than-expected processing speed as well as challenges and possible cognitive decline in the domains of executive functioning and cognitive flexibility, divided attention, selective attention, and working memory. Furthermore, she appeared to show significant difficulties filtering out irrelevant details as well as a degree of impaired judgment which was likely to affect her capacity to solve problems effectively.

The First Assessment: Contributions of the Rorschach

Tuula's complete Rorschach protocol transcribed verbatim and including documentation on response location, the Sequence of Codes and the Structural Summary are presented in Appendix E at the end of the book. The Rorschach was administered and scored according to Exner's Comprehensive System (Exner, 2003).

Given her generally average to above-average cognitive performance, Tuula's Rorschach protocol was suspect in terms of validity. She produced only fourteen responses, with *Lambda* = 1.80, no *Blends*, a surprising lack of adaptive resources (*EA* = 2.5), including significant deficits in emotional mentalization (*WSumC* = 0.5). Given her intelligence and level of education, she also showed a limited tendency to integrate ideas and percepts (*DQ+* = 4). These features aligned with her apparent effort to portray herself as mentally healthy, free of alcohol problems, and occupationally fit—similar to what she had successfully conveyed on the MMPI. At the same time, such constriction may reflect neurocognitive impairment, which was mildly to moderately present across a limited range of functions.

Distinguishing between deliberate defensiveness and neuropsychological constriction was challenging. Given Tuula's history of recurrent depression, prior hospitalization for psychotic depression, history of alcohol abuse and dependence, and repeated complaints from patients, some signs of psychopathology were anticipated, and the Rorschach—as an implicit method—was in a unique position to bypass deliberate attempts to control assessment outcomes. When protocols are heavily constricted to suppress psychopathology, low scores may be invalid due to reduced "signal," but elevated scores—especially those unaffected by *R*—tend to retain interpretive value.

Tuula's protocol featured a positive Coping Deficit Index (*CDI* = 4), a high *Lambda*, a low *EA*, a passive active-to-passive movement ratio (*a:p* = 0:2), and a positive Snow White syndrome (*Ma:Mp* = 0:2), suggesting limited adaptive resources; avoidant, concrete, and simplistic problem-solving; and a tendency to rely on fantasy under stress. All these indicators could stem from situational constriction or more enduring dysfunction.

No obvious problems with perception, thinking, or reality testing were observed, and the overall level of psychopathology appeared low (*PTI* = 0; *EII-2* = –0.26; Diener et al., 2011)—surprisingly so, given her clinical history. However, *EII-2* is considered less valid in high-*Lambda* protocols (Perry, 2006), and short records offer fewer opportunities to detect disordered thinking. Moreover, the total absence of critical contents, and the presence of only two *FQ–* responses is a rare occurrence, especially in clinical samples, further suggesting defensive test-taking.

Because an elevated *CDI* is more likely in high-*Lambda* protocols, it was difficult to determine whether Tuula's constriction reflected a situation-related defensive strategy or more chronic conditions such as developmental immaturity, attachment trauma, or neuropsychological decline, for example. Both possibilities—or a combination of the two—fit the assessment context. What was clear, however, was her success in presenting herself as psychologically healthy but with constriction, overcontrol, and avoidance at levels unexpected for someone with her intellectual and educational background.

Despite her relatively healthy presentation on self-report and cognitive testing, certain Rorschach findings did clearly suggest underlying dysfunction. Although Tuula was interested in people (*SumH* = 4), she did not anticipate positive and cooperative interactions with others (*COP* = 0), and half her human representations were poor (*GHR:PHR* = 2:2), including one *M*– response. The latter was her only response to Card III (R4): "A loving couple. Two people . . . a bow in between . . . the bow here hints to the fact that they are in good terms." Instead of the very frequent popular response, she perceived each popular human figure with legs for each in D5 and Dd30—instead of the common perception of legs in D5 and arms in Dd30—reflecting a significant perceptual distortion. This emotionally charged, interpersonally meaningful representation included intellectualization, color avoidance, denial, projection, and idealization. A pattern of alternating idealization and devaluation—characteristic of splitting—was also seen in response sequences R4 to R5 and R12 to R13 to R14 (Smith & Gacono, 2022), suggesting maladaptive interpersonal functioning, impaired affect regulation, and possible attachment issues. Furthermore, although Tuula's protocol was affectively constricted (*WSumC* = 0.5), her affective ratio was elevated (*Afr* = 0.75), suggesting attraction to emotionally arousing stimuli rather than avoidance. As clarified in the extended inquiry (Appendix E), she expressed interest in emotional engagement. However, this proved problematic. Her only color response (R13, "flowers") included denial, some degree of idealization, and perceptual inaccuracy, suggesting that attempts to integrate emotions tended to be associated with perceptual inaccuracy. This was consistent with her low performance on the Picture Completion subtest of the WAIS-R, suggesting left temporal dysfunction (Peiffer et al., 2014) and impaired social cognition. In addition to executive deficits associated with alcoholism (Lyvers, 2000), women with a history of alcohol abuse often show persistent social-cognitive impairments, even after long abstinence (Valmas et al., 2014). Finally, Tuula's *Ma:Mp* ratio (0:2) reinforced a defensive pattern of substituting fantasy for reality under stress.

The First Assessment: Final Observations and Conclusions

The initial assessment prompted by Valvira suggested that Tuula was intent on convincing us—and Valvira—that she was not currently struggling with mental health or alcohol-related problems and was fit to continue working in private practice. Clinical interviews and the MMPI portrayed her as cooperative but tense, likely mentally healthy, motivated to control the outcome of the assessment, and largely succeeding in doing so.

Only through performance-based methods did underlying vulnerabilities emerge. While Tuula's neurocognitive test results were generally in the high average to superior range for her age, mild to moderate weaknesses were evident in processing speed, executive functioning, attention, working memory, and aspects of perceptual judgment. Her Rorschach was notably constricted, possibly reflecting a simplistic, avoidant coping style. Yet, given the context, this also raised validity concerns, suggesting a possible "fake good" bias. However, some Rorschach variables less susceptible to distortion through constriction, along with qualitative observations, pointed to maladaptive interpersonal functioning, emotional detachment, and the use of passive, escapist coping strategies in response to stress.

Tuula attended the day hospital five days a week for three weeks, participating in therapeutic group activities, including therapeutic discussions, relaxation exercises, and rotating patient responsibilities. She was consistently cooperative, followed rules, and maintained a good mood, drawing little attention to herself.

However, on the final day of the assessment at the day hospital, staff found her asleep on a sofa, wearing the same clothes as the previous day and smelling of alcohol. A breath alcohol test revealed a markedly elevated blood alcohol concentration. Tuula admitted to spending the previous night drinking at a bar and was sent home to rest.

Until that point, the report would have noted mild to moderate cognitive decline in specific domains and emotional-interpersonal issues but remained inconclusive about their impact on Tuula's alcohol use or occupational capacity. Her overall strengths and vulnerabilities would have supported the view that her functioning was fragile, with a recommendation for continued outpatient follow-up and treatment as needed. The final binge-drinking episode, however, removed any remaining ambiguity: Tuula was deemed occupationally impaired and unfit to continue working in private practice without appropriate treatment and supervision.

The Second Assessment: Self-Report and Neuropsychological Assessment Findings

As noted earlier, five years after her initial assessment, Tuula's condition had further deteriorated, and she was again referred to the same day hospital for an evaluation of her occupational capacity—this time seeking early retirement for mental health reasons. She appeared significantly distressed and reported marked cognitive decline and serious relationship difficulties. Although she had remained in outpatient treatment and had substantially reduced her alcohol consumption, her partner had become increasingly violent, and she felt severely occupationally impaired.

In line with her more candid presentation in interviews, Tuula's MMPI profile had changed markedly from her initial assessment. While validity scales (L, F, K) still indicated rigidity and concerns with self-control, she now openly reported emotional distress and moderate symptoms, yielding a valid profile. Although she was applying for disability, there were no signs of symptom exaggeration. Her clinical scales produced a 273 code-type, with additional elevations on Scales 8, 1, 4, and 6—typically reflecting moderate to severe emotional distress marked by dysphoria, guilt, anxiety, and somatic complaints. She appeared self-deprecating, passive, and dependent in stressful contexts, often feeling helpless and needing support. She also presented as alienated, introverted, and mistrustful. Profiles of this type are commonly associated with attention and memory issues as well as a tendency to give up easily. When substance abuse is present, it is usually secondary to an underlying mood disorder.

Additional self-report measures supported this picture. The Beck Depression Inventory indicated moderate depression (BDI-II = 25/63; Beck et al., 2004), and the Symptom Checklist (SCL-90; Holi et al., 1998)) confirmed predominant depressive symptoms alongside cognitive complaints (e.g., attention, memory, and decision-making). The Alcohol Use Disorders Identification Test (AUDIT; Babor et al., 2001) confirmed that her alcohol consumption had been under control over the past year (AUDIT = 7/40). Current AUDIT points reflected drinking two to three times weekly. She reported past alcohol-related accidents (though none recently) and acknowledged that several physicians and other people had previously urged her to reduce or stop drinking—though not within the past year. She also described undergoing an exercise stress test the year before, which revealed high blood pressure and elevated coronary risk, prompting lifestyle changes, including a healthier diet, exercise, and reduced alcohol intake.

Tuula reported significant cognitive decline in recent years, with difficulties in concentration and memory. "I feel like I can't deal with things, or carry responsibility," she stated. "There are days when I don't know how to make coffee . . . or I start doing something but just don't follow through."

Her performance on cognitive tests had indeed declined substantially since the previous assessment. On verbal tasks, she remained in the average to above-average range, despite a slight deterioration of her performance on the Similarities subtest (SS = 8, previously 12). In contrast, her Performance IQ dropped from 108 to 75 (WAIS-III; Wechsler, 2005). Picture Completion improved (SS = 9, previously 5), but her scores on Block Design, Matrix Reasoning, and Picture Arrangement were in the low average to well-below-average range, and her Digit Symbol-Coding performance was extremely low (SS = 3). She was also markedly slow on TMT-A, TMT-B, and the Stroop test, where she made four interference errors—three in the second half. Processing speed was about 3 SD below the mean.

On the Wisconsin Card Sorting Test (Heaton et al., 1993), Tuula's performance was well below average (SS = 79), with an excessive number of perseverative responses and errors (SS = 76), and low average on Conceptual Level Responses (SS = 83). Additionally, she failed to maintain set once in the second half of the test.

Her memory had deteriorated significantly. On the WMS-R, her Verbal Memory declined from well above average to low average (SS = 123 → 84), Visual Memory from well above average to extremely low (SS = 123 → 67), and General Memory from well above average to well below average (SS = 126 → 78). Delayed Recall was also well below average (SS = 71). Finally, her Attention/Concentration fell from average to extremely poor (SS < 51), with digit span forward at 3 and backward at 2.

In summary, Tuula showed a pronounced decline across multiple cognitive domains over five years, especially in executive functions, cognitive flexibility, attention (divided, selective, sustained), working memory, processing speed, and both verbal and visual memory. Her verbal abilities remained largely intact, though there was a mild deterioration in abstract reasoning.

Interestingly, her ability to distinguish between essential and non-essential features in visual stimuli seemed to have improved. Also, it is important to note that Tuula's delayed recall was only marginally inferior to her immediate recall on both verbal and visual tasks of the WMS-R, making it improbable that her decline was specifically associated with a dysfunction of the entorhinal cortex or the hippocampus, as is typically the case in the early stages of dementia of the Alzheimer's type, for example. Given available background information, it is likely that Tuula's cognitive decline was associated with an excessive consumption of alcohol spanning most of her adult life, cardiovascular vulnerabilities which had more recently come to light—and which increased the risk of both ischemic and hemorrhagic strokes—as well as her recurrent episodes of moderate to severe depression. Regardless of etiology, Tuula's dramatic cognitive decline had a profound impact on her capacity to carry out daily tasks, and it was clear that she had become occupationally impaired.

The Second Assessment: Contributions of the Rorschach

Tuula's second Rorschach protocol transcribed verbatim and including documentation on response location, the Sequence of Codes and the Structural Summary are presented in Appendix F at the end of the book. Like the first Rorschach, the second Rorschach was administered and scored according to the Comprehensive System (Exner, 2003).

This time, Tuula was significantly more engaged with the Rorschach and produced a valid protocol with an average number of responses (*R* = 22). Interestingly, despite improved engagement, her protocol continued to reflect an avoidant coping style and simplistic information processing, nearly identical to the first assessment (*Lambda* = 1.75, previously 1.80; *Blends* = 1, previously 0). She still showed an unusual lack of adaptive resources (*EA* = 4.0, previously 2.5) and marked deficits in emotional mentalization (*WSumC* = 2.0, previously 0.5). Given the more transparent assessment context and candid self-reporting, these findings were no longer attributable to situational defensiveness, but rather to stable coping vulnerabilities, low stress tolerance, and limited emotional insight—likely also present during the first assessment.

As before, her performance was consistent with significant neurocognitive impairment. Again, the *CDI* was elevated (= 4), reflecting both reduced adaptive resources (*EA*) and poor social skills. Although Tuula remained interested in people (*SumH* = 5, previously 4), she continued to lack expectations for positive or cooperative interactions (*COP* = 0 in both assessments), showed deficits in her capacity to integrate emotions into problem-solving (*WSumC* = 2.0), and relied heavily on external sources (alcohol, other people) for support, reassurance, and guidance (*Fd* = 1; oral-dependent language [ODL] = 32 percent; Meyer et al., 2011, p. 362). Such pronounced dependency needs were almost totally absent from her first Rorschach (*Fd* = 0; *ODL* = 7 percent), suggesting an earlier denial of such needs. Moreover, the previously observed Snow White syndrome (*Ma* < *Mp*) was no longer part of Tuula's second Rorschach, suggesting a shift from passive attitudes and escapist fantasy to a better integration of her anxious attachment style. In essence, Tuula was now openly telling us that she needed help.

As in the first assessment, there were no indications of significant problems with reality testing or thinking, and the overall level of psychopathology remained only mildly to moderately elevated (*PTI* = 0; *EII-2* = 0.60, previously –0.26). This time, the protocol included some critical contents and a normative proportion of perceptual inaccuracies (*X–%* = 0.23, previously 0.14), suggesting that Tuula was no longer actively attempting to control or suppress the emergence of mild to moderate psychopathology.

Despite Tuula's highly controlled and constricted first Rorschach, some psychological issues had emerged already then that were still evident in her second Rorschach. This confirmed their validity as relatively stable elements in the structure and dynamics of Tuula's personality. Additionally, some of these features appeared to be more pronounced in the second testing, which further confirmed her more candid engagement in the task. First, most of her human representations were now poor in quality (*GHR:PHR* = 1:4). Also, like the first time, one of these was an *M–*. However, the *M–* was no longer the "loving couple" on Card III but a response on Card IX (R15): "Two guys with their backs against each other, wearing hats," followed by "four apples or four fruits" (R16). An even more pronounced alternation between idealization and devaluation, characteristic of splitting, was also noted (from R2 to R3, from R6 to R7, from R9 to R10, from R12 to R13, from R16 to R17, and from R21 to R22; Smith & Gacono, 2022), suggesting wounded narcissism and problems with self-esteem regulation. Finally, several aggressive contents were present (R7, R9, and R14), suggesting that Tuula might have considered aggression as a normal part of human interaction (Gacono & Smith, 2022).

These findings and qualitative observations seemed to make it even clearer than the first time that Tuula tended to engage in maladaptive interpersonal behavior and that her maladaptive behavior probably included mild peculiarities in thinking (R1, R7, and R8) as well as perceptual inaccuracies. The affective distancing was apparent this time through the back-to-back position of the "guys" in R15 and was followed by the emergence of dependency needs (*Fd*). Hence, Tuula's ambivalence and immaturity in relationships emerged once again. Moreover, her problematic relationship with her emotional life was confirmed. Not only was Tuula largely detached from her emotions (*WSumC* = 2.0, previously 0.5) and hasty in seeking gratification of her primitive needs (*FM* = 0 and a high *Lambda* in both Rorschachs), but the rare times she would be in touch with her emotions and attend to them, she would keep their expression tightly under control (*FC:CF* + *C* = 4:0). Her Rorschach also confirmed once again how, despite these difficulties, she tended to be exceedingly attracted to emotionally arousing stimuli (*Afr* = 1.20, previously 0.75; also note the expressed preference for chromatic color cards in the extended inquiry of both Rorschachs). This created significant inner conflict, as Tuula—despite her impaired ability to integrate emotions with thinking and decision-making—actively sought out and engaged in emotionally arousing situations. This helped illuminate the dynamics underlying her "stormy" relationships and dependent behavior.

Interestingly, however, no evidence was found in Tuula's second Rorschach of a tendency to distort things and become disorganized when she did attempt to verbally and semantically process her emotions. Her four *FC* responses were all perceptually accurate. This suggested improvement in her capacity to integrate her emotional reality into her problem-solving activities in adaptive ways, although it was not occurring with the generally desired frequency (*WSumC* < 2.5). Furthermore, improvement in this area was consistent with the significant improvement of her judgment on the Picture Completion subtest of the WAIS. Taken together, and despite widespread cognitive decline in attention, executive functions, and memory, these findings suggested improvement in Tuula's left temporal cortex mediated verbal-semantic processing abilities, as well as possible improvements in social cognition.

These few notable positive changes might have been the result of Tuula's reduced alcohol intake over the previous year. They might have also been the result of her having concurrently found new ways of thinking and being, possibly with the help of psychiatric treatment and treatment at the specialized addiction clinic. While in her first Rorschach there was little to suggest depressive thinking or a negative self-image (*MOR* = 0), her second Rorschach let these elements transpire (*MOR* = 2), while also suggesting she was possibly more involved with herself than she had previously been (*Ego Index* = 0.64, previously 0.43). Her *MOR* responses included "a bigfooted bear wearing high-heels, and its arms are somewhat poorly developed" on Card IV (R7), and a "torn rug" following a "butterfly" response on Card VIII (R13). Together these responses convey a sense of seeing oneself as odd, immature, defective, and broken. Finally, as mentioned earlier, her second Rorschach no longer included a Snow White syndrome (*Ma* = *Mp*), suggesting she had started to have a more active approach in finding solutions to stressful life situations, despite her pronounced dependency needs (*Fd* = 1; *ODL* = 32 percent). Also, despite her avoidant, overly simplistic and concrete approach to problem-solving, it looked like she was more actively "connecting the dots" in her life (*DQ+* = 7, previously 4). Her verbalization on the extended inquiry (see Appendix F) probably best illustrates how this new and more candid way of thinking and being—where Tuula began to share her emotional neediness and vulnerabilities with others—also brought considerable discomfort. This could be seen particularly in the way she related to the achromatic cards on the Rorschach. As she said in acceptance of her situation, referring to the gray and black colored cards at the end of the extended inquiry: "I'd rather remove those dark ones. I can't remove the dark shades from life either now."

The Second Assessment: Final Observations and Conclusions

The picture that emerged from this second assessment—prompted by Tuula's sense of occupational impairment and her wish to seek early retirement for disability—was that her stress tolerance and functional capacity had deteriorated significantly. This time, she was far more candid. She no longer tried to control the outcome, and her test results confirmed her own impressions of cognitive decline, depression, and other mental health and relational problems. Her Rorschach was no longer constricted to the point of questionable validity but still showed significant coping vulnerabilities and a simplistic, avoidant problem-solving style. At the same time, positive changes were noted, including improved ability to process and integrate emotional experiences into decision-making and a more active, less escapist approach to stressful situations.

Changes in Tuula's Rorschach profile over five years aligned with shifts in her behavior at the day hospital and in how she dealt with her dysfunctional relationship. She attended the full five-week program at the day hospital as planned and was notably more engaged—participating actively in therapeutic group discussions and openly sharing her depression, difficult relationship, and other stressors.

Midway through the program, Tuula experienced a major confrontation with her partner, resulting in an episode of domestic abuse in which she feared for her life. She cried out for help until a neighbor called the police, and her partner was arrested. She sustained severe bruising and received support from her older daughter, law-enforcement authorities, and the day hospital. Tuula ultimately ended the relationship and changed her locks. A final report recommended that she be granted early retirement due to depression and significant neurocognitive deterioration.

In Conclusion

Tuula, a 43-year-old general practitioner in private practice, was initially referred to our psychiatric day hospital for an occupational assessment after multiple patient complaints to the Finnish National Supervisory Authority for Welfare and Health (Valvira) over suspected alcohol use at work and professional misconduct. Although superficially cooperative, she firmly denied any alcohol use on the job. Her MMPI clinical scales were within normal limits, but validity scales suggested rigid self-control and repression of even minor weaknesses, casting doubt on the profile's validity while also highlighting Tuula's capacity to present herself as mentally healthy.

Her Rorschach was notably brief and constricted, possibly reflecting an effort to "fake good." Yet her neurocognitive testing showed mild impairment in processing speed, attention, working memory, and frontal-executive functions—suggesting that her Rorschach constriction may also have reflected genuine coping deficits. The protocol indicated some distorted perceptions of self and others, a passive and dependent coping style, and a paradoxical attraction to emotional stimulation despite difficulty processing emotion adaptively.

Although performance-based measures raised concerns about Tuula's fitness to practice, the results of this first assessment remained inconclusive—until she arrived inebriated at the day hospital on the final day. This unanticipated event exposed the severity of her alcohol dependence and clarified her occupational impairment. None of the assessment methods had predicted this incident, but self-report tools, including the MMPI, had been particularly ineffective in detecting the nature and extent of her underlying issues.

Five years later, the context of Tuula's second assessment was very different. Now 48, she was seeking early retirement due to cognitive decline, depression, and an overwhelmingly stressful life situation, including an abusive relationship. She had significantly reduced her alcohol intake in the past year following a diagnosis of high blood pressure and elevated cardiac risk. Her neurocognitive testing now confirmed a moderate to severe, widespread decline. The MMPI and other self-report tools—which all appeared to be valid this time—revealed moderate to severe depression, emotional distress, somatic anxiety, interpersonal mistrust, insecurity, and pronounced dependent tendencies.

Although she was now more engaged and candid on the Rorschach (*R* = 22), most features of constriction observed earlier remained. These findings were now more clearly attributable to cognitive decline along with other coping deficits, but they also raised questions: Had her initial protocol already reflected early neuropsychological deterioration? Or was it primarily defensive? Could it have stemmed from long-standing coping vulnerabilities?

All three explanations likely contributed to her performance on the Rorschach. First, her *CDI* and *Lambda* profiles in the first testing may have reflected early cognitive decline, especially given her exceptionally low *EA*, which remained low in the second assessment. Second, as with the MMPI, Tuula had likely attempted to influence the outcome of her first Rorschach by limiting responses and successfully avoiding indicators of psychopathology. This was supported by the absence of critical contents in the first protocol and a low percentage of *FQ*– responses, both of which increased in the second testing. Third, her long history of emotional struggles, avoidance, and relational difficulties suggested more enduring personality-based vulnerabilities.

Tuula exhibited a simplistic, concrete, and avoidant coping style in handling emotionally charged or complex situations. Her alcohol use appeared to serve as a maladaptive coping strategy to manage painful emotions and stress. Both Rorschach assessments pointed to deep interpersonal difficulties that probably exacerbated her symptoms and drinking—forming a vicious cycle that destabilized her psychological functioning. This cycle, alongside chronic stress, excessive alcohol consumption, cardiovascular risk, and a long-standing mood disorder, all likely contributed to the marked cognitive decline observed over five years.

In the first assessment, Tuula worked hard to convince us she was occupationally capable but ultimately gave in to her addiction on the final day. In the second, after psychiatric treatment and confronting both her partner and her alcohol use, she had begun to change—cutting back on alcohol and developing a more flexible, emotionally honest way of relating to herself and others.

Ultimately, Tuula had managed to control the outcome of her first MMPI, producing a healthy profile, but both her first and second Rorschach pointed to significant psychological issues and vulnerabilities in terms of her coping, her thinking, her emotional life, and her relationship to herself and to others. Although her first Rorschach was suspect in terms of validity given its degree of constriction and the circumstances of the assessment, all the key findings later proved to hold true. Furthermore, the Rorschach allowed us to make a more comprehensive assessment of

Tuula's psychology, beyond what could be achieved by self-report and neurocognitive testing alone, and to reach a deeper understanding of her strengths and vulnerabilities, as well as a deeper understanding of the changes that had occurred in her psychological buildup over time. In our collaborative summary/discussion session with Tuula, these insights enabled us to empathize more deeply with her plight, while also helping her see herself better and feel more deeply seen, accepted and understood. This time we were all on the same page, exploring life's dark shades.

Notes

1 Personal details and background information have been altered or withheld to protect the patient's identity and ensure confidentiality.
2 In Finland, only the original version of the MMPI has been translated into Finnish. Although reference data for Finland has never been collected, US reference data for the original MMPI was collected in areas of the Midwest with a significant Nordic and Finnish cultural heritage, and many clinicians in Finland find it to be both useful and justified in clinical practice.

References

American Psychiatric Association. (1994). *Diagnostic and statistical manual of mental disorders* (4th ed.). American Psychiatric Association. doi:10.1176/appi.books.9780890423349.

American Psychiatric Association. (2013). *Diagnostic and statistical manual of mental disorders* (5th ed.). American Psychiatric Association.

Babor, T. F., Higgins-Biddle, J. C., Saunders, J. B., & Monteiro, M. G. (2001). *AUDIT: The Alcohol Use Disorders Identification Test: Guidelines for use in primary care* (2nd ed.). World Health Organization.

Beck, A. T., Steer, R. A., & Brown, G. K. (2004). *BDI-II: Beckin depressioasteikko, käsikirja* [*BDI–II: Beck Depression Inventory, manual*] (S. A. Hautala & K. Alanne, Trans.). Psykologien Kustannus Oy.

Diener, M. J., Hilsenroth, M. J., Shaffer, S. A., & Sexton, J. E. (2011). A meta-analysis of the relationship between the Rorschach Ego Impairment Index (EII) and psychiatric severity. *Clinical Psychology & Psychotherapy*, 18(6), 464–485. doi:10.1002/cpp.725.

Exner, J. E. (2003). *The Rorschach: A comprehensive system—volume 1: Basic foundations and principles of interpretation* (4th ed.). Wiley.

Gacono, C. B., & Smith, J. M. (2022). The extended aggression scores: Assessing aggressivity with Comprehensive System-Revised. In J. M. Smith, Y. Weinberger-Katzav, & P. Fontan (Eds.), *The Rorschach: A comprehensive system—revised. Supplementary scales handbook* (pp. 22–36). Rorschach Workshops.

Greene, R. L. (2011). *The MMPI-2: An interpretive manual* (2nd ed.). Allyn & Bacon.

Hathaway, S. R., & McKinley, J. C. (1943). *The Minnesota Multiphasic Personality Inventory*. University of Minnesota Press.

Hathaway, S. R., & McKinley, J. C. (n.d.). *Minnesota Multiphasic Personality Inventory.* Psykologien Kustannus Oy.

Heaton, R. K., Chelune, G. J., Talley, J. L., Kay, G. G., & Curtiss, G. (1993). *Wisconsin Card Sorting Test manual: Revised and expanded.* Psychological Assessment Resources.

Holi, M. M., Sammallahti, P. R., & Aalberg, V. A. (1998). A Finnish validation study of the SCL-90. *Acta Psychiatrica Scandinavica*, 97(1), 42–46.

Lyvers, M. (2000). "Loss of control" in alcoholism and drug addiction: A neuroscientific interpretation. *Experimental and Clinical Psychopharmacology*, 8(2), 225–249. doi:10.1037/1064-1297.8.2.225.

Meyer, G. J., Viglione, D. J., Mihura, J. L., Erard, R. E., & Erdberg, P. (2011). *Rorschach Performance Assessment System: Administration, coding, interpretation, and technical manual.* Rorschach Performance Assessment System LLC.

Meyers, J. E., & Meyers, K. R. (1995). *Rey Complex Figure Test and Recognition Trial: Professional manual.* Psychological Assessment Resources.

Peiffer, A. M., Laurienti, P. J., Koch, K. R., & Timmerman, L. (2014). Merging the Wechsler Adult Intelligence Scale picture completion subtest with fMRI in adult learners: A pilot study. *International Journal of Innovative Technology and Exploring Engineering*, 3(11), 122–126.

Perry, W. (2006, October). *The Rorschach Ego Impairment Index* [Seminar]. The Finnish Rorschach Association, Turku, Finland.

Reitan, R. M. (1958). Validity of the Trail Making Test as an indicator of organic brain damage. *Perceptual and Motor Skills*, 8(3), 271–276. doi:10.2466/pms.1958.8.3.271.

Smith, J. M., & Gacono, C. B. (2022). Cooper, Perry, & Arnow (1988) Rorschach defense scales: Revisiting the coding of defenses. In J. M. Smith, Y. Weinberger-Katzav, & P. Fontan (Eds.), *The Rorschach: A comprehensive system—revised. Supplementary scales handbook* (pp. 22–36). Rorschach Workshops.

Stroop, J. R. (1935). Studies of interference in serial verbal reactions. *Journal of Experimental Psychology*, 18(6), 643–662. doi:10.1037/h0054651.

Tort-Merino, A., Falgas, N., Allen, I. E., Balasa, M., Olives, J., Contador, J., Castellví, M., Juncà-Parella, J., Guillén, N., Borrego-Écija, S., Bosch, B., Fernández-Villullas, G., Ramos-Campoy, O., Antonell, A., Rami, L., Sánchez-Valle, R. & Lladó, A. (2022). Early-onset Alzheimer's disease shows a distinct neuropsychological profile and more aggressive trajectories of cognitive decline than late-onset. *Annals of Clinical and Translational Neurology*, 9(12), 1962–1973. doi:10.1002/acn3.51689.

Valmas, M. M., Ruiz, S. M., Gansler, D. A., Sawyer, K. S., & Oscar-Berman, M. (2014). Social cognition deficits and associations with drinking history in alcoholic men and women. *Alcoholism: Clinical and Experimental Research*, 38(12), 2998–3007. doi:10.1111/acer.12566.

Wechsler, D. (1992). *WAIS-R Wechslerin aikuisälykkyysasteikko: Käsikirja* [*WAIS-R Wechsler Adult Intelligence Scale: Manual*] (T. Järvinen & J. Häkkinen, Trans.). Psykologien Kustannus Oy.

Wechsler, D. (1997). *Wechsler Memory Scale, Revised (WMS-R): Käsikirja [Wechsler Memory Scale—Revised manual]* (M. Ruoppila, T. Era, & K. Heikkinen, Trans.). Psykologien Kustannus Oy.
Wechsler, D. (2005). *WAIS-III: Käsikirja [Wechsler Adult Intelligence Scale—Third Edition]*, (M. Mattila, H. Hakala, & J. Määttä, Trans.). Psykologien Kustannus Oy.

Appendixes

Appendix A

Catherine's Rorschach Protocol, Sequence of Codes and Structural Summary from the Initial Assessment (Comprehensive System; Exner, 2003)

Table A.1 Catherine's (female, forty-nine years) first Rorschach protocol

Card#	*R#*	*Response Phase*	*Inquiry Phase*
I	1	For me it's the pelvis . . . [looks at back of card, laughs]. E: Look closely.	E: [Rpts Ss resp] What made it look like that? S: In relation to this thing here [shows outline of W]. I don't know.
	2	Or then an island.	E: [Rpts Ss resp] What makes it look like that? S: To be able to escape. E: What do you mean? S: Because there are already separations [shows white parts in the middle: location W].
II	3	Two different islands.	E: [Rpts Ss resp] What made it look like that? S: Both are the same [shows both sides of W]. E: The same? S: I don't know.
	4	Or then one could imagine two little bears [laughs].	E: [Rpts Ss resp] What made it look like two little bears? S: These two, with their little snouts there, well . . . little ears [both sides of D6]. It sounds very childish what I'm saying, but, oh well.
III	5	[Looks at me] We're going to talk about the stomach again [laughs, points to D3].	E: [Rpts Ss resp] What makes it look like that? S: It has to be more like this [shows other shape with finger in D3 area]. E: More like how? S: Maybe the pain. E: The pain? S: At one point we had some problems. I had restrictions on certain things, and I was eating less.

Card#	*R#*	*Response Phase*	*Inquiry Phase*
	6	It could represent, uh . . . the lungs [shows D3].	E: [Rpts Ss resp] What makes it look like lungs? S: Well, since I know that . . . that is, with all the problems and everything, I was always trying to do well and . . . E: What makes it look like lungs? S: The shape and uh . . . Dad's illness.
	7	Here there are bats if you like [D2 on both sides]. Ultimately, I think I relate everything to illness now [laughs]. There it looked like two bats. Otherwise, well, I don't see any other . . .	E: [Rpts Ss resp] What made them look like bats? S: Well, I'm afraid of bats. E: Okay, but what makes them look like bats? S: Well, the tail and the head here.
IV	8	I can't see anything. A landscape of a coast or something like that, no? [laughs silently, looks at me].	E: [Rpts Ss resp] What makes it look like that? S: I don't really know. I can't remember. E: Where is it? S: All this here I suppose [shows outline of W].
	9	If you want, you can also imagine a monster. If not, I don't know.	E: [Rpts Ss resp] What makes it look like a monster? S: The monster for me is a miser. E: A miser? S: An evil being. E: What makes it look like that? S: Well, the eyes [points to upper middle area]. Someone who's out to get you.
V	10	A bat. . . . If not, I don't know.	E: [Rpts Ss resp] What makes it look like a bat? S: Well, a bat flies, and I've always been afraid of bats.
VI	11	Doesn't it represent an island? No? E: Everyone sees different things in it.	E: [Rpts Ss resp] What made it look like an island? S: The shape of . . . of this. E: This [circular gesture over card to indicate whole blot]? S: No not that [shows D3, therefore only D1].
	12	It could also be a sheep-skin or another kind of skin, and once it's spread out, uh . . .	E: [Rpts Ss resp] What made it look like that? S: Sheepskin is a skin that is soft. E: Soft? S: Yes, sheep are soft, pleasant animals. E: What makes it look like that to you? S: Me, uh, well, in principle I like animals, so . . . E: Okay, but what makes it look soft? S: Maybe it's a reflex.

Card#	*R#*	*Response Phase*	*Inquiry Phase*
VII	13	One can imagine two people talking to each other based on certain things here.	E: [Rpts Ss resp] What makes it look like that? S: Here. We see that it's two people talking. The heads are quite representative. They are chatting away, so there you have it. I think I'm falling back into childhood here.
	14	Or the lower abdomen [shows D4].	E: [Rpts Ss resp] What makes it look like the lower abdomen? S: There. Me, I see it like this. E: What about it makes it look like that? S: Maybe a maternity or I don't know, I couldn't tell you exactly.
	15	Otherwise, it could be little devils. The little heads [laughs, referring to D3s]. Ultimately, I am much more negative.	E: [Rpts Ss resp] What makes it look like little devils? S: They scare me. The eye here. They are in the process of . . . it's scary.
VIII	16	I prefer this one because it's richer in colors, and it feels good. Otherwise, this could also be the pelvis [shows D2], right . . .	E: [Rpts Ss resp] What makes it look like the pelvis? S: I see it that way, according to me. I don't know.
	17	It could also be the lungs [shows D5] . . . it doesn't exactly have this shape but, well . . .	E: [Rpts Ss resp] What makes it look like the lungs? S: Yes [shows D5], to my father with silicosis.
IX	18	It's not obvious, is it . . . I can't really see. E: Take your time. Maybe a Corsican landscape.	E: [Rpts Ss resp] What made it look like a Corsican landscape? S: Already the colors and . . . and then I know that Corsica is a beautiful country.
X	19	It's not a Corsican landscape, is it? You don't know?	E: [Rpts Ss resp] What makes it look like a Corsican landscape? S: Yes, with the two islands on the side [shows D9 on both sides] . . . or then it could be heads.
	20	Here there are some nasty creatures [D1 on both sides] that want to eat [shakes legs, laughs nervously]. No, I can't see [looks worried].	E: [Rpts Ss resp] What makes them look like that? S: I don't like them. E: You don't like them? S: Their legs and all that. I'm falling back into childhood. E: You said they were nasty creatures. What makes them look nasty? S: They don't inspire me.

Table A.2 Catherine's (female, forty-nine years) first sequence of codes.

Card	*Resp. No.*	*Loc. and DQ*	*Loc. No.*	*Determinants and Form Quality*	*2*	*Contents*	*Pop*	*Z Score*	*Special Scores*
I	1	Wo	1	Fo		An		1.0	
	2	WSv	1	Fu		Ls			
II	3	Wv	1	Fu	2	Ls			
	4	Do	1	Fo	2	A	P		
III	5	Do	3	F–		An			DR2, PER
	6	Do	3	Fo		An			DR2, PER
	7	Do	2	F–	2	A			PER
IV	8	Wv	1	Fo		Ls			
	9	Wo	1	Fo		(H)	P	2.0	DV, GHR
V	10	Wo	1	Fo		A	P	1.0	ALOG, PER
VI	11	Dv	1	Fu		Ls			DR
	12	Do	1	Fo		Ad	P		PER
VII	13	W+	1	Mpo	2	H	P	2.5	DR, GHR
	14	Do	4	F–		An			DR
	15	Do	3	Mpu		(Hd)			DR, PHR
VIII	16	Do	2	F–		An			
	17	Do	5	Fo		An			DR2, PER
IX	18	Wv	1	CFo		Ls			PER
X	19	Dv	9	Fu	2	Ls			DR2
	20	Do	1	FMp–	2	A			DR

RATIOS, PERCENTAGES, AND DERIVATIONS

R = 20	L = 4.00	
EB = 2 : 1.0	EA = 3.0	EBPer = N/A
eb = 1 : 0	es = 1	D = 0
	Adj es = 1	Adj D = 0
FM = 1	SumC' = 0	SumT = 0
m = 0	SumV = 0	SumY = 0

AFFECT

FC:CF+C	= 0 : 1
Pure C	= 0
SumC' : WSumC	= 0 : 1.0
Afr	= 0.33
S	= 1
Blends:R	= 0 : 20
CP	= 0

INTERPERSONAL

COP = 0		AG = 0
GHR:PHR		= 2 : 1
a:p		= 0 : 3
Food		= 0
SumT		= 0
Human Content		= 3
Pure H		= 1
PER		= 7
Isolation Index		= 0.30

IDEATION

a:p	= 0 : 3	Sum6	= 11
Ma:Mp	= 0 : 2	Lvl-2	= 4
2AB+(Art+Ay)	= 0	WSum6	= 45
MOR	= 0	M-	= 0
		M none	= 0

MEDIATION

XA%	= 0.75
WDA%	= 0.75
X-%	= 0.25
S-	= 0
P	= 5
X+%	= 0.50
Xu%	= 0.25

PROCESSING

Zf	= 4
W:D:Dd	= 8:12:0
W : M	= 8 : 2
Zd	= -3.5
PSV	= 0
DQ+	= 1
DQv	= 6

SELF-PERCEPTION

3r+(2)/R	= 0.30
Fr+rF	= 0
SumV	= 0
FD	= 0
An+Xy	= 6
MOR	= 0
H:(H)+Hd+(Hd)	= 1 : 2

PTI = 1	☐ DEPI = 3	☑ CDI = 5	☐ S-CON = 4	☐ HVI = No	☐ OBS = No

Figure A.1 Catherine's (female, forty-nine years) first structural summary (lower section)

Source: Reproduced by special permission of the Publisher, Psychological Assessment Resources, Inc., 16204 North Florida Avenue, Lutz, Florida 33549, from the Rorschach Interpretation Assistance Program: Version 5 by John E. Exner, Jr., Ph.D., Irving B. Weiner, Ph.D., and PAR Staff, Copyright 1976, 1985, 1990, 1994, 1995, 1999, 2001, 2003 by Psychological Assessment Resources, Inc. (PAR). Further reproduction is prohibited without permission of PAR.

Appendix B

Catherine's Rorschach Protocol from the Follow-up Assessment at Twenty-Six Months (Comprehensive System; Exner, 2003)

Table B.1 Catherine's (female, fifty-one years) second Rorschach protocol

Card#	*R#*	*Response Phase*	*Inquiry Phase*
I	1.	A small island . . . [looks at me]. E: Take your time. Try to find something else, maybe. S: What else can I say? See you soon? Ah, it's a bit . . . [looks to the side]. . . . No, it can't be an island? E: Yes, but look carefully. It can maybe be something else as well. S: . . . I can't remember anymore . . . E: Can't you see anything else besides an island? S: No, I can't really see.	E: [Rpts Ss resp] What makes it look like an island? S: Yes. E: Is it the whole thing? S: Yes. E: What makes it look like that? S: That's it. For me, that was it. E: Yes, but what made it look like a small island? S: Like this [vaguely pointing at different parts of the whole blot]. E: Help me see it like you do. S: Here [points vaguely to the outline of the right side of the blot].
II	2.	. . . I can't remember anymore . . . E: What does it look like to you? S: Like two little dogs [laughs]. E: Apart from that? S: I don't know anymore.	E: [Rpts Ss resp] Where are the dogs? S: [Points to D6 on both sides]. E: What makes it look like two little dogs? S: Because basically the two dogs are [makes gesture of pinching her mouth while smiling]. E: They are what? S: Kiss! [laughs] It's a shame when you can't recover.

Card#	*R#*	*Response Phase*	*Inquiry Phase*
III	3.	. . . Uh . . . maybe little . . . I don't know anymore. E: Little? S: I can't remember. E: Take your time. Take a good look at the card and try to figure out what it looks like. What might it be? S: . . . I can't remember anymore. E: Just take your time. See if you can see something. S: I just can't remember, damn it! E: Do you think it doesn't look like anything? S: Like two little characters. E: Ok. Something else maybe? S: Uh . . . I don't know what to say.	E: [Rpts Ss resp] Where did you see the two little characters? S: There and there [shows D9 on both sides]. E: What makes them look like two little characters? S: I don't know. E: Just help me see them like you do. What makes them look like that? S: I don't know.
IV	4.	. . . Uh . . . shoot! [shows D1 area] . . . I can't see what it represents. E: What might it be? S: A chimpanzee [laughs].	E: [Rpts Ss resp] What makes it look like a chimpanzee? S: It's just an idea. E: Sure, but what makes it look like that? S: Well, there's the grind like that [vaguely shows the whole blot, including central areas]. E: Grind? S: I don't know. E: What makes it look like a grind? S: I don't know. [The word used in French here was *mouture*, which can be translated as "grind" in English and primarily refers to the process of grinding or the ground product itself [as with coffee or grain], suggesting texture or granularity rather than form or shading. The use of the word is inappropriate here but also suggests a possible reference to the impression of shading as texture.]
V	5.	A . . . how do they call that? . . . Is it a chimpanzee? No . . . I can't figure it out.	E: [Rpts Ss resp] S: I don't think so. E: What makes it look like a chimpanzee? S: I don't know.

Card#	*R#*	*Response Phase*	*Inquiry Phase*
VI	6.	I don't know, what is this? E: It's an inkblot, but what does it look like? S: A unicorn.	E: [Rpts Ss resp] Where's the unicorn? How do you see it? S: There [points to the upper part of the blot]. E: What makes it look like a unicorn? S: It's what it reminds me of. E: Yes, but how do you see it? S: I can't remember. E: What is a unicorn, by the way? S: It's a thing with . . . a thing with horns. E: A thing? S: Ah, it's complicated.
VII	7.	It . . . it . . . looks like an island. E: Okay. Take your time. Could it be anything else, besides an island?	E: [Rpts Ss resp] Where do you see it, the island? S: Here [points to D1 on the left]. E: Just this part here? S: No. The whole thing. E: Okay, and what makes it look like an island? S: I don't know.
	8.	Or two characters.	E: [Rpts Ss resp] What makes it look like two characters? Where do you see them? S: Here [points to both sides of the blot]. E: What makes them look like two characters? S: I can't remember.
VIII	9.	Here there are two little mice, right? E: Okay. Anything else? S: And here [points to the lower part of the blot], what is that then? E: It's up to you. It can be many things.	E: [Rpts Ss resp] Show me the mice. S: There and there [shows D1 on both sides]. E: What makes them look like mice? S: Like this here [shows different parts of D1]. E: Okay. So what makes them look like mice to you? S: [long pause]
IX	10.	. . . I can't see what it looks like. E: Take a good look. Everyone sees different things anyway. S: I can't remember. E: Take your time. S: I can't find it. E: Isn't there something that comes to mind when you look at it? S: The lower back? [laughs]. No, no, not the lower back.	E: [Rpts Ss resp] Where's the lower back? S: Back here [shows her own lower back]. E: No, I mean here on the card. S: Oh. Here [shows both sides of the blot].

Card#	*R#*	*Response Phase*	*Inquiry Phase*
X	11.	. . . I can't remember . . . This is [points to D11] . . . what is this? E: What does it look like to you? S: . . . I can't remember . . . E: Take your time. I want you to find something for me. S: Something on the lower back? [looks at me] [The expression used in French on both R10 and R11 was *les reins*, which can refer both to the lower back or to the kidneys. Although the former might be more likely here, given her reference to her own back in the inquiry on R10, the correct translation remains unclear.]	E: [Rpts Ss resp] What makes it look like something on the lower back? Where is it? S: I don't know [points toward top left area of D9]. No, not there. E: You pointed to this part here previously [I show area D11]. S: I don't know.

Appendix C

Ville's Rorschach Protocol, Sequence of Codes and Structural Summary (Comprehensive System; Exner, 2003)

Table C.1 Ville's (male, twenty-one years) Rorschach protocol.

Card#	*R#*	*Response Phase*	*Inquiry Phase*
I	1.	A butterfly.	E: [Rpts Ss resp] What makes it look like that? S: The butterfly's body [D4], the wings [W].
	2.	A bat's head. Can't make out anything else. My imagination stops there.	E: [Rpts Ss resp] S: The whole thing. The eyes [DdS30], the teeth [DdS29], the bat's ears [Dd34].
	3.	Some person leaning. A monk carrying something.	E: [Rpts Ss resp] S: Here [D7]. It's carrying something [D4], with a cloak on. Here's the other leg [bottom section of D2, so the person is D2].
	4.	Some woman standing behind branches and stretching her arms upwards.	E: [Rpts Ss resp] S: The legs [D3], the torso [central area of D4], the hands [D1]. E: And the branches? S: Here on the sides [both sides of W]. E: What made them look like that? S: I don't know. Just these different shapes here [shows outlines of D2].
II	5.	Christmas elves with their hands against each other.	E: [Rpts Ss resp] S: The hat, hands against each other. They're sitting [W].
	6.	A face. The mouth and the eyes, the nose in between.	E: [Rpts Ss resp] S: Here and here, and the nose [points to DS5, DdS30s and D4; the entire face is WS].
	7.	A human's pelvis.	E: [Rpts Ss resp] S: Here [D3]. E: What makes it look like a pelvis? S: The shape.

Card#	*R#*	*Response Phase*	*Inquiry Phase*
III	8.	They are carrying something. A cockroach's head [D7]. A grasshopper's head. Women wearing high heels.	E: Here you said they are carrying something. A cockroach's head. A grasshopper's head . . . S: Or birds, breasts, carrying something. It could be a cockroach's head, eye, eye, spike, jaws [D7].
	9.	Could also be birds carrying a cockroach's head, wearing high heels [laughs].	[no further inquiry].
IV	10.	A tree.	E: [Rpts Ss resp] S: The trunk in the middle and the leaves go like this [points to D4s and D6s, all together W].
	11.	A three-legged creature.	E: [Rpts Ss resp] S: The three legs [D6s and D1], the arms [D4s], the head [D3].
	12.	. . . A middle finger on both sides.	E: [Rpts Ss resp] S: The knuckles and the middle finger [Dd21].
	13.	. . . The ears of a dog [D4s].	E: [Rpts Ss resp] S: The ears, not together. The ears of a dog. Not a dog.
V	14.	A bat.	E: [Rpts Ss resp] S: The wings [W].
	15.	It could also be a moth or a butterfly.	E: [Rpts Ss resp] S: Same thing [W].
VI	16.	A squashed fox, the whiskers. Got run over by a car.	E: [Rpts Ss resp] S: The tire of the car went over it, and it got squashed [W]. E: What made it look like that? S: The shape.
	17.	The muzzle of a bear right there, from a cartoon, not quite . . .	E: [Rpts Ss resp] S: Here, the face of the bear. The muzzle, the eye, the muzzle [shows outline of Dd24 on the left, but also broader area encompassing most of the bottom left side and the same on the right side, therefore Dd99].
VII	18.	Two Indians kissing again.	E: [Rpts Ss resp] S: About to kiss. E: How do you see them? S: The profiles here with the feather [D1s].

Card#	*R#*	*Response Phase*	*Inquiry Phase*
	19.	A strange-looking monster, the mouth right there. Very angry. It's angry.	E: [Rpts Ss resp] S: The mouth, the nose, the eye, the hat. Both middle parts [D3].
VIII	20.	Lizards climbing that tree or something else.	E: [Rpts Ss resp] S: Lizards walking [W, with lizards in D1]. E: What makes it look like that? S: The shape.
IX	21.	Something's hanging. A creature with a hanging trunk.	E: [Rpts Ss resp] S: The eyes [DdS23], the nose [Dd30], peeking from behind a bush [D11, all together DdS99].
X	22.	Crabs with their claws.	E: [Rpts Ss resp] S: Crabs and claws [D1s]. E: What makes them look like crabs? S: It's not precise.
	23.	The pelvic bone.	E: [Rpts Ss resp] S: The gray part [D11]. I don't know. Could also be lungs. E: What made it look like that? S: The shape.
	24.	The shoulder blades.	E: [Rpts Ss resp] S: Here [D6]. E: What made it look like that? S: Also the shape.
	25.	Eyes. A mustache.	E: [Rpts Ss resp] S: Here [D2s] and here [D10].
	26.	A flower there.	E: [Rpts Ss resp] S: The stem. A yellow and red flower [D15].

Table C.2 Ville's (male, twenty-one years) sequence of codes

Card	*Resp. No.*	*Loc. and DQ*	*Loc. No.*	*Determinants and Form Quality*	*2*	*Contents*	*Pop*	*Z Score*	*Special Scores*
I	1	Wo	1	Fo		A	P	1.0	
	2	WSo	1	Fu		Ad		3.5	
	3	D+	2	Mao		H, Cg, Id		4.0	GHR
	4	W+	1	Ma. FD–		H, Bt		4.0	PHR
II	5	W+	1	Mpo	2	(H), Cg		4.5	GHR
	6	WSo	1	F–		Hd		4.5	PHR
	7	Do	3	F–		An			
III	8	D+	1	Ma–	2	H, Cg, Ad	P	3.0	COP, FAB2, PHR
	9	D+	1	Ma–	2	A, Ad		3.0	COP, FAB2, PHR
IV	10	Wo	1	Fo		Bt		2.0	
	11	Wo	1	Fu		A		2.0	INC
	12	Ddo	21	F–	2	Hd			PHR
	13	Do	4	F–		Ad			
V	14	Wo	1	Fo		A	P	1.0	
	15	Wo	1	Fo		A	P	1.0	PSV
VI	16	Wo	1	Fo		A		2.5	MOR
	17	Ddo	99	F–	2	(Ad)			DV
VII	18	D+	1	Mao	2	Hd, Art	P	3.0	COP, GHR

Card	*Resp. No.*	*Loc. and DQ*	*Loc. No.*	*Determinants and Form Quality*	*2*	*Contents*	*Pop*	*Z Score*	*Special Scores*
	19	D+		Mau	2	(Hd), Cg		1.0	AG, PHR
VIII	20	W+	1	FMau	2	A, Bt	P	4.5	
IX	21	DdS+	99	FMp. FD–		Ad, Bt		5.0	
X	22	Do	1	Fo	2	A	P		
	23	Do	11	F–		An			
	24	Do	6	F–		An			
	25	Do	2	F–		Hd			PHR
	26	Do	15	FCo		Bt			

RATIOS, PERCENTAGES, AND DERIVATIONS

R = 26	L = 1.60	
EB = 7 : 0.5	EA = 7.5	EBPer = N/A
eb = 2 : 0	es = 2	D = +2
	Adj es = 2	Adj D = +2
FM = 2	SumC' = 0	SumT = 0
m = 0	SumV = 0	SumY = 0

AFFECT

FC:CF+C	= 1 : 0
Pure C	= 0
SumC' : WSumC	= 0 : 0.5
Afr	= 0.37
S	= 3
Blends:R	= 2 : 26
CP	= 0

INTERPERSONAL

COP = 3	AG = 1
GHR:PHR	= 3 : 7
a:p	= 7 : 2
Food	= 0
SumT	= 0
Human Content	= 9
Pure H	= 3
PER	= 0
Isolation Index	= 0.19

IDEATION

a:p	= 7 : 2	Sum6	= 4
Ma:Mp	= 6 : 1	Lvl-2	= 2
2AB+(Art+Ay)	= 1	WSum6	= 17
MOR	= 1	M-	= 3
		M none	= 0

MEDIATION

XA%	= 0.54
WDA%	= 0.61
X-%	= 0.46
S-	= 2
P	= 7
X+%	= 0.38
Xu%	= 0.15

PROCESSING

Zf	= 17
W:D:Dd	= 11:12:3
W : M	= 11 : 7
Zd	= -6.5
PSV	= 1
DQ+	= 9
DQv	= 0

SELF-PERCEPTION

3r+(2)/R	= 0.35
Fr+rF	= 0
SumV	= 0
FD	= 2
An+Xy	= 3
MOR	= 1
H:(H)+Hd+(Hd)	= 3 : 6

PTI = 3	☐ DEPI = 2	☐ CDI = 1	☐ S-CON = 2	☑ HVI = Yes	☐ OBS = No

Figure C.1 Ville's (male, twenty-one years) structural summary (lower section)
Source: Reproduced by special permission of the Publisher, Psychological Assessment Resources, Inc., 16204 North Florida Avenue, Lutz, Florida 33549, from the Rorschach Interpretation Assistance Program: Version 5 by John E. Exner, Jr., Ph.D., Irving B. Weiner, Ph.D., and PAR Staff, Copyright 1976, 1985, 1990, 1994, 1995, 1999, 2001, 2003 by Psychological Assessment Resources, Inc. (PAR). Further reproduction is prohibited without permission of PAR.

Appendix D

Pekka's Rorschach Protocol, Sequence of Codes and Structural Summary (Comprehensive System; Exner, 2003)

Table D.1 Pekka's (male, forty-eight years) Rorschach protocol

Card#	*R#*	*Response Phase*	*Inquiry Phase*
I	1.	The head of a cat.	E: [Rpts Ss resp] What made it look like that? S: The outline fits [W].
	2.	Or two heads of dogs on each side.	E: [Rpts Ss resp] Where? S: Here [shows D7 on both sides] E: What made it look like that? S: Again, the outline, the shape.
II	3.	Two vague human figures facing each other.	E: [Rpts Ss resp] Show me. S: Their hands together. E: Can you show me more precisely? S: Like their heads are here [D2s]. Pretty vague.
III	4.	Two. A pot in the middle.	E: [Rpts Ss resp] S: The body, the hands [D9s], the pot in the middle. E: A pot in the middle? S: Here [D7]. They're cooking something there.
	5.	A bow in the middle and . . .	E: [Rpts Ss resp] S: Yes here [D3] E: What made it look like a bow? S: The outlines.
IV	6.	. . . Some old man.	E: [Rpts Ss resp] S: The whole thing. The feet, the face, but the overall impression. If you look carefully, no. E: What made it look like an old man? S: Maybe because he's lying down on his back.
	7.	Or some giant.	E: [Rpts Ss resp] S: The same thing. Big feet.

Card#	*R#*	*Response Phase*	*Inquiry Phase*
V	8.	A bat.	E: Here first you said a bat, then a butterfly. S: The wings suggested a butterfly, but the ears a bat.
	9.	Or a butterfly.	[no additional inquiry].
VI	10.	A hide. The top part doesn't really stand out.	E: [Rpts Ss resp] S: The hide of a bear. E: What made it look like the hide of a bear? S: It's like the extremities would be the paws, something on the floor, then the details support it [points to outlines], the paws, the head.
	11.	Some bird. The bird's head. Something like that.	E: [Rpts Ss resp] S: Beak-like, the wings.
VII	12.	A face.	E: Here in the beginning, you said a face. S: Here, you have to leave these out [shows D3 without Dd21], the face, the eyes, the mouth. I don't know about the bottom part.
	13.	Here a clenched fist with the thumbs upwards.	E: [Rpts Ss resp] S: Yes, a little vague [shows only D1 on the left].
VIII	14.	As a whole, this could be a bear < >.	E: [Rpts Ss resp] S: The face [top part], the body [D5 + D2], and the hands [D1]. It's rising up. You can't see the feet, so the upper body.
	15.	^ On the sides, two rats.	E: [Rpts Ss resp] S: Or something. > < > < Like this. Four limbs.
IX	16.	. . . > ˅ [looks at the back of the card] Two hippopotamus heads of some kind.	E: [Rpts Ss resp] S: The head of a hippopotamus, let's leave this out [leaves 1/3 of D1 out, close to D3].
	17.	˅ This could be the head of an elephant.	E: [Rpts Ss resp] S: Here, the ears [D6].
	18.	˅ Or the head of a hairy dog [D6].	E: [Rpts Ss resp] S: Yes, hairy dogs. E: Hairy? S: It's not a flat surface, there are additional dimensions. E: Additional dimensions? What do you mean? S: The surface is vague, the colors are lighter there, it gives a more hairy impression.

Card#	R#	Response Phase	Inquiry Phase
X	19.	. . . ˅ ˄ . . . Vague creatures.	E: [Rpts Ss resp] S: Here [D1s] and here [D8s]. E: What made them look vague? S: I don't know. The shape is somehow vague. E: Were there one or two answers here? S: Here are these [D1], and then these here [D8].
	20.	[other two vague creatures coded as separate response, based on inquiry for R19].	[no additional inquiry].
		As a whole, I can't make anything of it.	E: At the end you said that, as a whole, you can't make anything of it. S: I'm trying to look, but . . . for me nothing stands out clearly enough.

Table D.2 Pekka's (male, forty-eight years) sequence of codes

Card	*Resp. No*	*Loc. and DQ*	*Loc. No.*	*Determinants and Form Quality*	*2*	*Contents*	*Pop*	*Z Score*	*Special Scores*
I	1	Wo	1	Fo		Ad		1.0	
	2	Do	7	Fu	2	Ad			
II	3	Wo	1	Fo	2	H		4.5	GHR
III	4	D+	1	Mao	2	H, Hh	P	3.0	COP, GHR
	5	Do	3	Fo		Cg			
IV	6	Wo	1	Mpo		H	P	2.0	GHR
	7	Wo	1	Fo		(H)	P	2.0	GHR
V	8	Wo	1	Fo		A	P	1.0	
	9	Wo	1	Fo		A	P	1.0	PSV
VI	10	Do	1	Fo		Ad, Hh	P		
	11	Do	3	Fo		A			
VII	12	Ddo	99	F–	2	Hd			PHR
	13	Do	1	Mau		Hd			PHR
VIII	14	Wo	1	FMa–		Ad		4.5	INC
	15	Do	1	Fo	2	A	P		
IX	16	Ddo	99	Fu	2	Ad			
	17	Do	6	Fu		Ad			
	18	Do	6	FT–	2	Ad			
X	19	Dv	1	Fu	2	A			
	20	Dv	8	Fo	2	A			

RATIOS, PERCENTAGES, AND DERIVATIONS

R = 20	L = 3.00	
EB = 3 : 0.0	EA = 3.0	EBPer = N/A
eb = 1 : 1	es = 2	D = 0
	Adj es = 2	Adj D = 0
FM = 1	SumC' = 0	SumT = 1
m = 0	SumV = 0	SumY = 0

AFFECT

FC:CF+C	= 0 : 0
Pure C	= 0
SumC' : WSumC	= 0 : 0.0
Afr	= 0.54
S	= 0
Blends:R	= 0 : 20
CP	= 0

INTERPERSONAL

COP = 1	AG = 0
GHR:PHR	= 4 : 2
a:p	= 3 : 1
Food	= 0
SumT	= 1
Human Content	= 6
Pure H	= 3
PER	= 0
Isolation Index	= 0.00

IDEATION

a:p	= 3 : 1	Sum6	= 1
Ma:Mp	= 2 : 1	Lvl-2	= 0
2AB+(Art+Ay)	= 0	WSum6	= 2
MOR	= 0	M-	= 0
		M none	= 0

MEDIATION

XA%	= 0.85
WDA%	= 0.89
X-%	= 0.15
S-	= 0
P	= 7
X+%	= 0.60
Xu%	= 0.25

PROCESSING

Zf	= 8
W:D:Dd	= 7:11:2
W : M	= 7 : 3
Zd	= -5.0
PSV	= 1
DQ+	= 1
DQv	= 2

SELF-PERCEPTION

3r+(2)/R	= 0.45
Fr+rF	= 0
SumV	= 0
FD	= 0
An+Xy	= 0
MOR	= 0
H:(H)+Hd+(Hd)	= 3 : 3

PTI = 0	☐ DEPI = 3	☐ CDI = 3	☐ S-CON = 3	☐ HVI = No	☐ OBS = No

Figure D.1 Pekka's (male, forty-eight years) structural summary (lower section)

Source: Reproduced by special permission of the Publisher, Psychological Assessment Resources, Inc., 16204 North Florida Avenue, Lutz, Florida 33549, from the Rorschach Interpretation Assistance Program: Version 5 by John E. Exner, Jr., Ph.D., Irving B. Weiner, Ph.D., and PAR Staff, Copyright 1976, 1985, 1990, 1994, 1995, 1999, 2001, 2003 by Psychological Assessment Resources, Inc. (PAR). Further reproduction is prohibited without permission of PAR.

Appendix E

Tuula's First Rorschach Protocol, Sequence of Codes and Structural Summary (Comprehensive System; Exner, 2003)

Table E.1 Tuula's (female, forty-three years) first Rorschach protocol

Card#	*R#*	*Response Phase*	*Inquiry Phase*
I	1.	Some animal. For me it's a bat. [Puts card down on table] E: Take your time. S: [Picks card up, looks at it a little more, puts back down] I don't see anything else. E: Look at it a little longer. I'm sure you can see something else. S: Okay . . .	E: [Rpts Ss resp] What makes it look like that? S: The whole thing. The wings [W].
	2.	In the middle the shape of a person, the feet [Dd31], the hands [D1], the head [upper central area] [D4].	E: [Rpts Ss resp] What makes it look like that? S: The legs, the waist [central part of D4], the hands up, the nose. E: What about the head? S: I wish there was something. Now there's a driveway in the middle [shows central axis]. E: Okay. Let's focus on what you saw in the first round. S: Sure.
II	3.	˅ Some bug, the antennae, the head [D3], the wings [D6], the legs [D2s].	E: [Rpts Ss resp] S: Yes, the wings [D6], the legs [D2s]. E: The legs? S: Yes, here [D2s]. The antennae made me think of that.
III	4.	A loving couple. Two people. A bow in between.	E: [Rpts Ss resp] S: Here [D9s], the legs [shows two legs for each [D5 and Dd30]. The bow here [D3] hints to the fact that they are in good terms. E: What made it look like a bow? S: The shape.
IV	5.	A cruel-looking creature, with big feet, wings. The torso right there [central area].	E: [Rpts Ss resp] S: The feet [D6s], the wings [D4s], the eyes [in D3 area], sharp. E: You said it was cruel-looking? S: Yes. The color and the shape [W].

Card#	*R#*	*Response Phase*	*Inquiry Phase*
V	6.	This looks more like a bird. A living creature, a bird.	E: [Rpts Ss resp] S: The wings, the feet, the head [W].
VI	7.	> ˅ The head is missing, but this person has bought themselves a winter coat. The legs [D6]. The head is hidden under the coat.	E: [Rpts Ss resp] S: The legs opposite each other [D6]. E: What makes it look like a coat? S: Clearly. A zipper [D5], the head is not visible, inside the coat are the hands and body [W].
VII	8.	Two Christmas elves looking at each other.	E: [Rpts Ss resp] S: Both have caps [D5s], a body, you can see one hand [D3]. E: Is the lower section part of it? S: It's part of it, some kind of skirt or something [W].
VIII	9.	A face, eyes.	E: [Rpts Ss resp] S: The eyes [upper central area of D2], the face [D2]. It could be the face of a cat.
	10.	Two animals, dogs. I don't see anything in the upper part.	E: [Rpts Ss resp] S: A badger or a wild animal. [D1s]. E: What makes it look like that? S: Just the shape.
IX	11.	˅ < ˅ < An elephant, the eyes, the big ears, the coat [D1s], the pants [D3s], a city-elephant.	E: [Rpts Ss resp] S: The eyes, the head, the ears [D6]. It's dressed in clothes. A city-elephant, the coat, and the pants. E: What made it look like that? S: The head of the elephant made me think of that.
X	12.	> ˄ . . . Blue crabs.	E: [Rpts Ss resp] S: Because of the legs [D1s].
	13.	Flowers [D15s and D13s]. Here also [D2s].	E: [Rpts Ss resp] S: Here [D15s and D13s], except for the stem [D7s]. Six flowers. E: What makes them look like flowers? S: The shape and the different colors.
	14.	Two little bugs facing each other.	E: [Rpts Ss resp] S: The antennae, the eyes, and the mouth [D8s].

Extended inquiry:

E: [Lays all ten cards on the table] Which were the two cards that you liked the least?
S: This one and this one [IV and I].
E: Why?
S: Because it's just a black bat. I want colors.
E: Okay. And which were the two cards that you liked the most?
S: This one and this one [X and III].
E: Okay, why?
S: Here you have the loving couple and here you have colors, flowers, it's positive.

Table E.2 Tuula's (female, forty-three years) first sequence of codes

Card	*Resp. No*	*Loc. and DQ*	*Loc. No.*	*Determinants and Form Quality*	*2*	*Contents*	*Pop*	*Z Score*	*Special Scores*
I	1	Wo	1	Fo		A	P	1.0	
	2	Do	4	Fo		H			GHR
II	3	Wo	1	Fu		A		4.5	
III	4	D+	1	Mp–	2	H, Hx, Cg		4.0	AB, PHR
IV	5	Wo	1	FC'o		A		2.0	
V	6	Wo	1	Fo		A		1.0	
VI	7	W+	1	FDu		Hd, Cg		2.5	PHR
VII	8	W+	1	Mpo	2	(H), Cg	P	2.5	GHR
VIII	9	Do	2	Fu		Ad			
	10	Do	1	Fo	2	A	P		
IX	11	W+	1	Fu		A, Cg		5.5	FAB
X	12	Do	1	Fo	2	A	P		
	13	Do	13	FC–	2	Bt			
	14	Do	8	Fo	2	A			

RATIOS, PERCENTAGES, AND DERIVATIONS

R = 14	L = 1.80	
EB = 2 : 0.5	EA = 2.5	EBPer = N/A
eb = 0 : 1	es = 1	D = 0
	Adj es = 1	Adj D = 0
FM = 0	SumC' = 1	SumT = 0
m = 0	SumV = 0	SumY = 0

AFFECT

FC:CF+C	= 1 : 0
Pure C	= 0
SumC' : WSumC	= 1 : 0.5
Afr	= 0.75
S	= 0
Blends:R	= 0 : 14
CP	= 0

INTERPERSONAL

COP = 0	AG = 0
GHR:PHR	= 2 : 2
a:p	= 0 : 2
Food	= 0
SumT	= 0
Human Content	= 4
Pure H	= 2
PER	= 0
Isolation Index	= 0.07

IDEATION

a:p	= 0 : 2	Sum6	= 1
Ma:Mp	= 0 : 2	Lvl-2	= 0
2AB+(Art+Ay)	= 2	WSum6	= 4
MOR	= 0	M-	= 1
		M none	= 0

MEDIATION

XA%	= 0.86
WDA%	= 0.86
X-%	= 0.14
S-	= 0
P	= 4
X+%	= 0.57
Xu%	= 0.29

PROCESSING

Zf	= 8
W:D:Dd	= 7:7:0
W : M	= 7 : 2
Zd	= -1.0
PSV	= 0
DQ+	= 4
DQv	= 0

SELF-PERCEPTION

3r+(2)/R	= 0.43
Fr+rF	= 0
SumV	= 0
FD	= 1
An+Xy	= 0
MOR	= 0
H:(H)+Hd+(Hd)	= 2 : 2

PTI = 0	☐ DEPI = 3	☑ CDI = 4	☐ S-CON = 2	☐ HVI = No	☐ OBS = No

Figure E.1 Tuula's (female, forty-three years) first structural summary (lower section)
Source: Reproduced by special permission of the Publisher, Psychological Assessment Resources, Inc., 16204 North Florida Avenue, Lutz, Florida 33549, from the Rorschach Interpretation Assistance Program: Version 5 by John E. Exner, Jr., Ph.D., Irving B. Weiner, Ph.D., and PAR Staff, Copyright 1976, 1985, 1990, 1994, 1995, 1999, 2001, 2003 by Psychological Assessment Resources, Inc. (PAR). Further reproduction is prohibited without permission of PAR.

Appendix F

Tuula's Second Rorschach Protocol (Five Years Later), Sequence of Codes and Structural Summary (Comprehensive System; Exner, 2003)

Table F.1 Tuula's (female, forty-eight years) second Rorschach protocol

Card#	*R#*	*Response Phase*	*Inquiry Phase*
I	1.	It could be two Santa Clauses facing each other, and the Santa Claus has angel wings.	E: [Rpts Ss resp] Show me. What makes it look like that? S: Angel wings [Dd34], the triangular hat [Dd28, all together D7].
	2.	And a Christmas tree . . . E: Sorry? S: Here and here [bottom halves of D2]. I don't see anything else. E: Take your time. You might see something else.	E: [Rpts Ss resp] S: It goes from here and this edge here is a bit worse [refers to outline] E: Where exactly? S: Here, both of these [Dd99, bottom half of D2].
	3.	Hands. Hands reaching upwards.	E: [Rpts Ss resp] S: Hands asking for help there [D1].
II	4.	This is a bat.	E: [Rpts Ss resp] S: The blackness makes it look like that. The head and the wings. The whole black area [D6].
	5.	Then here you have two dog heads with their muzzles facing each other. I can't get anything else from this one.	E: [Rpts Ss resp] S: Here and another one here [D1s], their muzzles facing each other, the ears.
III	6.	Here clearly two female figures. There's a butterfly in the middle.	E: [Rpts Ss resp] S: A butterfly in the middle [D3] and there are the women [D1]. E: Are these two separate responses? S: No. In the same image, the same whole. A high heel there [Dd33] and there [Dd31] some big boot, shoe, felt slipper or something. E: What about the butterfly? S: The wings and the central part [D3].

Card#	R#	Response Phase	Inquiry Phase
IV	7.	This is a big-footed bear wearing high heels, and its arms are somewhat poorly developed.	E: [Rpts Ss resp] S: Poorly developed arms [D4s], high heels [D6s], and this whole lump is the bear [W], and it's the backside of the bear, it doesn't have eyes. E: You said this whole lump? S: The whole lump is the one bear. E: Poorly developed arms? S: Because you have the big feet [D6s] and the arms and such stumps [D4s].
V	8.	A bat. I don't get anything else from this.	E: [Rpts Ss resp] S: In my opinion that's what it looks like. The wings, then the antennae, although I don't know if bats have antennae or not [W].
VI	9.	This is the hide of a predatory animal, so, the skin. It could be a wolf, based on that snout.	E: [Rpts Ss resp] S: This whole thing [W], the spine [D5], looked like a wolf because of the snout [D3]. E: What made it look like skin? S: Maybe the symmetry, a clear hide.
VII	10.	Two Christmas elves.	E: [Rpts Ss resp] S: This hat [D5] makes it look like that. Otherwise, it could just be some girl. It looks just like a decoration. Could even be a Christmas ornament [W]. E: What makes it look like an ornament? S: The face [D9], the hat [D5], the hand [Dd21], the waist [border between D3 and D4], the lower body [D4]. I'm not worried that there are no feet, it's just the way I see it. It could be placed on a table to stand, for example.
VIII	11.	The pink ones are two animals [D1s], badgers, for instance.	E: [Rpts Ss resp] S: Two legs, a tail, and . . .
	12.	The lower part in terms of color looks like a butterfly.	E: [Rpts Ss resp] S: This right here [D2]. The wings and the symmetry. E: You said it looked like a butterfly in terms of color? S: Yes, the color also plays a role.

Card#	*R#*	*Response Phase*	*Inquiry Phase*
	13.	In the middle there's a torn rug.	E: [Rpts Ss resp] S: Torn apart. E: What makes it look like it's torn apart? S: One part here, another there [shows both sides of D5], and in the middle, those torn-up . . . a blue rug [D5].
IX	14.	At the top, two crabs [D3s].	E: [Rpts Ss resp] S: The orange ones [D3s]. E: What made them look like that? S: The shape and the claws.
	15.	. . . There are those blue or greenish, two guys with their backs against each other, wearing hats.	E: [Rpts Ss resp] S: The hats are like this, the head, the hand on the chin, like this [shows gesture]. The whole green part then is the guy [D1, with head and hat in lower part of D3].
	16.	At the bottom I see four apples or four fruits.	E: [Rpts Ss resp] S: Four [D6]. E: What makes them look like that? S: The shape. The shape and the color.
X	17.	The blue ones are spiders.	E: [Rpts Ss resp] S: These [D1s]. E: What makes them look like spiders? S: The legs.
	18.	The red ones are the map of some country.	E: [Rpts Ss resp] S: Clearly. Sweden or Norway or something [D9]. E: What makes it look like that? S: Well, maybe this coast and inland. E: Coast and inland? What about it makes it look like that? S: This is colored differently; the sea would be here [white space around D9]. E: Colored differently? S: It's darkened. I can't say exactly.
	19.	Those yellow ones are flowers.	E: [Rpts Ss resp] S: The stem part [D7] and the flower [D15]. E: What makes it look like a flower? S: It just looks like it. The petal is light, and this is the heart of the flower.

Card#	*R#*	*Response Phase*	*Inquiry Phase*
	20.	That green is a wig.	E: [Rpts Ss resp] S: These flipped things and the shape of the head [D10].
	21.	Over there are two bugs, something . . .	E: [Rpts Ss resp] S: The antennae, the eyes. I don't know what species. The tail, the legs [D8].
	22.	There are two bunny rabbits.	E: [Rpts Ss resp] S: The ears, the nose, the front paws [D12].

Extended inquiry:
E: [Lays all ten cards on the table] Okay, now tell me which were the two cards you liked the least, as well as the two cards you liked the most, and why.
S: This is bad, dark [I]. Santa Clauses that don't fit and hands asking for help. It made me feel uncomfortable. Then in this one there's nothing [V]. I just saw that bat. It also doesn't please me.
E: Okay. And the two you liked the most?
S: This was the best of them [X].
E: Why?
S: It has colors and details. There's a lot of everything in it.
E: Pick another one.
S: This is better [IX], it's more open. This one is crumpled together [VIII]. Otherwise, I might have chosen this one [VIII].
E: Good, thank you. What did it feel like to do this test?
S: Not bad at all, but I'd rather remove those dark ones. I can't remove the dark shades from life either now.

Table F.2 Tuula's (female, forty-eight years) second sequence of codes

Card	*Resp. No*	*Loc. and D*	*Loc. No.*	*Determinants and Form Quality*	*2*	*Contents*	*Pop*	*Z Score*	*Special Scores*
I	1	D+	7	Fu	2	(H)		6.0	INC, PHR
	2	Ddo	99	F–	2	Bt			
	3	Do	1	Mao		Hd			PHR
II	4	Do	6	C'F–		A			
	5	D+	6	Fo	2	Ad	P	3.0	
III	6	D+	1	F–	2	H, Cg, A		3.0	PHR
IV	7	W+	1	Fu		A, Cg		4.0	FAB, MOR
V	8	Wo	1	Fo		A	P	1.0	INC
VI	9	Wo	1	Fo		Ad, An	P	2.5	
VII	10	W+	1	Fo	2	(Hd), Cg, Art	P	2.5	DR, GHR
VIII	11	Do	1	Fo	2	A	P		
	12	Do	2	FCo		A			
	13	Do	5	FCu		Hh			MOR
IX	14	Do	3	Fu	2	A			
	15	D+	1	Mp–	2	H, Cg		4.5	PHR

Card	*Resp. No*	*Loc. and D*	*Loc. No.*	*Determinants and Form Quality*	*2*	*Contents*	*Pop*	*Z Score*	*Special Scores*
	16	Do	6	FCo	2	Fd			
X	17	Do	1	Fo	2	A	P		
	18	DdS+	99	FYu	2	Ge		6.0	
	19	Do	15	FC.FYu	2	Bt			
	20	Do	10	Fu		Cg, Art			
	21	Do	8	Fo	2	A			
	22	Do	12	F–	2	A			

RATIOS, PERCENTAGES, AND DERIVATIONS

R = 22	L = 1.75	
EB = 2 : 2.0	EA = 4.0	EBPer = N/A
eb = 0 : 3	es = 3	D = 0
	Adj es = 2	Adj D = 0
FM = 0	SumC' = 1	SumT = 0
m = 0	SumV = 0	SumY = 2

AFFECT

FC:CF+C	= 4 : 0
Pure C	= 0
SumC' : WSumC	= 1 : 2.0
Afr	= 1.20
S	= 1
Blends:R	= 1 : 22
CP	= 0

INTERPERSONAL

COP = 0	AG = 0
GHR:PHR	= 1 : 4
a:p	= 1 : 1
Food	= 1
SumT	= 0
Human Content	= 5
Pure H	= 2
PER	= 0
Isolation Index	= 0.14

IDEATION

a:p	= 1 : 1	Sum6	= 4
Ma:Mp	= 1 : 1	Lvl-2	= 0
2AB+(Art+Ay)	= 2	WSum6	= 11
MOR	= 2	M-	= 1
		M none	= 0

MEDIATION

XA%	= 0.77
WDA%	= 0.80
X-%	= 0.23
S-	= 0
P	= 6
X+%	= 0.45
Xu%	= 0.32

PROCESSING

Zf	= 9
W:D:Dd	= 4:16:2
W : M	= 4 : 2
Zd	= +5.0
PSV	= 0
DQ+	= 7
DQv	= 0

SELF-PERCEPTION

3r+(2)/R	= 0.64
Fr+rF	= 0
SumV	= 0
FD	= 0
An+Xy	= 1
MOR	= 2
H:(H)+Hd+(Hd)	= 2 : 3

PTI = 0	☑ DEPI = 5	☑ CDI = 4	☐ S-CON = 4	☐ HVI = No	☐ OBS = No

Figure F.1 Tuula's (female, forty-eight years) second structural summary (lower section)
Source: Reproduced by special permission of the Publisher, Psychological Assessment Resources, Inc., 16204 North Florida Avenue, Lutz, Florida 33549, from the Rorschach Interpretation Assistance Program: Version 5 by John E. Exner, Jr., Ph.D., Irving B. Weiner, Ph.D., and PAR Staff, Copyright 1976, 1985, 1990, 1994, 1995, 1999, 2001, 2003 by Psychological Assessment Resources, Inc. (PAR). Further reproduction is prohibited without permission of PAR.

Index

Note: Page numbers in *italic* and **bold** refers to figures and tables, respectively; Page numbers followed by "n" refer to end notes.

achromatic color (*C'*) 108
Acklin, M. W. 44, 107, 150
active inference 8
active human movement (*Ma*) 99–100
AD *see* Asperger's disorder (AD)
adaptive resources 29, 32, 33, 158, 184, 188–189; *CDI* 34–37; deficits in 9, 68
ADHD *see* attention-deficit/hyperactivity disorder (ADHD)
ADHD/C *see* attention-deficit/hyperactivity disorder combined type (ADHD/C)
ADHD/PI *see* attention-deficit/hyperactivity disorder of the inattentive type (ADHD/PI)
AdjD 34
affect 108; mentalization 104–110; negative 92
Affective Difficulty Index 34
Affective Ratio (*Afr*) 52, 105–106, 111n22
AGC see aggressive content (*AGC*)
age-adjusted standard scores 33, 40
aggressive content (*AGC*) 101, 190
agnosia 49, 62, 81n4
AG response 34, 74, 145
Aita, J. A. 22, 68
alcohol/alcoholism: abuse 156; Tuula's case 180, 184–186, 188, 190; Ville's case 156, 159, 160
Alcohol Use Disorders Identification Test (AUDIT) 187
Ales, F. 42, 47
Allen, J. G. 101–102
Allison, J. 43–44
ALOG 49–50, 64, 173
Alzheimer's disease 146, 151; Aricept for 147, 151, 153n3; early-onset 152–153; *see also* dementia of the Alzheimer's type (DAT)
ambivalence 5, 160, 161, 163, 190
amnesia 61, 81n4
amphetamine-induced physiological stress 108
amygdala(r); activity 93, 94; dysfunction 96; emotional input 95; enlargement 92; modulation 95; structure 91–96, 102, 119
Anderson, A. K. 92
Ando, A. 74, 76–77, 102
anorexia nervosa 177
anosognosia 64, 147, 149, 153
An response 46, 51
anxiety 36, 68–69, 73, 76–79, 122, 144, 153, 166, 169, 176–177, 187, 193
aphasia 81n4
apperception 4, 5, 11n4
apraxia 61–62, 81n4
Aricept (donepezil) 147, 151, 153n3
Art 46, 51
Asari, T. 93–95, 110n9
ASD *see* autism spectrum disorder (ASD)
Asperger's disorder (AD) 77, 176
attention-deficit/hyperactivity disorder (ADHD) 73–77, 122; current assessment 156–157; multidisciplinary and multimethod assessment 161; neuropsychological and self-report-based assessment findings

157–158; psychotherapy for 162; rehabilitation and treatment targets 162–163; Rorschach protocol 158–161, **207–209**; sequence of codes **210–211**; structural summary *212;* summary/discussion session with 163–164
attention-deficit/hyperactivity disorder combined type (ADHD/C) 75
attention-deficit/hyperactivity disorder of the inattentive type (ADHD/PI) 75
AUDIT *see* Alcohol Use Disorders Identification Test (AUDIT)
auditory verbal hallucinations (AVH) 92
autism spectrum disorder (ASD) 75, 77–81, 122; associated with autism spectrum disorder 176; cognitive testing using WAIS-R 174–175; comprehensive treatment plan 177; neuropsychological assessment findings 168–169; Rorschach assessment and treatment 166–168; Rorschach protocol 171–174, **213–215**; self-report-based and other assessment findings 169–171; sequence of codes **216**; structural summary *217;* TAT performance 175–176
automatic phrases (*AP*) **20**, 22, 69
autosomal recessive disorder 66, 81n10
AVH *see* auditory verbal hallucinations (AVH)

Batterie d'Évaluation Cognitive 96 (BEC96) 32, 48–50, 53n5, 53n14, 142, 148–149, 153n1
Bayton, J. A. 43
BDI-II *see* Beck Depression Inventory (BDI-II)
BEC96 *see* Batterie d'Évaluation Cognitive 96 (BEC96)
Beck Depression Inventory (BDI-II) 121, 158, 169, 187
Beck, S. J. 31, 97
Beck System 5
Belyi, B. I. 70
Bender–Gestalt Test 22
Berry, B. A. 71
binomial theorem 111n19
Blatt, S. J. 43
Blend(s) 41, 62, 63, **128–129**
Bleuler, E. 4–5
borderline personality disorder (BPD) 92, 95, 96, 110n12
borderline personality organization (BPO) 95, 110n12
bottom-up processing 111n25
BPD *see* borderline personality disorder (BPD)
BPO *see* borderline personality organization (BPO)
Broca, P. 15
Brugger, P. 71–72
Buschke, H. 143, 148

Caputo, J. S. 24
Cardwell, G. F. 43
Cattelani, R. 68
caudate 50, 93
CDI see Coping Deficit Index (*CDI*)
CDR scale *see* Clinical Dementia Rating scale (CDR scale)
CHI *see* closed head injury (CHI)
cholinesterase inhibitor 151
chromatic responses 105
Clinical Dementia Rating scale (CDR scale) 63, 81n7
closed head injury (CHI) 68, 69, 81n11
cognitive-behavioral therapy 80, 163
cognitive codes 31, 49–50, 62, 101, 159
cognitive complexity 42–43, 104
cognitive deficits 47, 144, 151; Catherine's case 146; *CDI* 35–37; individuals with 32–33, 122; MMSE 81n3; *Vg* responses 43
cognitive deterioration 152, 153; final observations 185–186, 191–194; first structural summary *221*, *228;* follow-up occupational assessment 181–182; psychiatric day hospital in 180–181; Rorschach protocol 183–185, 188–191, **218–219**, **222–225**; self-report and neuropsychological assessment findings 182–183, 186–188; sequence of codes **220**, **226–227**
cognitive disarray 68
cognitive disintegration 151
cognitive function(ing) 29, 91; assessment 121; Catherine's case 147; correlation with *EA* 32; *Det* linked to 41–42; *LSO* correlation with 42; Luria's motor sequences

149; *M* responses 120; Rorschach variables related to 28, 51–52, 122; Ville's case 163
Cognitive Mediation 28
cognitive neuroscience research 50
cognitive performance variables 29
cognitive sophistication 38, 97, 106
Cognitive Triad 28
cognitive variables 9, 44
collaborative/therapeutic assessment 4
color-determinants 104–110
color-naming/nomination (*Cn*) 18, **19**, 21, 22, 68, 109, **125**
color nomination (*Cn*)
color responses 107
color shock 108
Complexity 28–29, 38–39, 100, **128**; roots of 39; variables contributing to 47; verbal and nonverbal processing abilities 41
composite international reference data 35
Comprehensive System (CS) 4, 8, 11, 15, 17, 28, 60, 90, 123, 142, 183
Comprehensive System—Revised (CS-R) 34, 60
conceptual confusion 24
confabulation 24
confusion 65, 68, 148, 150, 176
Conklin, A. C. 101
CONTAM 49, 64
Contents (*Cont*) 39–40
conventionality 16, 48–50
cooperative movement (*COP*) 34, 37–38, 51, **130**
Coping Deficit Index (*CDI*) 29, 33, 34, 36–38, 76, **128**, 184
cortical–subcortical group 18, 21
Cotugno, A. J. 73–74, 76
Cronbach, L. J. 29
crystallized intelligence 33, 41–42
CS *see* Comprehensive System (CS)
CS-R *see* Comprehensive System—Revised (CS-R)

Damasio, A. R. 108–109
DAT *see* dementia of the Alzheimer's type (DAT)
Dauphin, B. 47
DBS *see* deep brain stimulation (DBS)
Ddo 44
De Araújo, C. A. 36, 41, 78
deep brain stimulation (DBS) 60
definite dementia 15, 16
dementia 15, 40, 122; definite 15, 16; praecox 5; senile 16, 21; typical epileptic 15
dementia of the Alzheimer's type (DAT) 50, 61–62; acknowledging memory difficulties 141–142; cardinal neuropsychological signs 61, 81n4; contributions of Rorschach protocol in 144–147, **198–200**; diagnoses, summary/discussion session, and treatment plan 147, 151–152; first sequence of codes **201**; first structural summary *202*; follow-up assessments 148–151; individuals with moderate 63; medical and neuropsychological assessment findings 142–144; qualitative perspective 152–153; response processes in 62; second Rorschach protocol **203–206;** see also Alzheimer's disease
dementia with Lewy bodies (DLB) 65–66
de Mol, J. 67
DEPI see Depression Index (*DEPI*)
depression 34, 36, 68–69, 144, 153, 176, 188, 191, 193
Depression Index (*DEPI*) 34, 69
depth psychology 5
Determinants (*Det*) 39–42
Developmental Index (*DI*) 46
Developmental Quality Plus/Synthesis (*DQ+/Sy*) **125**
Developmental Quality Vague/Vague percent (*DQv/Vg%*) **126**
developmental trauma 72
de Villemor-Amaral, A. E. 104
DI see Developmental Index (*DI*)
Diagnostic and Statistical Manual of Mental Disorders (DSMs); DSM-III-R criteria 80; DSM-IV criteria 147; DSM-IV-TR criteria 80; DSM-5 criteria 82n17; DSM-5-TR criteria 73, 77
disordered thinking 24, 49–50, 62, 64–66, 74–75, 79–80, 95, 100, 172
disorientation 50, 143
DLB *see* dementia with Lewy bodies (DLB)
L-Dopa treatment 22
Dörken, H. 65

dorsal attention network 47
Do scores 44
DQ+ responses 42, 43, 45, 64, 80, 172
DQo responses 43, 80
DQv/+ responses 43, 44
DQv responses 43
DR1 response 50
DR2 response 50, 146
Drohocki, Z. 18, 20–21
DSMs *see* Diagnostic and Statistical Manual of Mental Disorders (DSMs)
dual-code theory 71
Dykens, E. 79–80

EA see Experience Actual (*EA*)
EEG *see* electroencephalogram (EEG)
Egocentricity Index 52
Ego Impairment Index (*EII*) 91; EII-*2* 50, 159; *EII-3* 50
ego strength 6, 31, 52–53n3
EII see Ego Impairment Index (*EII*)
electroencephalogram (EEG) 22, 67, 98, 120
elevated *CDI* 36–38, 76, 184
Ellis, D. W. 68
embodied mentalization 8, 32, 96–103
embodied simulation 98–101
emotional/emotion 108; disintegration 21; distress 68; interference 91–96; processing 107
empathy 9, 32, 101; magnifier 65; markers of 100; MNS 98
entorhinal cortex 188; epilepsy 15, 21, 142
epileptic seizures 18, 20–21
es 33, 41, 64, 69, 74
executive function(ing) 10, 28, 36–37, 50, 90, 142, 148, 150, 151, 156, 183, 186, 188, 190
Exner, J. E. 4, 6, 29, 31–32, 38, 43, 46, 61, 69, 90, 96–97, 100, 104–105, 183; Comprehensive System 4, 8, 11, 15, 17, 28, 60, 90, 123, 142, 183, 188; conceptualization of Rorschach 7; CS 25; positive *CDI* 34–35
Experience Actual (*EA*) 31–35, 37–39, 65, 67, 69, 106, 123, 184, 189, 193
experiential field 40
eye-tracking study 42

F% value 28–29, 41, 46, 52, 75
F– (poor form quality) 110n5
F+% (percentage of good form responses) **19**
F+ (perceptually accurate responses) 110n5
FAB2 response 79–80, 159
factor analysis 23, 44–45
FD see Form Dimension (*FD*)
Fd responses 38, 190
FD responses 46
Fechner-Bates, S. 44
feeling(s) 32, 98, 100, 108, 158, 175, 182
"feeling of movement" 101
"felt movement" 96
Finn, S. E. 72, 104, 166
first unrotated principal component (FUPC) 40
fluid intelligence 169
FM response 62, 64, 98, 172
fMRI *see* functional magnetic resonance imaging (fMRI)
Fonagy, P. 108–109
fonction du réel 17
Form-Color (*FC*) 60
formal operational thought 53n10
Form Dimension (*FD*) **129**
form quality 15, 21–22; codes 110nn5–6; factors 45
Fouques, D. 74
FQ-% score 29, 46
FQ–responses 91, 93–94
FQu% responses 77, 93–94
French School method 79
Freud, S. 4
Friedman, H. 43
Friston, K. J. 8
Full-Scale IQ (FSIQ) 33, 68, 168, 182
functional magnetic resonance imaging (fMRI) 90, 96, 102, 107, 110n1
functional neuroimaging studies 92
FUPC *see* first unrotated principal component (FUPC)
fusiform gyrus 92, 110n7

Gacono, C. B. 35
Gainotti, G. 71
general intelligence (g) 33, 41, 43, 44, 50, 53n6
GHR 146, 160, 174, 185, 189
Giromini, L. 46, 90, 98, 102–103, 107, 150
Gold, J. M. 52, 122

Gorske, T. T. 123
Greenberg, R. P. 43
Grober and Buschke memory test 143, 148
Grober, E. 143, 148

Hachinski's Ischemic Score 142
Hachinski, V. 142
Halstead-Reitan Impairment Index 69
Halstead–Reitan Neuropsychological Test Battery (HRNTB) 44, 45
hemispheric activation 71, 95
hemispheric asymmetry 70–73
Hertz System 5–6
heterogeneity: of ASD 77; in Pekka's performance 174
hippocampus 142, 153n2, 188
Holaday, M. 77–79
HRNTB *see* Halstead–Reitan Neuropsychological Test Battery (HRNTB)
Human Movement (*M*) **124**
human movement response (*M*) 8, 17, **19**, 31–32, 45, 60, 91, 96–103
Hyper-Vigilance Index (*HVI*) 159–161
hypervigilant information processing style 162
hypochondriasis 69, 169

ICD *see* International Classification of Diseases (ICD)
ID *see* intellectual disability (ID)
ideation 28, 97
Ilonen, T. 36–38, 67
impaired reality testing 110n3
implicit self 107
impotence (*Imp*) **20**, 22, 68, 150
inferior parietal lobule 98
information processing 16, 28
inkblot test 3, 5, 16, 46, 64, 66, 80, 111n25, 144, 188
INS *see* International Neuropsychological Society (INS)
insula 96
intellectual disability (ID) 60–61
intellectual passivity 21
intelligent/intelligence 25n1, 29, 91–92; individuals 28; Rorschach variables related to 51–52; test 3, 10, 121–122
intentions 32
International Classification of Diseases (ICD) 176
International Neuropsychological Society (INS) 4
International Society of the Rorschach and Projective Methods (ISR) 3
Ishibashi, M. 107
Isolate/R 38
ISR *see* International Society of the Rorschach and Projective Methods (ISR)

Judgment of Line Orientation Test 53n7
Jung, C. G. 4

Kanwisher, N. 98
Keller, R. 78
Kelley, D. 97
Kimoto, A. 65–66
Kishimoto, N. 80
Kissel, S. 43
Kleiger, J. H. 31, 49–50, 96, 101
Klopfer, B. 97
Klopfer System 5
Kourtzi, Z. 98
Kraepelin, E. 5
Kral, V. A. 65
Kutz, A. S. 75–76

Lambda 28–29, 33, 38, 41, 66–67, 74, 76, 80
Lambda/Form percent (*Lambda/F%*) **127**
Landis, T. 72–73
Larsen, J. K. 107
lateralized tachistoscopic presentations of inkblots 70, 72
left hemisphere, functions of 104–110
left inferior frontal gyrus (LIFG) 102
Level 2 Cognitive Codes (*Lvl-2*) 49
Lewy bodies 81n8
Lezak, M. D. 23–24
LIFG *see* left inferior frontal gyrus (LIFG)
linguistic and executive perseveration errors 63
lobectomies 24
Location, Space, and Object Qualities (*LSO*) 39, 42, 71
Locke, S. R. 74
LSO *see* Location, Space, and Object Qualities (*LSO*)

MADRS *see* Montgomery and Åsberg Depression Rating Scale (MADRS)

magnetic resonance imaging (MRI) 93, 105, 110n2, 142
Marsden, G. 44
MC 31–33, 39, 77, 106
McGuire, P. K. 50
Meehan, K. B. 76
mental disorders 16, 24, 74, 122, 142
mentalization 29, 32, 101; embodied 32; networks 8
Meyer, G. J. 8, 31, 33, 35, 39–41, 150, 152
Mihura, J. L. 3, 42, 63
mind–body dichotomy 5
Mini-Mental State Exam (MMSE) 41, 53n8, 61, 81n3, 142, 153n1
Minnesota Multiphasic Personality Inventory (MMPI) 4, 11n2, 121, 169, 178n2, 182, 194n2
Minor, S. W. 70–71
minus responses *see FQ–* responses
Miron, T. 101
mirror neuron system (MNS) 8, 96–103
Mitolo, M. 96
MMPI *see* Minnesota Multiphasic Personality Inventory (MMPI)
MMSE *see* Mini-Mental State Exam (MMSE)
MNS *see* mirror neuron system (MNS)
Montgomery and Åsberg Depression Rating Scale (MADRS) 142, 144
Mouren-Simeoni, M. -C. 74
MRI *see* magnetic resonance imaging (MRI)
MT+ regions 111n18
multi-method approach 180–181
multidisciplinary rehabilitation program 156
Mu suppression 99, 111n14

Nasu–Hakola disease *see* polycystic lipomembranous osteodysplasia with sclerosing leukoencephalopathy (PLOSL)
National Institute of Neurological and Communicative Disorders and Stroke and the Alzheimer's Disease and Related Disorders Association (NINCDS-ADRDA) 61
neurocognitive deficits/disorders 32, 51, 91, 122, 169
neurocognitive functioning 122; *Afr* 52; *CDI* variables associated with 36, 37; correlations with *DI* scores 46; *M* responses 9, 96, 106; *SI* responses 42
neurocognitive variables 49, 120
neurodevelopmental disorders 36, 51, 60, 96
neurodualism 10
neuroimaging: Rorschach research 32, 91; studies 92; technologies 25; *see also* Rorschach variables, neuroimaging studies of
neurological populations, Rorschach research history with 24–25
neuropsychoanalysis 10, 107
neuropsychological assessment findings 142; in Pekka's case study 168–169; of TBI patients 67–68; in Tuula's first assessment 182–183; in Tuula's second assessment 186–188; in Ville's case study 157–158
neuropsychological studies 106
neuropsychological test 143; standard 64, 150, 162; traditional 7, 10, 121–122
neuropsychotherapy 162, 164n4
neuroscientific theories 92
NINCDS-ADRDA *see* National Institute of Neurological and Communicative Disorders and Stroke and the Alzheimer's Disease and Related Disorders Association (NINCDS-ADRDA)
"nonorganic" mental disorders 16
nonverbal forced-choice task 72–73
nonverbal learning disorder/disability (NVLD) 75, 77
NVLD *see* nonverbal learning disorder/disability (NVLD)

Oberholzer, E. 17, 21
object recognition 90, 148–149
ODL see oral dependent language (*ODL*)
O'Neal, C. C. 75
oral dependent language (ODL) 90, 160, 189
"organic" mental disorders 16
"organic" schizophrenia 21
organicity 18; cerebral 22; pathognomonic sign of 21; Rorschach signs of 24
organic psychotic disorders 15
organizational perseverations 62, 171, 176

Parker, R. S. 67
Parkinson's disease 60
passive forms of human movement (*Mp*) 99–100
pastel-colored cards 105
percentage of popular responses (*P%*) **19**
Perceptanalysis 21
perceptual distortions (*FQ–*) 8
Perceptual Organization (PO) 36
perceptual/perception 4, 11n4; accuracy 16, 48–50; of color 109; perceptual–cognitive activity 43; perceptual–cognitive engagement 38; perceptual–cognitive problem-solving task 7, 90; of three-dimensionality 41
Perceptual-Thinking Index (*PTI*) 48, 50, 91, 159, 164n3
performance-based methods/tests 7, 10, 72, 185–186
Performance IQ 36, 44, 45, 168, 183, 187
perplexity (*Plx*) **20**, 22–24, 68
Perry, W. 44–45, 61–65, 108
Perseveration (*PSV*) 62, 78, **126**
personality: disorders 3, 35, 92; functioning 24, 67, 73, 77, 81, 90, 120–122; tests 8, 10, 11n1, 23, 121
PET *see* positron emission tomography (PET)
PHR 146, 160, 185, 189
Piagetian techniques 44, 53n9
Picture Completion subtest 168, 182, 185, 187, 190
Pineda, J. A. 99
Piotrowski System 6
Piotrowski, Z. 17, 48, 61, 68, 92, 96–97, 104, 109, 150; organic signs 17–24, **19–20**; seminal work 21
PLOSL *see* polycystic lipomembranous osteodysplasia with sclerosing leukoencephalopathy (PLOSL)
PO *see* Perceptual Organization (PO)
polished façade 63–64
polycystic lipomembranous osteodysplasia with sclerosing leukoencephalopathy (PLOSL) 66–67
Porcelli, P. 97, 99–101, 103, 111n15
positive *CDI* 34–36, 38
positron emission tomography (PET) 98, 111n13
post-traumatic stress disorder (PTSD) 95
potential space 150
PPI analysis *see* psychophysiological interaction analysis (PPI analysis)
prefrontal cortex 101
prefrontal lobotomies 24
process approach 61
projections 12n6
PSV see Perseveration (*PSV*)
psychiatric evaluation 180
Psychodiagnostics (Rorschach) 4–5, 15
psychological test batteries 67
psychopathology 24, 90–91, 159–161; *FQ*–responses in patients with 91, 93–94; hemispheric asymmetry and 72; Pekka's case 169; and psychological resources 31; social coping and verbal processing deficits 36; Tuula's case 184, 189, 193; in Ville's case 163
psychophysiological interaction analysis (PPI analysis) 94, 110n10
psychotic disorders 22, 49, 78, 79, 94, 95, 122, 166, 175
psychotic phenomena 9, 9 4, 45, 49, 50, 78, 159, 164n3
psychotic symptoms 49, 72, 91–92, 168, 170
PTI see Perceptual-Thinking Index (*PTI*)
PTSD *see* post-traumatic stress disorder (PTSD)
Pure C 31, 67, 105
Pure H (whole and non-fictional human content) 51, 74, 75, **131**

R (total number of responses) **19**, 45
Ramires, V. R. R. 80
Rapaport, D. 40, 97
Rapaport–Schafer System 6
Raven's Colored Progressive Matrices—Special Scale *see* Raven's Scale
Raven's Scale 46, 53n12
Receiver Operating Characteristic curves (ROC curves) 66, 81n9
reflection responses **130**
Regard, M. 71–73
Reitan, R. M. 25, 68
repetition (*Rpt*) **19**, 22, 68
repetitive transcranial magnetic stimulation (rTMS) 91, 102, 110n2, 111n17
Resende, A. C. 46
resource 31, 158; adaptive 9, 29, 32–34, 37, 68, 158, 184, 188–189; cognitive

65, 103, 162; internal 74, 76; neuropsychological 109; psychological 29, 31–32, 35, 62
response patterns 24, 61
response process 4, 7, 42, 44, 62, 90–91, 106, 122
resting-state fMRI 96
Rey-Osterrieth Complex Figure test (ROCF test) 50, 157, 183
Ridley, S. E. 43
right-hemispheric perception 71
Ritzler, B. 152
ROC curves *see* Receiver Operating Characteristic curves (ROC curves)
ROCF test *see* Rey-Osterrieth Complex Figure test (ROCF test)
Rorschach assessment 120; client information 9; measures individual's explicit self-representation 121–122; neurocognitive correlates in geriatric population 11; in neuropsychology 121, 122–123; sensitivity to postinjury cognitive and personality changes 68; shading responses 108; theoretical scatter plot model *30*
Rorschach, H. 3, 15, 28, 39, 64; coded movement 96; correlations with cognitive performance variables 29; Exner's conceptualization 6–7; history research with neurological populations 24–25; Searls's description about 4–5; seminal work 15–17
Rorschach inkblots method/test 3–5, 29, 47, 71, 90, 93, 98–99; advantages 9–10; Meyer and Friston's Bayesian model of brain function 8–9; R-PAS conceptualization 7; reconceptualization of 7–8
Rorschach Perceptual Accuracy 44, 53n11
Rorschach Performance Assessment System (R-PAS) 7–9, 11, 11n3, 60, 71, 90, 123, 137; ADHD diagnosis 76; *Afr* in 52, 111n22; categories of space 42; and *CDI* 38–39; in Cognitive Triad examination 28–29; *Complexity* in 39, 47; *CritCont* in 101; *EII-3* in 50; *FQ–%* 91; FQ– response 110n5; *LSO* variables in 82n15; and *MC* 31; *M* response 97–98; oral content responses 90; *PEC* in 49; and Piotrowski's findings 17–18; *PPD* in 40; Rorschach variables 31, **124–136**; *SI* in 44; *Sy* in 42; *TP-Comp* 50; *Vg* in 43; *V* responses 106; *WSumC* in 106
Rorschach protocol: Catherine's case **198–200**, **203–206**; Pekka's case 171–174, **213–215**; Tuula's case 183–185, 188–191, **218–219**, **222–225**; in Ville's case 158–161, **207–209**
Rorschach Research Council (RRC) 40
Rorschach Response Process 44–45
Rorschach theory 52, 122
Rorschach variables, neuroimaging studies of 90–91; amygdalar structure and function 92–96; embodied mentalization 8, 32, 96–103; emotional interference 92, 95, 96; human movement response 8, 17, **19**, 31–32, 45, 60, 91, 96–103; mirror neuron system 8, 96–103; with neuropsychological correlates and guidelines **124–136;** related to cognitive functioning 28, 51–52, 122; related to intelligence and cognitive functions 51–52; unique perception 91–96
R-PAS *see* Rorschach Performance Assessment System (R-PAS)
RRC *see* Rorschach Research Council (RRC)
rTMS *see* repetitive transcranial magnetic stimulation (rTMS)
Ruth, J. M. 68

Schachtel, E. G. 40, 109
schizophrenia 15, 24, 95; Bleuler's view 5; MMPI and HRNTB 44; "organic" 21; positive *CDI* 36; Skalweit's protocols 21
Schizophrenia Index (*SCZI*) 69, 162, 164n3
schizophrenia spectrum disorders 94
SCZI see Schizophrenia Index (*SCZI*)
SD *see* standard deviations (SD)
Searls, D. 4–5
self-report-based assessment findings: in Pekka's case study 169–171; in Tuula's first assessment 182–183; in Tuula's second assessment 186–188; in Ville's case study 157–158
semantic cuing 143

senile dementia 16, 21
sensorimotor cortex 98–99, 101
sequence of codes: Catherine's case **201**; Pekka's case **216**; Tuula's case **220**, **226–227**; Tuula's second **226–227**; Ville's case **210–211**
SI see Space Integration (*SI*)
Skalweit, W. 21
skepticism 4, 98
Smith, N. M. 44
Smith, S. R. 121, 123
Snow White syndrome 100, 184, 189
Society for Personality Assessment (SPA) 3, 100
somatic markers 109
SPA *see* Society for Personality Assessment (SPA)
Space Integration (*SI*) 42, 44, 47, 71
space responses/Space Integration (*S*/*SI*) **127**
Space Reversal (*SR*) 42, 47, **127**
spatial disorientation 24
Spender, K. 76
SPM *see* statistical parametric mapping (SPM)
SR see Space Reversal (*SR*)
S response 42, 70
standard deviations (SD) 48, 65, 183
Standard Score (SS); in Catherine's case 143; in Pekka's case 168; in Tuula's case 182; in Ville's case 157
statistical parametric mapping (SPM) 94, 110n11
stimulus-boundedness 23
STN *see* subthalamic nucleus (STN)
Strickland, V. L. 74
Stroop test 183, 187
substance abuse 156, 162, 163, 180, 187
subthalamic nucleus (STN) 60, 81n1
Sum6 response 65
sum of human content responses (*SumH*) 51, 64, 69, **131**
sum of *M* and weighted sum of color responses (*WSumC*) **124–125**
superior temporal sulcus 98, 102
Sx responses 46, 51–52

T (texture response) **19**, 46
tachistoscopy 82n14, 107
TAT *see* Thematic Apperception Test (TAT)
TBI *see* traumatic brain injury (TBI)
TCI see Trauma Content Index (*TCI*)
temporal lobe epilepsy 92, 142
temporal pole 94–95, 102
Thematic Apperception Test (TAT) 23, 170–171, 174, 175
Thought and Perception Composite (*TP-Comp*) 50, 77, 111n16
Thought, Language and Communication Disorder Scale (TLC Disorder Scale) 79, 82n18
thought organization 5–6, 48–50
TLC Disorder Scale *see* Thought, Language and Communication Disorder Scale (TLC Disorder Scale)
TMS *see* transcranial magnetic stimulation (TMS)
TMT-A *see* Trail Making Test A (TMT-A)
TMT-B *see* Trail Making Test B (TMT-B)
top-down processing 8, 111n25
TP-Comp see Thought and Perception Composite (*TP-Comp*)
traditional Rorschach theory 122
Trail Making Test A (TMT-A) 157, 183
Trail Making Test B (TMT-B) 157, 183
transcranial magnetic stimulation (TMS) 98, 111n13
trauM see traumatic human movement (*trauM*)
Trauma Content Index (*TCI*) 145
trauma flashbacks 95–96
traumatic brain injury (TBI) 15, 17, 67–70, 122, 156, 156–157
traumatic human movement (*trauM*) 101

unilateral brain lesions 70–73
unique perception 91–96
Unique Response Ratio (URR) 93–95, 110n9
unusual responses (*FQu*) 8, 91
URR *see* Unique Response Ratio (URR)

validity of eye-tracking findings 47
validity scales 169, 182, 186, 192
Valtonen, J. 10
VC *see* Verbal Comprehension (VC)
Vecchio, A. 90
VEM *see* Verbal Memory (VEM)
Verbal Comprehension (VC) 33, 40, 44, 52

verbal disorganization 50
Verbal IQ (VIQ) 33, 168
Verbal Memory (VEM) 183, 188
verbal processing skills 41–42
Vg responses 43
VIM *see* visual memory (VIM)
VIQ *see* Verbal IQ (VIQ)
Vista (*V*) responses 46, 106
Vista Shading (*V*) **129**
visual-grasping types 16, 25n1
visual attention 71, 90
visual memory (VIM) 37, 49, 143, 157, 183, 188
Vitolo, E. 47
voxel-based morphometry 93, 110n8

WAIS *see* Wechsler Adult Intelligence Scale (WAIS)
WAIS-R *see* Wechsler Adult Intelligence Scale—Revised (WAIS-R)
Wartegg Drawing Completion Test 23, 121
WCST *see* Wisconsin Card Sorting Test (WCST)
Wechsler Adult Intelligence Scale (WAIS) 43, 157
Wechsler Adult Intelligence Scale—Revised (WAIS-R) 36, 44, 45, 68, 168, 174, 185
Wechsler Intelligence Scale for Children—Revised (WISC-R) 33
Wechsler Intelligence Scale for Children (WISC-III) 36
Wechsler Intelligence Scale for Children—Revised (WISC-R) 33
Wechsler Memory Scale (WMS) 157
Wechsler Memory Scale—Revised (WMS-R) 36, 183, 188
weighted sum of Cognitive Codes (*WSumCog*) 49
weighted sum of color responses (*WSumC*) 31–32, 91, 105–106, 108–109
weighting system for color responses 111n26
Weiner, I. B. 35
Wernicke, C. 15
whole inkblot responses (*W*) 42
Whole responses/Whole response percent (*W*/*W%*) **127**

Winnicott, D. W. 150
WISC-III *see* Wechsler Intelligence Scale for Children (WISC-III)
Wisconsin Card Sorting Test (WCST) 36, 142, 144, 148, 149, 157, 187
WISC-R *see* Wechsler Intelligence Scale for Children—Revised (WISC-R)
WMS *see* Wechsler Memory Scale (WMS)
WMS-R *see* Wechsler Memory Scale—Revised (WM-SR)
Wood, J. M. 45
W responses 39, 42–45, 65, 68, 70–71, 77
WSum6 49–50, 62, 64, 69, 74, 80, 82n16
WSumCog see weighted sum of Cognitive Codes (*WSumCog*)
Wu-Holt, P. 107, 150

X–% score 45, 46, 48
X+% score 45, 46, 48, 76
Xy response 46, 51

Yalof, J. 79, 80
Yazigi, L. 104

Zahn, B. S. 68
Zd score 52, 66
Zillmer, E. A. 4, 44–45
Z score frequency (*Zf*) 45, 64, 69, **126**

For Product Safety Concerns and Information please contact our EU representative GPSR@taylorandfrancis.com Taylor & Francis Verlag GmbH, Kaufingerstraße 24, 80331 München, Germany